TM

MW00558956

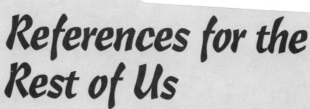
References for the Rest of Us

COMPUTER BOOK SERIES FROM IDG

Are you intimidated and confused by computers? Do you find that traditional manuals are overloaded with technical details you'll never use? Do your friends and family always call you to fix simple problems on their PCs? Then the *". . . For Dummies"*™ computer book series from IDG is for you.

". . . For Dummies" books are written for those frustrated computer users who know they aren't really dumb but find that PC hardware, software, and indeed the unique vocabulary of computing make them feel helpless. *". . . For Dummies"* books use a lighthearted approach, a down-to-earth style, and even cartoons and humorous icons to diffuse computer novices' fears and build their confidence. Lighthearted but not lightweight, these books are a perfect survival guide to anyone forced to use a computer.

> *"I like my copy so much I told friends; now they bought copies."*
>
> Irene C., Orwell, Ohio

> *"Quick, concise, nontechnical, and humorous."*
>
> Jay A., Elburn, IL

> *"Thanks, I needed this book. Now I can sleep at night."*
>
> Robin F., British Columbia, Canada

Already, hundreds of thousands of satisfied readers agree. They have made *". . . For Dummies"* books the #1 introductory level computer book series and have written asking for more. So if you're looking for the most fun and easy way to learn about computers look to *". . . For Dummies"* books to give you a helping hand.

IDG BOOKS

UPGRADING &
FIXING MACs
FOR
DUMMIES™

UPGRADING & FIXING MACs FOR DUMMIES™

by Kearney Rietmann and Frank Higgins

IDG BOOKS

IDG Books Worldwide, Inc.
An International Data Group Company

San Mateo, California ♦ Indianapolis, Indiana ♦ Boston, Massachusetts

Upgrading & Fixing Macs For Dummies

Published by
IDG Books Worldwide, Inc.
An International Data Group Company
155 Bovet Road, Suite 310
San Mateo, CA 94402

Library of Congress Catalog Card No.: 94-77184

ISBN: 1-56884-189-2

Printed in the United States of America

10 9 8 7 6 5 4 3 2 1

1D/QX/RR/ZU

Distributed in the United States by IDG Books Worldwide, Inc.

Distributed in Canada by Macmillan of Canada, a Division of Canada Publishing Corporation; by Computer and Technical Books in Miami, Florida, for South America and the Caribbean; by Longman Singapore in Singapore, Malaysia, Thailand, and Korea; by Toppan Co. Ltd. in Japan; by Asia Computerworld in Hong Kong; by Woodslane Pty. Ltd. in Australia and New Zealand; and by Transword Publishers Ltd. in the U.K. and Europe.

For general information on IDG Books in the U.S., including information on discounts and premiums, contact IDG Books at 800-762-2974 or 415-312-0650.

For information on where to purchase IDG Books outside the U.S., contact Christina Turner at 415-312-0633.

For information on translations, contact Marc Jeffrey Mikulich, Foreign Rights Manager, at IDG Books Worldwide; FAX NUMBER 415-286-2747.

For sales inquiries and special prices for bulk quantities, write to the address above or call IDG Books Worldwide at 415-312-0650.

For information on using IDG Books in the classroom, or for ordering examination copies, contact Jim Kelly at 800-434-2086.

 is a registered trademark of IDG Books Worldwide, Inc.

 The text in this book is printed on recycled paper.

About the Authors

Kearney Rietmann

Kearney Rietmann was the Editor of *Macworld* magazine for the first two years of the life of the Macintosh, and she's been using and writing about Macs for over ten years. She bought one of the original Macintosh computers in early 1984, and since then, she's bought two more desktop Macs and a PowerBook. She's also upgraded her machines with storage, memory, modems, printers, video cards, and an AppleTalk network.

Kearney has also worked with Apple Computer on introducing over 30 Mac products ranging from Quadras, PowerBooks, and Performas to printers, scanners, mice, monitors, keyboards, speakers, and microphones. One of her favorite activities is interviewing Macintosh users to find out exactly what they do with their Macs. She has interviewed hundreds of people, and she's always amazed by how much people's work and personal lives change when they buy a new Mac, a new upgrade, or a new software package.

When she's not writing about Macs or upgrading her machines, Kearney plays Tetris 1 and 2 on her daughter's Nintendo Game Boy and attends as many aerobics classes a week as she can. She also voraciously reads books on history, mystery, and fortune telling.

Frank Higgins

Frank Higgins is the president and owner of Yoyodyne Systems, a Macintosh consulting firm in the San Francisco Bay area. Frank's company is dedicated to helping people get the most out of their Macs. He was also the Macintosh hardware specialist at Raynet Incorporated, where he was responsible for troubleshooting, repairing, upgrading, and maintaining over 900 networked Macs and peripherals.

Frank has a bachelors degree in German Language and Culture from the University of California at Santa Cruz. Before he began working with the Macintosh, he tried out a variety of jobs, including performing juggling and magic on the streets of Freiburg, Germany; pouring hot wax into candle molds; and playing video games professionally. When Frank's head isn't buried deep down inside the Mac, he enjoys cycling, surfing, and medieval German literature.

Welcome to the world of IDG Books Worldwide.

IDG Books Worldwide, Inc., is a subsidiary of International Data Group, the world's largest publisher of business and computer-related information and the leading global provider of information services on information technology. IDG was founded more than 25 years ago and now employs more than 5,700 people worldwide. IDG publishes more than 200 computer publications in 63 countries (see listing below). Forty million people read one or more IDG publications each month.

Launched in 1990, IDG Books is today the fastest-growing publisher of computer and business books in the United States. We are proud to have received 3 awards from the Computer Press Association in recognition of editorial excellence, and our best-selling ...*For Dummies* series has more than 7 million copies in print with translations in more than 20 languages. IDG Books, through a recent joint venture with IDG's Hi-Tech Beijing, became the first U.S. publisher to publish a computer book in the People's Republic of China. In record time, IDG Books has become the first choice for millions of readers around the world who want to learn how to better manage their businesses.

Our mission is simple: Every IDG book is designed to bring extra value and skill-building instructions to the reader. Our books are written by experts who understand and care about our readers. The knowledge base of our editorial staff comes from years of experience in publishing, education, and journalism — experience which we use to produce books for the '90s. In short, we care about books, so we attract the best people. We devote special attention to details such as audience, interior design, use of icons, and illustrations. And because we use an efficient process of authoring, editing, and desktop publishing our books electronically, we can spend more time ensuring superior content and spend less time on the technicalities of making books.

You can count on our commitment to deliver high-quality books at competitive prices on topics customers want to read about. At IDG, we value quality, and we have been delivering quality for more than 25 years. You'll find no better book on a subject than an IDG book.

John J. Kilcullen

John Kilcullen
President and CEO
IDG Books Worldwide, Inc.

Acknowledgments

We'd like to thank Bill Grout, our most excellent agent. Also, thanks to Oliver Thompson for his comments and insight. And many thanks to Jahna Michaelsen, Olivia Rodriguez, and all the other folks at Apple Service Training.

At IDG Books, we thank Kristin Cocks, the most accessible, available, and accommodating editor we know. Also, thanks to William Barton, Colleen Rainsberger, Becky Whitney, and Dennis Cohen for all the time and care they put into the manuscript. And thanks to Janna Custer, Megg Bonar, Mary Bednarek, Beth Jenkins, Diane Steele, and Tracy Barr.

And Ken, Carla, Camille, Rene, and Nadine Periat, Mike Prather, Mike Holm, Susan and Woody Higgins, Ed Higgins and Stacy Bliss, Dallas and Pam, and Gas and Peg Periat, we thank them for their support. And thanks to Janet Periat, because without her, this book wouldn't have happened. Finally, thanks to Claire, our favorite eight-year-old.

(The publisher would like to give special thanks to Patrick J. McGovern, without whom this book would not have been possible.

Dedication

To Janet, Claire, and Bill, the people we love most

Credits

Publisher
David Solomon

Managing Editor
Mary Bednarek

Acquisitions Editor
Janna Custer

Production Director
Beth Jenkins

Senior Editors
Tracy L. Barr
Sandra Blackthorn
Diane Graves Steele

Production Coordinator
Cindy L. Phipps

Associate Acquisitions Editor
Megg Bonar

Associate Project Editor
Kristin A. Cocks

Editors
William A. Barton
Colleen Rainsberger
Becky Whitney

Editorial Assistant
Laura Schaible

Technical Reviewer
Dennis Cohen

Production Staff
Chris Collins
Tyler Conner
Sherry Gomoll
Angela Hunckler
Drew R. Moore
Steve Peake
Carla Radzikinas
Kathie Schnorr
Gina Scott
Robert Simon

Cover Design
Kavish + Kavish

Illustrator
Accent Technical Communications

Proofreader
Michelle Worthington

Indexer
Sherry Massey

Book Design
University Graphics

Contents at a Glance

Cartoons at a Glance
By Rich Tennant

page 8

page 9

page 389

paae 119

page 67

page 173

page 400

page 213

page 212

page 231

Table of Contents

Introduction

• •

*W*elcome to *Upgrading & Fixing Macs For Dummies* — also known as "Cool Mac Stuff You May Want to Add to Your Machine," "Fear No Upgrade 101," and "Saving Your Upgrade Money (by Doing the Upgrades Yourself or by Getting Them Done for Free or for the Best Price Possible)."

If you're reading this book, you've likely made it successfully through the first stages of Mac ownership. And that's no small feat. Congratulations on choosing the Mac and on getting it up and running.

You probably bought your Mac, unpacked it, set it up on your desk, and even hooked it up to a printer. Great! You've powered up the machine many times by now, and you're undoubtedly a whiz at opening files, saving them, and closing them. You know the difference between a diskette and a hard disk, and maybe you've even survived a few disasters, such as forgetting to save a document or throwing the wrong file in the trash. You should be feeling pretty confident about your Mac abilities by now. And rightfully so. You've accomplished a lot.

But now you may be ready to get even more out of your Mac. If so, this book is for you.

Before we go on to upgrading and fixing the Mac, we should probably slow down here for a second to say that if you *haven't* yet bought a Mac, used it for a few months, and done at least a couple of the things we mentioned in the preceding paragraphs, you probably don't want this book just yet. Instead, you really should take a look at *Macs For Dummies* by David Pogue, also published by IDG Books. That book is full of all the great introductory Mac info you need. So spend a little time first just with your Mac and with *Macs For Dummies*, and then come back to this book. It'll still be here when you're ready.

Why You Need This Book

If you bought your Mac 3, 6, or 18 months ago, the chances are good that you've already jumped over the major start-up and learning hurdles, and that, in general, things between you and your Mac are going fine.

But maybe you're also facing some of the following situations:

- ✔ Some of the Mac equipment that tempted you when you first bought your system — which you rejected at the time as too expensive — has now come down in price. (Remember that laser printer and the scanner you wanted but didn't go for?)

- ✔ You tried to save a file and discovered that your hard disk is full — yeah, do you *believe* it? That same 40MB hard disk that seemed so huge when you bought it.

- ✔ Your Mac is telling you too often that it's out of memory and that you can't open all the applications you want.

- ✔ You've decided to add more memory but you don't want to pay a technician to install it. You just need some simple instructions so you can do it yourself.

- ✔ You've been hearing about CD-ROM drives and multimedia and you're wondering how to use these items with your Mac.

- ✔ You're tired of looking at a tiny half-page of work on-screen and you're dreaming about a bigger monitor.

- ✔ Your office mate has bragged one too many times about the great, new, speedy PowerPC accelerator card he or she just installed (whatever that is, anyway; you just know that it sounds like a big deal). In a fit of Mac envy, you decide that you must get that card for your Mac, too.

- ✔ You just inherited a small fortune and you've decided to invest in the biggest, most wonderful color monitor you can find — something to rival the screen at your favorite movie theater.

- ✔ You'd like to add some cool stuff to your Mac, but no way in the world are you going to take a screwdriver, open up your computer, and *install* a piece of hardware. Don't worry, we'll tell you about tons of easy upgrades that plug right into your Mac, with nothing to take apart or close up at all.

- ✔ You absolutely *hate* the color of your PowerBook trackball and you're wondering just what you can do about it.

Or maybe you have no specific ideas at all about anything you want to add to your Mac. You've just heard something vague about *upgrades* and *add-ons*. What the heck *are* those anyway? Well, in short, they're items of computer hardware that enable you to do even more with your Mac than you've done so far, as well as to improve how you work with it — for example, a large-screen monitor, a new hard disk, more memory, a color printer, or even stereo speakers.

Upgrades, large and small, can provide more workspace on your Mac screen, add the extra document storage you need, eliminate those pesky Mac out-of-memory messages, improve the appearance of your printouts, and enable you to blast your neighbors with stereo music from your Mac instead of from your CD player. (But, hey, keep the volume down — your neighbors need some sleep, too, you know.)

The Answers to a Couple Good Questions

But doesn't it cost a *lot* of money to add new stuff to my Mac, you ask? And isn't it hard to install all this extra Mac gear?

Good questions. Prices keep coming down, so you may actually be surprised at how much stuff you can now afford to add to your Mac. And one good way to save money is to do the upgrades yourself instead of paying a technician to do the work for you.

As for Mac gear being hard to install, well, in this book, we tell you all about *outside upgrades*, such as hard disks, CD-ROM drives, scanners, printers, speakers, fax modems, and monitors — upgrades that you plug into the back of your Mac. No screwdrivers are required, nor is taking apart your Mac. These upgrades are quite easy, and we tell you where and how to plug them into your Mac.

You don't even need to worry about what we call *inside upgrades*, such as additional memory, internal storage, or expansion cards. (If these terms sound like gibberish to you now, don't worry — we explain all these pieces of hardware to you throughout the book. We also give you helpful advice on how to purchase them.) You can choose to have a technician install the inside upgrades for you or install them yourself.

If you decide to go with a technician, we tell you how to choose a good one, how to work with a technician after you've found one, and how to get good service and prices. We even offer some suggestions about how to get your upgrades installed for free. And if you do decide to install your upgrades yourself, we provide you with simple, step-by-step instructions. Essentially, we hold your hand every step of the way.

How to Use This Book

The first rule is this: Don't read *anything* you don't really need to read. And don't pick up this book and read it straight through, cover to cover — unless, of course, you really *want* to. You can use the book to quickly find the specific information you need for your Mac and the upgrades you're interested in.

In these pages, we cover all the Mac models, old and new, from the compact, all-in-one Macs to the modular two-piece Macs and the PowerBooks. We've designed the book so that you can easily find where specific information about your Mac or Macs appears. Just read the sections that cover your machine.

If you own a PowerBook, go directly to the PowerBook chapters and sections. (Do not pass go, do not collect $200.) If you're interested in monitors, modems, or memory, look at those chapters or sections. If you want to find out about working with a technician or about getting free upgrade help, Chapter 2 is your chapter. Or if you're worried about damaging your Mac instead of improving it when you upgrade, check out Chapter 3 for safety procedures.

If you want installation instructions, just read those. If you want upgrade recommendations for your Mac, just read the recommendations. Or if you want technical background info, read that. We put the technical stuff in boxes so you'll spot it right away. Or skip the techno-babble if it's not for you. You don't need any of it to upgrade your Mac successfully.

How This Book Is Organized

The book contains seven major parts, an index, many, many cross references, and a detailed table of contents that directs you right to the chapters and sections you need.

Part I: Getting Ready

This part does just what it says — it gets you ready to upgrade. You learn about some quick Mac fixes and how to determine whether you need to repair your Mac or upgrade it. You also learn how to decide whether to do an upgrade yourself or hire a technician for it. And if you're not sure whether you really want to upgrade your Mac or just buy a new machine, well, we help you make that decision, too.

If you decide to install hardware in your Mac yourself, we tell you the few, simple tools you'll need and, most important, we give you the details about doing the upgrade safely for both you and your Mac. Even though installing upgrades inside means you work around electrical components, don't worry about zapping yourself or your Mac. And we understand any hesitation you might have, but a little nervousness means you'll take the proper precautions we outline for you.

Part II: The Cavalcade of Macs and Upgradeability

Here's where you find an overview of the Mac models. Look in these chapters to determine just how upgradeable your Mac is and to find recommendations on which upgrades to make. For the older Mac models, we also tell you whether we think you should consider buying a new Mac instead of spending time and money on upgrading.

Part III: Easy Outside Upgrades and Fixes

These are the upgrades you plug into your Mac — those that don't require you to open up and get inside your Mac at all. Take a look at the chapters in this part if you're interested in adding more storage, printers, monitors, modems and fax modems, or network capabilities to your Mac. You find purchase suggestions, tips on using these upgrades, and advice about fixing and maintaining them.

Part IV: Easy Inside Upgrades and Fixes

Look in this part for information about the upgrades that go inside your Mac. These upgrades include memory and internal storage, video cards, and upgrades that make your Mac and your work faster. We again give you purchase pointers, tips, and maintenance and repair advice.

Part V: Software Upgrades

In this part, you receive information about the Mac System, tips for upgrading the System, and information about the software you need to run hardware like printers, modems, and monitors. We also discuss how to use software to speed up your Mac, and we offer you tips for backing up your files and applications and advice about recovering from a hard disk crash as quickly and inexpensively as possible.

Part VI: Opening Up the Mac and Installing Upgrades

Look in this part for easy, step-by-step instructions for inside Mac upgrades, such as installing memory, internal storage, or hardware to speed up your Mac. First, we cover these upgrades for the compact, all-in-one Macs. Then we cover those for the modular, two-piece Macs, and, finally, for the PowerBooks. The different sections are clearly marked so that you can easily refer to only those that discuss your Mac and the particular upgrade or upgrades you want to make.

Part VII: The Part of Tens

You may want to read this part first. It's full of easy tips, tricks, and insider upgrade information. We point out which are the hardest Mac upgrades so that you know which ones to avoid attempting yourself and for which you're best off working with a professional technician. If you own a PowerBook, make sure that you check out our top ten favorite PowerBook upgrades. (We think you'll especially love our tips for getting longer battery life). And to improve your Mac's performance, don't miss the section on making your Mac run better.

Icons Used in This Book

We've used several eye-catching icons, or pictures, in this book to get your attention and spotlight items we urge you to read and those that you can skip if you want. Here are those icons and what they mean:

We've loaded each chapter with cool tips and tricks that you can use as short-cuts. Read these whenever you come to them. They'll improve the work you do with your Mac and give you ways to show off your Mac skills to your neighbors at home or in the office.

Read the technical stuff only if you want to — or come back to it later, when you have time to digest some background information. Although some of these sections are pretty technical, we try to keep the jargon to a minimum and we explain everything we tell you. The point here is to inform you, not to create barriers between you and getting your work done with your Mac.

This icon is pretty straightforward. We use this one whenever we want to remind you of something we talked about earlier or to remind you to do something *very* important — such as back up your files. (You probably can never get too many reminders to back up. Backing up is definitely *not* a case of too much of a good thing.)

 We use this icon only a few times in the book, so we want you to make sure that you read these warnings carefully whenever they appear. They usually involve working around the electrical components inside the Mac, and we want you to perform that work safely. If you follow the instructions we provide, you should experience *no problemo* at all.

Best of Luck with Your Upgrades — and Have Fun

Whether you're a do-it-yourself upgrader or someone who wants upgrades done for you, this book gives you the tools you need. Take the information presented in these pages and run with it to get more work, and more fun, out of your Mac. One word of advice: If you think you need an upgrade, you probably do. If the upgrade makes your computing faster, easier, or more enjoyable, it's well worth the time, expense, and effort you put into it. So good luck, and we really mean it when we say: "Have fun!"

The 5th Wave

By Rich Tennant

"GARY AND SOME OF HIS FRIENDS WANTED TO BOB FOR APPLES THIS YEAR.
I GUESS IT CAN'T HURT AS LONG AS THEY'RE NOT PLUGGED IN."

Part I
Getting Ready

"NOT ONLY DID WE GET YOU AN APPLE WITH A MOUSE, LIKE YOU ASKED, WE ALSO GOT YOU A BANANA WITH A LIZARD."

B *In this part...*

efore you upgrade or fix your Mac, you need to know what your options are. First, is it possible to even upgrade or fix your Mac? If so, what are your choices? And can you do it yourself, or should you call a technician?

And if you've never even thought of opening your Mac, don't worry. In this part, we first get you familiar with the basic elements of your Mac, from front to back, inside and out. Words like "scuzzy" and "Ethernet port" won't be foreign for long.

Chapter 1

Finding the Problem
(and Some Easy Solutions)

. . . .

In This Chapter

▶ Checking and fixing your ailing Mac

▶ Finding the problem

▶ Deciding if a fix requires a repair or an upgrade

▶ Calling for help

. . . .

The computing corollary to Murphy's law goes something like this: "If a computer is going to crash, it does so at the most inconvenient time and at the very moment that causes you the most frustration."

Problems with your Mac are *really* a drag. And what you need are ways to fix those problems — and fix them fast. In this chapter, you learn how to isolate several basic problems, and you learn a few simple tricks to get your Mac going again. Using these fixes, you even stand a good chance of solving your Mac problems yourself, without needing to call for help. This chapter also helps you decide if what you really need to do is repair or upgrade your Mac to solve a particular problem. Finally, you get some help in determining whether it's time to call in an expert, and you receive some pretty handy advice on choosing a good technician.

Basic Mac Checks and Fixes

What any Mac user wants is a Macintosh that's well-behaved and gets work done on time. But sometimes your Mac stubbornly refuses to do anything for you. The most common problem users experience is a Mac that fails to start or a machine that *crashes* — which means that it simply stops running right in the middle of your work.

If your Mac doesn't act the way you want, try some of the following checks and fixes to get your machine back to work. We've found that these fixes cure many of the problems you're likely to encounter.

Is everything connected?

Sometimes the Mac malfunctions simply because a cable comes loose from the back of the machine. (This may seem kind of silly, but such situations happen more often than you may think. In fact, a large computer manufacturer once told its technicians to handle service and repair calls in the following manner: If they went on a call to a customer's office and saw that a power cord was unplugged, the technicians were just to plug the cord back in when no one was looking. Then they were to open the machine, pretend to make a few adjustments, and show the customer that the machine was now fixed. The idea was to not embarrass the customers by letting on that they missed something so obvious.)

Several problems can result from a loose connector. Usually a quick check suggests an easy solution.

- The screen is completely black.

  Check the power cord. On modular Macs, which have a separate screen, check the cable or cables from the monitor to the Mac, too.

- The mouse, keyboard, or other plug-in hardware like a modem doesn't work.

  Check that the cable or cables for these devices are firmly connected at both ends.

- The Mac isn't printing or can't find the printer.

  Check the printer or network cable and make sure that the cable is connected at both ends.

Always shut down the Mac before you connect or disconnect any cables. (Pull down the Special menu, choose Shut Down, and turn off the power switch if your machine requires it.)

After you check a cable, disconnect it from the Mac and check for any bent pins, cat hairs, cobwebs, or misplaced ham sandwiches lodged in the connector. As you replace the cable, make sure that the plug lines up correctly with the connector on the Mac and then push it firmly into place. Refer to the section "Your Mac from the Back," in Chapter 4 for more information about the cable connectors on the back of your machine. Some cable plugs, such as the SCSI cable and the external diskette drive cable, come with thumb screws on either side. (Sounds rather medieval, doesn't it?) You tighten these screws with your thumb and finger to keep the cable from accidentally disconnecting.

Does your Mac start?

If your Mac seems completely unresponsive or dead after you first try to start it, try starting it again. Does it beep or make any noise at all after you turn on the power switch or press the Power key, depending on your Mac model? (The Power key is the one marked with a triangle and located at the top center or top right of the keyboard.) If you hear no beep or no noise at all, check the cables as described in the preceding section. If any are loose, reconnect them and try again.

If your Mac remains completely unresponsive even after you make certain that all connectors are secure, you probably have a pretty serious problem and need to call a technician to take a look at your machine.

If your Mac beeps but the screen remains blank, look for the brightness dial on your monitor. Sometimes this dial gets turned all the way down so that the screen looks like it's not working at all. Turning the dial back up shows you whether this is the cause of your problem.

On most compact black-and-white Macs, you can find the brightness dial on the front panel in the lower-left corner. On Macs with color monitors, look on the right side of the monitor, near the top. PowerBooks use a slider, a dial, or up-down buttons located on the right, below the screen.

If you use a non-Apple monitor with your Mac, look for a dial or knob behind an access door, on the front of the monitor along the bottom, or on either side. A symbol that looks like a shining sun usually accompanies the knob.

 If the screen on the Mac Classic, the Mac Classic II, or the Performa 200 is completely dark, you probably have a serious problem and should see a technician. The reason for this situation is that these Macs have no brightness dial. Instead, you control the screen brightness with the Brightness control panel, which is part of the Mac system software. Because you control the brightness from the screen, you can't turn the screen completely dark.

After you find the brightness knob, try adjusting it as far as it goes in either direction. If your screen lights up, you've solved the problem. If not, your problem may be serious and you may need to call a technician for help.

What about a flashing question mark icon?

If your Mac starts but flashes a question mark at you, *don't panic.* The question mark just means that the Mac can't find a disk — either hard disk or diskette — containing the system software it needs to start.

In this case, first check all the cables that connect any hardware, such as external hard disks or scanners, to the *SCSI port* on the back of the Mac. (The SCSI port is a connecting point where you plug hardware into your Mac.) For more information about this port, see the section "Your Mac from the Back," in Chapter 4; for now, however, you should recognize the SCSI port from its icon, which appears as a diamond with a horizontal bar through one side.

Make sure you switch off your Mac before you connect or disconnect any cables.

Because you can connect as many as six external pieces of hardware to the SCSI port, each linked to another in a chain, any one cable can easily come un-plugged anywhere along the line. Make sure that all the cables connect firmly. See Chapter 8 for more information about connecting hardware to the SCSI port and for guidelines on linking so many cables. If the question mark still flashes at you after you check the cables, however, skip to the section "Using Disk First Aid," later in this chapter.

Checking for recent additions to your Mac

If you recently added new hardware or software to your Mac, the newcomer may cause a conflict with some other Mac component . The conflict must be resolved before the Mac can work correctly. If you think that a hardware upgrade may be causing your start-up problem, refer to the section "What to Do if Something Goes Wrong," in the chapter that describes the kind of upgrade you added.

A hardware upgrade problem typically causes the Mac to sound an error chime on start-up instead of its usual beep. A sad Mac icon — letting you know the Mac's sorry it can't get along with the new hardware — and some numbers also appear on your screen. Or, your Mac may function normally until you actually try to use the new hardware, at which point the problem may rudely surface. Again, see the section "What to Do if Something Goes Wrong," in the chapter that describes your particular upgrade.

An upgrade to your system software may cause the Mac to freeze or crash during start-up or cause a system error dialog box to appear on-screen. If your Mac freezes or crashes at start-up, try pressing Shift while you restart your machine. Pressing this key prevents new additions to the system software from loading as you restart the Mac.

If starting with Shift pressed does get your Mac up and running, you need to identify which new addition to your system software is the culprit — and then remove it or update to a new version that eliminates the bug. See Chapter 17 for more information on working with system software.

Getting out of a crash

When your Mac crashes or freezes, you don't necessarily lose all the work you did in the past hour. Often you can restore the Mac to a usable condition long enough to save your work and restart normally. Several relatively simple fixes may do the trick if your Mac crashes:

✔ Wait a few minutes. Some operations take longer than you expect. The Mac may just need a few extra moments to complete a task. You shouldn't need to wait more than two or three minutes, however, for this fix to work.

✔ Press and hold the Command key (also known simply as ⌘) while you press the period key. Pressing these keys together is how you tell your Mac to stop the current task, if possible. Most people use this key sequence to cancel a long printing job, and the combination sometimes even works as a generic cancel command, depending on the application you're using. Some applications substitute Escape (or Esc) for the ⌘-period combination, so try pressing Esc, too.

✔ Press ⌘, Option, and Esc simultaneously. With System 7, this key combination forces the crashed application to quit. Unfortunately, this trick doesn't work with System 6. Using this key combination doesn't enable you to save work done in the application you quit, but may enable you to save changes made in other open applications.

System 6 and System 7 are two different versions of what's known as the Mac operating system. Think of the operating system as the software that runs and controls your Mac and your applications. You know, somebody always has to run the show, and with the Mac it's the operating system.

System 6 is an earlier version of the operating system than System 7, which means that System 7 lets you do more things with your Mac, such as use the trick we mention here to get out of a crash or use more memory. If you use System 6, you might want to think about upgrading to System 7. See Chapter 15 for more information.

Note: If none of the preceding suggestions work, press the Interrupt switch, which is marked with the word *Interrupt*, a small circle, or a line with a dip in the middle. A blank dialog box containing a > prompt appears. Type **G FINDER** after the prompt and press Return. If this process works, your Mac returns to the Finder, and you see the desktop with your hard disk and the trash icons. You may be able to save some work and restart normally. Figure 1-1 shows the Interrupt dialog box and what you type in it.

If you still have no luck getting out of the crash, press the Reset button, which is marked with either the word *Reset* or a left-facing triangle. Pressing this button restarts the machine. We're sorry to say that, you'll lose any unsaved work with this technique, but you do regain control of your Mac.

If your Mac doesn't have a Reset button or an Interrupt switch (the Mac LCs and the Mac IIsi don't), press and hold ⌘ and then press the Power key. (This key is marked with a triangle and is located either at the top center or top right of the keyboard.) Pressing these two keys has the same result as pressing the Interrupt switch. Pressing ⌘-Control-Power is the same as pressing the Reset button. Again, you'll lose any unsaved work, but you'll get control of your Mac.

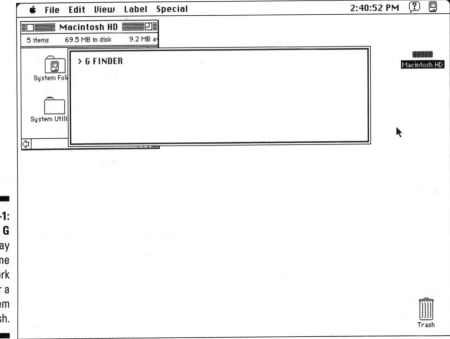

Figure 1-1:
Typing **G Finder** may save some of your work after a system crash.

Use the on/off switch or button at the back of the Mac only as a last resort. Using the Special menu's Shut Down or Restart command ensures that the Mac puts away all your work neatly so that it opens correctly the next time you want to use it. Turning the power switch off and on, on the other hand, does not put your work away and can result in problems later on.

For more information about the keys, buttons, and switches mentioned in this section, see Chapter 4.

Checking for viruses — another fix

Computer viruses can cause the Mac to crash or act strangely — such as your cursor bouncing wildly over the screen when you press the mouse button or funny (or not-so-funny) joke messages popping up while you're trying to work. Even worse, viruses also can irreparably damage your files and applications. Your Mac catches these strange diseases from diskettes that you insert in the diskette drive or, very occasionally, from software you get from computer bulletin boards or on-line services.

The best defense against viruses is to use virus-protection software regularly. If you don't have a virus-protection program of some kind, we suggest you get one now. Several good commercial packages are available, as is the freeware program Disinfectant by John Norstrad. You can obtain Disinfectant free of charge from user groups, or you can download it from most computer bulletin boards and on-line services. If you buy a commercial virus-protection product, make sure that you send in the registration card to receive updates for any new viruses that appear.

Before you download a file from an electronic bulletin board or an on-line service, read the description of the file to make sure the file has been scanned for viruses.

If you suspect that a virus is infecting your hard disk, use your virus-protection program on the disk to detect and remove the virus. Then disinfect all your diskettes and backups to avoid reinfecting your files. Make sure that you save a copy of the antivirus program's report telling you which files were infected. If you still notice strange behavior as you work with any of these files or applications, replace the files with copies from your backups.

Applying Disk First Aid

Disk First Aid — the Mac equivalent of a box of Band-Aids with dinosaur pictures on them — is one of the handiest pieces of software supplied free with every Macintosh. A fact of Macintosh life is that, as you use your machine, *stuff* builds up on the hard disk and may one day cause the disk to crash. This buildup is much like the grime that accumulates in your kitchen drain pipes, eventually stopping up your sink.

Fortunately, Mac system software (System 6 and higher) includes this Disk First Aid utility. This software helps get rid of dirty hard disk grime. If you don't find this utility installed on your system, local Mac user groups can usually provide copies. (For a fee, Apple will mail you a diskette containing the utility, but they often take their own sweet time getting it to you.)

Disk First Aid may prove helpful in correcting the following kinds of problems:

- ✔ Flashing question mark icon at start-up
- ✔ Problems opening files
- ✔ Random application crashes
- ✔ Crashes at start-up

If Disk First Aid finds a problem and reports that it fixes the problem, run the program again to make sure that the hard disk is really fixed. Sometimes one problem can hide another problem, and you must run Disk First Aid twice or more to take care of everything. Keep running Disk First Aid until the program reports that your hard disk is OK.

Although quite useful, Disk First Aid is not the end-all and be-all of hard disk-repair utilities. The commercial disk-repair utilities we mentioned earlier do the same job, although each utility takes a slightly different approach. Commercial utilities usually fix a wider range of problems than Disk First Aid can, but sometimes Disk First Aid is the only solution due to the approach it takes to hard disk repair.

How to use Disk First Aid correctly

Start your machine using the Disk Tools (System 7) or the Utilities 1 (System 6) diskette that came with your Mac (depending on your system version). After the Mac starts, double-click the Disk First Aid icon to start the utility.

Now you need to select the hard disk you want to fix (Disk First Aid works on both diskettes and hard disks, but we'll refer to hard disks only here). If you own the old version of Disk First Aid, click the Drive button in the Drive Selection dialog box until the name of the drive you want appears in the dialog box and then click Open, as shown in the following figure.

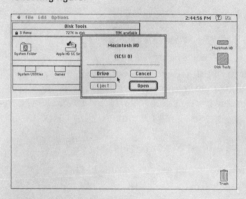

After you select the hard disk to fix, the Disk First Aid status window appears; click the Start button in this window, as shown in the following figure.

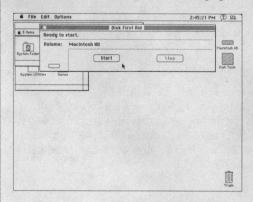

If you own the new version of Disk First Aid, the Disk First Aid window appears on-screen after you start the utility. As the following figure shows, this one window combines the functions of the Disk Selection dialog box and the status window of the old version.

To select a hard disk to fix with the new version, select the icon for that disk from the list of available hard disks shown in the window. After you select the hard disk, click the Repair button.

After you click the Repair or Start button, depending on your version of the utility, Disk First Aid scans the hard disk for problems. If Disk First Aid finds a problem, it asks if you want to fix the problem. Click the OK button to have the utility do the repair. Then, if Disk First Aid can fix the problem, a message appears telling you that the hard disk has been fixed.

If Disk First Aid cannot fix the problem, it tells you that, too. (Gee, thanks, but no thanks, you say. So what do I do if it can't fix the problem?) If Disk First Aid finds a problem but can't fix it, you may want to try a commercial disk-first-aid-type utility, such as Symantec's Norton Utilities or Central Point's MacTools. Or call a user group or technician for help. See the section "When — and Who — to Call for Help," later in this chapter for more information.

Reinstalling system software

This fix may be a last resort if nothing else works and you suspect a problem exists with your system software. Reinstalling your system software is most likely to work in the following situations:

- ✔ On a system you recently upgraded to System 7 without doing a clean install
- ✔ On a system infected by a virus (but reinstall the system software *only* after the virus has been destroyed but you still experience problems with crashes or start-up failure)
- ✔ If Disk First Aid reports that the system file has been damaged

See Chapter 15 for information on reinstalling system software.

Simple Steps for Isolating a Problem

The first step in fixing a problem is to pin down exactly what's going wrong. You need to know what's broken before you can start fixing or replacing parts. Following these steps can help you determine what exactly is causing the problem with your Mac and provide you with suggestions on how to fix it.

1. Check out anything new you've added to your system.

Sometimes new hardware or software causes problems to crop up on a Mac that has run flawlessly before.

Your Mac can be like an aquarium full of tropical fish. Usually, all the fish live together with no problems. Sometimes, however, adding a new fish can upset the entire ecosystem. If you recently added an upgrade, the new hardware or software should always be your first suspect in tracking down any problem with your system. See the section "What to do if something goes wrong," in the chapter that covers your particular upgrade for more information.

2. Determine exactly when the problem occurs.

Does it happen at start-up? Does it happen when the Mac tries to access an external device? Does it happen as you try to open a certain application? Think about exactly what you did just before the problem occurred. Did your Mac crash after you opened your word processor? If so, and your word processor never crashed before, try to figure out what was different this time.

3. **Try to duplicate or recreate the problem.**

   Try to repeat any actions you took preceding the problem and note what happens just before something goes wrong. By duplicating the problem, you can usually isolate exactly what is going wrong. Then you can tell a technician what you did just before the problem surfaced so that he or she is better able to fix your Mac quickly and correctly.

4. **Change the circumstances one by one to further isolate the problem and help you figure out exactly what is causing it.**

   After you recreate the problem, try variations on the steps preceding the problem. These variations may further help you pinpoint exactly what's causing the problem.

   The following example illustrates how you can isolate a problem by trying to repeat it and then changing the circumstances surrounding it:

   Suppose that your Mac crashes while you're writing a letter to Cousin Fredrik, who recently arrived from the Old Country. You remember that, just before you started your letter, you opened your Hungarian translation desk accessory to find a good Hungarian greeting. You also remember that your word processor crashed just as you returned to the translator for a closing line.

   You restart your Mac and try to repeat the crash by opening first your Hungarian translation desk accessory and then your word processor. Then you switch from the word processor to the translator, which is the point at which the original crash occurred. You try this operation with other applications, such as another word processor and a graphics application. If the crash occurs again with each application, always at the point of switching from the application to the translator, you can pretty much confirm that switching from an open application to your Hungarian translator desk accessory causes the application to crash.

   Now that you've isolated the problem, you use the Get Info command in the Finder to check the date on your translator. Sure enough, the Get Info information says that the translator was created in 1989, so it's been around for a while. You call the software company that makes the translator, and the representative tells you that a newer version that corrects the problem you're experiencing is now available. The new version of your Hungarian translator desk accessory arrives the next week, and you finish your letter to Cousin Fredrik without any further hitch.

5. **Try replacing whatever is causing the problem with another version of the same thing that you know works correctly.**

   After you isolate a piece of software or hardware that you think is causing the problem, try substituting another copy of the software or a different piece of the same hardware to see if the problem persists.

You may, for example, suddenly find that you can no longer type lower-case letters in any application — just as if your Caps Lock key is active. Pressing the key to release it, however, has no effect. You restart your Mac, but the Caps Lock key still doesn't seem to function. You decide to borrow another keyboard from a friend. After you start your Mac with your friend's keyboard attached, lowercase letters again appear normally. The keyboard, therefore, is the likely culprit, and you can take it to a technician for repairs.

To use an example of a software problem, suppose that your page-layout program begins crashing each time you try to work with it. More specifically, every time you open a newsletter template file, the Mac freezes up and you must restart the machine. You try opening a different template file, however, and the program works just fine. Unfortunately, you need to use your newsletter template file to finish your work by the deadline. You replace your original template file with a copy from a backup disk — and it works fine again. The problem, therefore, was with the copy of the template file on your hard disk, and you solved it by using the fresh copy from your backup.

By isolating a problem, you may discover an easy solution that you can apply right away. Even if you can't fix things yourself, you can still give a technician valuable information that helps him or her solve the problem quickly.

A Repair or an Upgrade (Which is the Solution?)

Sometimes you run into a problem that initially appears to call for repair work — but turns out that an upgrade is what you really need. If, for example, your complaint is that an application runs too slowly on your machine to be useful, you may actually need to upgrade your system with a speed accelerator — or even buy a new Mac. And if you keep getting error messages that claim that you don't have enough memory to open the application or that your hard disk is full, well, your Mac just may be trying to tell you that you need to upgrade its memory or add a nice new hard disk to the system.

You can, however, attempt several temporary solutions to the problems these error messages represent. Turn on virtual memory, for example, to get rid of any "not enough memory" error messages. (Refer to Chapter 15 for more information about virtual memory.) Dragging files to the trash and emptying the trash should eliminate the "disk full" error message. Be aware that these quick fixes do have their drawbacks: virtual memory slows down your Mac. And what if you want to keep every file on your hard disk and not throw away perfectly good work? Upgrading your system's memory or adding another hard disk are the only long-term solutions to these types of problems.

If you take your Mac to a technician for repairs and discover that fixing it costs almost as much as buying a new computer, you should seriously consider investing in a new Mac instead. You can bet good money that since you bought your current Mac, plenty of new models — both faster and cheaper than your old work horse — have appeared on the market. Scope out the features and performance of the new Mac models that fall in the price range of your estimated repair costs. You may find that, instead of repairing your old machine, you can get a better, faster, newer Mac for the same money.

When — and Who — to Call for Help

Knowing when and who to call about a problem you're experiencing with your Mac is one of the most important steps to getting your machine back up and running.

First, of course, you want to try all the basic checks and fixes listed at the beginning of this chapter before putting out any distress signals. If those suggestions don't solve your problem, however, consider it time to call in the cavalry, John Wayne, and a holsterful of computer tools!

Before you call for help, be prepared to explain your problem in detail. If you isolate the glitch the way we describe earlier in this chapter, you should have no trouble. You should also write down and have ready the following information:

- ✔ The name of your Mac model
- ✔ The amount of memory in your Mac
- ✔ The size of the hard disk in your Mac
- ✔ The version of system software you're using (for example, System 6.0.5 or System 7.0.1)

If you're having trouble with application software, make sure that you have the application's name and version number on hand as well.

Help for your Mac while it's still under warranty

Where exactly you seek help often depends on how old your Mac is.

When you buy a new Macintosh, a warranty covers the machine for one year from the date of purchase. If anything on the computer stops working because of a manufacturing defect, Apple fixes it free of charge. (That means that if you buy a new Mac today, and five months from now the diskette drive stops reading diskettes, you don't pay anything to get the drive fixed — what a deal! But then, who wants Mac hardware problems, even if you get a great deal on fixing them.)

So if you encounter a problem while your Mac's warranty is still good, take advantage of the opportunity: Get an Apple-authorized technician (or service provider, as these fix-it folks like to be called) to do the fixing for you.

Only Apple is the expert on the Apple warranty, but here's what we suggest. . . .

In general, the Macintosh warranty is a good thing, because it ensures that you get free repairs during the first year you own your computer. But the warranty also restricts you from playing around too much inside your computer during the warranty period. The idea is that, if you break something inside your Mac while you make an installation on your own, Apple isn't obliged to fix it for you.

If you want to make any of your own upgrades or changes inside your Mac during the warranty period, we suggest that you first call the following Apple customer-assistance number: 800-776-2333. Tell the representative who answers exactly what you plan to do, such as install a new memory card or an expansion card. Then ask for — and follow! — this person's advice on whether to make the change yourself or have an authorized service provider do it.

You don't want to do anything inside your Mac that may cause Apple to say that you voided the warranty. In general, however, you should be able to install expansion cards without breaking anything. The expansion slots into which these cards fit are designed so that you can easily expand and improve your machine. So your warranty shouldn't be voided if you make that upgrade yourself. But go ahead and ask about it anyway before you do anything — after all, it's a toll-free call.

Depending on your Mac model, installing memory can become a bit more involved than merely installing an expansion card. So if your warranty is still good, you may not want to perform this installation yourself.

As for installing a new internal storage drive, think twice — or three times — before you attempt this change during the warranty period. According to the Apple customer-assistance representative we talked to, Apple considers installing a storage drive as servicing, *not* upgrading. If you make this type of change yourself during the warranty period, Apple may no longer honor the warranty. We suggest, therefore, that you wait until *after* the warranty period to make any internal storage changes yourself.

After the warranty period is over, however, you have no more free repairs to consider, so you can either make any changes inside your Mac yourself or take your machine to a service provider for assistance — the choice is all yours.

One final note: Making external upgrades to your Mac — connecting an external hard disk, an external CD-ROM drive, a modem, or a large monitor, for example — is not the same as installing hardware inside your machine. These outside upgrades should not affect your warranty. But, again, if you have any questions at all about what upgrades you can install yourself, call the Apple customer-assistance number provided here *before* you begin any work.

So how do you locate a service provider? First, you can take your machine back to its old home: the place you bought it. If that's not possible (say you've moved to Hawaii for better sun), you do have one other alternative — and that's right, only one. Call this number at Apple Computer: 800-538-9696.

If you call, tell the folks you talk to your product model and your zip code, and they can give you information about the nearest authorized resellers in your area (database magic in action). Then you can contact the reseller, find out about available repair services and prices, and arrange for the fix.

The *best thing* about using this Apple phone number is that you can be certain that any repair service names you get are authorized by Apple to work on your machine. These service providers also honor your Mac warranty and do not try to make you pay for any parts the warranty covers.

By the way, if you call that 800-538-9696 number again, you can also learn about other Mac services in your area, such as training and user groups. And you don't need to wait until a certain time to call. The lines are open 24 hours a day, seven days a week.

If you're into asking for references, we suggest that you secure a list of the user groups in your area. Then, after you discover which service providers can help with your repairs or upgrades, check with these user groups for information on which of these providers are the most reliable and offer the best prices.

Note: You can also call 800-SOS-APPL, Monday through Friday from 6:00 a.m. to 6:00 p.m. Pacific Time. The representatives who answer this number can provide information about Apple hardware and software products and also answer questions about using your Mac.

If you own a PowerBook, call the 800-SOS-APPL number. Describe your PowerBook problem to the representative who answers; if the machine is under warranty, Apple repairs it for you at no cost to you.

After Apple agrees to fix your PowerBook, the service that follows is not only free but is truly wonderful: Apple pays a delivery service to drop off a special packing box at your machine's location, and you pack up your PowerBook while the delivery person waits. The delivery service then flies your PowerBook off to an Apple repair center, and it (your PowerBook, not the delivery service) gets repaired. Finally, within just a day or two, your computer arrives back at your location all fixed — and you haven't paid a dime. We've used this service with our PowerBooks, and we suggest you go ahead and call. This is the best way ever to fix your PowerBook.

In general, the SOS APPL PowerBook free repair service applies only to PowerBooks under warranty. Certain problems, such as screen flicker on particular models, however, may qualify for this free repair service even if the machine's warranty has expired. If you experience any problems at all with a PowerBook, call this service as your first step toward a solution.

Note: You can still use this service after your machine is out of warranty, but you have to pay for it. The service is so professional, however, that you may want to go ahead and use it even though you do pay. But check first with service providers in your area to compare their services and charges to those of the SOS-APPL services.

In nearly all cases, your best bet if something stops working within one year of purchase is to get your Mac fixed under warranty. Warranties apply only to hardware problems, however. Most service providers don't even try to fix a problem if they suspect software as the culprit. So, as we pointed out earlier, being able to recreate any problems you experience with your Mac *before* you take it in for repairs is very important. If a technician runs standard diagnostic tests and doesn't find the problem, you're likely to get your Mac returned to you with the explanation that it's a software problem. If, however, you can recreate the problem and help the technician recreate it, too, you stand a far better chance of getting your machine repaired.

After the honeymoon (warranty) is over

After the magical first year of the warranty is over, you're on your own if you need anything fixed on your machine. The best place to look for help at this time is in a Macintosh user group. Again, call 800-538-9696 to locate a user group in your area.

A good user group should have all the dope on the best repair places in town, as well as on where to get the best deals on upgrade equipment. As a matter of fact, user groups are an excellent source of information on just about any aspect of the Mac. The best plan is to join a user group before anything goes wrong so that you know who to ask for help when a problem does arise.

Try contacting a user group about fixing your Mac. Some of the larger user groups also include among their members technicians who can fix your machine for very reasonable fees. These people may or may not be authorized by Apple. (If they're not, ask others in the user group for advice and opinions about these technicians' skills before you entrust your machine to them.)

After you obtain a list of service providers from the user group, you face two alternatives: the authorized Apple resellers we've already mentioned or independent repair shops. Apple resellers are in business to move products out the door. Because service does not bring in much revenue, some resellers provide repair services only because Apple requires them to do so. Instead of helping you with repairs, these resellers may try to guide you toward purchasing new equipment. Other resellers, however, pride themselves on providing excellent repair service and go to great lengths to fix your problem. If you are lucky enough to find one of these places, stick with it. Good service is as valuable as gold.

Independent repair shops also can offer a good value by repairing parts rather than replacing them with new ones. If a chip goes bad on your Mac's logic board, for example, a repair shop may simply replace the chip, whereas a reseller is more likely to replace the entire logic board. Needless to say, replacing the logic board is much more expensive than replacing one little chip.

Just as you probably do when you need car repairs, you should shop around for a good price on repairs to your Mac. Charges often vary substantially for the same repair, depending on where you take your machine, so make sure that you get an estimate in writing and that the technician thoroughly explains to you any deviations from the estimate. Make sure, too, that you ask the provider how long your Mac must stay in the shop (and do so before you leave it). Some service providers often have a backlog of several days on repairs — and possibly even longer if they need to order parts. As we stated earlier, the goal in fixing your Mac is to get it fixed and fixed quick so you get can back to work as soon as possible. And the suggestions we've offered in this chapter should assist you in doing just that.

Chapter 2

Why Should You Upgrade (and Should You Do It Yourself?)

• •

In This Chapter

▶ Reasons to upgrade

▶ How to install your upgrade

▶ When to upgrade and when not to upgrade

▶ When to upgrade and when to buy a new Mac

• •

See Jane. See Mac. See Jane work at Mac. See Mac run out of memory. See Jane run out of patience. Upgrade, Jane, upgrade!

Reasons to Upgrade

This section gives you some reasons why you might want to upgrade your Mac and tells you why other Mac owners have taken the upgrade path.

You've only got two reasons to upgrade

Although many situations may induce you to upgrade, you really have only two basic reasons:

✔ To do new things on your Mac

✔ To do the things you're already doing better or faster

Why people upgrade

The following situations provide vivid examples of the two reasons why you — and other users — may want to upgrade your Macs.

Example 1: Your friend Joe works in an accounting department. He constantly makes changes to huge spreadsheets, and the recalculations take forever. He decides to install a math coprocessor in his Mac so that he doesn't need to spend so much time waiting on the calculations.

Example 2: You keep receiving "disk full" error messages and must constantly throw files in the trash to make more room for new documents on your hard disk. But you don't want to keep throwing important work away, so instead you pile up stacks of diskettes containing old, stored files. Finally — before you end up neck-deep in diskettes — you decide to add a larger hard disk, either internal or external, to your system.

Example 3: You realize that cutting and pasting information between several different applications — such as your word processor, your e-mail program, and your database — could save you a bundle of time. Unfortunately, whenever you try to open all these applications at once, you receive a "not enough memory" error. To solve the problem, you install more memory in your Mac.

Example 4: You find yourself often needing to transfer files from your PowerBook to your desktop Mac. You normally save your PowerBook files onto a diskette and then insert the diskette into your Mac whenever you want to work with those files at your desk. The problem with this approach is that you can't transfer very many files at a time — and you can't transfer really large files at all. Buying AppleTalk network connectors to link your PowerBook and your Mac makes your file transfers go faster and easier than continuing to use floppies for the task. (For more information about AppleTalk and networking, see Chapter 11.)

Example 5: Your older compact Mac just doesn't run today's software as fast as you want. Documents take forever to open and scroll through, and your spell-checker seems to take forever to chug through even your shortest letters. Installing an accelerator puts the pep back in your Mac. (For more information about accelerator hardware and speeding up your Mac in general, see Chapter 14).

Example 6: Jack's company owns Macintosh computers for each employee but only two laser printers for the entire office. Everyone in the office must use a laser printer for printing documents, but the company doesn't have enough money to buy a laser printer for each employee. Instead, the company installs an AppleTalk network so that everyone can share the two laser printers. After the employees begin using AppleTalk, they also learn that they can use the file-sharing capabilities of System 7 to send documents back and forth to each other — an added bonus. (For more information about sharing printers and networking, see Chapters 9 and 11.)

How to Install Your Upgrade

If you decide to upgrade your Mac, your options for installing the upgrade hardware are as follows:

- ✔ Install the upgrade yourself
- ✔ Have a professional install the upgrade for you
- ✔ Put your Mac under your pillow and see if the Upgrade Fairy will do the upgrade for you

When to Upgrade and When Not to Upgrade

You have to know when it's time to install an upgrade and when it's not. Here are some ways to help you decide.

Why you can upgrade your Mac yourself

With the help of the instructions we give in this book, installing most Mac upgrades is a piece of cake — chocolate, our favorite. Except for the black-and-white compact Macs, most Mac models are designed to be easily upgradeable. The modulars and the color compacts are especially easy. The modulars have plenty of room inside, and you can easily locate where everything goes. The color compacts are made with upgrading in mind — most parts snap together like Legos.

Contrary to popular belief, upgrading a Macintosh does not involve using a soldering iron; most

Mac models, in fact, don't require any special tools beyond a screwdriver for upgrading. And many outside upgrades require no tools at all, because you simply plug a cable into the back of the Mac and immediately start using the new hardware. How's *that* for convenience?

Finally, don't worry about breaking your computer. Just follow the instructions that come with your upgrade hardware and the guidelines we give you in this book, and you'll make out just fine.

When to upgrade

Go ahead and upgrade if any of the following scenarios apply to you:

- You continually see "not enough memory," "disk full," "not enough memory to keep window open" or "Having a great time in Florida; wish you were here. Love, Mac" messages popping up on-screen

- Everything you do with your Mac is slow, and you're always waiting for something to happen, such as software to load or files to open — or Christmas to come so you can check under the tree for a new Mac

- You need to do something new with your Mac that it doesn't do now, such as scan photos, display colors, or telecommunicate

- You can't run new software on your old Mac

- You hear about a new product that really sounds fun and the price is right . . . but your Mac just doesn't fit the requirements

- A bunch of other Macs in your department at work get upgraded

Getting some help upgrading, maybe even for free . . .

You can get help with your upgrade from several different sources, such as from the reseller where you buy the upgrade hardware, from the technical support department of the company that makes upgrade, or from local Mac user groups.

These are our suggestions:

- Have the reseller where you purchase the upgrade install it for you. The charge should be reasonable — or maybe you can get the installation done for free. Even if you don't mind installing the hardware yourself and you're all psyched up to do it, if a dealer offers to upgrade your Mac for free — hey, why not? You can always install the next upgrade yourself.

- If you purchase hardware through a mail-order company, you can pay the service department of an Apple-authorized reseller to install it.

- You can hire a consultant who is authorized to work on Mac hardware and have him or her do the upgrade for you.

- You can contact the Mac user groups in your area for help. These groups sometimes offer memory or expansion card installation services, and they occasionally conduct clinics where you can bring in your machine and have upgrades installed by group members.

- Contact the technical support department of the company that makes the hardware you're installing. A support person may walk you through the upgrade over the phone, or the company may make recommendations about consultants or resellers in your area who are specially trained to work with its products.

Finally, see Chapter 1 for suggestions on finding service locations, technicians, and consultants you can trust.

> ✔ Your computer starts to appear in antique shops or in the medieval history section at the local museum

When not to upgrade

Don't upgrade if any of the following scenarios seem familiar to you:

> ✔ Everything works fine just the way it is — that is, you get the results you want from your Mac in a reasonable amount of time
>
> ✔ Your neighbor buys the latest Mac model, and you're feeling more than a twinge of Mac envy
>
> ✔ You're pressured by pushy sales people who try to tell you what a savvy shopper you are by purchasing the very latest upgrade
>
> ✔ Anybody advises you to spend tons of money on an upgrade, whether the person is a trusted friend, a highly recommended consultant, or an overly-assertive salesperson (Always get a second opinion first!)
>
> ✔ Well-meaning technology-lovers tell you about the latest, greatest thing — but you can't even figure out what in the world they are *talking* about, much less what you'd do with it if you could
>
> ✔ You've just read glowing magazine reviews about high-priced equipment with features you don't even need (Such reviews are often useful, but you must remember that some of the most hard-core computer lovers write these articles, and they sometimes lose perspective about what's really needed in the "real" world.)

Should You Upgrade or Buy a New Mac?

Another decision to make is whether to upgrade your Mac or just break down, sell your existing system, and buy an entirely new Mac. We use the following formula to help make such a momentous choice:

The total cost of the upgrade

versus

The cost of a new Mac *minus* the selling price of the old Mac

The following examples should give you some idea of how to apply this formula to real-life situations. Any time you consider upgrading, we suggest you go through this process so that you can really be sure that upgrading is the right step. The formula is also worth applying if you need to justify an upgrade or a new Mac purchase to the person in your company who authorizes such equipment expenditures.

The prices we give in these examples are *all approximations*. Actual prices, of course, vary from time to time and from place to place. Most importantly, we simply want you to learn the process of applying this formula whenever you must decide between upgrading your old machine or buying a new Mac.

Example 1: Jane owns an old Mac SE that she's used since college. She works a great deal with page layouts, and she's frustrated by the computer's small screen and slow speed. She also needs a high-density diskette drive so that she can exchange files on diskette with her co-workers.

Jane decides that she needs an accelerator with a video card for a 19-inch black-and-white monitor, a high-density diskette disk drive, and a larger hard disk. Her friend George suggests that she also look into new Mac prices, because he's recently spotted some great deals at local computer stores.

Here's how Jane applies the formula to determine if an upgrade or a new Mac best meets her needs:

Total Upgrade Cost	Cost of New Mac
Accelerator with video: $800	Quadra 610, 8MB memory, 240MB* hard disk: $1,900
19-inch black-and-white monitor: $900	19-inch black-and-white monitor: $900
High-density disk drive upgrade: $400	**Sale price of her Mac SE: $400**
Hard disk: $400	
Total: $2,500	Total: $2,400
	*comes with a high-density diskette drive

After getting price quotes and determining how much she can get from selling her Mac SE, Jane decides that she may as well buy the new Mac. She'll actually save $100 by doing this.

Example 2: Peter is an accountant and uses a Mac IIci for his work. In general, he's happy with the system, but he wishes it were faster. He prices new Macs and decides that he doesn't want to spend so much money, so he looks at accelerators.

Total Upgrade Cost	*Cost of New Mac*
Accelerator: $800	Quadra 650, 8MB memory, 240MB hard disk: $2,300
	Sale price of his Mac IIci: $1,000
Total: $800	Total: $1,300

Peter decides that buying the accelerator to speed up his current machine is his best bet until he can set aside more money for a new system.

Example 3: Penelope works in a small office and is constantly frustrated by "not enough memory" and "disk full" error messages. She uses a Mac SE/30 with 5MB of memory and an 80MB hard disk. She wants to upgrade to 8MB of memory and a 400MB hard disk. She would love a new Mac, but doesn't think her boss will go for it.

Total Upgrade Cost	*Cost of New Mac*
Hard disk: $500	Quadra 660av, 8MB memory, 500MB hard disk: $2,500
More memory: $200	
Total: $700	Total: $2,500

Penelope's boss approves the $700 upgrade, but not the $2,500 for a new Mac. (The sale price of Penelope's old Mac doesn't figure in here, because her company keeps the old Macs to give to new employees. Sure hope *we* don't end up with a job there.)

Example 4: Fritz owns a Mac IIsi with 5MB of memory and an 80MB hard disk. He's starting to work on multimedia productions, but his Mac IIsi just isn't up to the job. Because his IIsi includes only one expansion slot, he'd need to purchase an expansion chassis to hold all the expansion cards necessary for his new work. His friends advise him to buy a new Mac with more expansion slots.

Total Upgrade Cost	Cost of New Mac
External expansion chassis: $1,500	Quadra 950, 64MB memory, 1.2GB hard disk: $6,200
Professional sound card $900	Accelerated video card: $ 1,700
Accelerated video card: $ 1,700	CD-ROM drive: $700
Extra Memory: $2,200	**Sale price of his Mac IIsi:** $600
Larger hard disk: $1,000	
System accelerator: $1,200	
CD-ROM drive: $700	
Total: $9,200	Total: $8,000

Because of all the hardware features Fritz needs, he discovers that he can buy a new Mac for $1,200 less than it would cost to upgrade his Mac IIsi to the same level. Fritz figures that he can use his current monitor and keyboard with the new Mac Quadra 950 and further learns that he does not need to buy a separate sound card with the new system, because the Quadra 950 comes with all the sound capabilities built-in that he needs. And with the new Quadra 950, he'll have a much more stable system than with an upgraded IIsi. Fritz cashes in some bonds and sets up his multimedia studio complete with a brand new Mac.

Okay, now it's your turn: Use the following table to work out the formula for deciding whether to upgrade your existing Mac or to buy a new one.

Total Upgrade Cost	Cost of New Mac
	Sale price of old Mac:
Total:	Total:

How to determine the value of your old Mac on the used market

To determine the going rates for Macs in your area, read the want-ads in your newspaper for a couple of weeks before you actually price your used equipment.

For a national perspective on used-Mac prices, take a look at the magazine *Macworld*. *Macworld*'s news section lists the going rates for used Macs every month. This information comes from the American Computer Exchange of Atlanta, Georgia, a company that runs a database used to match up used-Mac sellers and buyers. Refer to the rates listed in the magazine to price your own Mac. And if you're not having any luck selling your Mac locally, you may even want to give this company's service a try yourself (although we haven't tried the service ourselves, so can't offer any experienced counsel on it). American Computer Exchange charges the seller ten percent of the Mac's selling price. To learn more about the service, call the company at 800-786-0717.

Chapter 3

Approaching Your Mac with Care

· ·

In This Chapter

▶ Backing up before an upgrade

▶ Identifying your workspace and your tools

▶ Grounding yourself and your Mac

▶ Following safety tips

· ·

*W*e really want you to read this introduction The reason is (gasp!) electrostatic discharge. (Insert frightening Hollywood monster movie music here.)

The term *electrostatic discharge* may sound really technical, but it's actually a very common, simple phenomenon. Electrostatic discharge is what you feel if you scuff your feet on a carpet on a cold winter day and then touch a metal door knob — *(zap!)* You probably know that zap you feel as static electricity. Static electricity doesn't usually hurt you, but it sure can kill your Mac.

Because the silicon chips in your computer contain such tiny elements, the relatively minor zap you feel from touching a door knob would have the same effect on a computer chip that dropping a bomb would have on your neighborhood. In fact, tiny amounts of static electricity that you can't even feel can kill a chip. Worse — it can cripple a chip, and the damage may not show up until weeks later.

What can you do to prevent electrostatic discharge? Glad you asked. You must ground yourself and your Mac — no, we don't mean sending your Mac to bed without any supper and taking away its driving privileges. And you do it by using a grounded antistatic mat for your Mac and a grounding wrist strap for yourself. (See the section, "Your tools," later in this chapter for information on these handy items.)

Note that the electrostatic discharge information we cover in this chapter, as important as it is, applies to *inside* Mac upgrades only, such as installing memory, an internal hard disk, or expansion cards. When you do outside upgrades, such as plugging an external hard disk, a modem, or a scanner into the back of your Mac, you don't need to follow the special procedures for grounding yourself. Just be sure to leave your Mac plugged in but turned off. Then, before you plug in the outside upgrade, touch any exposed metal piece on the back area of the Mac. Touching the metal will drain away any electrical charge that might be present on your body.

Backing Up Before You Upgrade

You've been told a thousand times to back up. Make this a thousand and one. Backing up is especially important if you're about to upgrade your system. Back up *all* your software — both your applications and all your documents. The reason is simple: you need an extra copy of all your work in case something happens to your hard disk as you upgrade. For more information on backing up, see Chapter 16.

Backing up is especially important when you upgrade, because changing your Mac or any of its components creates a slight chance that you could damage the applications and files on your hard disk.

Of course, right about now you may be thinking, "But all my files and applications are on my hard disk, and I'm not upgrading my hard disk, so do I still need to back up?" Yes, because seemingly unrelated upgrades can cause problems with the entire system. In the worst of all possible worlds, for example, just plugging in a scanner to the back of your Mac could cause your hard disk to fail. Or, in adding memory, you could wind up with a faulty chip that causes a catastrophic failure in your entire Mac system. The chance of these disasters occurring is small, but the point is that they *could* happen, so why take the risk? By backing up all your data you make sure that you don't lose your vital — and even your not so vital — files.

We can't emphasize this enough — you *must* back up your files. Always. (And *especially* before you upgrade.) Even experts can sometimes encounter problems in which a full backup could have saved them much unnecessary anguish — had they but remembered to follow this simple rule.

Identifying the Ideal Workspace and the Tools You Need

Before you upgrade your Mac, you need a place to work and the right tools to get the job done.

Your workspace

The following characteristics describe a good location to work on your Mac:

- No commotion
- No traffic — so don't try to do your upgrade in the middle of 5th and Main during rush hour
- Enough space to spread out the parts of your Mac and the new upgrade parts
- Good lighting so that you can easily see small parts
- A place you don't mind getting dirty

(The table or bench on which you work should be flat and about twice as big as you think it needs to be. And you don't want to work on a metal, plastic, or vinyl surface. Good surfaces to work on are wood or Formica. You'll be laying down your antistatic mat on the work surface when you do upgrades inside your Mac. The section, "Your tools, " gives more information about this mat.)

Your tools

Imagine yourself elbow deep in a Macintosh and you drop a screw into the heart of the machine. You can see it, but you can't touch it. If only you had picked up a magnetic screwdriver before you started. Now you have to run out to the hardware store and buy one right in the middle of your upgrade. And after you get back? Now let's see, just *what* part of the upgrade were you doing before you dropped that screw?

Back when Frank worked in a busy company repairing Macs, having all the right tools ready beforehand was critical. Otherwise, if he went looking for a tool in the middle of an upgrade, someone could have just come in and walked off with a part of the Macintosh while he was away and installed it in another computer!

Safety tools to use with all Mac models

You need the following tools to create a static-free environment to work safely inside any Mac model:

- ✔ A grounding wrist strap
- ✔ An antistatic mat
- ✔ A grounding wire for your Mac

  (This wire has a clip on both ends. One clip attaches inside the Mac, and the other end connects to an electrical grounding point.)
- ✔ A electrical outlet tester

Electricity and safety tools and terms explained

Electrical ground or ground — noun; an electrical connection that safely conducts static electricity from your Mac to the earth. You create the connection by attaching a wire between the object you want to ground and a metal stake in the earth. Sometimes the metal water pipes in a building are used instead of a metal stake. The stake or the water pipes make up the main grounding point for a building. The lower round hole in electrical outlets or the outlet cover screw are wired to the building's main grounding point.

Ground — verb; to connect an object, such as your Mac, yourself, or your work surface, to an electrical ground. For example, when you work inside your Mac, you must ground yourself, your Mac, and your work surface. Grounding puts all three at what's called the same electrical potential, so that no static electrical charges flow between you, your Mac, or your work surface.

Grounding wrist strap — an elastic band that you wear on your wrist when you work inside your Mac. The band has a metal plate that touches your skin and that also attaches to a wire that connects to the grounding point at an electrical outlet.

You buy a wrist strap packaged in a kit with an antistatic mat. Keep reading for more information about this kit.

Antistatic mat — a mat made of materials that do not conduct electricity. When you work inside your Mac, you should place an antistatic mat over your work surface and connect the mat to the grounding point on an electrical outlet. Then the mat can drain static-electric charges away from you and your Mac.

You buy an antistatic mat and a wrist strap together in a kit. The kit we recommend is the "Techni-Stat Field Service Kit," available from Techni-Tool. The part number is 205ST010, and the cost is about $40. The phone number is 215-941-2400.

Grounding wire for the Mac — a wire that grounds your Mac when you work inside the computer. This tool is a piece of wire with alligator clips on both ends. To ground your Mac, you attach one clip to the metal chassis inside the Mac. You attach the other clip to a metal snap on the antistatic mat or to the metal screw on a grounded electrical outlet cover. You can buy this kind of wire at Radio Shack or at an electronics store for a dollar or two. When you go to the store, ask for a wire lead or a jumper wire with alligator clips on both ends.

Electrical outlet tester — a small device that plugs into an electrical outlet. Lights on the tester let you know if the outlet is wired properly for safe grounding. You can buy one of these testers at a hardware store for about five dollars.

Before you ground yourself, your Mac, and your work surface, you need to test the electrical outlet that you plan to use for grounding. You want to make sure the outlet is wired properly for safe grounding. To test the outlet, plug in an electrical outlet tester to find out if the outlet is safe. If the outlet is safe, the tester's lights will indicate that the outlet is wired correctly for grounding, which means you can use either the lower round hole or the outlet cover screw. If the outlet isn't safe, the tester lights will let you know.

If you find out that the outlet isn't wired safely for grounding, you'll have to contact an electrician to rewire the outlet.

Note that even though the one outlet you test is safe for grounding, the others in your building may not be safe. Be sure to test any other outlet you plan to use for grounding.

Grounding creates a safe environment for working inside your Mac. It may seem like going against good judgment to connect yourself to an electrical outlet, but after you verify that the outlet is wired safely for grounding, you can safely connect to the outlet with a grounding wrist strap.

If you don't have much experience with grounding, you can read more about this very important procedure in the section, "Grounding Yourself and Your Mac," later in the chapter.

The exact tools required for the upgrade itself depend on the type of Mac you're upgrading — compact, modular, or portable. You can purchase almost all the tools you need from a hardware store. You can order certain specialized tools through the mail from Macintosh hardware vendors.

Tools for upgrading black-and-white compact Macs

If you're upgrading a black-and-white compact Mac, you need the following tools:

- A long-handled Torx number 8 screwdriver
- A magnetic Phillips number 2 screwdriver
- A large flat blade screwdriver
- A wire for grounding your Mac; the wire should have alligator clips at either end (you can find this kind of wire at Radio Shack or other electronics stores)
- A Pony 3201 spring clamp (or what people call a Mac case cracker)
- Needle-nosed pliers
- An egg carton for holding screws

- ✔ A wire cutter designed for electronics that cuts at the tip of the tool rather than in the middle of the cutting blades

- ✔ Safety glasses

  (If the CRT inside a black-and-white compact Mac is damaged, it may implode and shower glass over the surrounding area, including you. The safety glasses protect your eyes.)

- ✔ A rabbit's foot or four leaf clover, just in case

If you have problems getting ahold of some of the specialized tools for working on a black-and-white compact Mac, you can order the Mac Tool Kit from Mac Warehouse. The kit includes a spring clamp to open the Mac case and a Torx screwdriver. Rabbit's foot not included. The Mac Warehouse phone number is 800-255-6227.

Tools for upgrading color compact Macs

If you're working on a color compact Mac, you need the following tools:

- ✔ A magnetic Phillips number 2 screwdriver
- ✔ Needle-nosed pliers
- ✔ A Torx number 8 screwdriver (either long- or short-handled)
- ✔ An egg carton for holding screws

Tools for upgrading modular Macs

If you're working on a modular Mac, you need the following tools:

- ✔ A magnetic Phillips number 2 screwdriver
- ✔ Needle-nosed pliers
- ✔ An egg carton for holding screws

Tools for upgrading PowerBooks

If you're working on a PowerBook, you need the following tools:

- ✔ A Torx number 8 screwdriver (either long- or short-handled)
- ✔ A Torx number 10 screwdriver
- ✔ A magnetic Phillips number 2 screwdriver
- ✔ A jeweler's flat-blade screwdriver
- ✔ Needle-nosed pliers
- ✔ An egg carton for holding screws

If you have trouble finding some of the tools for working on a PowerBook, you can order a PowerBook tool kit from Mac Warehouse. The Mac Warehouse phone number is 800-255-6227.

Grounding Yourself and Your Mac

Electrostatic discharge prevention guidelines — say that five times really fast! Grounding prevents electrostatic discharge.

You always want to ground yourself, your Mac, and your work surface when you work inside the computer. There's only *one* exception to this rule: when you discharge the CRT, or picture tube, in a black-and-white compact Mac. When you discharge the CRT, make sure that neither you, nor Mac, nor your work surface are grounded. See Chapter 19 for the instructions for discharging the CRT.

Here's how to ground yourself, your Mac, and your work surface so that you don't zap your Mac with static electricity:

1. Use an electrical outlet tester to verify that the electrical outlet you use as a grounding point is safely wired for grounding.

   Don't use the outlet as a grounding point if the tester indicates the outlet isn't safe. If you connect to an unsafe outlet, you run the risk of standing your blackened hair on end, feeling your eyes bug out in pain, and having thick dark smoke pour out of your ears. Get the picture? Contact an electrician to rewire the outlet for grounding.

2. Place your antistatic mat on your work surface and connect it to an electrical ground.

3. Put on your grounding wrist strap and connect it to the electrical ground as well.

4. Open your Mac and clip one end of the Mac grounding wire to the metal *chassis.* (The chassis is the metal frame inside your Mac that holds everything together.) Clip the other end to a metal snap on your antistatic mat or to the screw on a grounded electrical outlet cover. See Chapters 17 through 19, for the instructions for opening your Mac model.

With this setup, you, your Mac, and your work surface are at the same electrical potential, and you leave no chance of damaging the computer chips from static discharge.

Feel like taking a gamble with your Mac?

No matter who's Mac you're upgrading, make sure that you carefully follow the preceding electrostatic discharge prevention guidelines to prevent static electricity from damaging the computer. Grounding yourself and your Mac is essential for performing any upgrade. Failing to take the correct electrostatic discharge prevention precautions before upgrading your machine is like a surgeon forgetting to scrub up before operating on a patient. And the procedure can become extremely hazardous to the health of the patient.

Note: Suppose that you worked on your Mac during the warranty period (the first year after purchase) and you killed your computer with static electricity. You take the machine to a technician for service under warranty. If, however, the technician suspects that you worked on your Mac in a nongrounded environment, he or she may refuse to honor the warranty. Of course, you don't need to worry about the warranty in such a case if your Mac is more than a year old. But you should worry about damaging your Mac — and about any repair costs that result from that damage. (*Zap!*) Refer to Chapter 1 for more information about your Mac warranty.

Some people may claim you can get by without following electrostatic discharge prevention guidelines, because, after all, they upgraded their Macs without a wrist strap, and things worked out just fine. Hey — they got *lucky*. And the unfortunate thing about luck is that it usually changes (often for the worse).

Companies that make computers and upgrade hardware, including Apple, follow strict guidelines to prevent electrostatic discharge from plaguing their assembly lines. The bottom line is that companies spend time and money on these procedures because the people working in the companies know it's necessary.

Ground (ing) rules for preventing electrostatic discharge

Follow these rules to keep electrostatic discharge from damaging your Mac:

- ✔ Always work on a grounded work surface like an antistatic mat.

- ✔ Always wear a grounding wrist strap, except to discharge the CRT of a black-and-white compact Mac. (See Chapter 17 for more information about discharging the CRT in a compact Mac.)

- ✔ Open the antistatic packaging on expansion cards or memory SIMMs only on a grounded work surface like an antistatic mat. See Chapter 12 for more information on memory and SIMMs.

✔ Always use *static-shielded bags* to transport expansion cards, memory SIMMs, and any other circuit boards. (These are the silver or pink bags in which the products are packaged.)

✔ Be careful not to touch the components on expansion cards or memory SIMMs.

✔ Don't put upgrade boards or parts of your Mac on metal surfaces during an upgrade. Metal surfaces attract static electricity and can cause an electrical short in components.

✔ Do not wear clothes made of synthetic fabrics while you work on a Mac.

✔ Do not open shrink-wrapped packages around an open Mac or near upgrade components.

✔ Keep items such as Styrofoam coffee cups, plastic bags, scotch tape, plastic wrap, vinyl, inflatable Godzillas, and almost any other plastic item away from an open Mac. These items cannot be grounded but can generate and hold a static charge that can damage your Mac.

✔ Don't use a vacuum cleaner inside your Mac. The moving parts inside a vacuum cleaner work much like a static electricity generator.

✔ Keep other people who are not wearing grounding wrist straps away from your open Mac. Anybody not grounded can pass a charge on to you or your Mac and damage your chips.

What exactly does "grounding yourself" mean?

Grounding yourself and your Mac is essential if you want to make certain that you don't accidentally damage the Mac's sensitive electronic components. But what does grounding something really mean?

We can start out by reiterating our earlier example of touching a metal door knob after scuffing your shoes across a carpet on a dry day. Scuffing your shoes on the carpet builds up an electrostatic charge on your body that puts you at a much higher *electric potential* than the door knob — didn't know you had so much potential in life, did you? If two objects with different levels of electric potential (such as your hand and the door knob) touch, a spark (or *zap!*) generates as static electricity. The spark jumps from one of the objects to the other to equalize this difference in potential — and you get a shocking surprise.

The amount of static electricity that flows between you and a door knob is quite enough to trash a computer chip. But by connecting yourself and your Mac to the *earth ground* in your home or office electrical system, you equalize the electric potential between yourself and your Mac so that no charge flows in either direction.

One way to get a good earth ground is with a metal stake pounded into the ground and a wire attached to it. The metal water pipes in buildings often serve the same purpose as the metal stake. Using the ground that is already built into a building's electrical system is much simpler by far. The round hole on most wall outlets (the one beneath the two vertical slots where you insert the prongs on an electrical plug) connects to an earth ground and doesn't carry any current. Most modern grounding systems either plug right into this hole or connect in some other way, such as to the screw that holds the outlet cover on.

Safety Tips for Upgrading the Mac

To keep your Mac safe from harm, always follow the electrostatic discharge prevention guidelines given in the preceding section.

And to keep yourself safe while doing an upgrade, follow these tips:

- ✔ Always unplug your Mac before you start any hardware upgrade.
- ✔ Never open a Mac that is plugged in or running.
- ✔ Watch out for metal edges inside the Mac; they can be sharp enough to cut your fingers if you slip.
- ✔ Watch out for hot parts inside the Mac. The CRT in black-and-white compact Macs can be quite hot right after you turn off the Mac. And the larger hard disks in older Mac IIs can generate enough heat to burn you.
- ✔ Always wear safety glasses when you work inside black-and-white compact Macs.
- ✔ Keep away from the power supply or the analog board in black-and-white compact Macs. (The *analog board* provides power for the CRT. You'll recognize it because it's the largest circuit board inside the Mac and the only one with wires running to the CRT.)
- ✔ If you have long hair, keep it tied back while you work inside a Mac. This precaution not only eliminates a possible static electricity problem, but also keeps your hair from getting caught inside the Mac.
- ✔ Remove your grounding wrist strap and any metal jewelry you're wearing before you discharge the CRT on a black-and-white compact Mac.

We've emphasized the importance of grounding yourself with a wrist strap and an antistatic mat. The only situation in which you don't want to be grounded is when you discharge the CRT on a black-and-white compact Mac. Make sure that you are not wearing your grounding wrist strap if you do this. For more information about discharging the CRT, see Chapter 17.

Chapter 4

Basic Mac Anatomy

• •

• •

*I*n this chapter, you become familiar with the different parts of your Macintosh. You aren't doing any upgrading yet, so put away those saws, hammers, putty knives, and toothpicks — you don't need them at all (yet!). Here you learn all about the Mac, inside and out, so you'll be ready to upgrade when the time comes.

The Three Types of Macs

Macintosh computers come in three basic flavors: compact, or the all-in-one Macs; modular, or the Macs with detached monitors; and the portable PowerBooks. The following sections describe the features of these different models so you always know what type of Mac is sitting there before you.

Mac-in-a-box

Compact Macs have the screen built into the main box, or *case*. This type of Mac is the original computer that many people think of when they hear the name Macintosh.

Many people like the compact Macs because the computers are easy to move around, and they provide all the hardware you need in a small, neat package. The main disadvantage of black-and-white compact Macs is their limited upgrade capability, which means that you can't really install many add-ons. The black-and-white compact case is a bit difficult to open, too. But if you own one of the new color compacts, you're in luck — they're much easier to upgrade than the black-and-whites, thanks to their design. (Refer to Chapter 5 for more information about the different compact Mac models and their upgrade possibilities.)

Modular Macs

Modular Macs feature a separate screen and a bigger main unit with ample room inside for adding stuff to improve memory, speed, and video.

Many Mac users like the modular Macs because they can use any size screen, either color or black and white. Because these Macs are roomy inside, they're easy to upgrade or repair, and many upgrade possibilities are available. See Chapter 6 for more information about each modular Mac and its upgrade capabilities.

PowerBooks — the flat Macs

The PowerBooks are the anywhere, anytime Macs. Battery powered with a built-in screen, these units are small, lightweight, and work great on your lap in an airplane seat or at the beach. But please, do not bury your PowerBook in the sand!

Like the compacts, PowerBooks are self-contained, complete packages. They offer somewhat limited upgrade capabilities. To compensate for these limitations, however, many PowerBook upgrades simply plug into the back of the machine. For more information about each different PowerBook and its upgrade possibilities, see Chapter 7.

Looking Around Outside Your Mac

This section reviews the outside of your Mac. Some of the easiest ways to upgrade your Mac involve upgrading its exterior features — such as adding a new keyboard or mouse. Take it from our experience: an ergonomic keyboard — one designed to protect the health of your hands and wrists — can really make typing much easier and more comfortable. And all you do to achieve this upgrade is buy the new keyboard and plug it in.

The information in this section acquaints you with the outside of your Mac so that you know what we're talking about in terms of outside or external upgrades and where to attach them. Refer to Part 3 of this book for more information about the specific hardware you can add on to the outside of your machine.

Finger stations

Most of the keyboards you see on a Macintosh are one of two kinds — standard or extended. Figure 4-1 shows these two Mac keyboards.

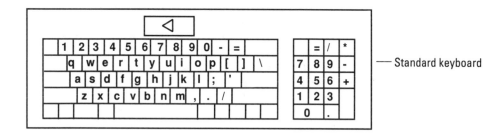

— Standard keyboard

Figure 4-1:
Two kinds
of Mac
keyboards:
standard
and
extended.

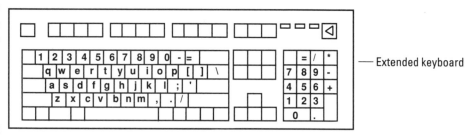

— Extended keyboard

The *standard keyboard* contains all the normal typewriter keys, plus a numeric keypad on the right. The *extended keyboard* includes a row of function keys across the top, four cursor keys, and other miscellaneous keys that make this keyboard look like a keyboard for IBM PCs and compatibles. The rumor is that Apple designed the extended keyboard to make people who switch from the PC to the Mac feel more at home.

Note: On certain Macs, such as Mac IIs and Quadras, you use a large key with the triangle on it, called the *Power* key, to turn on the machine. You'll find this key in one of two places: in the top center of the standard keyboard or in the upper-right corner of the extended keyboard.

Mousing around

The mouse is the one hardware component that truly makes a Mac a Mac. It enables you point politely, click OK buttons, pull down menus, and drag objects around the screen. Just try using your Mac sometime without the mouse and see how much you can actually do. Chapter 9 gives you information about upgrading your mouse.

When your fingers do the rolling

The PowerBook's keyboard is built-in and looks like a standard keyboard with the numeric keypad cut off. The keys are full-sized, however, and work just fine. The trackball on the PowerBook works exactly like an upside-down mouse, but instead of rolling the ball along the table, you roll it with your finger. Turn over your mouse sometime and move the ball around, and you'll see what we mean. The PowerBook has two buttons, one above and one below the trackball. The two buttons work like the one button on the mouse, and you can use them interchangeably — the choice is yours. Figure 4-2 shows a PowerBook keyboard, trackball, and the trackball's buttons.

Figure 4-2: The PowerBook keyboard, trackball, and buttons.

Buttons

Trackball

Face to face with your Mac

On the front of modular and compact Macs, you find a diskette drive slot in which you insert your diskettes.

On most PowerBooks, the diskette drive is located on the right side. The PowerBook Duos and the PowerBook 100 models, however, do not come with a built-in diskette drive, but you can attach an external diskette drive if you need one. See Chapter 8 for information about this upgrade.

Located to the right of the diskette drive's slot is the emergency diskette-eject hole. (On PowerBooks with internal diskette drives, this hole is in the lower-right part of the drive area.) If a diskette gets stuck in the drive, you can poke a straightened paper clip into this handy little hole as a last resort to release the diskette. Carefully push the paper clip into the hole and push against the manual eject lever inside. Make sure that you push it straight in so that the paper clip doesn't slip off the metal tab inside the hole.

On some compact Macs, such as the SE and the Mac Plus, you also find a screen-brightness knob on the lower-left corner of the front panel.

When the going gets rough, switch!

Many Macs feature *Reset* and *Interrupt* switches, sometimes located on the front of the Mac, sometimes on the side. Some people call these switches the programmer's switches. The Reset switch, or button, is usually labeled with a triangle, and the Interrupt switch is labeled with a circle or a line with a V-shaped dip in it. On the PowerBooks, these "switches" are actually two small holes on the back panel of the machine. The holes are labeled with a triangle (Reset) and a circle (Interrupt), just like on the regular Macs. The holes are tiny, and you must insert the end of a paper clip in them to use them.

So just what do you do with these switches? Well, you can often use them to get your Mac out of a freeze-up or a system crash. (For more information about getting out of crashes, refer to Chapter 1.) The Reset button turns off the power momentarily and makes the Mac restart itself. The Interrupt switch is not quite so radical; it simply enables you to exit to the Finder, from which you may be able to save your work before actually restarting the machine. Most people just use these two switches for getting their Mac out of a crash, but if you ever get into programming, you may also use the Interrupt switch for debugging your programs — which means getting rid of any problems in a program that cause it not to run right.

Note: Macs like the IIsi and the LCs don't have these two switches. You press Û-Control-Power key to carry out the reset function, and you press Û-Power key to carry out an interrupt.

Your Mac from the Back

The back of your Macintosh presents many opportunities for easy outside upgrades and add-ons. The back is where you plug in your external hardware, such as a new keyboard or mouse, a large monitor, a modem, an external hard disk, or an external CD-ROM drive.

At first glance, the back of your machine may look like a jungle of cables and dust bunnies with strange hieroglyphics scattered across the plastic and metallic terrain. If you look closer, however, you notice that these symbols actually form a road map for connecting add-ons to your Mac. In fact, if you match these pictures with the components they represent and make sure that the plug is right side up, connecting add-ons to the Mac is much easier than trying to attach the right speaker cable to the connectors on your stereo.

Located below each symbol is a connecting point, or *port*, into which you plug add-ons for your Mac. Each cable coming from an add-on depicts a symbol on its plug that matches the icon above the port that it connects to. You may also notice that each plug has a flat side or an arrow to show you which side goes up. If you look closely at the ports, you can see that almost all of them are oriented so that plugs can be connected only one way — the flat side or the side with the arrow goes up.

The ADB port? It's where you catch the bus

The first port we're going to examine is the *Apple Desktop Bus* (ADB) port. Some Macs have one of these ports on the back, and some have two. You plug in your mouse and keyboard into the ADB ports.

The keyboard also has a free ADB port that you can plug your mouse into if you want to. If your Mac has only one ADB port on the back, you have to use the port on the keyboard for your mouse.

Figure 4-3 shows the ADB ports. If you want to add joysticks, game controllers, trackballs, or drawing tablets to your Mac, you plug them into these ports as well. See Chapter 9 for more information about these upgrades.

The Mac 128K, Mac 512K, Mac 512Ke, and Mac Plus do not have ADB ports. Instead, they have a mouse port on the back and a keyboard connector on the front.

Figure 4-3:
ADB ports.

Mac, print that letter, get that phone

The printer and modem ports of the Mac were originally designed for use by a printer, such as the ImageWriter, and an external modem. (For those of you who don't know, a *modem* is a device your Mac uses to talk with other computers over the phone lines.) But many things can connect to these two ports: various printers, modems, sound digitizers, some scanners, and networks. You can connect only two devices at a time, however. Figure 4-4 shows the printer and modem ports on the back of your Mac. Notice the handy printer and modem icons above each port.

Figure 4-4:
Many
different
upgrades
connect to
the printer
and modem
ports.

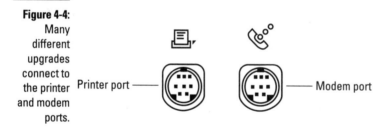

Printer port —————— ————— Modem port

Note: The printer port also links your Mac to an AppleTalk network (a *network* lets computers communicate with each other, but not over the phone lines like with a modem. The network connects computers via cables). People often get confused by this use of the printer port, because many AppleTalk networks use the same kind of wire as a telephone and may even plug into a phone jack. People reason that, if the network cable plugs into the wall like a phone, it should be connected to the Mac port displaying the telephone icon (the modem port). But nooooo — an AppleTalk network works *only* if it's plugged into the printer port — go figure.

On newer Macs, such as the Quadra 660av and 840av, the modem port is called the *Geoport.* This port enables you to carry out modem-like activities, such as telecommunicating and faxing, without a modem. You do, however, need a special adapter to connect to the phone line.

Be very careful not to confuse the plugs that go into the mouse and keyboard ports (the ADB ports) with the plugs that go into the printer and modem ports. All these ports are round, but each type has a different number of pins and they *are not* interchangeable. We once saw the result of someone forcing a network connector into the keyboard port — a $40 purchase had to be tossed because the plug's pins were completely mangled. Miraculously, this mistake didn't fry the Mac — a much more costly repair. Refer to Figures 4-3 and 4-4 to avoid confusing the mouse and keyboard ports (ADB ports) with the printer and modem ports.

Why your floppy disk isn't a flop

The *diskette port* enables you to connect an external diskette drive to your Macintosh. These days, external diskette drives aren't such a big deal, but before hard disks became part of every Mac, two diskette drives were essential. An extra diskette drive is still handy if you regularly copy information from diskette to diskette, but otherwise, you probably won't find much use for this port. Figure 4-5 illustrates the Mac's diskette port. The icon above the port represents a diskette. For more information about external diskette drives and external storage in general, see Chapter 8.

Figure 4-5:
The Mac's
diskette
port.

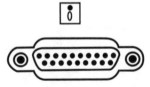

You may have heard diskettes called floppies. As you know, Macintosh diskettes aren't floppy. In fact, they're actually pretty rigid. The term carries over from the early days of computers when large, flexible, bendable disks were used for storage.

Want an audio output, Jack?

The *audio output port* functions the same as a headphone jack does on a Walkman. This port enables you to connect headphones or external speakers to your Mac so that you can work more quietly — or loudly, depending on your work environment. Depending on your Macintosh model, this audio output may be in stereo or mono. Regardless of how you hear the sound, audio output can be useful. Figure 4-6 shows the audio output port. The speaker symbol above the port represents its sound function.

Figure 4-6:
The audio output port.

When "scuzzy" means fast, not bad

To us, the best port of all is the *SCSI port!* The name of this port is truly one of the best examples of computer techno-babble we've ever heard. It stands for *Small Computer System Interface* and is pronounced *scuzzy*. SCSI is one of those lovely names that tell you absolutely *nothing at all.* This port, however, enables you to add all kinds of cool stuff to your Mac without ever cracking open the case. Among the devices you can connect to this port are hard disks, scanners, CD-ROM drives, tape drives, and other storage devices.

The SCSI port connects to big, fat cables that transmit information back and forth very quickly between your Mac and other pieces of hardware like hard disks or scanners. Figure 4-7 shows the SCSI port. The icon represents different kinds of hardware linked together in a chain. Chapter 8 provides more information about SCSI.

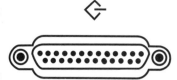

Figure 4-7:
The SCSI port.

Other ports of call

Some Macintosh models come with additional input/output ports that enable you to engage in such cool activities as recording sound or video or linking up to sophisticated business networks. Your Macintosh may or may not have these ports — take a look and see. The following sections describe some of these ports.

Microphone input port: karaoke anyone?

If your Mac features a microphone input port, you can record sound without adding any special equipment. Apple sells a special microphone to plug into this port, or you can pick up a cheap one from Radio Shack that works just as well. Figure 4-8 shows the microphone input port; notice the microphone icon.

Figure 4-8:
The
microphone

A few Macintosh models, such as the Quadra 660av and Quadra 840av, include connectors for stereo sound input, much like the connectors on your stereo music system. These connectors enable your Mac to capture high-quality stereo sound from audio tapes, CDs, video cassettes, or a microphone. The sound is useful for multimedia applications. The stereo sound input ports are shown in Figure 4-9. Notice the arrow icons that represent the right and left stereo channels.

Figure 4-9:
The stereo
sound input
ports

A plug for your monitor

Most modular Macs have a monitor port to plug in the cable from your monitor. Which monitors work with your machine depends on your Macintosh model. Figure 4-10 shows the monitor port with its monitor icon. See Chapter 10 for information on monitor upgrades.

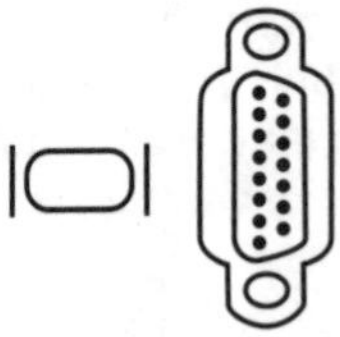

Figure 4-10:
You find this
monitor port
on most
modular
Macs.

Making Macintosh funniest home videos

Some Macs, such as the Quadra 660av and Quadra 840av, can accept and transmit video images as well as sound. You'll see two sets of *video input* and *video output* ports — for a total of four ports. You'll know these ports by their video camera icons. The first set of two ports is for *standard composite video*, one input and one output. The second set is for high-quality *S-video*, again with one input and one output port.

The standard composite video ports you find on these Macs are the same as the jacks you find on most VCRs and camcorders. The S-video ports are like the jacks on higher-quality video components such as laserdisc players and expensive camcorders. The video input ports and video output ports enable your Mac to connect to VCRs, camcorders, laserdisc players, and television sets. Figure 4-11 shows the video input and output ports with their icons indicating input and output.

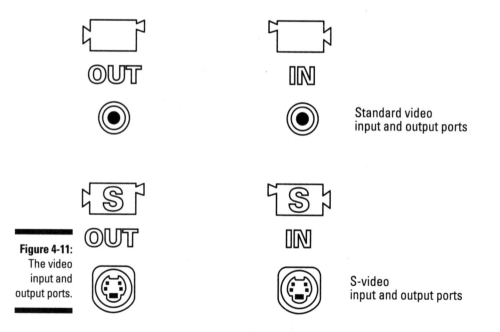

OUT

IN

Standard video
input and output ports

Figure 4-11:
The video
input and
output ports.

OUT

IN

S-video
input and output ports

Ethernet — not for catching fish (or ether, either)

The *Ethernet port* enables the Mac to connect to a fast kind of network, called *Ethernet*, that is built into high-end machines such as the Quadras and the Power Macintoshes. Figure 4-12 shows the Ethernet port. Its icon represents a stream of information flowing back and forth between different computers.

Figure 4-12:
The Ethernet port provides fast networking.

In work environments in which several computers — or even hundreds of them — need to talk to each other and share information, the computers and hardware like printers are often linked together by cables. The computers' software enables them to communicate via the cables. All the computers shoot information back and forth between each other; the entire system is called a network.

Of course, network users (or you sitting at your own computer) want fast transmission speeds for documents and data, so many companies use an Ethernet network. You must connect a box called a *transceiver* to the Mac's Ethernet port to connect your machine to the Ethernet cables and the network. Chapter 11 gives you more information about network upgrades.

A PowerBook inspection

Although the PowerBooks are small, they contain the same number of ports that other Macintosh models do. The PowerBooks do incorporate their own special versions of some of these ports, but although the PowerBook versions look different, they function exactly the same as their larger counterparts. Figure 4-13 shows these PowerBook ports.

Docking in port ... or porting in dock?

PowerBook Duos come with a printer port on the back for connecting to a printer or a network. They also have one large connector that links up to what's known as a *dock*. Figure 4-14 shows you this large connector.

PowerBook 160/180

Figure 4-13:
The ports on
the back of a
PowerBook.

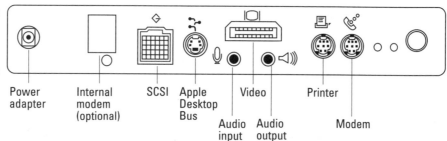

Power   Internal   SCSI   Apple   Video   Printer
adapter   modem   Desktop
               (optional)   Bus
                                                Audio Audio   Modem
                                                input output

Figure 4-14:
This large
connector
on the back
of the
PowerBook
Duos links
the Duos to
a dock.

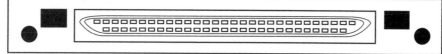

If you haven't seen one, a dock is a Macintosh with the brains — the processor
and logic board — removed. It's a box or shell that sits on your desk, to which
you can connect a monitor, printer, and hard disks in the same way that you
connect these devices to a standard Mac. In the front of the box is a large slot,
sort of like the slot in a VCR. You can slip a PowerBook Duo right into the slot,
which is called *docking* your PowerBook — your Duo does dock, but unlike a
boat, it doesn't float.

After the Duo is securely in the slot, the dock has received a brain transplant,
so to speak, and can perform all the functions of a standard desktop Macintosh.
If you finish working at your desk and want to take your portable somewhere
else, simply remove the Duo and take it with you. (See Chapter 7 for more
information about the PowerBook Duos and the Duo docks.)

Journey to the Center of the Mac

When most people look inside a Macintosh for the first time, the reaction is usually along the lines of: "Is that *all?*" A modular Mac — particularly one that's not already full of add-on boards — probably looks especially empty inside. After you become familiar with the machine's basic parts and how they appear, the Mac's interior terrain really is not that complicated at all.

The power supply (the heart of the Mac)

You may wonder why the Mac even needs its own power supply; after all, it *does* plug into a wall socket. What this interior power supply actually does, however, is convert the AC power from the wall plug to the lower-voltage DC power used by the Mac's hardware components. By the way, AC and DC stand for *alternating current* and *direct current*, not active computer and dead computer — at least, we hope not. *And* this is not a plug for DC Comics, publisher of the Superman, Batman, and other superhero comic books such as The Hacker, which — too bad — bit the dust.

The Mac's power supply provides power for all the other components inside the machine. You probably won't upgrade the power supply, but you might replace it if it dies.

In PowerBooks, the battery takes the place of the power supply.

Your hard disk — the Mac's filing cabinet

The hard disk is the Macintosh filing cabinet where all your applications and documents get stored. You can't actually see the hard disk, because it's enclosed in an airtight metal case to keep out dust and contaminants. The hard disk connects to an internal version of the SCSI port. One of the most common Mac upgrades is to install a new internal hard disk. For more information about hard disks, see Chapters 8 and 12; and for instructions on installing an internal hard disk, see Chapters 17 through 19, depending on your Mac model.

The diskette drive behind the slot

The diskette drive is located behind the slot in the front of desktop Macs and on the side of the portables. You undoubtedly know this slot well, because you insert your diskettes into it. And we hope that's all you insert in it; remember — you do *not* need to feed your Mac coins to get it to work. The drive is enclosed in a metal bracket and is usually located next to or under the hard disk inside the Mac. For more information about diskette drives, see Chapter 8.

Note: If you add an internal hard disk to a Macintosh SE that contains two internal diskette drives, you must first remove the upper diskette drive to make the upgrade. See Chapter 17 for the instructions on removing the diskette drive and installing a hard disk in the SE.

Thanks for the memory

Memory is the workspace for your Mac. If you think of the hard disk as a filing cabinet, the memory is the table on which the Mac spreads out the contents of the files so that it can work on them. You add memory to desktop Macs by plugging in small circuit boards called *SIMMs* (*Single In-line Memory Modules*); these circuit boards contain memory chips. For more information on memory and on SIMMs, see Chapter 12.

Memory banks are groups of sockets that hold the SIMMs. Sockets come in two different kinds, angled and vertical. A bank of memory can consist of one, two, or four SIMM sockets. Different desktop Mac models need different types and speeds of SIMMs. PowerBooks use special compact memory cards that require less power and occupy less space than do regular SIMMs. Figure 4-15 shows the two different types of SIMMs sockets, angled and vertical. For instructions on installing memory, see Chapters 17 through 19, depending on your Mac model.

SIMMS

Figure 4-15: To add memory to desktop Macs, you plug in small circuit boards containing memory chips called SIMMs.

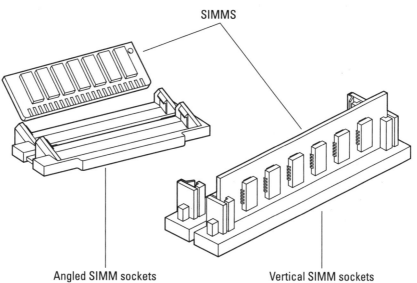

Angled SIMM sockets   Vertical SIMM sockets

Some desktop Macs use special SIMMs to increase the number of colors the monitor can display. This type of memory is called *video memory*, or *VRAM*. Chapter 15 provides more information on video memory upgrades. For instructions on installing video memory in color desktop Macs, see Chapters 17 and 19, depending on the Mac model you're upgrading.

Playing cards and the slots

Expansion cards are special circuit boards you use to customize and modify the capabilities of your Mac. By installing these cards, you can make your Mac perform faster, connect it to larger monitors, connect it to scientific instruments, or add to older models features that are now built into the newer Macs, such as an Ethernet connection or a video digitizer.

Cards fit into the *slots* on the *logic board* inside your Mac. These slots look like long bars with several rows of holes in them. The following section, "Mac logic in control," offers more detail on the logic board and its slots. Chapters 17 and 19 provide instructions for installing expansion cards.

Mac logic in control

The Mac contains a *logic board* — and, no, we don't mean a committee of Vulcans, chaired by Star Trek's Mr. Spock, charged with pronouncing all Mac operations logical or not. The Mac logic board is the big circuit board that sits at the bottom of your computer and ties all the parts of the machine together to make it work. Think of the board as an electronic air traffic controller, because it makes sure that signals keep moving back and forth between the different Mac hardware components — so your computer can boldly go where no Mac has gone before.

The logic board contains the power and cable connectors for the hard disk, the diskette drive, the SIMM sockets, and the expansion cards. The board also contains the *central processing unit*, or *CPU*, which is the true brain of your Mac. You can see a typical logic board illustrated in Figure 4-16. Notice the various slots and connectors. You must remove the logic board to carry out quite a few upgrades on compact Macs. See Chapter 17 for instructions on removing and reinstalling the logic board in the compacts.

Knowing where the CPU is located on the logic board isn't really necessary for most upgrades, but you can sure impress your friends if you can point out which chip is the brain of your Mac. Look at the drawing of the logic board shown in Figure 4-16, and you can see the CPU. The CPU is usually the largest chip on the board and is in the shape of a square or a long rectangle.

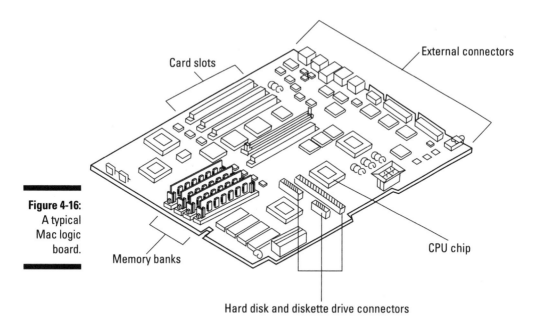

Card slots

External connectors

Figure 4-16:
A typical
Mac logic
board.

Memory banks

CPU chip

Hard disk and diskette drive connectors

Unless your Mac is a Power Macintosh, the chip is labeled with the word
Motorola and the numbers 680X0 on it. (The *X* is actually the number 0, 2, 3, or
4, depending on your Mac model.) Other letters may appear in this number, but
if the number starts with 68 and ends with 0, you can be pretty sure you've
found the CPU chip.

In the Power Macs, the chip is clearly labeled *Power PC.* The chip may be
manufactured by Motorola or — surprise — IBM! Who would have thought
we'd see the day when the "computer for the rest of us" was powered by a chip
made by Big Blue. Truth is stranger than fiction.

Part II
The Cavalcade of Macs and Upgradeability

"MY GOSH BARBARA, IF YOU DON'T THINK IT'S WORTH GOING A COUPLE OF WEEKS WITHOUT DINNER SO WE CAN AFFORD A POWER MAC, JUST SAY SO."

In this part...

You've probably noticed that Macs come in three flavors: compacts, or all-in-one Macs; modulars, which basically means a separate monitor and computer unit; and portables, the best of which are the PowerBooks. Here's where you find out how your own Mac or Macs fit into the product line, what expansion options you have, and what upgrades we recommend.

In these chapters, you learn how to make the right *decisions* about upgrading your Macintosh for your needs, be they work, education, or entertainment. Also, if you are thinking about buying a new or used Mac, use these chapters as your buyer's guide.

Finally, if we recommend an upgrade, such as an accelerator, a video card, or a high density floppy diskette drive, and you don't know what it is, see Parts 3 and 4 of this book for explanations.

Chapter 5

Compact Macs

• •

In This Chapter

▶ Descriptions of the compact Macintosh models

▶ Upgrade possibilities for each compact Mac

▶ Recommended upgrades, if any, for each compact

• •

*T*he original Macs were all compact Macs, and many people still think of this particular Mac flavor in terms of those machines: either old and slow or black and white only. But, really, the concept "compact Mac" doesn't have to equate to a negative. In fact, some of the newest, greatest color Macs are compact machines.

A few of the older black-and-white models retain some useful add-on possibilities, and we cover the possibilities for you in this chapter. The oldest compacts, however, are simply horrendous to upgrade, and your options in this area are quite limited. If you own one of these older babies, you may quickly notice that we're not at all shy about suggesting that you go out and buy a new machine if we really feel such an old clunker isn't worth attempting to upgrade.

For some reason, however, after the compacts started coming out in color, they also became very easy to upgrade. If you own a color compact, in fact, you should find upgrading a breeze, with many, many options available to you. So read about your compact in this chapter and learn exactly what improvements — if any — you can make to your particular model. As you read, you'll notice that for each Mac we give the processor, the upgrade possibilities, and upgrade recommendations. You'll also notice that we've grouped the Macs according to case style — which means that you'll find the Macs that look alike on the outside all in one place.

The 128K, 512K, 512Ke, and MacPlus Macs

The Macs in this section are similar. They share the same case and the same processor. The illustration in Figure 5-1 gives you an idea of what these original Macs look like.

Figure 5-1:
The 128K,
512K, 512Ke,
and
MacPlus
Macs look
like this.

Macintosh 128K (January 24, 1984 to April 14, 1986)

This machine is *the* original Macintosh. Apple called it "The computer for the rest of us," because it was a complete, self-contained system that was easy to use. Before the Mac hit the market, computers were difficult to work with at best and required you to open them up and play with chips and circuits and other technical items all the time. With the Macintosh, however, all the components inside were preset at the factory, and, in fact, you couldn't even open the case without special tools. The problem with this closed design, unfortunately, is that you can't easily add new pieces to the machine to keep up with the rapid pace of technology — hence, these first Macs offer an extremely limited upgradeability.

Processor: 68000, 8 MHz

Upgrade possibilities: None. Clean up this machine, put it in the closet, and in ten years or so, you may have a collector's item that's actually worth more than what you paid for it.

Recommendations: Buy a new Macintosh.

What do all these processor numbers mean?

By now, you're probably wondering about all these *processors*, which are also known as chips. If you talk about processors, you're actually talking about the speed of your computer. The speed of your particular Macintosh model is determined by both the megahertz, abbreviated *MHz*, and the processor number.

The processors that keep the Mac running are the *Motorola 68000*, the *68020*, the *68030*, and the *68040*. (The last two numbers indicate the processor's generation—the bigger this number is, the newer and faster the chip is.) The megahertz numbers range from 8 to 40. (Again, the bigger the megahertz number, the faster the chip.)

To tell which Mac is faster than another machine, first look at the processor generation number (for example, 68030 or 68040). If the generation numbers are the same, look at the megahertz (for example, 25 or 33).

The Power Macs use the PowerPC processor. This chip is faster and less expensive than the 68040 and uses what is known as *RISC technology*. RISC stands for *Reduced Instruction Set Computer*, and what that means is . . . well, if you hear the term RISC bandied about, you just know that it means fast, cheaper, and a good thing.

Macintosh 512K (September 10, 1984 to April 14, 1986)

Called the "Fat Mac," this machine gave Macintosh users additional memory with which to work.

Processor: 68000, 8 MHz

Upgrade possibilities: Extremely limited. You probably don't want to upgrade this Macintosh, and it probably won't ever be as valuable as the Mac 128 as a collector's item. If you keep it around, however, your children can still use it to create MacPaint drawings.

Recommendations: Buy a new Macintosh.

Macintosh 512Ke (April 14, 1986 to August 1, 1986)

This Mac is a Mac 512K that is enhanced (hence the "*e*") to use 800K floppy disks.

Processor: 68000, 8 MHz

Upgrade possibilities: Not many. Consider this Mac in the same league as its nonenhanced brothers and sisters when it comes to upgrades.

Recommendations: Buy a new Macintosh.

Macintosh Plus (January 16, 1986 to October 15, 1990)

Remarkably, the Mac Plus still runs most of the software available today, although it runs it very slowly and has only a tiny nine-inch screen on which to display it. You might find one of these used, but we really wouldn't recommend that you buy one of these machines. Of course, if someone happens to offer you one for free and you need a basic Mac, don't turn it down.

Processor: 68000, 8 MHz

Upgrade possibilities: You can upgrade the memory to a maximum of 4MB. You can't install an internal hard disk, but you can add unlimited external hard-disk storage. You can also speed up the machine, but not very cheaply or effectively.

Recommendations: Our first recommendation is to buy a new Macintosh. If the slow speed of the machine and its small screen don't bother you, however, go ahead and upgrade to the maximum 4MB of memory. Adding a new hard disk is also a good idea so that you can store more documents.

Try to save up for a new Mac, but if you just can't get together the money for a new machine and you feel OK about spending money on this one, you can double its speed fairly inexpensively. The one speed upgrade we recommend is the Brainstorm Accelerator, from Brainstorm Products. You can't install this upgrade yourself, however, because only Brainstorm resellers are authorized to do it.

SE, SE FDHD, and SE/30 Macs

These three Macs look like the original Macs on the outside, but they're different on the inside because of the one expansion slot they each contain. The SE/30 runs faster than the other two SEs because of its 68030 processor. Figure 5-2 gives you an idea of what the SE Mac models look like.

Macintosh SE (March 2, 1987 to August 1, 1989) and SE FDHD (August 1, 1989 to October 15, 1990)

The SE FDHD differs from the plain vanilla SE only in that it includes an FDHD disk drive, also called a *SuperDrive*. This drive is a high-density floppy disk drive that gives you up to 1.4MB for storing many documents and also enables you to exchange floppy disks and information between your Mac and an IBM PC or compatible.

Processor: 68000, 8 MHz

Upgrade possibilities: Lots. The SE has many upgrade possibilities because of its one expansion slot.

Recommendations: Your money would probably still be best spent on a new Macintosh. But if you can't part with your old SE, the most practical upgrades include expanding the memory to the 4MB maximum and adding a new hard disk (either internal or external, depending on your machine). You could also install a video card in the expansion slot to connect a large external black-and-white monitor for viewing full-page layouts. The SE cannot produce color even on an external monitor, so if your needs go beyond the upgrades we suggest here, seriously consider buying a new Mac.

Macintosh SE/30 (January 19, 1989 to October 21, 1991)

This machine is still the speed champ of compact Macs. If you want a compact black-and-white Mac and find a used SE/30 for sale, we suggest you don't hesitate to buy it.

Processor: 68030, 16 MHz

Upgrade possibilities: Lots. The SE/30's capability to take on a ton of memory and to use a color monitor via an expansion card lead us to classify this machine as very upgradeable. Its only limitation is the single expansion slot.

Recommendations: Add as much memory as you need, up to the 128MB maximum; be aware, however, that you need special software to use more than 8MB (see Chapter 17). If you need a bigger screen, we also suggest adding a video expansion card so that you can connect an external color monitor or a large external black-and-white monitor. You can also add a new hard disk.

Note: An interesting fact is that the Mac SE/30 gets its name from the 68030 processor. This Mac is the only Mac that includes the processor number in its name. If Apple had applied the naming conventions it set for the Mac II series (Mac II, IIx, IIcx, and so forth), the SE/30 probably would have been named the SE/x.

Classic, Classic II, and Performa 200 Macs

The Mac Classic had a new Coca-Cola-style name but was actually the original Mac technology packed in a new case. The Classic II was intended to replace the SE/30. The Performa 200 is a Classic II with the Performa name and sold in consumer electronics stores. See Figure 5-3 for an idea of what the Classic Macs and the Performa 200 look like.

Macintosh Classic (October 15, 1990 to September 14, 1992)

The Classic came out as a low-cost replacement for the aging SE. Unfortunately, it lacks the SE's expansion slot, which seriously limits its upgradeability.

Processor: 68000, 8 MHz

Upgrade possibilities: Fair. The memory expands to 4MB, and you can replace the internal hard disk that comes in the machine with a larger one.

Recommendations: Upgrade the memory and add a larger hard disk.

Macintosh Classic II (October 21, 1991 to September 13, 1993)

This Macintosh was supposed to replace the SE/30, but as far as we're concerned — no way. The Classic II runs slower than the SE/30 and doesn't have an expansion slot.

Processor: 68030, 16 MHz

Upgrade possibilities: Fairly limited. This machine lacks a multipurpose upgrade slot, so your options are pretty limited. You can, however, add a math coprocessor to speed up certain number-crunching operations.

Recommendations: Add memory up to 10MB and add a new hard disk. If your work involves a significant number of spreadsheets and charts, you could add a math coprocessor.

Macintosh Performa 200 (September 14, 1992 to April 12, 1993)

The Performa 200 is the Macintosh Classic II with the Performa name on the case and sold in consumer electronics stores.

Processor: 68030, 16 MHz

Upgrade possibilities: The same as the Classic II.

Recommendations: The same as the Classic II.

The Color Classic Mac

This color Macintosh should have come out five years earlier. That Mac users had to wait until 1993 for the first compact Macintosh with a built-in color screen seems unbelievable. Figure 5-4 shows the Color Classic Mac.

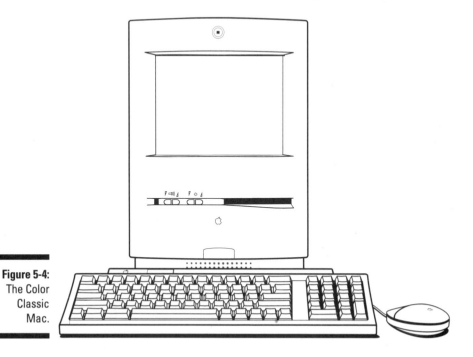

Figure 5-4:
The Color
Classic
Mac.

Macintosh Color Classic (February 10, 1993 to May 16 1994)

Yes, the color quality on the Color Classic screen is great, but the nine-inch size is too small, just like those of all the other compact Macs.

Processor: 68030, 16 MHz

Upgrade possibilities: Good. This Mac's design makes it very easy to upgrade, which is one point in its favor. You can add up to 8MB of memory, an external hard disk, and a large external color monitor via a connector card installed in its one expansion slot.

Recommendations: Install more memory and add a new external hard disk drive. Because the built-in screen is so small, you should probably also upgrade to a larger external monitor. Also, add a math coprocessor if you work with spreadsheets or CAD programs.

For some reason, a Macintosh called the Color Classic II is sold only in Japan. The processor for the Classic II is the same 68030, but it runs at 33MHz. Why this speedy, souped-up, hot rod of a Color Classic is available only in Japan and not in other countries is beyond us. We get monster movies with guys in rubber suits, and they get the Color Classic II?

The Mac TV, LC 500 series, and Performa 500 series Macs

These Macs have great color screens, built-in speakers, and even an optional internal CD-ROM drive. The machines are the ultimate in easy upgrading because of their design. Figure 5-5 shows you what these color compact Macs look like.

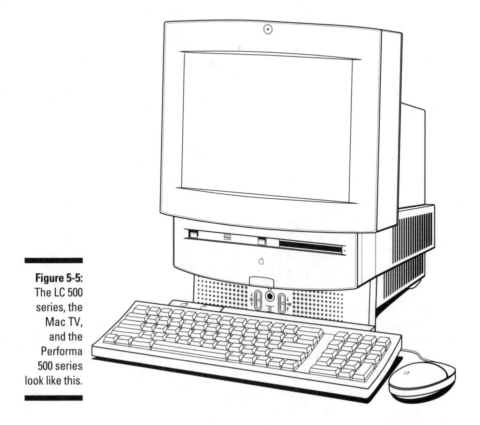

Figure 5-5: The LC 500 series, the Mac TV, and the Performa 500 series look like this.

Macintosh LC 500 series — LC 520 (June 28, 1993 to February 2, 1994), LC 550 (February 2, 1994), and LC 575 (February 2, 1994)

These color compact Macs all share the same case and a built-in, high-quality, 14-inch color monitor, and they come with internal stereo speakers and a microphone. You can also buy these machines with an internal CD-ROM drive. In our opinion, these are some of the most well thought out Macs Apple has ever produced. Normally, you can buy Macs with the LC name only through schools and universities, but don't feel left out if you're not in the academic world, because you can buy these same Macs under the Performa name in consumer electronics stores.

Processor: 68030, 25 MHz for the LC 520; 68030, 33MHz for the LC 550; 68LC040, 33MHz for the LC 575

Upgrade possibilities: Many. These Macs are an upgrader's dream, because their internal design offers extremely easy access to any components you want to change or add to. The memory expands to 36MB, and you can add video memory and a math coprocessor. The LC 520 and LC 550 contain one expansion slot, and you can choose from many reasonably priced expansion cards that let you connect an external monitor or a TV as a monitor, attach scientific instruments, or link up to high-speed networks. The LC 575 has the same kind of expansion slot as the other two LCs and also has a specialized slot designed for communications upgrades. The slot accepts special cards that contain high-speed modems or Ethernet networking features.

Recommendations: Add as much memory as you need, up to 36MB, and go ahead and install expansion cards to customize the machine for your work needs. You can upgrade the video memory to increase the number of colors that appear on your monitor and increase storage capacity with a new hard disk, either internal or external.

Macintosh TV (October 25, 1993)

It's cool. Its case is black. You can watch TV, use your VCR, play Nintendo, listen to music, write a report and illustrate it with graphics — all on this insanely great machine! (Sorry to be so enthusiastic, but we *like* this Macintosh.) The expansion slot in this Mac comes filled with the hardware that lets the machine function as a TV. A remote control unit switches between the computer and TV functions, and the Macintosh CD-ROM drive functions as a music CD player.

Processor: 68030, 32 MHz

Upgrade possibilities: You can add up to 8MB of memory and a hard disk.

Recommendations: Any Mac that enables you to hook a Nintendo to it needs no further upgrading, but for truly awesome sound, connect this Mac's audio to your stereo system.

Macintosh Performa 500 series — Performa 550 (October 18, 1993), Performa 560 (January 17, 1994), Performa 575 (April 25, 1994), Performa 577 (April 25, 1994), and Performa 578 (April 25, 1994)

The Performa 500 series brings all the awesome features of the LC 500s to consumers, not just teachers and students. If you want the built-in features of the LC 500s, such as the high-quality color monitor, internal speakers, and an optional internal CD-ROM you can buy one of the Performa 500 Macs at a consumer electronics store such as Sears or Circuit City. The Performa 550 and 560 are essentially the same Mac as the LC 550. And the Performa 575, 577, and 578 are basically the same as the LC 575. You'll find differences from model to model in hard disk size, the amount of memory installed, the kind of software included.

Processor: 68030, 33MHz for the Performa 550 and 560; 68LC040, 33MHz for the Performa 575, 577, and 578

Upgrade possibilities: These Performas offer the same easy upgrading as the LCs they're based on. The memory expands to 36MB, and you can add video memory and a math coprocessor. The Performa 550 and 560 contain one expansion slot, and as we said for the LC, you can choose from many reasonably priced expansion cards that let you connect an external monitor or a TV as a monitor, attach scientific instruments, or link up to high-speed networks. The 575, 577, and 578 have one expansion slot and a second, specialized slot designed for communications upgrades. The second slot accepts special cards that contain high-speed modems or Ethernet networking features.

Recommendations: See the upgrade recommendations for the LC 500 series — all the same recommendations apply to their Performa siblings.

Chapter 6
Modular Macs

● ●

In This Chapter

▶ Descriptions of all the modular Macintosh models

▶ Upgrade possibilities for each modular Mac

▶ Recommended upgrades for each model

● ●

*I*f you buy a modular Mac, you get your computer in two separate pieces: the monitor and the main computer box. The Mac II was the first modular Mac, and it's also the first Mac with major upgrade possibilities. Owners can expand their modular Macs and tinker with them all they want. This is especially true for business users, who usually want to add on options for networking, fast number crunching, and sophisticated graphics.

The modular Macs that you read about in this chapter range from the Mac II to the Power Macs containing the fast PowerPC processor. Modular Macs contain anywhere from one to six expansion slots so that you can add any number of capabilities you may need for specific tasks. Because you can customize these machines so extensively, two of the same-model Macs sitting side by side may look identical but actually boast very different capabilities. Differences between these look-alike machines may include the type of network installed for communicating with other computers, whether sound-editing capabilities are present, and the machine's capability to carry out business, engineering, or scientific applications.

In the computing world, you can never have a machine with too much memory or too big a hard disk. We recommend, therefore, that you add more memory and a larger hard disk to any modular Mac you may own. These two upgrades also are the best improvement you can make to your machine for the money you spend. For details on the specific upgrades that we think make the most sense for a particular Mac, check out our recommendations for each model. Also, as you read, you'll notice that we've grouped the Macs according to case style — which means that you'll find the Macs that look alike on the outside all in one place.

The II, IIx, and IIfx Macs

Here are the first Mac IIs — the first color Macs and the first Macs with major upgrade possibilities. Figure 6-1 shows what these Mac IIs look like.

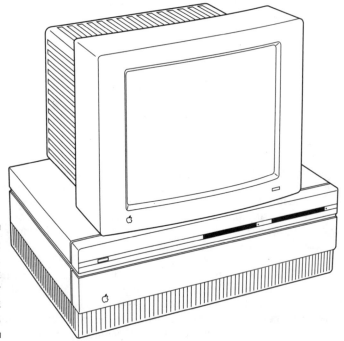

Figure 6-1:
The II, IIx, and IIfx modular Macs look like this.

Macintosh II (March 2, 1987 to January 15, 1990)

This machine is the Macintosh reinvented — the first color Mac. The graphics standard set when the machine came out was incredible, and you could use many more colors than you could on other computers. Sixteen colors was the standard at the time, for example, but by installing the right expansion card, you could use as many as 256 on the Mac II. The machine is very flexible in terms of upgrading too, but its major limitation is its slow speed.

Processor: 68020, 16 MHz

Upgrade possibilities: Many. The memory expands to 8MB, and six expansion slots enable you to add many, many different capabilities to the Mac II. Most people in business add fast networking and communications capabilities and one or more video cards for attaching large monitors. The Mac II is so flexible, in fact, that you can upgrade it to current state of the art. Doing so, however, would probably cost you twice as much as just buying the latest Mac.

Recommendations: If your work requires more speed, buy a new Macintosh. If the slow speed doesn't bother you and you need the flexibility of this Mac II's six expansion slots, add a new hard disk and possibly an accelerator card. You can definitely add more memory, although expanding the memory beyond 8MB is really a pain (see Chapter 18). If you intend to work extensively with complex image processing (which requires a much higher processor speed than this machine can muster), we recommend that you simply buy a new Mac.

Macintosh IIx (September 19, 1988 to October 15, 1990)

This Mac is the next step up from the Mac II and runs twice as fast. The machine also comes with a high-density disk drive that provides more disk storage space than does the Mac II as well as more flexibility for moving files around.

Processor: 68030, 16 MHz

Upgrade possibilities: The memory expands to 128MB, and like the Mac II, this machine has six expansion slots, which offer you many, many upgrade possibilities.

Recommendations: Unlike the plain vanilla Mac II, the Mac IIx's 68030 processor runs the machine fast enough to make it worth keeping around and upgrading. Add more memory, a new hard disk, and possibly an accelerator card if you crave more speed. (Or just buy one of the latest, speediest modular Mac CPUs, such as the Power Macintosh 7100/66 or 8100/80, and use it with your Mac IIx monitor and keyboard.) The IIx also makes a good file server or print server for a small workgroup with modest speed requirements. So definitely keep this machine around even if you do buy a new modular Mac.

If you own a modular Mac, you can often save money by buying just a new CPU and using your old monitor, keyboard, and mouse with the new unit.

If this is the first chapter you've read in Part 2, you may at this point be wondering about all these processor numbers that we keep bandying about for each modular Mac. If you care about such things and want to read more about processors, refer to the sidebar in Chapter 5 entitled, aptly, "What do all these processor numbers mean?"

Macintosh IIfx (March 19, 1990 to April 15, 1992)

When the Mac IIfx came out, it was supposed to be the wicked, fast, bad boy, high-end, graphics workstation. The IIfx has its own unique design quirks, true, but overall it's a good machine.

Processor: 68030, 40 MHz

Upgrade possibilities: Many. The memory expands to 128MB, and the six expansion slots offer lots of upgrade options.

Recommendations: Making this fast machine run even faster is definitely possible. But speeding it up may not be as economical as just buying the latest Macintosh, which would give you speed plus other state-of-the-art sound and video features. Compare the cost of accelerating this Mac to the cost of purchasing a brand new Mac before you decide to upgrade. The IIfx still makes a good machine for general business use, but buy a new Mac if you plan on doing oodles of graphics.

The IIcx, IIci, and Quadra 700 Macs

The Mac IIcx, IIci, and Quadra 700 take up about half the space that the Mac II and IIx take up on a desk, which is great for giving people more work space. But the smaller physical size of these Macs means room for fewer expansion slots. Figure 6-2 shows what these machines look like. Notice the smaller size compared to the relatively hulking modular Macs shown back in Figure 6-1.

Macintosh IIcx (March 7, 1989 to March 11, 1991)

This Mac is a smaller version of the Mac IIx. Limiting the machine to only three expansion slots gives this Mac its small size, or what some people call *footprint*. Because of this model's design, you can easily access the components you want to upgrade inside the machine. Its diminutive size, however, does somewhat limit its upgrade possibilities.

Processor: 68030, 16 MHz

Upgrade possibilities: The memory expands to 128MB, and the three expansion slots give you room to add a few expansion cards. You can also add a math coprocessor.

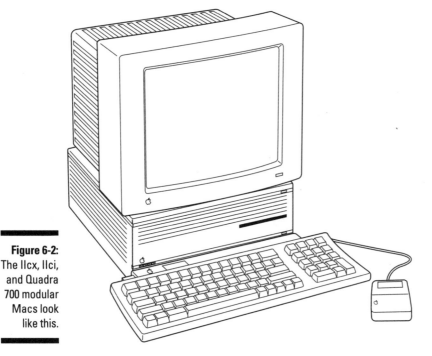

Figure 6-2:
The IIcx, IIci,
and Quadra
700 modular
Macs look
like this.

Recommendations: The Mac IIcx is a good machine for word processing and general home and business use. But if you need more than a moderate amount of computing power, you're probably better off picking up a new Mac.

Macintosh IIci (September 20, 1989 to February 10, 1993)

This machine became almost a standard for business use and, as a result, had one of the longest life spans of any Mac model. The IIci was also the first Mac to include built-in video capabilities so that you could connect a monitor to it without putting a video card in one of the expansion slots. Essentially, the built-in video means that you get an extra expansion slot to fill.

Processor: 68030, 25 MHz

Upgrade possibilities: The memory expands to 128MB, and three NuBus expansion slots accept expansion cards. The IIci also includes a memory cache slot so that you can install cache cards to increase your system speed.

NuBus is the official name for the expansion slots in the modular Macs. This kind of slot accepts expansion cards that give your Mac the ability do things like connect to external monitors, link to other Macs via a network, and connect to scientific instruments. Some modular Macs have other kinds of slots as well. We cover the other slots under each specific Mac model.

Recommendations: For faster system performance, take advantage of the cache card slot and install either a cache memory card or an accelerator card that can use this slot. If you need even more colors on-screen, a larger monitor, or faster graphics redraws than you get with the machine's built-in video capabilities, install a video card in one of the NuBus expansion slots. (Another benefit of installing a video card is improved system performance.)

Macintosh Quadra 700 (October 21, 1991 to March 15, 1993)

The Quadra 700 was the first Macintosh to use the 68040 processor, which at the time the machine was introduced meant *speed*.

Processor: 68040, 25 MHz

Upgrade possibilities: The memory expands to 68MB. Two NuBus expansion slots and one 68040 processor-direct slot accept expansion cards. The machine's video sockets enables you to add up to 2MB of video memory so that you can connect large monitors and work with many colors on-screen.

A *processor-direct slot* is an expansion slot that accepts expansion cards that speed up your Mac. For more information on speeding up your Mac, see Chapter 14.

Recommendations: Besides adding memory and a hard disk, if you think you need more speed, you can add a PowerPC accelerator card.

The Mac IIsi

The Mac IIsi is basically a slowed-down Macintosh IIci in a smaller case. Figure 6-3 shows this Mac.

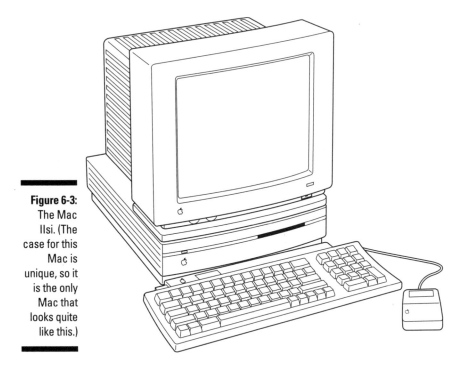

Figure 6-3:
The Mac
IIsi. (The
case for this
Mac is
unique, so it
is the only
Mac that
looks quite
like this.)

Macintosh IIsi (October 15, 1990 to March 15, 1993)

This computer is unique in that it is the only Mac model to use this particular case design.

Processor: 68030, 20 MHz

Upgrade possibilities: The memory expands to 65MB. The IIsi has one processor-direct slot that accepts cards designed specifically for the IIsi. This slot also accepts cards designed for the SE/30 if you install an SE/30 card adapter, and it accepts NuBus cards if you install a NuBus card adapter. The NuBus adapter card for the IIsi includes a math coprocessor.

Recommendations: If you crunch enough numbers, install either a math coprocessor card or the NuBus adapter that contains a math coprocessor.

The IIvi, IIvx, Performa 600 and 600 CD, Centris 650, Quadra 650, and Power Macintosh 7100/66 Macs

Amazingly, these Macs all look alike on the outside, even though the power that's packed inside each machine is different. Figure 6-4 illustrates these Mac models.

Macintosh IIvi (October 19, 1992 to February 10, 1993)

In case you've never seen a Mac IIvi, don't feel bad — this model was sold only outside the USA.

Processor: 68030, 16 MHz

Upgrade possibilities: The memory expands to 68MB, and three NuBus expansion slots and one 68030 processor-direct slot accept cards. You can install a math coprocessor and upgrade the video memory to a maximum of 1MB. You can also add an internal CD-ROM drive or a removable storage drive. If you've been drooling over the fast PowerPC processor, you can even upgrade your IIvi to the Power Mac 7100/66 via a logic board upgrade.

Recommendations: Adding a CD-ROM is a great option for this machine, and if you crunch numbers, you can also add a math coprocessor.

Macintosh IIvx (October 19, 1992 to October 21, 1993)

The IIvx was intended to replace the IIci in the Mac lineup, but had a short life span due to the success of the Quadra and Centris lines, which came out soon after this machine.

Processor: 68030, 32 MHz

Upgrade possibilities: The memory expands to 68MB. Three NuBus expansion slots and one 68030 processor-direct slot accept expansion cards. The video memory expands to a maximum of 1MB. You can install an internal CD-ROM drive or other storage drives. As with the Mac IIvi, if you're dreaming about the PowerPC processor, you can upgrade your IIvx to the Power Mac 7100/66 via a logic board upgrade.

Recommendations: As for the IIvi, adding a CD-ROM is a great option for the IIvx.

Figure 6-4:
The Ilvi, Ilvx,
Performa
600 and 600
CD, Centris
650, Quadra
650, and
Power
Macintosh
7100/66
modular
Macs look
like this.

Macintosh Performa 600 and Performa 600 CD (September 14, 1992 to October 18, 1993)

These Macs are really just one Mac. The Performa 600 CD comes with an internal CD-ROM drive, while the Performa 600 doesn't have the drive installed when you buy the computer — of course, you can always install the CD-ROM drive later. This machine is essentially a Mac IIvx without a math coprocessor and packaged with software for consumers. By the way, the Performa 600 CD was the first Macintosh to contain a built-in CD-ROM drive.

Processor: 68030, 32 MHz

Upgrade possibilities: The memory expands to 68MB. Three NuBus expansion slots and one 68030 processor-direct slot accept expansion cards. The video memory expands to 1MB. You can install an internal CD-ROM drive to the Performa 600. And if you want PowerPC processor speed, you can upgrade this machine to the Power Mac 7100/66 via a logic board upgrade.

Recommendations: Adding a CD-ROM drive is a great option for the Performa 600. If you crunch numbers, you can also add a math coprocessor.

Macintosh Centris 650 (February 10, 1993 to October 21, 1993)

The Centris name was used for only six months, and then the Centris Macs were rolled over into the Quadra line. The high-end configurations of this model came with built-in Ethernet capabilities and an integrated math coprocessor in the 68040 chip. The low-end configuration of the Centris 650 used the low-cost version of the 68040 chip, the 68LC040, which does not include a math coprocessor.

Processor: 68040, 25 MHz

Upgrade possibilities: The memory expands to 136MB, and the machine has three NuBus slots and one 68040 processor-direct slot. The video memory expands to 1MB. You can install an internal CD-ROM drive or other storage drives. To install a math coprocessor in the low-end configuration of the Centris 650, you must remove the 68LC040 processor chip and replace it with a full 68040 processor that includes the math coprocessor. If you covet the speed of the PowerPC processor, you can upgrade your Centris 650 to the Power Mac 7100/66 via a logic board upgrade.

Recommendations: Depending on your needs, you may want to add more video memory or expansion cards. The CD-ROM is also a great upgrade.

Macintosh Quadra 650 (October 21, 1993)

The Quadra 650 is really the Centris 650 with a faster processor and a name change.

Processor: 68040, 33 MHz

Upgrade possibilities: Same as the Centris 650.

Recommendations: Same as the Centris 650.

Power Macintosh 7100/66 (March 14, 1994)

The Power Macintosh 7100/66 is one of the first of three Macintosh computers to use the PowerPC processor. This machine's case is based on the Quadra 650 design.

Processor: PowerPC 601, 66 MHz

Upgrade possibilities: The memory expands to 136MB, and the machine features three NuBus slots, one processor-direct slot, and one level 2 cache slot for an optional cache memory card to speed up processing. You can also install an internal CD-ROM drive or other storage drives. This machine is also available in an audio-video (AV) configuration, which means that an AV card comes installed in the processor-direct slot.

A *level 2 cache slot* is an expansion slot that accepts special expansion cards containing high-speed cache memory to speed up Mac processing.

Recommendations: Installing an internal CD-ROM drive is a good idea for this machine. If you want to work with many colors on-screen or you want to use a larger monitor, upgrade the video memory. If you plan to use this machine as a graphics workstation, also install an accelerated video card. To improve performance — that is, if the PowerPC performance isn't already fast enough for you — install the level 2 cache card.

The Centris 610, Quadra 610, AWS 60, Quadra 660av, Power Macintosh 6100/60, and WGS 6150 Macs

Besides containing the number *6* in their names, these Macs all come in the same flat case, all contain one expansion slot, and have room for an internal CD-ROM. Figure 6-5 gives you an idea of what these Macs look like.

Figure 6-5:
The Centris 610, Quadra 610, AWS 60, Quadra 660av, and Power Macintosh 6100/60 modular Macs look like this.

What's the RISC in the PowerPC anyway?

The PowerPC brings *RISC* (*R*educed *I*nstruction *S*et *C*omputing) to the Macintosh. In a word, RISC means *fast*. The Power Macs that use the PowerPC chip can run up to two to four times faster than can other personal computers if these souped-up machines use software that is written specifically for them. The word software gurus like to throw around for software written specifically for a particular computer is *native*. One of these insiders, for example, may say something like "I wish those software developers would hurry up and bring out more native applications for the Power Mac!"

If you upgrade your current Mac to use the PowerPC and run your old software, you can expect Quadra-like performance and speed. For true PowerPC action, however, make sure that you also upgrade your software to the versions designed for this processor. Oh, and the Power Macs also enables you to run Macintosh, DOS, and Windows applications all at one time on one machine. Well-worth the added RISC, we'd say.

Macintosh Centris 610 (February 10, 1993 to October 21, 1993)

The Centris 610 is one of the two original Centris models — along with the 650. The machine became the Quadra 610 in October 1993.

Processor: 68LC040, 20 MHz

Upgrade possibilities: The memory expands to 68MB, and the video memory expands to 1MB. The machine has only one expansion slot that accepts either processor-direct cards designed for the Centris 610 or seven-inch NuBus cards with an adapter. You can install an internal CD-ROM drive or a removable storage drive. You can also add the DOS Compatibility Card, which enables your machine to run Macintosh and DOS or Windows applications.

Because of the internal design of the Macs covered in this section, you have to install seven-inch NuBus cards in the expansion slot. The NuBus cards designed for the other modular Macs are too long to fit in the Macs in this section. However, you can use the seven-inch cards can in any modular Mac with NuBus slots.

Recommendations: Adding the CD-ROM is an excellent upgrade for this machine. If you need the speed of the PowerPC processor, you can upgrade to the Power Mac 6100/60 via a logic board upgrade. If you work in both the Macintosh and DOS or Windows worlds, add the DOS Compatibility Card.

Macintosh Quadra 610 (October 21, 1993)

The Quadra 610 is an upgraded Centris 610 with a faster processor and a name change.

Processor: 68040, 25 MHz

Upgrade possibilities: Same as the Centris 610. This Mac can be upgraded to the Apple Workgroup Server 60.

Recommendations: Same as for the Centris 610.

Apple Workgroup Server 60 (March 22, 1993)

The Apple Workgroup Server 60 is also known as the AWS 60. The machine is the same as the Quadra 610 and comes bundled with network server software.

Processor: 68040, 25 MHz

Upgrade possibilities: Same as the Quadra 610.

Recommendations: See the recommendations for the Quadra 610. Upgrade the machine's storage capacity, too, to make available on the network as many files as possible. We also recommend adding a tape backup drive for network backups if your machine doesn't already have one.

Macintosh Quadra 660AV (July 29, 1993)

This Mac was introduced in July 1993 as the Centris 660AV, but Apple changed its name to Quadra 660AV in October 1993 after the entire Centris line was rolled into the Quadra line. The "*AV*" in 660AV stands for audio-video and refers to the machine's capability to import and export sound and video.

Processor: 68040, 25 MHz

Upgrade possibilities: The memory expands to 68MB. The machine offers the same processor-direct slot as do the Quadra and Centris 610. The slot accepts cards designed specifically for it and also accepts, with an adapter, seven-inch NuBus cards. The machine's GeoPort technology enables you to connect a GeoPort Telecom adapter pod that sets up the computer to function as a fax, a modem, and a telephone. For more information about the GeoPort, see Chapter 4. You can add an internal CD-ROM to this machine, and if you want PowerPC processor speed, you can upgrade your Quadra 660AV to the Power Mac 6100/60 or the Power Mac 6100/60AVvia a logic board upgrade.

Recommendations: GeoPort technology is still evolving, so if you fax or telecommunicate via modem regularly, we suggest you buy a good fax/modem instead of the GeoPort Telecom adapter pod.

Macintosh Quadra 610 DOS-Compatible (February 28, 1994)

This machine is a Macintosh that also offers MS-DOS and Windows compatibility, which means that you can run both Macintosh and DOS or Windows applications at the same time and cut and paste information between the two environments. You switch back and forth between the environments by pressing two keys, or you can connect two monitors to your computer and view both the Mac and DOS or Windows environments.

Processor: 68LC040, 25 MHz, and Intel 486SX, 25 MHz

Upgrade possibilities: The memory expands to 68MB, and the video memory expands to 1MB. The one internal expansion slot contains the DOS Compatibility card, so you can't add any expansion cards to this machine — unless, of course, you grow tired of DOS compatibility and remove the card. You can add an internal CD-ROM drive to this machine, and if you dream about the PowerPC processor, you can upgrade your DOS-compatible Centris 610 to the Power Mac 6100/60 via a logic board upgrade.

Recommendations: If you add the CD-ROM drive, you can access DOS-formatted CD-ROMs when you work in the DOS/Windows mode — pretty neat, huh?

Power Macintosh 6100/60 (March 14, 1994) and WGS 6150 (April 25, 1994)

The Power Macintosh 6100/60 is one of the first three Macintosh computers to use the PowerPC processor. This machine is based on the Quadra 610 case design. (For more information about the PowerPC processor, see the sidebar "What's the RISC in the PowerPC anyway?" earlier in this chapter, and also refer to Chapter 25.) The Workgroup Server 6150 is the network server version of the Power Mac 6100/60.

Processor: PowerPC 601, 60 MHz

Upgrade possibilities: The memory expands to 72MB. The machine has one expansion slot that accepts either processor direct cards designed for the Power Macintosh 6100/60 or, with an adapter, seven-inch NuBus cards. The machine also has one level 2 cache slot for an optional cache memory card to speed up processing. You can install an internal CD-ROM drive or other storage drives. This machine is also available in an audio-video (AV) configuration, which means that an AV card comes installed in the processor-direct slot. In the AV configuration, the expansion slot is filled and can accept no other expansion cards.

Recommendations: Installing an internal CD-ROM drive is a good idea for this machine. If you want to work with many colors on-screen or you want a large monitor, upgrade the video memory. If you plan to use this machine as a graphics workstation, install an accelerated video card. To improve performance — that is, if PowerPC performance still isn't fast enough for you — install the level 2 cache card.

The Quadra 800, Quadra 840AV, AWS 80, Power Macintosh 8100/80, and WGS 8150 Macs

If you want fast computing speed, the Macs in this section are for you. Figure 6-5 shows you what the Quadra 800, Quadra 840AV, AWS 80, and Power Macintosh 8100/80 Macs look like.

Macintosh Quadra 800 (February 10, 1993 to March 15, 1994)

This machine is the successor to the Quadra 700 and offers more internal-storage options.

Processor: 68040, 33 MHz

Upgrade possibilities: The memory expands to 136MB, and the computer includes three NuBus expansion slots and one 68040 processor-direct slot. The video memory expands to 1MB. You can add up to three internal storage devices, such as hard disk drives, CD-ROM drives, or tape cartridge drives. This Mac can be upgraded to the Apple Workgroup Server 80. If you want PowerPC processor speed, you can upgrade this machine to the Power Macintosh 8100/80 via a logic board upgrade.

Recommendations: Go ahead and upgrade to the Power Mac.

Figure 6-6:
The Quadra
800, Quadra
840AV, AWS
80, and
Power
Macintosh
8100/80
Macs look
like this.

Macintosh Quadra 840AV (July 29, 1993)

This Quadra is a fast version of the Quadra 800. The "*AV*" in 840AV stands for audio-video and refers to the machine's capability to import and export sound and video.

Processor: 68040, 40 MHz

Upgrade possibilities: The memory expands to 128MB, and the machine has three NuBus expansion slots and one 68040 processor-direct slot. The video memory expands to 2MB. The computer's GeoPort technology enables you to connect a GeoPort Telecom adapter pod that sets up your computer to function as a fax, a modem, and a telephone. Adding an internal CD-ROM is an excellent upgrade for this machine, and if you want PowerPC processor speed, you can upgrade your Quadra 840av to the Power Mac 8100/80 or the Power Mac 8100/80av via a logic board upgrade.

Recommendations: GeoPort technology is still evolving, so if you use fax or modem functions on a regular basis, we suggest you buy a good fax/modem instead of the GeoPort Telecom adapter pod.

Apple Workgroup Server 80 (March 22, 1993)

The Apple Workgroup Server 80 is called the AWS 80 for short. The machine is based on the Quadra 800 and comes bundled with network server software and hardware.

Processor: 68040, 33 MHz

Upgrade possibilities: Same as for the Quadra 800.

Recommendations: See our recommendations for the Quadra 800. Upgrade the storage to make available on the network as many files as possible. We also recommend adding a tape backup drive for network backups if your machine doesn't already have one.

Power Macintosh 8100/80 (March 14, 1994) and WGS 8150

The Power Macintosh 8100/80 is one of the first three Macintosh computers to use the PowerPC processor and ranks as the most powerful of the three. This machine's case is based on that of the Quadra 800 and 840av case designs. (For more information about the PowerPC processor, see the sidebar "What's the RISC in the PowerPC anyway?" earlier in this chapter, and refer also to Chapter 25.) The Workgroup Server 8150 is the network server version of the Power Mac 8100/80.

Processor: PowerPC 601, 80 MHz

Upgrade possibilities: The memory expands to 264MB, and the machine has three NuBus slots, one processor-direct slot, and one level 2 cache slot for an optional cache memory card to speed up processing. You can add up to three internal storage devices, such as hard disk drives, CD-ROM drives, or tape cartridge drives. This machine is also available in an audio-video (AV) configuration, which means an AV card comes installed in the processor-direct slot.

Recommendations: Installing an internal CD-ROM drive is a good idea for this machine. If you want to work with many colors on-screen or you want a large monitor, upgrade the video memory on the internal video card. If you plan to use this machine as a graphics workstation, install an accelerated video card.

The Quadra 900, Quadra 950, AWS 95, and WGS 9150

These Macs have speed and lots of slots inside for expansion cards. See Figure 6-7 to find out what the Quadra 900, Quadra 950, AWS 95, and WGS 9150 Macs look like.

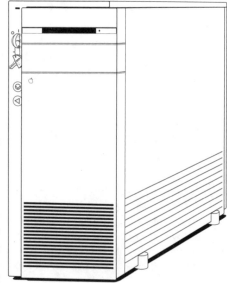

Figure 6-7:
The Quadra 900, Quadra 950, AWS 95, and WGS 9150 Macs look like this.

Macintosh Quadra 900 (October 21, 1991 to May 18, 1992)

The Macintosh Quadra 900 was the high end of the Quadra line for a very short time. It includes six expansion slots for maximum upgradeability.

Processor: 68040, 25 MHz

Upgrade possibilities: The memory expands to 256MB. You have ample room for expansion with five NuBus expansion slots and one 68040 processor-direct slot. The video memory expands to 2MB, and you can also install up to five internal hard disks. You can speed up your Quadra 900 by installing a PowerPC-based accelerator card.

Recommendations: Along with the Quadra 950, this machine is the most expandable of the Quadra line, so go ahead and fill the five expansion slots — but with built-in Ethernet and built-in video, what else could anyone really want?

Macintosh Quadra 950 (May 18, 1992)

This Quadra replaced the Quadra 900 and uses a faster version of the 68040 processor.

Processor: 68040, 33 MHz

Upgrade possibilities: The memory expands to 256MB, and the machine features five NuBus expansion slots and one 68040 processor-direct slot. The video memory expands to 2MB, and you can also install up to five internal hard disks. This Mac can be upgraded to the Apple Workgroup Server 95. You can also speed up the Quadra 950 with a PowerPC based accelerator card.

Recommendations: Like the Quadra 900, this machine is the most expandable of the Quadras, so don't hesitate in filling its five expansion slots with whatever strikes your fancy. But, again like the Quadra 900, with its built-in Ethernet and built-in video, what else could anyone really want?

Apple Workgroup Server 95 (March 22, 1993)

The Apple Workgroup Server 95, called the AWS 95 for short, is based on the Quadra 950 and comes bundled with network server software and hardware.

Processor: 68040, 33 MHz

Upgrade possibilities: The memory expands to 256MB. The machine contains four NuBus expansion slots and one 68040 processor-direct slot. The video memory expands to 2MB, and you can also install up to five internal hard disks.

Recommendations: See those for the Quadra 950. Upgrade the storage capacity too to make available on the network as many files as possible. As with the other workgroup servers, we also recommend adding a tape backup drive for network backups if your machine doesn't already have one.

Work Group Server 9150 (April 25, 1994)

The Work Group Server 9150 is a PowerPC-based server that comes in the Quadra 900 case. It comes fully loaded with a CD-ROM and a tape drive. It comes with a bracket inside to hold up to five internal hard disks.

Processor: Power PC 601, 80 MHz

Upgrade possibilities: The memory expands to 264MB. The machine contains four NuBus expansion slots, one PowerPC level 2 cache slot, and one Power Mac video card slot. You can also install up to five internal hard disks.

Recommendations: Add as much memory and storage as your budget allows. Other than that, this baby has all the hardware it takes to make a great network server.

The LC, LC II, LC III, LC 475, Quadra 605, and Performa 400 series Macs

The LC's and their offspring give you the most bang for your computing buck. Figure 6-8 shows what the LC, LC II, LC III, LC 475, Quadra 605, and Performa 400 series Macs look like.

Figure 6-8:
The LC, LC II, LC III, LC 475, Quadra 605, and Performa 400 series Macs look like this.

Macintosh LC (October 15, 1990 to March 23, 1992)

The LC was the first low-cost color Macintosh. In fact, LC *stands* for low cost. The LC is basically the same computer as the Mac II, but in a smaller case.

Processor: 68020, 16 MHz

Upgrade possibilities: The memory expands to 10MB. The machine has one LC expansion slot, and its video memory expands to 512K.

Recommendations: Expand the video memory if you want more colors on-screen. If you want more speed, install an accelerator card in the expansion slot.

Macintosh LC II (March 23, 1992 to March 15, 1993), Macintosh Performa 400 (September 14, 1992 to April 12, 1993), Macintosh Performa 405 (April 12, 1993), Macintosh Performa 410 (October 18, 1993), Macintosh Performa 430 (April 12, 1993)

The LC II is basically the LC with a new processor, although the speed difference is very small between it and its "slower" sibling. The Performa 400, 405, 410, and 430 all are based on the LC II. The different Performa model numbers indicate different configurations, such as different hard disks, more or less video memory, and different bundled software. The Performas also come with a low-quality color monitor and some of them come with a fax/modem.

Processor: 68030, 16 MHz

Upgrade possibilities: The memory expands to 10MB. The machine has one LC expansion slot. The video memory expands to 512K.

Recommendations: Expand the video memory if you want more colors on-screen. You can install an accelerator card in the expansion slot if you want more speed.

What's the deal with all these Performas?

The Performas are usually Mac LC models packaged for sale in consumer electronics stores. The Performa package includes a low-quality color monitor, software, and sometimes a fax/modem. You may have noticed how consumer electronics stores often use the sales tactic of advertising that they will "meet or beat" the price of any competing store for the same product model. So in case you've wondered why so many otherwise identical Performas have different model numbers, it's so that different consumer stores can sell "different" models. That way, the stores never really have to make good on their claim of meeting or beating any other store's price.

Macintosh LC III (February 10, 1993 to February 14, 1994), Macintosh Performa 450 (April 12, 1993), Macintosh Performa 460 (October 18, 1993), Macintosh Performa 466 (October 18, 1993), Macintosh Performa 467 (October 18, 1993)

If you think of the LC as a reengineered Mac II, you can think of the LC III as a reengineered Mac IIci. Starting with the LC III, the expansion slot for the LC line was made larger to offer better expansion card performance. Even though the slot is larger, however, you can still install cards designed for the LC and LC II.

The Performa 450 is the same machine as the LC III and is sold with a low-quality color monitor, a fax/modem, and software. The Performa 460, 466, and 467 all are the same machine. They, too, are based on the LC III, but their processor is faster. These Macs also come with a low-quality monitor, a fax/modem, and software.

Processor: 68030, 25 MHz for the LC III and the Performa 450; 33 MHz for the Performa 460, 466, and 467

Upgrade possibilities: The memory expands to 36MB. The machine has one LC expansion slot in which you install cards designed for the LC III or for the LC and LC II. The video memory expands to 768K. You can also install a math coprocessor.

Recommendations: Expand the video memory if you want more colors on-screen. If you want more speed, install an accelerator card in the expansion slot.

Macintosh LC 475 (October 21, 1993), Macintosh Quadra 605 (October 21, 1993), Macintosh Performa 475 (October 18, 1993), Macintosh Performa 476 (October 18, 1993)

The LC 475 is the first computer in the Mac LC line to use a 68040 processor. The Quadra 605 comes in a Quadra-style case and looks different than the LC 475, but inside, these two are the same Mac. The Performa 475 and 476 are the same as the LC 475, but they come with a low-quality monitor, a fax/modem, and software.

Processor: 68LC040, 25 MHz

Upgrade possibilities: The memory expands to 36MB, and the video memory expands to 1MB. The machine has one LC expansion slot.

Recommendations: Expand the video memory if you want more colors on-screen. You can install an accelerator card in the expansion slot if you need more speed.

Chapter 7

Portable Macs

• •

In This Chapter

▶ Descriptions of the PowerBooks

▶ Upgrade possibilities for each modular Mac

▶ Recommended upgrades for each PowerBook

• •

*M*ost people think of portable or mobile Macintosh computing only in terms of the PowerBooks, which isn't surprising considering that about a million of them are out there in use. But before the PowerBooks came along, two other portables were available. If you own one of these early portables, see the section "The first Macintosh portables." For the most part, however, you learn about PowerBook upgrades here.

For upgrading purposes, the PowerBooks are all very similar. The major differences from model to model are processor speed and screen quality. Usually, the higher the machine's model number, the faster the speed and the better the screen quality you enjoy.

Your PowerBook can never have too much memory or too big a hard disk. So when you do finally decide to upgrade, first buy as much memory as you can afford and then pick up the biggest hard disk your budget allows.

The next essential addition for your PowerBook is an extra battery. Keeping an extra charged battery on hand doubles your time away from an electrical outlet. We also highly recommend obtaining a battery charger and a second AC adapter.

A good carrying case may not seem like an upgrade, but it keeps all your accessories together and protects your computer from dings, bumps, and rain during travel.

The final PowerBook add-on that we consider essential is an internal modem. The modem enables you to access data back at your office, read e-mail, or send a fax. Its capability to stay connected, no matter where you use your machine, is what the "power" in PowerBook is really all about.

Of course, these essentials aren't the only upgrades available to the PowerBook owner. Other handy add-ons include a network connector for plugging into a network; a printer adapter cable for enabling you to use whatever printer you find on the road; or — how about even a portable printer? An external battery pack can keep you charged up for 12 hours or more of computing time, and a cellular phone connector enables you to use your internal modem anywhere you find a phone.

Tons of options let you upgrade the PowerBook to a more powerful and flexible portable than it already is. One of the most amazing things we've seen is a portable image-scanning station for the PowerBook that enables reporters to send digitized images back to their newspaper offices. Beyond the basics, you can pick and choose other add-ons according to your particular needs.

As you read, you'll notice that, for each PowerBook, we give the processor, the upgrade possibilities, and upgrade recommendations.

The PowerBook 100

This first PowerBook is basically the same machine as the first Apple Macintosh Portable in a much smaller and lighter package. Figure 7-1 shows the PowerBook 100.

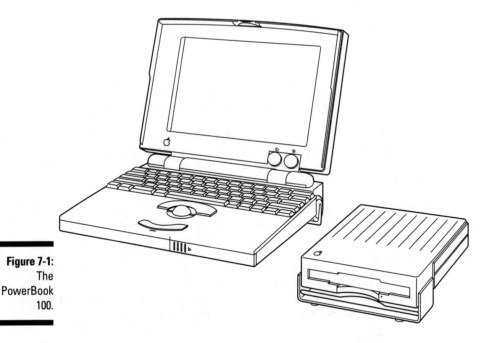

Figure 7-1:
The
PowerBook
100.

PowerBook 100 (October 21, 1991 to August 3, 1992)

The idea behind the PowerBook 100 was to sell tons of these low-cost units to students and consumers. The tactic backfired after most people bought the more high-powered, more expensive PowerBooks. The PowerBook 100 also has a docking mode, which is a feature that enables you to connect the machine to your desktop Mac as an external hard disk.

Processor: 68HC000 (low power 68000), 16 MHz

Upgrade possibilities: The memory expands to 8MB, and the machine contains an internal modem slot for adding telecommunications capabilities. You also can attach an external 1.4MB disk drive and use a docking cable to connect to your desktop Mac.

The first Macintosh portables

Macintosh Portable (September 1989 to February 1991)

This was the first portable Macintosh sold by Apple, and it went over like a concrete parachute. This may have been because the machine felt like it was made of concrete: it was too heavy and too big, at a time when PC laptops were starting to look more like the sleek, slim PowerBooks of today. The computer functioned just like any other Macintosh. Mainly, these portables were just too heavy to carry around — so heavy that they were also called the "luggables."

Processor: 68HC000 (a low-power 68000), 16 MHz

Upgrade possibilities: The memory expands to 9MB, and the machine has one expansion slot and an internal modem slot for those who want to telecommunicate while away from their usual work place. You can also install an internal hard disk or upgrade the existing one.

Recommendations: Despite the numerous upgrade possibilities, finding the parts to upgrade this machine is pretty much a dead end. If you need a portable Mac, see how much you can sell this portable for on the used computer market and apply the money to the price of a PowerBook. You won't be sorry.

Macintosh Backlit Portable (February 1991 to October 1991)

The display screen on this second portable Mac is backlit, which makes the screen easier to read under almost any lighting conditions.

Processor: 68HC000 (low power 68000), 16 MHz

Upgrade possibilities: The same as for the Macintosh Portable.

Recommendations: Buy yourself a PowerBook.

Recommendations: This is a very useful PowerBook. (Parts of this very book, in fact, were written on one of these handy little machines.) The general Power-Book upgrade recommendations listed at the beginning of this chapter all apply to this machine. If you need a modem, check to make sure that the modem is specifically compatible with the PowerBook 100 before you buy it. Some modems aren't compatible, much to the chagrin of any PowerBook 100 owner. The external disk drive is pretty much a must. We also suggest you use a docking cable to connect to your desktop Mac. This connection enables you use to your PowerBook 100 as an external hard disk for your regular Mac, and it also makes transferring files back and forth between the two machines quite easy.

The 100 Series PowerBooks

The PowerBooks have been phenomenally successful. In fact, by the end of 1993, over one million had been sold. If imitation is really the sincerest form of flattery, then the PowerBooks should definitely feel flattered — almost every laptop on the market now looks just like a PowerBook. Figure 7-2 shows what these PowerBooks look like.

Figure 7-2:
The 100
series
PowerBooks
look like this.

PowerBook 140 (October 21, 1991 to August 3, 1992)

The PowerBook 140 is one of the original three PowerBooks. This PowerBook puts the computing power of the Macintosh IIcx into a laptop unit. The 140 makes a great all-around machine for use on the road, even though newer models are faster.

Processor: 68030, 16 MHz

Upgrade possibilities: The memory expands to 8MB, and you can upgrade the hard disk. The machine also has an internal modem slot for telecommunications.

Recommendations: Again, the general PowerBook recommendations apply here. And if you need a new battery, look for the batteries sold for the PowerBook 165c and 185c. They give you about 20 percent more computing time than others do.

PowerBook 170 (October 21, 1991 to October 19, 1992)

This model is the third of the three original PowerBooks. It was designed as the high-end unit, with the fastest processor of the three and a screen that's easiest to read. Even though this machine has been around awhile, its superior screen quality keeps it in the high-end range.

Processor: 68030, 25 MHz

Upgrade possibilities: The memory expands to 8MB, and the machine contains an internal modem slot for telecommunications upgrades.

Recommendations: Again, see the general PowerBook recommendations. If you need new batteries for this machine, look for those sold for the PowerBook 165c and 185c. These batteries also give this machine about 20 percent more computing time than others do.

PowerBook 145 (August 3, 1992 to June 7, 1993)

The PowerBook 145 replaces the PowerBook 140. The 145 is basically the same machine as the 170, but with a lower-quality screen. In fact, if you set the 145 and more expensive 170 side by side, the only difference you notice is in the screen. Everything else is identical. Basically, Apple decided that the processor speed for the 140 was too slow, so the 145 inherited a faster chip.

Processor: 68030, 25 MHz

Upgrade possibilities: The memory expands to 8MB, and the machine has an internal modem slot for telecommunications.

Recommendations: Again, see the general PowerBook suggestions. And if you need new batteries, follow the recommendations for the PowerBook 140 and 170.

PowerBook 145b (June 7, 1993)

The PowerBook 145b replaces the PowerBook 145. This machine's internal design reduces manufacturing costs, which results in lower prices for consumers. If you compare the 145 and 145b, they look identical. Inside, however, the 145 has only 2MB of memory, whereas the 145b boasts 4MB. So right away, you can run larger applications and use larger documents on the 145b. And you get more memory for a lower price.

Processor: 68030, 25 MHz

Upgrade possibilities: The memory expands to 8MB, and the machine has an internal modem slot for telecommunications.

Because of the PowerBook 145b's design, you could actually install a total of 10MB of memory. Installing this much memory would be a mistake, however, because the machine can only use up to 8MB. In other words, stick with 8MB, and don't buy more memory than you need. (See Chapter 14 for more information about memory.)

Recommendations: The same as for the PowerBook 145.

PowerBook 160 (October 19, 1992 to August 16, 1993)

The PowerBook 160 includes a connector for attaching an external monitor. It is also one of the first PowerBooks with a built-in screen that's capable of *grayscale display*, which means that you actually see shades of gray on-screen, instead of just black and white.

Processor: 68030, 25 MHz

Upgrade possibilities: The memory expands to 14MB, and the machine offers built-in video support for color, which means that you can connect an external color monitor. You can also install an internal modem for telecommunications.

Recommendations: Again, the general PowerBook recommendations apply. Because this PowerBook has built-in video capabilities, go ahead and connect it to an external monitor, either color or black-and-white, if your work requires this type of display.

PowerBook 180 (October 19, 1992 to May 16, 1994)

Like the PowerBook 160, the 180 includes a connector for an external monitor. The screen in the 180 is capable of grayscale display, also like the 160, but the 180's quality is much higher. The main thing that you'd notice if you viewed the 160 and the 180 side by side is that the screen on the 180 displays much sharper images. This screen provides a wider viewing angle, too, which, practically speaking, enables you to slouch more as you type while sitting on the couch. The PowerBook 180: machine of choice for couch potatoes — what a recommendation! The wider screen also makes sharing your work with others who work next to you and try to look over your shoulder much easier.

Processor: 68030, 33 MHz

Upgrade possibilities: The same as for the PowerBook 160.

Recommendations: The same as for the PowerBook 160.

PowerBook 165 (August 16, 1993)

This PowerBook replaces the PowerBook 160. It boosts the processor speed to the same level as that of the 180. All other features are the same as those of the 160. The 165 just inherited the faster chip from the 180. We believe that, by giving the 165 the faster chip, Apple simplified their manufacturing process, because the 165 and 180 share the same logic board.

Processor: 68030, 33 MHz

Upgrade possibilities: The same as for the PowerBook 160.

Recommendations: The same as for the PowerBook 160.

PowerBook 165c (February 10, 1993 to December 13, 1993)

This PowerBook is the first one with a color screen. But the mediocre screen quality, which makes looking at it hard on the eyes, and the machine's short battery life are decided drawbacks. Everyone, it seemed, wanted to wait for a better color screen, so sales of this model just didn't take off.

Processor: 68030, 33 MHz

Upgrade possibilities: The same as for the PowerBook 160.

Recommendations: The same as for the PowerBook 160. Because of the poor screen quality, however, you may want to connect an external monitor to use this PowerBook at your desktop.

PowerBook 180c (June 7, 1993 to March 14, 1994)

The PowerBook 180c keeps the promise of high-quality color on a PowerBook that the PowerBook 165c is unable to provide. What's known as an *active matrix display* gives the 180c a better, though smaller, screen than that of the 165c. The 180c's screen provides a wider viewing angle and crisp, bright colors. Even though the screen is physically smaller than that of the 165c, it displays more and smaller dots to create its images. These tiny dots mean that you see larger portions of a document on-screen. The 180c's screen is one of those rare cases in which less really *does* mean more.

Processor: 68030, 33 MHz

Upgrade possibilities: The same as for the PowerBook 160.

Recommendations: The same for as the PowerBook 160.

The 500 Series PowerBooks

The 500 series PowerBooks carry on the successful tradition of the 100 series PowerBooks. The coolest thing about the 500s is the touch pad that replaces the trackball on the 100s. The 500s are also the first PowerBooks to use an 68LC040 processor, and we've heard promises about an upgrade path to the PowerPC.

Included as built-in features on the 500 series are: speakers, an Ethernet port, a video port for external monitors, a two-battery bay, and an expansion slot. That's right, you heard correctly, an expansion slot! The 500s are the first PowerBooks to include a slot for expansion cards. The slot is located in the left battery bay, so you can either use two batteries or use one battery and an expansion card. Another thing the 500s let you do is use PCMCIA cards. To use these cards you plug an adapter module into the expansion slot. To find out about PCMCIA cards, read "PCMCIA Explained" in this chapter.

PCMCIA Explained

PCMCIA. Help — to buy one of these expansion cards, you practically have to recite the whole alphabet. If you really have to know what the letters stand for, here you go: *P*ersonal *C*omputer *M*emory *C*ard *I*ndustry *A*ssociation. Yes, the PCMCIA is actually a standards committee — only a committee could come up with a name like PCMCIA. The committee publishes a list of standards that PCMCIA cards must use in order to work with laptop computers.

PCMCIA cards are credit card-sized expansion cards used in DOS-compatible laptops and the Newton. People like these cards because they're so small. The cards contain memory, modems, and networking circuitry, which you can use to upgrade your 500 series PowerBook. Now you know.

PowerBook 520 and 520c (May 16, 1994)

These two PowerBooks are the least expensive models in the 500 series. The 520 is the black-and-white version and the 520c is the color machine.

Processor: 68LC040, 50/25 MHz (the first processor speed refers to how fast the processor runs; the second speed refers to how fast data moves back and forth between the processor and other components in the Mac)

Upgrade possibilities: The memory expands to 36MB. A connector inside lets you install an internal modem. An expansion slot accepts special low power expansion cards or a PCMCIA adapter module.

Recommendations: Refer to the general PowerBook recommendations section at the beginning of this chapter. Go ahead and fill the expansion slot if you want to. These babies come fully loaded, so it's hard to think of something that isn't already there.

PowerBook 540 and 540c (May 16, 1994)

The 540 has an easy-to-read black-and-white screen, and the 540c displays thousands of colors and produces near photographic-quality images.

Processor: 68LC040, 66/33 MHz (the first processor speed refers to how fast the processor runs; the second speed refers to how fast data moves back and forth between the processor and other components in the Mac)

Upgrade possibilities: The same as the PowerBook 520 and 520c.

Recommendations: The same as the PowerBook 520 and 520c.

The PowerBook Duos

The Duos are also known as the 200 series PowerBooks. Figure 7-3 shows you what a typical dynamic Duo looks like.

PowerBook Duo 210 (October 19, 1992 to October 21, 1993)

The Duos are PowerBooks that are smaller and lighter than other PowerBooks. The Duos also use a different battery that lasts longer than those of the regular PowerBooks. This Mac's main feature — and the reason for the Duo name — is

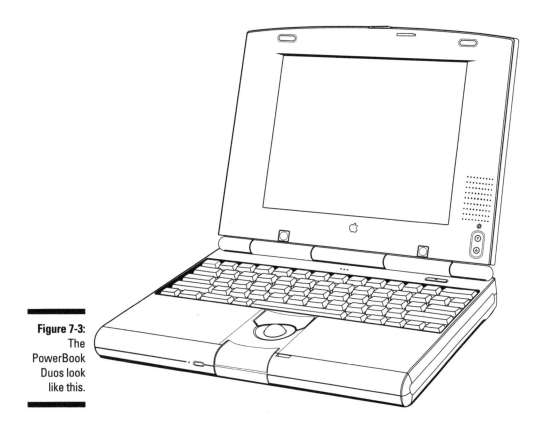

Figure 7-3:
The
PowerBook
Duos look
like this.

that a Duo is actually two machines in one: a PowerBook on its own and a desktop Mac after you plug the Duo into a piece of hardware called a *Duo Dock*. The section "More information on the Duo Dock," at the end of this chapter tells you more about this piece of hardware.

The Duo offers you a great deal of flexibility, because you can plug it into different kinds of docks to do different kinds of work. You can transform your Duo into a desktop Mac, for example, by plugging it into the Duo Dock. Or you can plug the Duo into a portable dock that enables you to connect the machine to other kinds of equipment, such as a video projector system for presentations. (This is one of those multimedia applications that everybody talks about, but one that no one seems to really know how to do.)

Processor: 68030, 25 MHz

Upgrade possibilities: The memory expands to 24MB. A connector on the back of the machine enables you to attach different docks, and an internal connector enables you to install an internal modem.

Recommendations: Again, refer to the general PowerBook recommendations section at the beginning of this chapter. This baby's speed and screen can be upgraded to those of the Duo 250 or Duo 270c for about $2000. (If you need the faster speed and a better screen, upgrading is cheaper than buying a new, higher model Duo.)

Every Duo owner should at least own the *Floppy Adapter*, which is a piece of hardware that enables you to connect an external disk drive and a second keyboard or a mouse. Other docks from Apple and other companies provide additional connectors for special applications, such as the multimedia application we mentioned earlier.

PowerBook Duo 230 (October 19, 1992)

The Duo 230 is much the same as the Duo 210 but with a faster processor that provides a small improvement in speed. The 230 is identical in every other way to the 210. The Duo 230 sold better than the 210, however, because of its faster speed.

Processor: 68030, 33 MHz

Upgrade possibilities: The same as for the Duo 210.

Recommendations: The same as for the Duo 210.

PowerBook Duo 250 (October 21, 1993 to May 16, 1994)

The PowerBook Duo 250 is just like the Duo 230 but sports a higher-quality active-matrix screen that provides better viewing and is much easier on the eyes than those of earlier-model Duos. You see sharp images, because the screen offers improved contrast and a wider viewing angle over those of its older brothers.

Processor: 68030, 33 MHz

Upgrade possibilities: The same as for the Duo 210.

Recommendations: The same as for the Duo 210.

PowerBook Duo 270c (October 21, 1993 to May 16, 1994)

This machine is the first color Duo. The 270c's screen is capable of displaying photographic-quality images, which makes this Duo the Duo of choice if you need to display multimedia presentations on its built-in screen.

Processor: 68030, 33 MHz

Upgrade possibilities: The memory expands to 32 MB.

Recommendations: See the general PowerBook recommendations section. Again, we want to emphasize that every Duo owner should own at least the Floppy Adapter, that handy piece of hardware that enables you to connect an external disk drive and a second keyboard or a mouse. Also check out the other docks that Apple and other companies offer with connectors for special applications.

PowerBook Duo 280 (May 16, 1994)

The PowerBook Duo 280 is the first Duo to use the 68LC040 processor, which makes this machine really fast. Its best feature is its high quality black-and-white display.

Processor: 680LC40, 33 MHz

Upgrade possibilities: The memory expands to 40 MB.

Recommendations: See the general recommendations for the PowerBooks. Again, we want to emphasize that every Duo owner should own at least the Floppy Adapter, that handy piece of hardware that enables you to connect an external disk drive and a second keyboard or a mouse. Also check out the other docks that Apple and other companies offer with connectors for special applications.

PowerBook Duo 280c (May 16, 1994)

The Duo 280c replaces the Duo 270c. The computer's screen shares the same high quality of the screen on the PowerBook 540c, which means that the screen displays photographic-quality images. The Duo 280c is the Duo of choice for displaying color multimedia presentations.

Processor: 68LC040, 33 MHz

Upgrade possibilities: The memory expands to 40 MB.

Recommendations: See the general recommendations for the PowerBooks. Again, we want to emphasize that every Duo owner should own at least the Floppy Adapter, that handy piece of hardware that enables you to connect an external disk drive and a second keyboard or a mouse. Also, check out the other docks that Apple and other companies offer with connectors for special applications.

More information on the Duo Dock

The Duo Dock is part of the PowerBook Duo family, but it isn't really a separate computer. You can't work with the dock unless you plug in a Duo. The dock contains all the Macintosh connectors that enable you to attach such hardware as a keyboard, an external hard disk, or an external monitor to the Duo. The dock also gives the Duo the capabilities to use a second hard disk, a math coprocessor, and two expansion cards. In other words, attaching it to the dock is a handy way to upgrade your Duo.

Upgrade possibilities: You can install an internal hard disk, two expansion cards, and extra video memory to improve the images on your screen and to enable you to connect large monitors, either color or black-and-white, to the dock. You

can also add hardware that enables you to use the Duo's internal modem. The machine also accepts a math coprocessor for fast number crunching and graphics applications.

Note: You can use these upgrades only while your Duo is plugged into the dock.

Recommendations: Adding a second hard disk for the extra storage capacity is a good idea. The math coprocessor comes in handy for crunching the numbers in large spreadsheets. Add video memory to improve the graphics on your monitor screen or to attach a large monitor. If your office is wired for an Ethernet network, add an interface card to enable you to connect your dock to the network.

Part III
Easy Outside Upgrades and Fixes

The 5th Wave   By Rich Tennant

©RICH TENNANT

Mac Repairpersons camp out

...SO IT'S MY FIRST DAY ON THE JOB, AND THE BOSS SENDS ME OUT TO THE HOME OF PETER TOWNSHEND OF THE ROCK GROUP "THE WHO," SEEMS HE'S HAVING TROUBLE WITH HIS MAC, PRINTER AND HARD DRIVE. WELL YOU'VE SEEN WHAT HE DOES TO HIS GUITAR AT THE END OF A CONCERT? AND HE LIKES HIS GUITAR...

In this part...

1f you're a little unsure about opening up your Mac, or if all you need to do is upgrade your storage capacity, then the chapters in this part are for you. We tell you about all sorts of different types of external upgrades, such as using graphics, buying new mice, improving your printed output with different fonts and better printers, and more.

And don't worry — you don't need to open up your Mac to do these upgrades.

Chapter 8

External Storage Upgrades

● ●

In This Chapter

▶ What are storage devices?

▶ Assessing your storage needs

▶ SCSI basics

▶ What to do if something goes wrong

▶ Maintenance tips

● ●

*Y*ou need storage because the memory your computer uses to perform its work only functions when the power is turned on. Storage enables you to keep and maintain your data after you turn off the computer. One way you can acquire more storage is to plug an external storage device, such as a hard disk, into the back of your Mac. This chapter describes your options.

Storage Devices Explained

Diskette drives, hard disks, removable cartridge drives, CD-ROM drives, tape drives, optical drives — these are all storage devices. Some of them you probably use every day, and others you may never have heard of. Some you may never use at all. All this hardware comes in both internal and external versions, but right now we're talking about the external flavors, because they're so easy to use — you just plug them into your Mac. (Chapter 12 discusses internal storage upgrades.)

Diskette drive

All desktop Macs come with one internal diskette drive. This drive is the place where you insert your diskettes. Yeah, we know you knew that, but we wanted to say it anyway. The diskette drive is also the original storage drive for the Mac — the first Macs didn't come with hard disks, strange as that may seem today.

Mac diskette drives come in three sizes: 400K, single-sided, 800K, double-sided, and 1,440K (1.4MB), high-density

The 400K drives came on the Macintosh 128k, and 512. The 800K drives came on the Mac 512Ke, Mac Plus, early Macintosh SEs, and Mac II. If you're still using a Mac with 800K drives and you frequently exchange files on diskette with people who own newer Macs, you ought to consider upgrading to a high-density diskette drive.

The high-density diskette drive is the current standard. One advantage to the high-density drive is that it enables you to store more files than the other drives. The high-density drive also enables you to exchange diskettes with DOS and Windows computers — and co-existing with the DOS and Windows world is something we're all doing more and more of these days.

Hard disks

People take hard disks for granted these days. Because hard disks are a standard Mac item, you may wonder why you need to consider one for an upgrade. The reason is that, at some point, your hard disk may fill up with all your work and you may need more room to store your files. You'll know the hard disk is filling up because you'll be getting "disk full" messages from your Mac when you try to save your work. That's when it's time to upgrade your hard disk

Physically, the inside of a hard disk is like the inside of a diskette. Inside the diskette's plastic case is a flexible plastic disk coated with a magnetic substance that your data is recorded onto. And inside the hard disk's sealed metal enclosure is a rigid metal disk that's coated with a magnetic substance. The coated metal disk records your data similar to the way a cassette recorder records music on a tape.

Floptical, Moptical, and Peter Cottontail

You may have heard about *floptical disk* storage. A floptical disk looks just like a high-density diskette, but the technology inside is different. A floptical disk holds 21MB of data, and a diskette holds 1.4MB. Floptical storage kind of missed out on the storage market in terms of timing; by the time it came out, newer storage systems offered better prices. The *optical* in floptical refers to the optical positioning technology that's used to pack large amounts of data into small spaces on a magnetically coated plastic disk.

The rigid metal disk in the hard disk enables you to store large amounts of data and gives you much, much faster access to your data than you have with diskettes. With technology continually evolving and new products coming out all the time, the storage capacity of hard disks keeps getting larger and larger. You can find hard disks that store as much as four gigabytes today, which is 4,000MB. And in the future, we're sure to find even larger sizes as manufacturers cram more capacity into their products.

When you upgrade your hard disk storage, you can upgrade to an internal hard disk or an external hard disk. For more information about internal hard disk upgrades, see Chapter 12.

The advantages to an external hard disk upgrade are the following:

> ✔ It's easy. You just plug the hard disk into the SCSI port on the back of your Mac. No need to open the machine.

> ✔ You can keep the internal storage space that came with your Mac and you gain the new storage you plug in. (An internal hard disk upgrade usually involves taking out your original hard disk and replacing it with the new one. You have to copy your data from the old hard disk to another storage medium, such as diskettes, and then copy to the new hard disk. What a pain — we're sure you can think of much better things to do than sit around and copy data from one place to another.)

The one disadvantage to an external hard disk upgrade is that the extra hardware box takes up space on your desk, and it's one more piece of equipment that you have to remember to switch on when you power up your Mac.

If you need to work on several Macs in different locations, just unplug your external hard disk and take it with you. This way, you have your documents, applications, and your customized system folder no matter where you work — at the office, on the airplane, at Disney World, or accompanying your kids on a school field trip. Hey, it's OK to take a break now and then.

Removable cartridge drives

Removable cartridge drives combine the large storage capacity of a hard disk with the transportability of a diskette. Cartridges come in different sizes, ranging from 44MB to as much as 270MB of data and for sure you'll be able to store much more in the near future. The cartridge sizes are 5 ¼-inch and 3 ½-inch, which make the cartridges as easy to carry around as diskettes.

Another advantage is that you get fast access to your data the same way you do with a hard disk. And because you can buy more cartridges as you fill them up, the cartridges give you virtually unlimited storage.

One more thing: the removable cartridges are used by service bureaus that give you professional-quality printed material. If you have page layout or graphics files that you want printed with a higher quality than is possible with a laser printer, for example, you can have the bureau print the files for you. The reason that the bureaus use cartridges and not diskettes is that files designed for high-quality printing are usually too large to fit on a diskette.

CD-ROM

When most people hear *CD-ROM*, they think multimedia. That's because so many games, encyclopedias, reference works, and educational programs come packaged on CD-ROM. CD-ROM has been adopted as storage for multimedia, because it stores large amounts of graphics, sound, or any other information. CD-ROM discs are also very cheap to duplicate. Getting information from CD-ROM is slow compared to using a hard disk; the good thing about CD-ROM is that you get a huge amount of information on one disc.

One thing Mac users need to understand is that you can't store any of your own information on CD-ROM — just like you can't record any sound or music on audio CDs. You use a hard disk for storing your own files.

The reason to get a CD-ROM drive is to use multimedia. CD-ROM is becoming so popular that we're almost positive you'll have a CD-ROM drive within a year or two if you don't have one already.

Tape drives

Tape drives are used almost exclusively for hard disk backup. In fact, we can't think of any other reason you'd want to use them. These drives are rather slow, but they store large amounts of data at a very low cost per megabyte. For most users, tape drives are the most practical and economical way to back up a hard disk.

Tape drives use a removable tape cassette that looks like an audio cassette. The amount of storage ranges from 40MB to 10,000MB, depending on the drive and the kind of tape. Of course, the storage amounts are always increasing.

The cost of tape storage is pennies per megabyte versus the cost of hard drive storage, which is about a dollar per megabyte. It's easy to see why tape drives are so economical for backup.

Optical drives

Optical drives use a laser beam to read and write data on removable optical cartridges. These cartridges look like CD-ROM enclosed in a plastic case. Service bureaus are beginning to accept optical cartridges, so people who work with lots of graphics and page layout are beginning to use optical storage for the same purpose that they use removable cartridge drives.

The big advantage to using optical drives is that you can store large amounts of data at a low cost per megabyte. The optical cartridges are also more rugged than magnetic removable cartridges. Optical cartridges offer a long storage life and are useful in situations where people need to store data for many years. Unlike magnetic media, such as hard disks and tape cartridges, which start to break down and lose data in 5 or 10 years, optical cartridges preserve data perfectly for 35 years or more. But then again, you probably won't care about the data you put on these cartridges 35 years from now — assuming you could even find a Mac and optical drive that hadn't completely rusted away.

The disadvantage to optical drives is that they are slow compared to hard drives. Their speed is similar to CD-ROM speed for accessing data. What a drag. As optical drives get faster, you'll probably see more people using them to store data on removable media.

WORM Drives

We're not kidding. WORM drives really exist! WORM stands for Write Once, Read Many. The cartridges that go in these drives are kind of like optical drive cartridges, but you can only record data on a WORM cartridge once. The data cannot be erased.

The drives are pretty outdated and have been replaced by optical drives that provide more storage flexibility. We only mention WORM drives so that if you hear people talking about them, you'll know they're not talking about fish bait.

Figuring Out Your Storage Needs

Different types of storage devices work best in different situations, depending on your needs. You have many choices when it comes to storage. Here are some general rules of thumb for the best use of storage types:

- *Diskettes* are best for transferring small- and medium-sized files between different computers. Diskettes are useful for creating a quick backup copy of one particular file. You can use diskettes to back up a hard disk, but the number of disks and amount of time it takes makes this a less-than-desirable way to back up.

- *Hard disks* are best for everyday storage needs. Hard disks are so standard these days that you probably can't imagine doing your work without them. Some people use a second hard disk as a backup system for their main hard disk, but this solution isn't ideal because of the high cost of data storage per megabyte. Also, data is generally more secure if stored with other storage devices.

- *Removable cartridge drives* are best for archiving files and transporting large files between computers and work sites. Because you can remove the cartridges, you can store important data in remote locations. The only drawback to this type of storage is that the cost per megabyte stored is relatively high.

- *CD-ROM* is best used to access multimedia information and programs. You can't store your data on CD-ROM, but it provides an easy and economical way for companies to distribute multimedia.

- *Tape drives* are the kings of backup devices. These drives offer the lowest cost per megabyte stored, and you can store the tapes long-term in remote locations. The one drawback is the slow speed.

- *Optical drives* are best for archiving data and transporting large files between computers and work sites. The long shelf life of optical cartridges makes this storage method good for long-term storage.

SCSI 101: Read if You Are Adding Just One External Storage Device

If you're just adding one device, this section is for you. Read the next section for more in-depth information or if you're adding more than one external storage device.

SCSI is a hideous acronym that stands for *Small Computer Systems Interface* and is pronounced "scuzzy." Believe it or not, you can connect up to six devices — storage or other kinds — to the Mac SCSI port. For information about the location of the SCSI port, see Chapter 4.

To connect an external storage device to your Mac through the SCSI port, you need a SCSI cable. When it comes to getting good SCSI cables, the thicker the better. The other thing you need is a terminator — not the movie guy — but a device that looks like the connector that plugs into the external drive but without the cable attached. The section covering SCSI 201 provides more information about termination if you need it.

The cable and terminator often come with the storage device you purchase. If you don't have a cable and terminator, buy them at a computer retail store.

When you look at your storage device, you see two SCSI ports, one stacked on top of the other. One port is for the Mac-to-SCSI cable, and the other is for the terminator. It doesn't matter which port you plug the cable or the terminator into, but you must plug in the terminator to signal to the Mac that the storage device is the only external device connected to the SCSI port.

Finally, if you're a PowerBook user, be sure to refer the PowerBook termination and SCSI cable information in the next section.

SCSI 201: Read if You're Adding Two or More External Storage Devices

Save yourself from some pretty techie stuff — read this section only if you're connecting more than one piece of hardware to the SCSI port on the back of your Mac.

Like we said in the SCSI 101 section, SCSI is a hideous acronym that stands for *Small Computer Systems Interface* and is pronounced "scuzzy." Every Mac since the Mac Plus includes the SCSI port.

The most important thing to know about SCSI and storage is that the one SCSI port, or connector, on the back of the Macintosh lets you plug in up to six storage devices. You can also connect other devices, such as scanners and printers, as long as the total is six or less. Chapter 4 provides more information about the location of the SCSI port.

You can connect six devices to one SCSI port because the devices link together in a chain. Each device has two SCSI connectors located on the back of the device, one located on top of the other. Cables link the devices together in the chain This linking process is sometimes called *daisy chaining*. The next time a techno-nerd tells you he or she is daisy chaining off the SCSI port, you'll understand, but you may not want to keep the conversation going for long.

SCSI cables come in two flavors: Mac-to-SCSI and SCSI-to-SCSI. You use the Mac-to-SCSI cable to connect the first device in your chain to the Macintosh and use the SCSI-to-SCSI cable to connect all the other devices to each other.

SCSI 201 continued: a few simple SCSI rules

To link storage devices together in a chain, you follow these simple SCSI rules:

Every external device needs its own unique ID number, ranging from 1 to 6.

The SCSI system allows for eight ID numbers, from 0 to 7. The Macintosh counts as one device, and its number is always 7. The internal hard disk always gets the number 0. This numbering scheme leaves the numbers 1 though 6 for external devices. If your Mac has a built-in CD-ROM drive, the CD-ROM drive gets the ID number 2 or 3.

The order of ID numbers in the chain isn't important, as long as each device is assigned a different number.

Assigning ID numbers to the devices in your SCSI chain isn't difficult at all. Each device comes with a dial or switch located near the SCSI connectors. The switch lets you to select the number you want to assign to the device.

The SCSI chain needs a terminator at both ends.

In SCSI lingo, a terminator is not a giant robot with an Austrian accent running around shooting people. Remember, we said that the devices in a SCSI chain each have two SCSI connectors. The last device, even if it is the only device you connect to your Mac SCSI port, has an open connector. The connector needs to be capped with a plug called a terminator so that data signals don't flow back along the chain and cause interference. Devices often come with terminators, or you can buy one when you buy SCSI cables. Terminators come in two flavors: *dead end* and *pass through*.

If your Mac has an internal hard disk, termination is built into the hard disk. Because the internal hard disk with termination is part of the same SCSI system as any external devices you add, the beginning of the chain is already terminated.

If your Mac does not have an internal hard disk, the computer may or may not have a terminator plug installed internally. You can open up your Mac and check on the logic board, or set up your SCSI chain as if your Mac had an internal terminator. If you experience problems, such as your Mac screen displaying the question mark icon on startup, your Mac probably doesn't have an internal terminator. So connect a pass-through terminator plug at the beginning of the chain. Then connect the pass-through terminator to the SCSI cable, and plug the cable and terminator into the SCSI port on the first device.

For Mac IIfx and Mac Plus users only

Two types of Macs have special termination considerations: the Mac IIfx and the Mac Plus. The Mac IIfx uses a special black terminator. When you purchase an external storage device for your Mac IIfx, make sure you get the black terminator.

The Mac Plus is fussy about which SCSI hard drive it accepts. Before you buy a hard disk for your Mac Plus, check with the manufacturer to be sure it works with your Mac.

The total length of all the SCSI cables may not exceed 18 feet.

Try to keep the cable length between 10 and 12 feet; longer chains tend to have problems more often, and the longer the chain, the more problems you're likely to experience.

Don't buy cheap SCSI cables.

Thin, improperly shielded cables can cause your SCSI chain to work poorly or not at all. Apple SCSI cables are excellent but expensive. You need well-shielded cables, and buying the thickest ones you can find will help ensure that you get well-shielded ones. In general, more expensive cables offer better quality, following the old saying, "You get what you pay for."

Use the same type of cable throughout your SCSI chain.

Guide to termination for PowerBook users

The internal hard disks in the 100 series PowerBooks have very limited built-in termination. This means that if you connect even one external device to the SCSI port on a 100 series PowerBook, you must supply proper external termination.

To do this termination, you need to use two terminator plugs. First, connect one pass-through terminator between the HDI-30 System cable and the external hard disk. Think of this HDI-30 System cable and terminator combination as one unit. Next, plug in the second terminator to the second SCSI port on the external hard disk. If you're connecting two or more SCSI devices in a chain, use the HDI-30 System cable and terminator combination to connect the first device. Plug the second terminator into the unused SCSI port on the last device in the chain.

Note that this termination information does not apply to the PowerBook Duos. The Duos do not have a SCSI port built in. Both the Mini Dock and the Duo Dock have termination built in so that when a PowerBook Duo is plugged into a Mini Dock or a Duo Dock, it follows the same termination rules as a desktop Mac.

SCSI cable connections for PowerBook users

PowerBooks have a special SCSI port on the back that uses a cable with a small square connector. This connector is called an HDI-30 connector, and the cables come in two flavors. The *HDI-30 System cable* lets you connect upgrade hardware, such as external hard disks, CD-ROM drives, and so forth to your PowerBook. The *HDI-30 Docking cable* lets you attach your PowerBook 100, 160, 165, and 180 to your desktop Mac and use the PowerBook's internal hard disk as an external hard disk on the Desktop Mac.

Another option for connecting upgrade hardware is to use a regular desktop Mac SCSI cable with a PowerBook SCSI adapter. The PowerBook adapter lets the regular Mac cable plug into the PowerBook SCSI port. So if you've got a regular SCSI cable, all you have to do is ask for a PowerBook SCSI adapter at a computer store or a mail order company.

Different kinds of cable in a SCSI chain can cause problems. Find a good cable that works and use it for your whole SCSI chain. You can solve many problems by using a set of high-quality cables of one kind from one source.

Here ends the course in SCSI basics.

What to Do if Something Goes Wrong

Do any of the following problems sound familiar to you? If so, read on for some possible solutions.

I just added an external hard disk to my Mac and now when I try to start it up, all I get is a flashing ? icon.

This is one of the two most common signs that something is wrong on your Mac's SCSI chain. Here are some probable causes and some fixes:

- ✔ *A loose or disconnected cable.* Make sure all the cables are firmly connected. Snap the wire bails on either side of the cable connectors in place to make sure cables don't come loose.

- ✔ *Two devices in the chain using the same ID number.* Check to make sure that each device has a different number. Also, remember that the Mac is number 7, the internal hard disk is number 0, and the internal CD-ROM is number 2 or 3.

✔ *A bad cable in the SCSI chain.* A bad cable may have a broken wire inside or may be too thin or poorly shielded. You need to swap out cables one at a time until you find the bad one. Doesn't this remind you of checking all your Christmas tree lights to find the one that made the whole chain go out?

✔ *The SCSI chain containing a variety of cables from different manufacturers.* Mixing cables in a SCSI chain is asking for trouble. Find a high-quality brand that works and stick with that brand. This advice especially applies to long SCSI chains.

✔ *One or more devices in the SCSI chain turned off.* Try turning all the devices in the chain off and then turn all the devices in the chain on again before starting up the Mac. Depending on the devices and their arrangement, you may or may not be able to leave unused devices turned off. The safest bet is to turn everything on before starting your Mac, even if you plan to use just one device.

✔ *A problem with termination.* A terminator is loose or broken, or too many terminators are in the chain. Make sure you don't have an internally terminated drive in the middle of the chain. To find out whether the drive is internally terminated, refer to the drive documentation.

If the manual doesn't help, call the technical support department at the company that makes the drive. If you give the model number, the support person can tell you whether it's internally terminated. Also, make sure you haven't double-terminated a drive by adding an external terminator plug to an internally terminated drive.

✔ *More or fewer terminators needed.* Sometimes with a very long SCSI chain (12 to 18 feet, for example) you need to add a pass-through terminator in the middle of the chain. With a very short chain (less than 18 inches) you may not need to terminate the last device. If you have only one external drive connected to a very short cable and are having problems, try removing the terminator.

✔ *One or more devices on your chain incompatible with another device or driver software.* Try removing all but one device and adding back devices one at a time until the problem appears. Then you'll know which device is the culprit and can contact the support department in the company that manufactures it.

✔ *The physical arrangement of the devices in the chain causing problems.* Try moving devices to different physical locations in the chain. For example, make the last external device the first, the first one the middle, and so on.

One of my storage drives isn't showing up on the desktop.

This problem is the second most common problem on the SCSI bus. The culprit may be software or hardware. To find out which it is, try using a SCSI utility like SCSI Probe. You can get this shareware utility from user groups, electronic bulletin boards, or on-line service. If the problem is software, SCSI Probe should allow you to identify and mount the device on your desktop. You can use Disk First Aid, MacTools, or Norton Utilities to help you. If you have no success, you'll probably have to consult a technician.

If the problem is hardware, meaning that SCSI Probe does not identify the device for you, try the solutions listed in the preceding question.

I can't figure out how to connect my hardware into a SCSI chain. And there's no way I'll ever get termination right.

SCSI chains and termination shouldn't stop you from getting the maximum from your SCSI port. Call the technical support department for the devices you're adding and get all the help you can from the support person on the phone. Or call a technician or consultant to help you.

Maintenance Tips

Follow these tips to help keep your storage devices in good running order:

- ✔ Keep magnets away from magnetic media such as diskettes, hard disks, and removable cartridges.

- ✔ Keep SCSI cable lengths as short as possible.

- ✔ Do not twist, kink, or step on SCSI cables.

- ✔ Do not use a damaged SCSI cable.

- ✔ Buy a good hard disk utility application, such as MacTools or Norton Utilities, and use it regularly to identify and fix minor problems before they become major. You can also use Disk First Aid, a utility included free with your Mac system software, although the commercial utilities include more features.

- ✔ Tape drive recording heads need to be cleaned periodically, depending on how much you use the drive. Refer to your drive's manual for details.

- ✔ Avoid dropping or jostling hard disks or removable cartridges. These items are very susceptible to damage from rough handling.

- ✔ Clean your diskette drive heads if you have trouble reading or writing to diskettes. Be sure to use an Apple-approved head cleaning kit. If you use some cleaning products too much, they can be abrasive and damage your Mac's drive heads. Don't bother to clean the heads unless you're having problems.

Chapter 9

Improving Your Output with Fonts, Printers, and Printer Upgrades

• •

In This Chapter

▶ Different types of printers

▶ Printer technology

▶ The printer-Mac connection

▶ PC printers and your Mac

▶ Fonts and your printed output

▶ Printer upgrade possibilities

▶ Some questions and answers about printers

▶ Printer maintenance

• •

*I*f you're buying a Mac, you probably need a printer, too. And after you've owned a Mac and a printer for a while, you're likely to want to improve your output. This chapter tells you how to improve your printing with new fonts or with a new printer. You also learn about memory and storage upgrades for your current printer that enable it to print faster, print larger documents, and use additional fonts.

Printer Types

Your choices of Mac printer types are many, including ImageWriter types, StyleWriter types, LaserWriter types, and other types such as thermal transfer, dye sublimation, solid wax, and daisy wheel printers. Table 9-1 describes each of these types of printer and what you need to know about it.

Table 9-1	Printer Types
Printer Type	*What You Should Know about It*
Dot matrix (ImageWriter type)	**Output:** The edges of text and graphics are jagged.
	Best use: Multipart forms where impact is needed to produce an imprint on several copies; situations in which a tractor-fed computer is required (you know, the paper with the tear strips and holes).
	How expensive: Inexpensive. Less than $400.
	Note: Some dot-matrix printers are classified as letter quality, which means that the dots are small and print close together. The output from these printers approaches laser printer quality.
Inkjet (StyleWriter type)	**Output:** Smooth text and graphics; the print quality depends on the paper used.
	Best use: Laser printer-quality printouts for black-and-white text and graphics; the print speed is slow; recommended for use with one Mac only, not on networks.
	How expensive: Inexpensive. Less than $400.
Color inkjet (color StyleWriter type)	**Output:** Smooth color text and graphics; as with black-and-white inkjets, the print quality depends on the paper used.
	Best use: Good-quality color output; the print speed is slow; recommended for use with only one Mac, not on networks; good for color transparencies.
	How expensive: The least expensive color printing. Less than $700.
Laser (LaserWriter type)	**Output:** Smooth text and graphics; laser-quality printing is now the standard against which all desktop computer printing is compared.
	Best use: Any black-and-white output, from text and drawings to photographs; works well as a personal desktop printer and on networks; good to use if durable black-and white-print is necessary, because toner doesn't scratch or smudge easily.

Printer Type	What You Should Know about It
	How expensive: Cost ranges from reasonable for personal desktop models (as little as $500) to very expensive for high-speed, high-quality workgroup printers.
Color laser	**Output:** Smooth color text and graphics, plus all the advantages of black-and-white laser output.
	Best use: Any color output, from text and drawings to photographs; good to use if durable color print is necessary, because toner doesn't scratch or smudge easily.
	How expensive: One of the most expensive color printing methods. $10,000 or more.
Thermal transfer	**Output:** Smooth text and graphics; nearly laser quality; susceptible to scratches and creases if the paper is folded.
	Best use: As a portable black-and-white printer for near laser-quality output while traveling; the speed depends on the printer model; some portable thermal transfer printers can print in color if a color cartridge is added, but the printing is very slow.
	How expensive: Inexpensive. Less than $500.
Color thermal transfer	**Output:** Smooth color text and graphics; good-quality color; susceptible to scratches and creases if the paper is folded.
	Best use: Good for general-purpose desktop color printing; good for color transparencies; the speed depends on the printer model.
	How expensive: Moderately priced color printing; a very attractive alternative to the high cost of color laser printing. Less than $1500.
Dye sublimation (color only)	**Output:** Very high quality; looks like a photograph.
	Best use: Used for proofing color layouts such as advertisements, brochures, and book and magazine pages.
	How expensive: Very expensive. $8000 to $10,000.

(continued)

Table 9-1 *(continued)*	
Printer Type	**What You Should Know about It**
Solid wax (color only)	**Output:** Smooth, sharp text and graphics; the quality is similar to that of thermal transfer.
	Best use: Very versatile in terms of the different kinds of paper on which it prints (in fact, we saw sample printouts from this printer done on sand paper!); the speed is reasonably fast.
	How expensive: Moderately priced color printing. Less than $1500.
Daisy wheel	**Output:** Macintosh equivalent of carving on stone tablets — Fred Flintstone was the first to pioneer this technology.
	Best use: Not at all; if you *really* needed to, however, you could possibly use this impact printer to print serial numbers on those thin metal tags that go on many products. The daisy wheel characters do make a nice, solid impression on the metal tag. (We've actually seen a daisy wheel printer and a Mac Plus used for this purpose.)
	How expensive: Hard to find new, but can be picked up dirt cheap used.

Printer Technology

Several standard printer technologies exist in the Mac printing world. Read the following descriptions primarily if you're interested in learning more about how your particular printer works — or are considering purchasing one of these other types.

Dot matrix

Dot-matrix printers are known for the jagged patterns of dots they produce on paper. Text and graphics print as a result of pins in a print head hitting a ribbon and leaving dots on the paper.

In a dot-matrix printer, the number of pins in the print head determines the quality of the printing. The ImageWriter, for example, uses only nine pins in its print head and is capable of producing 144 dots per inch (dpi). By contrast, the ImageWriter LQ uses 24 pins and produces 360 dots per inch. With nine-pin technology, you can easily recognize the individual dots in each letter or character. With the 24-pin print head, however, you see virtually no space between the dots on a page. You can't pick out the individual dots because they're so small and close together, but you can perceive the impression the pins make where they hit the paper: areas of all black look kind of shiny, and the paper looks flattened and thinned out.

Nine-pin print heads are hardier, more reliable, last longer, and are less prone to maintenance problems than are the 24-pin print heads.

If you own the second incarnation of the ImageWriter, the ImageWriter II, which is a nine-pin dot matrix printer, you can turn this printer into a color printer for very little money. You replace the black ribbon with a four-color ribbon and add a software driver to your Mac System folder. (The software for this is called MacPalette II, from Microspot.) In fact, you can replace the black ribbon of any dot-matrix printer with a one-color ribbon to add occasional splashes of color to your documents. By the way, with the one-color ribbon you don't need any special software. You can also install a card in the ImageWriter II so that you can share it on a network. Putting the ImageWriter II on a network is handy for workgroups with several people who need a dot matrix printer to print multi-part forms.

Inkjet

Inkjet printers are sometimes called "the poor man's laser printer" because they are less expensive than laser printers and because, if you use the right paper, inkjet printouts are almost indistinguishable from laser printouts. Inkjet printers use tiny nozzles to spray tiny droplets of ink that form dots on the paper. Inkjet printers are sometimes also called *bubble-jet printers* because of how the print head propels the ink to the paper. (The ink nozzle heats up until the ink begins to vaporize, and the vapor bubble forces a drop of ink out of the nozzle.)

You may need to experiment to find just the right paper for inkjet printers. Specially coated paper often seems to work best, because on most regular paper, the liquid ink tends to bleed along the paper fibers and make the print look slightly fuzzy. If you use low-cost ink refill kits to refill the inkjet's printer cartridge, this type of printer becomes the cheapest to use in terms of printing cost per page.

Laser

Laser printers operate the same as photocopiers. The only difference is that instead of copying a page from a book or page, the Mac tells the laser printer how the printed page is to look.

The laser printing process encompasses the following four steps:

1. A laser in the printer draws an image of the page to be printed on a light-sensitive cylinder inside the toner cartridge.

2. The cylinder picks up *toner* (the black powdery substance that a laser printer uses for ink), which clings to the image the laser produced in Step 1.

3. The toner image transfers to the paper.

4. Heat and pressure fuses the toner to the paper as the paper exits the printer.

Because a laser printer's plastic toner powder actually fuses to the paper, the page does not smear if it gets wet. Sometimes the toner flakes off the page if the paper is folded.

Thermal transfer

This printer technology shows up in both black-and-white and color printers. Thermal-transfer printers work much like dot-matrix printers, but instead of using an inked ribbon, the thermal printers use colored wax spread in a thin layer on a plastic strip or sheet. Heated pins melt very small dots of this wax onto the paper. The wax can be applied more precisely than ink can, and it produces sharper dots.

In color thermal-transfer printers, the wax transfers from a roll of plastic material. The roll employs an area of colored wax for cyan, magenta, and yellow, plus black. Combinations of the three colors produce just about any color you need, and black takes care of the text. The cost per page for color thermal-transfer printing is moderately high.

Some portable printers use a variation on the thermal-transfer technology. These printers use a cartridge that looks like a dot-matrix printer's ribbon, but it actually contains a wax-coated plastic strip. These printers are very small and are easy to carry around and use with a PowerBook. Some of these portable printers can also use color ribbons. The printed output from a thermal-transfer printer looks about the same as the output from an inkjet or laser printer. The wax can be scratched off the paper, however, and the pages don't take well to folding.

Dye sublimation

This printer technology is used only in very expensive color printers and produces prints that look almost like photographs. These printers use a special paper, and the printing costs run to $10 per page and up. One of the reasons dye-sublimation printouts look so good is that the dye, or ink, is actually absorbed *into* the paper instead of being laid down on the surface.

Solid wax

Solid-wax printer technology is used in color printers only. Solid-wax printers are similar in function to inkjet printers, but the output looks more like that of a thermal transfer. The ink used is solid wax, something like that of a crayon, and it is melted and sprayed onto the page. Because the wax doesn't bleed along the paper fibers as ink does, you get sharper images on a wider range of paper type. As is true of thermal-transfer printing, the pages produced by solid-wax printers can be scratched and do not fold well.

Daisy wheel

Daisy-wheel printers were the first letter-quality printers developed for computers. Because daisy-wheel printers can't print graphics, they didn't work well with the Mac. Daisy-wheel printers work like a computer-controlled typewriter. All the letters, numbers, and other characters are engraved around the edge of a type wheel inside the printer. The wheel spins around to the desired letter or character and types it onto the paper. To use a different font or font style, such as italic or bold, you must change type wheels. Changing fonts or styles this way is such a pain that we believe no one should ever bother doing it — if you *do* bother with one of these printers, your computer may go crazy and wind up jettisoning you into space as it sings "Daisy, Daisy. . . ." (Remember Hal in *2001*?)

Note: You may have seen or heard of *plotters*. Plotters print on regular size or oversize paper by using colored pens to mechanically draw lines on the page. They are mainly used for engineering or architectural drawings in which such oversized printouts are necessary to show details. The Mac usually requires special cables and software to connect to a plotter.

Making the Mac-Printer Connection

To connect your Mac to a printer, you need a cable connection, called either a *direct connect* or *network connection*, and software called a *driver*.

The cable connection

A *direct connect* cable connection links one Mac via cable to a printer. Most often, you use this method to connect a less-expensive personal printer to a single Mac. You plug the printer cable into either the printer or the modem port. If you want to use two direct connect printers with one Mac, such as a laser printer and a color inkjet printer, you can plug the printer cables into both ports.

A *network connection* enables a group of Macs to share the same printer via a network cable — as opposed to a *television* network connection, which so far gives you four options: ABC, CBS, NBC, and FOX. You usually find network connections used with printers designed to handle a large volume of printing generated by several Mac users.

A network connection gives you two hook-up options: AppleTalk or Ethernet. AppleTalk is more common than Ethernet, because AppleTalk comes built into all the Macs manufactured since the Mac Plus.

AppleTalk provides a cheap and easy way to connect Macs and printers: simply plug your AppleTalk connector into the Mac printer port. Ethernet, however, is faster than AppleTalk — and more expensive. Ethernet networks are normally used in businesses that most often employ more-expensive printers. The Ethernet connector plugs directly into the Ethernet port on the back of your Mac. If your Mac doesn't have Ethernet built-in, you can install a networking expansion card to add the capability. (To find out more about the Ethernet port, see Chapter 4, and for more information about networking, see Chapter 11.)

Note: Even with a network connection, you sometimes find a one-Mac-to-one-printer relationship. This setup still is different from that of a direct connect, because you can always add more Macs — and more printers — to the network.

Printer drivers

It would be nice if a chauffeur came with your printer, and a fancy limousine, too, but the term *driver* here refers to software that *drives* your printer. Your Mac requires this software to recognize the printer you're using. The driver carries out the first step in the printing process, which means that it translates the pages you create on your Mac into a form the printer can print. You need driver software for both direct connect printers and a network connection.

When you buy your printer, you also receive the driver on a disk. You then install the driver into your Mac System folder. Most drivers come with an installer program that places the driver in the correct location in the folder for you.

After you connect a printer to your Mac and install the driver software, make sure that you select the printer in the Chooser. (You find the Chooser in the Apple menu.) The box on the left side of the Chooser window shows the icons for the different printer drivers installed on your Mac. Several driver icons probably appear here, including the icon you installed and the icons for printer drivers that come standard with the system software. Select from this box the icon for the printer you want to use, and then select the listing for that printer from the box on the right.

Your Mac and PC Printers

Read this section only if you own a printer designed to run with a PC com-puter running DOS or Windows or you travel with your PowerBook and often find yourself needing to print documents in strange offices with non-Mac equipment — or if you simply can't put this book down without reading every single word we've written.

Your Mac and a PC printer aren't really the odd couple you might think they'd be. Printers designed for DOS or Windows machines are often cheaper than Mac printers, but we don't suggest you buy one just to save money. The special cables and software required to link your Mac to the PC printer will cost you, and you don't get the best performance in the world from these PC printers compared to Mac-only printers.

Still, if you really want to print on a PC printer, you can do so by using a special cable and software. To get the cable and software, just buy a product designed for this purpose, such as Apple's Macintosh Print Pack or GDT Softworks' PowerPrint.

Some laser printers are designed for use with both Macs and DOS- or Windows-compatible computers. Most printers with this capability automatically switch between DOS or Windows printing and Mac printing mode, but some require you to flip a switch or change a setting on the printer. Check the manual for the printer you want to use or call the manufacturer for instructions on using this type of printer with a Mac.

Fonts and Your Printed Output

In Mac printing, two kinds of fonts exist: *bitmapped* and *outline*. You may also want to buy additional fonts. See the end of this section for information about adding to your font library.

Bitmapped fonts

Bitmapped fonts are also sometimes called *screen fonts* because they're used mostly to display characters on the Mac screen. Bitmapped font technology is important, because at the time the original Mac came out, bitmapped fonts enabled the ImageWriter printer to print exactly the letters and characters that appeared on the Mac's screen. Bitmapped fonts worked great while the ImageWriter was the dominant Mac printer, but after laser printers became available, certain drawbacks came to light in the technology. Bitmapped fonts require a specially created font for every size of type you want to use, whether on-screen or on paper. Bitmapped fonts usually come with only a few point sizes, so very large or odd-sized characters appear rough and jagged. Also, when laser printers print bitmapped fonts, the printed letters look jagged no matter what their size.

Outline fonts

Outline font technology creates letters and characters from mathematical formulas. Outline fonts enable a printer to produce the sharpest possible letters and characters that the printer can print. These fonts also resize perfectly to any size you need. Two types of outline fonts exist: *PostScript* and *TrueType*.

PostScript

PostScript fonts are now a standard in the printing industry. These fonts enable the LaserWriter to produce high-quality, or *high-resolution*, text in any size.

Note: When people talk about fonts and printing, you often hear the word *resolution*. The term applies to the sharpness of the images that appear on both the Mac screen and on a printed piece of paper. Resolution is measured in dots per inch (dpi). The higher a printer's resolution, or the more dots it can print, the better your text or images appear. Some common resolution numbers you may encounter are 72 dpi (for the Mac screen), 300 dpi (for the LaserWriter), 600 dpi (for the LaserWriter Pro) and 1,200 dpi (for very expensive commercial printers used in print shops and service bureaus). You also hear the word *point* when people talk about printing. Fonts on the Mac are measured in points, which are a measurement that printers developed for measuring text. A point equals 1/72 of an inch. The Mac's screen resolution of 72 dpi is designed to correspond to this measuring system so that one dot on the Mac screen equals one point.

You may have heard of PostScript printers. These printers use the PostScript language developed by a company named Adobe. The printers come with a standard built-in set of PostScript fonts, such as Times, Helvetica, Bookman, and Symbol. A PostScript printer has its own internal computer brain that processes the PostScript text and graphics the printer produces. Because of this computer brain, PostScript printers usually print much faster than do non-PostScript printers.

Note: You may also have heard of font type called a *multiple master font*. This type of font is a PostScript font that enables you to create a variety of different-looking fonts from one master font. Typographers and professional desktop publishers are those who are most likely to work with multiple master fonts, because using these fonts requires that you know some pretty technical stuff about fonts and type.

TrueType

TrueType font technology was developed by Apple to compete with PostScript. Unlike PostScript fonts, TrueType fonts don't come built into a printer. Instead, these fonts come as part of the Mac system software.

TrueType fonts are important because they enable the Mac to create high-quality printed text even on inexpensive non-PostScript printers, such as the StyleWriter.

Adobe Type Manager and PostScript fonts on non-PostScript printers

Normally, you need a PostScript printer to run PostScript fonts. Even if you have only a non-PostScript printer, however, you can still use these fonts, thanks to Adobe Type Manager. Adobe Type Manager (or ATM) is an addition for the Mac system software developed by Adobe that enables non-PostScript printers to use PostScript fonts. You simply install the ATM software and any PostScript fonts you want to use in the System folder on your Mac.

ATM works by using PostScript fonts as a blueprint for drawing an image of our document's text in a format that a non-PostScript printer can use. The software then sends the image to the printer. ATM produces the highest quality output possible on whatever printer you use. The software also enables the Mac to use PostScript outlines to draw fonts of any size on-screen. In fact, many

people who use PostScript printers use ATM to view odd-sized fonts on-screen before printing them.

A new version of ATM, called Super ATM, lets you use multiple master fonts, which let you create many different looks from one master font. Super ATM also lets multiple master fonts stand in for fonts that are not present on your system so that documents created by other people on other Macs retain their original look. If you want to use multiple master fonts, you have to use Super ATM.

If you want ATM, you can get it from Adobe very inexpensively — for less than $10, as a matter of fact. Call Adobe at 800-521-1976, extension 4400, to order a copy. (This is really a deal. Frank bought ATM when it first came out for $99 and thought it was a bargain, even at that price.)

Additions to your font collection

What are some of the questions people usually ask when they consider buying new fonts? Read on.

Why would I need more fonts than those that come on my Mac and my printer?

If you like the look of your documents as they are, you don't need to add any fonts at all. But if you'd like a new look, a variety of looks, a fancier or different look to catch people's attention, or something a little more individual than the standard Mac fonts everybody uses, you should definitely go ahead and buy new fonts.

Should I buy PostScript or TrueType fonts?

The cost of these fonts is about the same, although PostScript fonts can be somewhat more expensive, especially for professional, commercial-quality fonts. What you want to buy depends largely on the kind of printer you use. If you use a PostScript printer or Adobe Type Manager, you should go for PostScript fonts. If you use a non-PostScript printer, buy TrueType fonts.

If you spot a really cool font that's not of the type you use with your printer, however, you can still go ahead and buy it. If, for example, you own a non-PostScript printer and want to use a PostScript font, you can install Adobe Type Manager and that particular PostScript font into your System folder and — voilà! — it's yours to use as you want. If you own a PostScript printer and want to use TrueType fonts, your job is even easier. If you Mac uses System 7, you simply add the new TrueType font to your System folder. If it uses System 6, you need to use the Font/DA mover and the TrueType extension to install and print the TrueType font. (Your Mac must have System 6.0.7 or later to use the TrueType fonts.)

Where can I buy fonts?

You can buy commercial fonts on disk at computer stores or from mail-order houses. Hundreds of shareware fonts also are available from user groups, on-line services, and shareware distribution companies. You can even purchase fonts on CD-ROM. Adobe, for example, sells a CD of fonts called Type on Call. You first buy the initial CD, which includes several fonts. Then, if you want more fonts later, you can call Adobe. After you authorize a credit card payment, Adobe gives you a password for access to even more fonts on the CD.

I just received an offer in the mail for a zillion fonts for a really cheap price, which seems to good to be true. Should I buy these?

The best-quality fonts come from professional type houses such as Adobe. Cheaper fonts and many shareware fonts lack the design detail that give fonts a professional appearance and that provide optimum readability. These fonts may also lack special characters, lowercase letters, and different styles such as italic and bold faces. If all you really want is many, many fonts that you plan to use only occasionally for documents that don't require top-quality appearance, go ahead and use shareware and cheaper fonts. But for professional-looking documents, we suggest that you stick with commercial fonts.

Installing your fonts in all the right places

Here's where you need to install your fonts, depending on the type of font you want to add and your specific system software:

✓ On a System 6 Mac, you must put bitmapped and TrueType fonts in the System file by using the Font/DA mover, and you install PostScript fonts in the System folder.

✓ On a Mac with System 7.0 or 7.0.1, you install bitmapped, TrueType, and PostScript fonts by dragging the icon for each font onto the system folder icon, and the system puts them

into the right place automatically. Bitmapped and TrueType fonts end up in the System suitcase and PostScript end up in the Extensions folder.

✓ On a Mac with System 7.1 and later versions, you install bitmapped, TrueType, and PostScript fonts by dragging the icon for each font onto the system folder icon, and the system puts them into the right place automatically. All three kinds of fonts end up in the Fonts folder located inside the System folder.

Printer Upgrades

If you think only in terms of upgrading the Mac, you may not realize that you can also upgrade certain printers. You can, for example, upgrade many printers' memory and can even add a hard disk to some printers.

Note: Within a product line of most Apple laser printers, such as the Laser-Writer II series or the Personal LaserWriter series, you can upgrade from one printer to a newer version's logic board by taking out the original logic board and installing the logic board for the newer version. This upgrade increases print resolution and speeds up printing.

If you add memory, you can print larger and more complex files. If you install an additional hard disk, you can store large numbers of fonts on your printer instead of on your Mac, which enables you to print faster with these fonts. An Apple product manager once told Kearney that you can actually add up to seven hard disks to the LaserWriter Pro 630, but we've never seen anyone do this. (That would be a *lot* of fonts, and who really needs that many anyway?)

You can't upgrade all printers, however, and it really is difficult sometimes to tell exactly which ones you can upgrade. To learn about the availability of upgrading your own printer, your best bet is to check its manual or call the manufacturer.

If you do decide to upgrade your printer memory or add an internal hard disk, you really need to contact a technician to make these upgrades. (Chapter 1 offers several tips on finding working with a technician.)

You also can add PostScript capability to any non-PostScript printer via a software upgrade. Hewlett-Packard, for example, sells this kind of software for the company's DeskWriter series of printers. Other products that add PostScript capability to non-PostScript printers include Freedom of Press, by Color Age, and T-Script, by TeleTypesetting Company. Using this software to print PostScript files, however, is a very slow process. In fact, you're likely to find printing PostScript files with this software too slow for most of your needs. The software also works best if you print PostScript files only occasionally. If you need the speed or if you print PostScript files frequently, you're probably better off just buying a PostScript printer.

Some Questions and Answers about Printing

Here are some questions people often ask about printers and the answers.

I try to print my document and I receive a message saying that the Mac can't find my printer. What can I do?

If you get this message, check first to make sure that the printer is switched on and warmed up. Then make sure that the cable or network connectors between your Mac and the printer are firmly connected. Finally, open the Chooser and make sure that you've selected the correct printer.

If these tips don't solve your printing problem, you may need to call for help. See Chapter 1 for information about finding help.

When I turn background printing on in the Chooser, my Mac has problems printing, but things print fine with background printing turned off. What's wrong?

Problems with background printing can result from a corrupt PrintMonitor file. The PrintMonitor file is part of the system software and it lets you continue working on one document while another prints in the background. You'll find the file in the Extensions folder inside your System folder. If you have background printing problems, try replacing your PrintMonitor file with a new copy from your Mac system diskettes.

For System 6, you'll find the PrintMonitor file inside the System folder. You need to replace the PrintMonitor file. You also need to replace the Backgrounder and LaserPrep files, which you find in the System folder.

I replaced the toner cartridge in my laser printer, but now all the pages come out blank. What should I do?

Toner cartridges usually come with a plastic strip inside that keeps toner from spilling during shipping. Check your printer manual for instructions on removing the strip or refer to the instructions that come with the cartridge. Unfortunately, the instructions that come with the cartridge are usually folded a zillion times into a tiny packet that contains at least 20 or 30 different languages and countless cryptic illustrations. Fortunately, the operation itself is fairly simple. It usually involves merely breaking off a plastic tab and pulling off the strip.

My Mac is on a network with several printers. I usually use the same printer all the time, but sometimes that printer is overloaded with work from other people. How do I set up my Mac so that it sends my documents to another printer?

You open the Chooser on the Apple menu. From the box on the left side, select the icon for the kind of printer you want to use, such as a LaserWriter. Then, from the box on the right, choose the actual name of the printer from the list of printers displayed. After you select this printer name, the Mac knows to use the printer you selected to print your documents, not the old one. Then close the Chooser.

Can I recycle my laser printer cartridge?

Yes, services exist that recycle printer cartridges in one of two ways: some services simply refill your cartridge with toner. Others actually remanufacture your cartridge, which means that they replace all the parts of the cartridge that can wear out and also refill the toner. Of the two services, remanufacturing gives you the best value for your money. These services are located in most metropolitan areas, so check the yellow pages of your phone book. If no service exists near you, check the classified ads in the back of Macintosh magazines for services that operate on a national level. Hewlett-Packard includes prepaid, preaddressed shipping labels in its toner cartridge package so that you can easily send your cartridge in to the company for refilling.

Can I recycle the ink cartridges for my inkjet printer?

Yes. Several kits on the market enable you to refill the cartridges with ink. These kits are available in computer stores, and you can also find others listed in the classified ads in the back of Macintosh magazines.

Every time I turn on my laser printer, it prints a start-up page. How can I stop this waste of paper?

A utility called LaserWriter Utility comes on disk with the LaserWriter. You can run this utility to turn the start page on and off. If you don't have the utility, you can get it from Apple or from on-line services. A similar utility should come with laser printers from other manufacturers. (We trust that they're concerned about saving paper, too.)

I bought some new fonts and installed them, but they don't appear on the Font menus of my Mac's applications. What happened to them?

That could happen if you bought PostScript fonts but did not install the corresponding bitmapped versions that come with the PostScript fonts. Go ahead and install the bitmapped versions. After you install the bitmapped versions, the fonts should appear in the Font menu. Another problem may be that the fonts are not installed in the right place. See the sidebar "Installing your fonts in all the right places," earlier in this chapter, for more information.

The fonts in my documents print right on my computer at home, but not at the office. What should I do?

The font or fonts you use at home are probably not installed on your Mac at the office. If this is the case, use fonts at home that you know you also have at the office or install the fonts from home on your Mac at the office. To be safe, stick with standard fonts.

The pages from my laser printer are coming out very light. Is it time to change my toner cartridge?

Before you spend money on a new toner cartridge, try a couple tricks that may give your cartridge a little extra life. First, try adjusting the toner switch or dial to a darker setting. If that doesn't work, remove the toner cartridge and rock it back and forth to evenly distribute the toner inside. If this doesn't work, your toner is empty — either that or maybe you rocked it to sleep.

Maintenance

Every printer requires some amount of maintenance beyond the simple needs of changing the ribbon, toner cartridge, or ink cartridge. Each printer has its own specific maintenance needs, however, so we suggest that you check your printer manual carefully for any special maintenance tips it offers to help keep your printer running in top form. Some laser printers' parts, for example, require cleaning every time you replace the toner cartridge. Inkjet printers may need the print head cleaned only periodically. In general, printers are low-maintenance items, but make sure that you faithfully perform any maintenance chores recommended in the manual so that your printed pages always look their best.

Chapter 10

Monitors, or Through the Looking Glass

● ●

In This Chapter

▶ Choosing a monitor

▶ Working with a monitor

▶ What to do when something goes wrong

▶ Maintenance tips

● ●

*T*he monitor creates two-way communication between you and your Mac. Your part of the communication comes from the keys you type and the mouse movements you make. The Mac responds to you through the monitor by showing the letters and numbers you type, the graphics you draw, the folders containing your files, the windows you work in, and the menus you can use to give commands. The monitor enables the Mac to comment on and warn you about what you're doing, as well as give you messages about what it's doing.

The monitor is the glass portal through which you enter the conceptual workspace of the Macintosh. It sounds a little like Alice stepping through the looking glass, doesn't it?

Choosing a Monitor

Color, black and white, large, small, two page display, full page display, partial page display — these are some of the characteristics of the monitors you can choose to go with your Mac.

Here's what most people think about when they choose a monitor.

✔ Black and white or color

✔ Size

✔ Picture quality

✔ Price

Of course, you have to consider several different factors when you choose a monitor. You may really want a 21-inch color monitor, but your budget dictates that you settle for a 14-inch color monitor. Or you'd love color, but your work demands large, full-page size, and with a budget that can't handle both features, you go with a black-and-white full-page monitor.

Everybody fantasizes about having a 21-inch color monitor of their very own sitting on their desk. But most of us have to live and work within the reality of a budget. If you can't afford the exact monitor you want right now, we hope you get it soon.

Monitor sizes

Mac monitor sizes range from the 9-inch built-in display on the black-and-white compacts to the 21-inch two-page display on detached monitors.

The size of your monitor dictates the size of the on-screen area you have to work in. Generally, the bigger the space, the easier it is to do your work. For example, creating a two-page brochure on a nine-inch compact Mac screen makes for a great deal of frustration. But doing the same job on a 21-inch two-page display is a breeze.

Mac screens come in standard sizes. If you know the standard sizes, you'll know what to look for and what to ask for when you shop. The different types of Mac screens and monitors are as follows:

✔ 9-inch, black-and-white, built-in compact Mac screen

✔ 10-inch, color, built-in Color Classic screen

✔ 12-inch black-and-white monitor

✔ 12-inch color monitor

✔ 14-inch color monitor

✔ 15-inch, black-and-white, full-page monitor (another term for full page is *portrait*; a full page or portrait monitor looks tall)

- ✓ 15-inch, color, full-page monitor

- ✓ 16-inch color monitor (this monitor shows about ¾ of a page up and down and 1½ pages across; not quite full-page, not quite two-page)

- ✓ 19-inch, black-and-white, two-page monitor (this monitor shows two full pages side by side)

- ✓ 20-inch, color, two-page monitor

- ✓ 21-inch, black-and-white, two-page monitor

- ✓ 21-inch, color, two-page monitor

Monitor screen size measurements are given in inches. The measurement is made diagonally across the screen from corner to corner. The measurement includes the entire glass surface, with the unused black border counted in the measurement.

Do you really need a color screen?

Color monitors look great and cost a lot. Looking great is definitely a bonus, but costing a lot is not. In our experience, everybody seems to *want* to work in color, but sometimes that's not how they actually do work. When people don't buy a color monitor, it's usually for two reasons: color is expensive, and black-and-white screens provides a clearer image.

What's the best kind of color monitor?

Several manufacturers now sell monitors that use the Sony Trinitron picture tube. This tube picture gives high-resolution, high-quality color.

All monitors use tiny dots to create pictures on-screen. On most color monitors, each dot is made up of three different colored dots — one red, one green, and one blue. Different colors are produced by varying the intensity of each group of three dots. Because round dots are used, the dots don't fit together completely and space is left between them. Therefore, the on-screen images look fuzzy.

Trinitron monitors, on the other hand, use square dots composed of three different colored bars — red, green, and blue. Because the square dots fit together so well, images on a Trinitron monitor appear sharper and more vibrant than on other monitors.

The one disadvantage to Trinitron monitors is that on every screen, a fine line appears about two thirds of the way down the screen. Most people are willing to ignore the line because of the overall Trinitron quality. You may notice this line more on some monitors than on others, but it is a normal Trinitron characteristic.

Most people who stare at a monitor for many hours each day agree that black-and-white monitors are easier on the eyes than color monitors. So if your work entails mostly word processing or page layout with black-and-white output, a black-and-white monitor is probably best for you.

Most people also agree that color is more fun. And if your work depends on color, you need a color monitor.

When you consider a large monitor, such as full-page or two-page, cost is a big issue. Unless your funds are unlimited, you have to decide — which do I need more, large size or color? Some people solve this dilemma by using two monitors: a small color monitor and a large black-and-white monitor. This way, you can do layout work on a large screen and also use color for graphics, and the solution is actually cheaper than buying a two-page color monitor.

When people think of monitor features, they usually think of the screen display. But monitors are not just display features in today's world of multimedia. The Apple AudioVision 14 Display, for example, contains a sound system made of two internal stereo speakers and a built-in microphone. You can't do much besides listen to sound and record sound with these features today, but as audio-video technology develops, you'll probably use them for telephone, voice mail, video conferencing, and speech-recognition applications.

Working with Your Monitor

Here's a bunch of information you always wanted to know about using your monitor but were afraid to ask.

What's a video card and do I need one?

Basically, a *video card* is an expansion card that enables you to connect your Mac to a monitor. If you have a Mac that works with a monitor, whether you know it or not, you already have a video card or built-in video capabilities, which enable your Mac to use that monitor.

You need a video card if

✔ You have an older Mac, such as the Mac II, IIx, or IIcx

✔ You're adding an external monitor to a compact Mac

✔ You want to use a monitor that's not supported by your machine's built-in video

✔ You want to connect an external monitor to a PowerBook that doesn't have a video port (for more information about PowerBook video, see Chapter 13)

✔ You want to see more colors on your monitor and your Mac can't accept any more video memory (for more information about adding colors, see Chapter 13)

✔ You want faster screen redraws (for more information about speeding up video, see Chapter 13)

Fine-tuning your monitor with control panel settings

One way to adjust your monitor is by using the brightness and contrast dials, located on the outside of the monitor. You can also control the monitor by using software control panels.

You can also change the number of colors that appear on-screen. To do so, you'd think you would open the Color Control Panel under the Apple menu, but you don't use this Control Panel for this purpose. Instead, use the Monitors Control Panel to change the number of colors. The Color Control Panel is where you set the color that selected text appears in.

You also use the Monitors Control Panel to select which monitor the menu bar is displayed in when you use more than one monitor at a time. And the Monitors Control Panel is where you find an option button that enables you to access any special functions that your monitor has, like zoom-in features that magnify text and images that appear on-screen. Depending on your monitor, you'll find several options or none at all.

Some non-Apple monitors come with software control panels that give you features like screen savers, screen capture, or a new layout for your desktop. The features you get in the control panels depend on the monitor you buy.

Using an external monitor with a PowerBook

With some PowerBooks, you can add an external monitor. Add a monitor to work in color or to work on a larger screen. Even if you have a color Power-Book, an external screen gives you a larger area to work in. Having two monitors also enables you to view two applications at one time.

The PowerBooks that have a video port so that you can connect an external monitor are the PowerBook 160, 165, 165c, 180, and 185c. You'll need a special cable to connect the PowerBook and the monitor. For information on how to use an external monitor with the other PowerBooks and the Duos, see Chapter 13.

Help! What Do I Do?

Here are the questions people ask most often about monitor problems. We also give some suggestions about fixes. But, like your TV set, computer monitors are very delicate and contain high-voltage components. If the fixes we suggest here don't work, we recommend that you have a technician take over.

My Mac is turned on and the screen is completely black. What do I do?

First, make sure that the monitor is plugged in and turned on. Then check to make sure the brightness dial isn't turned down all the way. If you have recently installed a video card or moved one to a different slot, your Mac may not recognize the card's location. To update the Mac about where the card is, you have to *zap the PRAM* in the computer. You zap the PRAM in one of two ways, depending on your system version.

In System 7, restart your computer while you hold down ⌘-Option-P-R. In System 6, hold down ⌘-Shift-Option when you choose the Control Panel option under the Apple menu. When a message asks you whether you want to zap the PRAM, click Yes.

If these suggestions don't work, it's time to call a repair technician.

The picture on my monitor is too dim, and the brightness is turned all the way up. What should I do?

As the monitor ages, the phosphor inside the tube glows less and less brightly. In order to compensate, the monitor needs to be adjusted so that more energy lights the phosphor. Initially, you can make small adjustments with the brightness dial, but as the phosphor continues to fade, the dial has less and less effect. At that point, you need to have a technician make larger adjustments inside the monitor.

The colors on my screen look washed out and they're not as bright as they used to be.

Usually a washed-out screen means that you need to adjust the brightness and contrast dials on your monitor. If adjusting the dials doesn't help, you should probably have a technician make adjustments inside the monitor for you.

On my black-and-white compact Mac, the screen stays black with a bright vertical line down the middle? Can I do anything about this?

Bright vertical or horizontal lines or other major distortions on the screen mean that your Mac has a serious problem. You'll need to take your Mac to a technician for repair.

What can I do about a flickery, jittery screen?

Nearby fluorescent lights can cause a flickery screen. Try moving the monitor as far away from the light as possible. Even a small move can make a difference. Sometimes appliances plugged in near the Mac can cause a flicker. Does your screen only flicker while you're making toast? Try to notice a pattern — which appliances are running when your Mac flickers? Don't run the Mac and the appliances at the same time, or try plugging your Mac into a different outlet. Also, a good surge protector with electrical noise filters can help solve the flicker problem.

The display on my Mac is pulsating. What should I do?

A pulsating or shrinking display may indicate a serious problem with the components inside your monitor. It's time to take it to a technician for repair.

Maintenance Tips

Monitors are pretty low-maintenance items. Usually you just have to clean fingerprints and smudges off the screen and case. By the way, compared to monitor repairs which are pretty difficult to do, maintenance is pretty easy.

- ✔ Don't use any harsh chemicals to clean your monitor.

- ✔ Don't spray glass cleaner directly onto the screen of either desktop Macs or PowerBooks. The cleaner can run down into the case and possibly cause a short circuit. Instead, spray a little cleaner onto a paper towel or cloth.

- ✔ The vents on top of the monitor are important for dispersing heat from the picture tube inside. Too much heat building up inside the case shortens the life of the electrical components, so keep the vents clear.

- ✔ Be careful not to spill anything in the vents on top of your monitor.

- ✔ Metallic confetti has a habit of maliciously finding its way into the vents on top of the monitor and causing serious damage by shorting out components inside. So when you plan office parties, don't buy metallic confetti, or else cover your computer.

- ✔ Be sure to leave enough space between your monitor and the wall so that the cable doesn't get squashed up against the wall. If the cable gets bent at a sharp angle, the wires inside can break. Then you'll lose the picture on your monitor and have to get a new cable.

Chapter 11

Using Modems, Faxing with Your Mac, and Networking

*W*hat modems and networking have in common is communication and connection between computers. But exactly how modems and networks get computers to connect and communicate is quite different. Modems connect computers via the phone lines, and networks connect them with cables.

What You Can Do with a Modem

E-mail, the Internet, faxes, America Online, CompuServe, bulletin boards, Prodigy, direct connections, remote control, and remote connects — they all relate to the use of your Mac together with a modem. (A *modem*, to refresh your memory, is simply a small piece of hardware that enables your Mac to connect to and communicate with other computers over the phone lines.)

E-mail: E-mail stands for electronic mail. Using e-mail enables you to send written electronic messages from your computer to other people's computers via a modem or a network.

Faxing: Because fax machines use the phone lines just as modems do, many modem manufacturers are beginning to adding fax capabilities to their products. You can fax any document you create on your Mac, to a fax machine via a fax modem. Using your Mac and a modem for faxing offers several advantages — saving paper, for example, because you don't need to print your document to fax it.

On-line services: America Online, eWorld, Prodigy, and CompuServe are all commercial on-line services. If you subscribe to an on-line service, you can use that service to make travel reservations, check stock prices, read electronic versions of your favorite magazines and newspapers, shop electronically, receive software, and send e-mail and files to other subscribers all on your computer.

The Internet: The massive, interconnected computer network known as the Internet gives you access to many diverse sources of information stored on computers all around the world. The information available on the Internet ranges from magazine and newspaper articles to scientific research, product information, and software that you can download to your own computer. The Internet also provides a way to send e-mail to other on-line services than those to which you subscribe or to people around the globe.

Bulletin boards: A bulletin board (aka *BBS*, for Bulletin Board Service) is the electronic version of the cork board at your supermarket. Electronic bulletin boards were also the forerunners of today's on-line services. Bulletin boards usually focus on a specific topic, such as a profession or hobby. Businesses, individuals, user groups, and practically any person or organization with a computer and a modem can set up a bulletin board dedicated to any topic they choose.

Direct connection: You can also use a modem to send files directly to another computer — a direct connection. Direct connections must be planned in advance with the person with whom you want to communicate so that the other user is available to set up the computer and modem on the other end.

Remote control: Have you ever thought about controlling your office computer from home or on the road? With the right software, a modem enables you to link up and control your Mac from a distance. You can perform such amazing feats as launching an application like Word or Excel, opening a file to access the information you need, and printing out the file on a printer at the office — all from miles away.

Remote connection: A remote connection enables you to connect your computer at home or on the road to an office network. After you're connected, you can access file servers and printers on the network. You can also use network services like e-mail and scheduling programs.

If you use a modem frequently, you may get complaints from your family and friends that you're hogging the phone. Installing a second phone line exclusively for your computer is often a good idea if you really get hooked on your modem — and want to avoid a lynching at the hands of the other phone users in your home.

Like the gift that keeps on giving, a modem is the upgrade that keeps on costing. Everytime you use your modem, you make a phone call, which goes on your phone bill just like long-distance calls. The first on-line service bill you get after you buy a modem can be a real shock. Your telephone bill itself may go way up, too, especially if your favorite bulletin boards are located far away and calls to them count as long-distance billings. Even if you're making only a local call to access your favorite on-line service, always remember that the service itself charges you for your connect time.

Yep, that ol' information superhighway we all keep hearing about is really a toll road.

Modem Basics and Buying a Modem

The two most important concepts you need to know about modems are *speed* and *standards*.

Speed relates to money

Modems keep getting faster and faster. Just a couple years ago, everybody was dying for what's known as a 1200-baud modem. Today, that speed is hardly respectable. In fact, 2400-baud is the slowest modem speed you can buy today — except used, of course. And even these modems are going the way of the Dodo bird (that is, extinct).

Even the terminology for modem speed is changing. *Baud* used to be the term everyone used to refer to the speed of a modem. Nowadays, you hear the terms baud and *bits per second* (bps), which also refers to speed, used interchange-ably. Technically, bps is the best way to refer to the speed of modems faster than 2400. So if you use the word baud around real technical types, you may get laughed at and called funny names. And if you go into a computer store and hear a salesperson say baud for modem speeds faster than 2400, you can smile smugly and know that you now know more about modems than does that poor soul.

The most popular modem speeds used today are, from slowest to fastest:

- 2400 bps
- 9600 bps
- 14,400 bps
- 28,800 bps.

Modem speed and your money are directly related. The faster the modem is, the more the modem costs. On the other hand, the faster your modem is, the shorter your phone call and the less money you spend on your phone bill and on connect charges for on-line services. Of course, some on-line services actually charge *more* if you connect with a high-speed modem — what a racket! — but even with the higher connect charge, the faster modem still saves you money.

Standards mean that you can communicate with other computers

Because a modem is a tool used solely to communicate with other computers, you need to buy a modem that sends and receives information the same way the modem at the other end of the phone line does.

An international committee defines how modems communicate with one another at each different modem speed. This committee is called the *ITU* (formerly known as the CCITT); the initials are in French, so don't even bother to worry about what they stand for. This committee establishes the *standards* that all modem manufacturers apply to their modems to make sure that the devices can communicate with the modems from all the other modem companies.

What all this standards information really means to you is that you want to make absolutely sure that the modem you buy complies with the ITU (or CCITT) speed standards. If your modem doesn't use these standards, you may experience problems attempting to connect to bulletin boards or on-line services. In fact, buying a modem that doesn't use ITU (or CCITT) standards is much like buying an old Betamax VCR now that all the videos for rent at the your local video store are VHS tapes — not a very good fit at all. To make sure that the modem you buy complies with these standards, look for the standard that you find printed on the modem package. See Table 11-1 for a list that shows you which standards apply to which modem speeds.

Table 11-1	ITU (CCITT) Standards and the Speeds to Which They Apply
If You See This Standard on the Modem Package	*It Means This Speed*
V.22bis	2400 bps
V.32	9600 bps
V.32bis	14,400 bps
V.34	28,800 bps

At certain points in the development of modem technology, the advent of new speeds can get somewhat ahead of the standards committee's ability to set new standards. Whenever this happens, modem manufacturers create their own interim standards. The interim standards, however, usually enable a modem to communicate only with another modem from the same manufacturer. The moral of this story is to stick to the ITU (or CCITT) standards.

At this point, you may ask: "Should I *ever* buy a modem that doesn't follow the standard?" Well, if you absolutely *need* the very fastest modem you can buy, and you *know* that your communications are to be limited to exchanging messages with other computers that use modems from the same manufacturer (so that you're sure the two modems are compatible), the answer is . . . yes. Say, for example, your company in San Francisco needs to exchange large files with an office in Los Angeles, and high-speed transmission is a must. In such a case, go ahead and purchase identical high-speed nonstandard modems for each office. If you use the modems for more than a couple months, the money that their high transmission speed saves you in phone charges will probably pay for both modems long before the ITU (or CCITT) gets around to setting a new standard.

Some nonstandard standards developed by modem manufacturers include HST, PEP, Express 96, V.32 terbo, V.Fast, and V.FC. Notice that some of these names look very much like the names of the ITU (CCITT) standards. Tricky, huh? Usually, you should avoid modems with these standards unless the modems also use the ITU (CCITT) standards.

Should I buy a fax modem?

If you want to send or receive faxes from your Mac, you really ought to consider buying a *fax modem.* Using a fax modem, you can send a document that you want faxed directly from your Mac to the recipient without first printing it on paper. (Another great way to save paper and move one step closer to the ubiquitous "paperless office" people always talk about but never quite seem to achieve.)

An additional benefit of using a fax modem is that if you receive faxes directly on your Mac, you can use your printer to print the document instead of messing with that slick, shiny fax paper (yuk!). And if your fax software includes *optical character recognition* (OCR) features, or you already own OCR software, perhaps the best thing about receiving a fax directly on your Mac is that you can change the fax to a text file that you can edit and use in your own work. You don't need to spend the extra time typing the text into a file as you would with a regular fax.

One caveat: If the modem you're looking at is really inexpensive, be aware that it may not have the capability to receive as well as send faxes. If all you do is send faxes, however, this kind of machine is probably sufficient. But if you need to receive faxes, too, pass this one by and take a look at some different models.

Other modem information

You see other numbers and letters floating around on modem packages when you shop for a modem, and you may wonder what they mean. (If you really don't care, however, just skip this section.)

In addition to speed standards, the ITU (CCITT) sets other standards, called *protocols*, for error correction and data compression. Error correction enables your modem to establish a reliable connection with another modem and then to transmit its data without any errors. Data compression enables your modem to increase the speed of its transmission by up to four times the modem's actual speed. (Such a four-fold increase, however, is hardly ever carried out, although it is theoretically possible. You're most likely to see a two- to three-fold increase if you're lucky.)

Among the numbers and letters you may encounter that relate to error correction and data compression are LAP-M, MNP4, MNP5, MNP 10, V.42, and V.42bis. MNP 10 involves using your modem with an unreliable connection like a cellular phone. Oh, and V.42 is an ITU (CCITT) standard for error correction, while V.42bis is an ITU (CCITT) standard for data compression. (And just to remind you, these particular standards have absolutely nothing to do with modem speed.)

Other considerations, besides speed, that you may want to keep in mind when you shop for a modem are its price, the software included, and the quality of the technical support provided by the manufacturer. User groups are great sources of information about modems and often can provide valuable insight on which ones to buy.

If you buy a modem with a speed of 9600 bps or faster, make sure you also get what is called a hardware handshaking cable. (Yeah, right! Like you, your Mac, and your modem are going to shake hands. Ha! Your Mac and your modem don't even have hands.) If you don't use this kind of cable, your Mac can't communicate with the modem at high speeds. The cable should come with the modem you buy, or, if not, ask for one specifically.

Communications Software

In the multifarious world of computing, we're sure you've noticed by now that you always need software to use your hardware. Modems, naturally, are no exception. To get your modem up and running, you must install what's called, logically enough, *communications software*. And if you fax with your Mac, you need fax software as well.

Communications speak

Connecting to an on-line service is also called *logging on* or *going on-line*, just in case you're interested in the lingo.

(By the way, the phrase *off-line* has assumed a rather interesting meaning in computer-industry jargon. In the statement "I'll talk to you off-line about that," for example, *off-line* actually means *separately* or *alone*, as in "I'll talk to you about that alone, after we get away from all the other people attending this meeting.")

After you finish using an on-line service, you *log off*, or disconnect. We hear the word *disconnect* used quite often among our computer friends — but in quite another context. If they say, "I think we got a disconnect," this usually means "I think we misunderstood each other."

On-line service software

America Online, Prodigy, CompuServe, and GEnie are all on-line services to which you can subscribe — and to which you can connect your computer via a modem and the phone lines. After you subscribe to an on-line service, you receive the communications software you need to handle two basic functions: establishing the modem-phone line connection to the service and, after you're connected, navigating the service's different information areas. You can link up to CompuServe and GEnie with standard communications programs, too, if you want. Most programs handle all the settings your modem needs to connect to the service, and they even place the call for you after you type in the phone number the first time you connect.

Each on-line service has its own unique look and feel. This look and feel is very important, because a large part of a subscriber's experience with an on-line service results in how easy — or difficult — it is to use. Unfortunately, this fact just doesn't seem to register with most on-line services. Instead of helping you navigate the service to find stock quotes, airline schedules, product tips, horoscopes, or other information, the service often seems to do its utmost best to confuse you and keep you from locating what you want. Being unable to find your way quickly around the service means that you must spend more time connected to it, which in turn means that the service charges you more money. Hmmmm, maybe they *do* get it after all. . . .

If you do subscribe to an on-line service but you find it too difficult to use, we suggest you drop your subscription and try another service. Most of these services offer much the same information, so you may as well be able to sit back and enjoy your experience instead of having to pay for all the extra connect time necessary to figure out how to get from one information area to the other.

America Online is one on-line service that was originally designed especially for Macintosh owners. As a result, it provides perhaps the friendliest face of all the on-line services. The service also offers plenty of news, product information, tips, technical support, and shareware programs just for Mac owners. And you can link up to the Internet via America Online as well. The service even talks to you through the Mac speaker by saying "hello," "good-bye," and another phrase or two, such as "you've got mail" or "file's done" after you finish downloading a file.

Communications programs

If you plan to link up to bulletin boards or connect directly with a friend, you need a communications program. Sometimes the modem you buy comes with its own communications software. Go ahead and use this program if you like it, although you may eventually want something with more features.

You can pick up some very decent communications shareware from user groups. Two good shareware programs we know are ZTerm, by David Alverson, and FreeSoft's Red Ryder. (In the realm of commercial programs, White Knight is FreeSoft's commercial version of Red Ryder.) You may also want to try Hayes' Smartcom II or Software Ventures' MicroPhone II.

If you own an integrated Mac program, such as ClarisWorks, you may already have communications software. The nice part about using the communications function of an integrated program is that you can easily cut and paste any text you download via your modem right into a word processing document created by the same program.

To save money when you send files via modem, compress the files so that they appear smaller and take less time to transmit. Less time communicating via modem translates to less money spent on the phone call and on any connect time charges that apply. The most popular file-compression programs are StuffIt, from Aladdin Systems and DiskDoubler, from Salient Software. (These are both commercial programs. StuffIt is also available as a shareware program called StuffIt Lite.)

"Free" software

Most on-line services give you access to a variety of different software, such as inexpensive shareware, commercial product updates, product demos, and images that include photographs, maps, and even video clips. You can *download* the software to your own computer, which means that your computer can receive the program; you can store it on your hard disk or on a floppy disk; and you can run the program later.

Many people consider the programs they download to be free software. Technically, the software *is* free, but keep in mind that you generate phone and on-line service connect-time charges while your computer receives the program. Long files take a long time to download, which means that you can spend quite a sum of money for the phone and connect time required to receive your "free" software.

Fax software

To use the fax capabilities of a fax modem, you must install fax software. Most fax modems come with this software. Two such programs are FaxSTF, from STF Technologies and Delrina FaxPRO, from Delrina. These programs come both separately and bundled with fax modems. Most fax software performs the job adequately, but we must admit that we're still waiting for the ideal program.

To fax a document by using your fax modem, you must first access the Chooser from your Apple menu. On the left side of the Chooser window is the Fax icon. Select this icon and then select the listing for your fax modem in the box on the right. After you fax a document, remember to use the Chooser again to select your printer instead of the fax modem. If you don't select the printer, you may end up faxing your document to the last person you faxed to instead of printing it.

Networking Basics

If you want to become a networking expert, many books exist on the subject. In this section, we're giving you the basics you need to get started, should you want to upgrade your one-Mac system to a network.

And, OK, to get the definition of a network out of the way, we'll just give it to you right now: a *network* is simply two or more Macs linked together by cable. And just for the record, although we specified *Macs* linked together, the network needn't really be limited to Macs — or even to computers, for that matter. A network can comprise Macs, DOS- and Windows-based computers (PCs), and even printers, all connected via cable.

Networks can span a few cubicles, an entire office, or even several buildings, all interlinked electronically. Or a network can consist of just a single Mac and one printer connected by network cables. Such a network is very, very small, but it's a legitimate network nonetheless.

Note: If your Mac connects to just a printer, with no way to connect any other hardware, well, we're sorry, but you don't have a network — even if your printing goes just fine. What you actually have is simply a Mac and a printer linked by a printer cable (also called a serial cable). By the way, the printers that connect directly to your Mac this way are the ImageWriter, the StyleWriter, and some of the inexpensive personal LaserWriters.

So what can you do on a network? Glad you asked. You can use a network to transfer files to others whose computers also are on the network; you can share files, such as large databases, with them; you can send them e-mail; and you can share printers. Not bad, huh?

Whatever your reason for installing a network, you have two main choices for the network to use with your Mac: AppleTalk and Ethernet. (If your office uses a lot of PCs, you may find your Mac connected to other types of networks, too.)

AppleTalk, the network you already have

AppleTalk is the networking software that comes with your Mac. Because every Mac ever made can connect to an AppleTalk network, even the original 128K Mac, AppleTalk is a cheap and easy way to build a network. All the hardware you need to connect your Mac to an AppleTalk network is a connector, such as the PhoneNET connector from Farallon Computing. The connector plugs into the printer port on the Mac and then connects your computer or printer to the network using the same kind of flat wire that connects your telephone to the wall jack.

Make sure that you plug your AppleTalk network connector into the printer port on the back of your Mac. Many people wrongly conclude that, because the connector is called a PhoneNET box and because the PhoneNET box connects to a cable that looks like phone wire, the connector should plug into the phone port on the Mac. But noooo. The network works only if the connector is plugged into the printer port.

Ethernet, a faster network

The other popular network option for the Mac is *Ethernet*. Ethernet moves files around much faster than AppleTalk can, but Ethernet is also more expensive to set up. How *much* faster? (You may ask.) Try roughly *40 times* faster!

You find Ethernet installed mostly in large offices and companies with hundreds of Macs and other computers, where people routinely transfer large files such as desktop publishing documents, color pictures, and large databases and spreadsheets. Because many new Macs include Ethernet as a built-in feature, however, and because the price for Ethernet keeps getting lower, this network is also rapidly becoming an option for small offices and home use.

To connect your Mac to an Ethernet network, you need one of three things: Ethernet circuitry built into your Mac, an Ethernet expansion card, or an Ethernet adapter box that plugs into the SCSI port or the modem or printer ports.

Some late-model Macs come with Ethernet already built in. The easiest way to determine if your Mac includes built-in Ethernet capability is to check the back for an Ethernet port. The icon near the Ethernet port looks something like this: **<ooo>.** If your Mac has this port, all you need to join the network is a box called a *transceiver* that plugs into the Ethernet port and provides the correct connectors for the network cable.

Most Power Macs, Quadras, and some Centris models contain built-in Ethernet circuitry. Performas, PowerBooks, LCs, Mac IIs, Classics, and the rest do not.

Ethernet can use several different types of cable for its network. The three most common are as follows:

- ✔ *Thin net* uses a type of cable similar to that used for cable TV. This cable is relatively cheap and easy to install, but finding and fixing problems with thin net is difficult.

- ✔ *Thick net* uses big, fat expensive cables. Thick net is not used much anymore because of the cost of the cables.

- ✔ *10baseT* is the very techie name for cables that are similar to the phone wiring used in your house but that contain more individual wires inside the outer insulation than phone wire does. Of the three cable types, 10baseT wiring is the cheapest to install, but it requires that each Mac connect to a central device called a *hub,* or a *concentrator.*

Ethernet also can run a network via fiber optic cables, and we should be seeing more of these cables in general use as prices fall and companies start making fiber optic Ethernet connectors.

Network topologies explained

Topolowhositz? *Topology* just refers to the pattern in which networks link together. Three basic Mac network patterns exist: daisy chain, bus, and star. (Kinda reminds you of elementary school, huh?)

The *daisy chain* topology, or pattern, is the simplest way to link a few Macs together in an AppleTalk network. First, you simply plug a PhoneNET-type connector into each Mac you want to link. Next, you plug a phone wire-type cable into the PhoneNET connectors on Mac numbers one and two. Then you plug in a cable to the other jack on the PhoneNET connector on Mac number two and connect it to Mac number three. Connect three to four, four to five, and so on. After you've connected all your Macs, add *terminating plugs* to the empty jacks on the PhoneNET connectors at both ends of the chain. Then if you want to add more Macs or printers to the chain later, you can.

Although the daisy chain pattern applies primarily to AppleTalk networks, devices such as Farallon Computing's EtherWave connectors enable you to link inexpensive 10baseT Ethernet cables in a daisy chain as well. The performance of daisy-chained 10baseT is not as fast as if its network were connected in a star pattern. However, the arrangement is certainly convenient, because setting up the network and adding machines to it is very easy.

The *bus* pattern uses one long cable as what's called a *backbone*, and each computer or printer connected to the network taps into this main cable. An example of this pattern can be found in any office with one long cable running through the walls connected to all the network's *data*

jacks. (These look like phone jacks but are used for the network.) People who want to connect their computer or a printer to the network simply plug a cable into the jack and tap into the bus or backbone. This bus arrangement is primarily used with thin net Ethernet cables, although AppleTalk networks also use this arrangement on occasion. The bus pattern's main weakness is that, if a break or a problem occurs in the line, every device, and therefore every person, past the break is affected.

Large AppleTalk networks and 10baseT Ethernet networks use the *star* topology. The phone company uses the same star scheme to connect telephones to the company's central office, or hub. In star topology, every telephone has its own wire that runs all the way to the main office. The cables you see on poles are actually bundles of many of these wires. The star pattern of a computer network uses the same type of arrangement so that every computer on the network has its own cable that connects to the central network hub. If a cable breaks, only one Mac experiences problems instead of half the network.

In reality, most networks are a hybrid of two or more of these patterns, such as a star typology with Macs daisy chained to it or a bus pattern connecting several stars.

A fourth pattern also exists: the *ring* topology. This setup is used mostly with DOS- and Windows-based computers and is called *token ring.* You can connect a Mac to a token ring network if you really need to, but the procedure is complex, and you must buy quite a bit of extra hardware and software to do so. Not a pretty situation, in our opinion.

Note: Before you connect your Mac to an Ethernet network, you need to know what kind of cable the network uses — thin net, thick net, or 10baseT — so that you can buy a transceiver or expansion card with the right kind of connectors.

If your Mac contains no built-in Ethernet capabilities, never fear; you can still connect your machine to an Ethernet network. You simply install an Ethernet expansion card in a slot inside your computer. Oh, an *inside upgrade,* you say. But don't worry. Installing an expansion card is easy (really!). Chapter 17 gives you the instructions for installing an expansion card in the compact Macs that have expansion slots. For modular Macs, you'll find complete instructions in the manual for your Mac.

Most Ethernet cards come with connectors for at least two different types of cables, although some cards have only the same type of connector as used for built-in Ethernet capability. With this second kind of card installed, you use the same transceiver as you do for a built-in Ethernet to connect your Mac to the network cables.

If your Mac has no expansion slot, if all its slots are filled, or if you own a PowerBook without built-in Ethernet capabilities, you can connect to an Ethernet network by using an external adapter box. Different versions of this box connect to either the SCSI port or to the modem or printer ports. These external adapters don't offer you the fastest Ethernet speeds possible, but they're certainly faster than AppleTalk and enable you to connect to Ethernet without installing a card.

AppleTalk and Ethernet compared

In comparing AppleTalk and Ethernet, everything comes down to this: When you think AppleTalk, think *cheap,* and when you think Ethernet, think *fast.* That's the difference in a nutshell — cheap and easy to set up versus higher prices and higher speeds. If you need "just a network," AppleTalk should probably work fine for you. If you need "a fast network," however, you really want Ethernet.

Is Ethernet worth the cost for home offices? It could be if you frequently move large files around among several computers. If you need a network and all your equipment is new enough to have built-in Ethernet capabilities, including the printers, installing an Ethernet network also may be worth your while. Remember, however, that most printers and the PowerBooks don't have built-in Ethernet and need special adapters. If you plan to use your network only occasionally and (or) most of your Macs lack built-in Ethernet, you're probably best off sticking to AppleTalk.

If all this networking stuff seems too daunting, and all you want to do is transfer a file from one Mac to another, fear not! You can always use the amazing *SneakerNet*! To operate this wondrous net, you simply copy a file from your Mac onto a floppy disk, put on your sneakers to carry the disk over to the other Mac, insert it, and — *ta daaaa!* — open the file! It's low tech, sure, but — hey! — *this* net *always* works (well, except if the file is too big to fit on a floppy . . .)!

What to Do if Something Goes Wrong with Your Modem or Network

Unfortunately, troubleshooting and fixing your modem or network go far beyond the scope of this book. Many experts have written huge tomes about the gruesome details of monitoring and maintaining networks and making your modem do what you want. If you experience problems with either of these upgrades, we suggest the old reliable: call for help. Or, how about reading *Modems For Dummies* by Tina Rathbone or *Networking For Dummies* by Doug Lowe? Also, Chapter 1 contains several suggestions about where to turn for expert advice and professional help. Good luck!

Part IV

Easy Inside
Upgrades and Fixes

The 5th Wave   By Rich Tennant

"WHO'S GOT THE COMPUTER WITH THE SLOW RESPONSE TIME?"

In this part...

This part takes the plunge and takes you to the inside of your Mac to perform upgrades. Need more memory for all your reports? Check out Chapter 14. Want to upgrade to color? Learn how much video memory to buy in Chapter 15. And what if you want to speed up your Mac? We tell you how fast your Mac can go.

But don't worry. These upgrades are easy and do not require that you own a pocket protector.

Chapter 12
Memory and Internal Storage

· ·

In This Chapter

▶ Understanding the benefits of adding memory

▶ Learning how to add memory

▶ Buying memory

▶ Purchasing an internal hard disk

▶ Getting started with your new hard disk

· ·

*E*verybody seems to confuse memory and storage all the time. So if you've felt kind of vague about the two, you're not alone. Memory and storage have very similar functions, such as holding your files and applications. But the Mac uses its memory and its storage systems for different purposes.

The Mac uses memory as its workspace — somewhat similar to how you probably use a desk. Just as you spread out your work on your desk, the Mac spreads out the files and applications you're working on throughout its memory hardware. You experience this particular Mac activity by having your files and applications open and running on your Mac screen. The amount of memory installed in the Mac limits the number of files and applications the Mac can work with at one time, just as the size of your desk limits the number of papers and other objects you can spread out on it to work on.

The Mac uses its storage system — usually consisting of a hard disk and a diskette drive — much the same way people in offices use a filing cabinet. After the Mac finishes working on and processing your files and applications in memory, it puts them away for safekeeping in its storage system. Similarly, after you finish working with papers and written documents at the end of the day, you gather them up from your desk and store them in a filing cabinet. Of course, if you're like many people, you simply leave everything piled up on your desk to work on again the following day; the Mac, however, is a much neater worker — which is most fortunate, as you'll learn in the following paragraph.

The reason the Mac needs a storage system in addition to its memory system is because of what happens after the computer's power shuts off: all your files and applications clear out of memory completely — poof! They're gone — dissipated into so many free electrons, along with all the work you did on them! Thanks to the Mac's storage system, however, you don't actually lose your work after your machine shuts off. Its storage system retains your files and applications even after power ceases to flow into the Mac's hungry little circuits. (This process is analogous to your making sure that you do store all your work in the filing cabinet at the end of the day to avoid the trauma of discovering in the morning that an overzealous janitor came in during the night and cleared off your desk, throwing out all your precious work.)

Finally, another reason people confuse memory and storage, besides their similarity in function, is because both are measured in megabytes. Some common memory sizes, for example, are 4MB, 8MB, and 16MB. Common hard-disk storage sizes include 40MB, 80MB, and 230MB.

Memory

Adding more memory is without a doubt the best upgrade you can make to your Mac. In addition to all the benefits we list below, adding memory lets you say good-bye to those bothersome "not enough memory" messages your Mac likes to send you when you start maxing out on the memory you've got.

What adding more memory does for you

- Enables you to open large, complex applications, such as page-layout and multimedia applications
- Enables you to open more applications at one time so you don't waste time opening and closing applications if you need to switch from one type of work to another
- Enables you to keep more files open at the same time within one application so that you don't need to spend time opening and closing the files on which you're currently working
- Enables you to open larger files within one application so that you can work with complex documents
- Enables you to speed up some applications' tasks, such as scrolling through long documents or loading a spelling checker
- Enables you to walk around the office saying, "My Mac's got more memory than your Mac," so that you get all the admiration that automatically comes with owning a fully loaded Mac. And, of course, we all know that this is the most important benefit of all.

Some people, especially those who often see the Mac's "disk full" message cropping up on-screen, may think that adding memory to their machines can give them more storage space and thus eliminate that pesky prompt. Not so. Only installing a larger hard disk can provide more storage and prevent that tiresome old message from popping up on-screen again and again to yak at you. (So if that's your problem, skip ahead to the section, "Internal Storage," later in this chapter.)

How to add more memory

To install extra memory in the Mac, you must actually install long, narrow circuit boards, or cards, called *SIMMs*. SIMM stands for *Single In-line Memory Module*, in case you're into knowing what all the acronyms in your life mean. (Table 12-1, by the way, explains this and an entire host of additional memory acronyms, in case you're really interested.) You plug the SIMMs into connectors on the Mac's logic board. These connectors are generally called *SIMM sockets*, although some people also call them *SIMM slots*. (For more information about the Mac logic board and its various components, see Chapter 4.)

Note to PowerBook users: If you're interested only in information on PowerBook memory, you can skip most of this section, because PowerBooks use special memory expansion cards instead of SIMMs. Just read the section, "Upgrading PowerBook memory" and then skip to the section, "How to buy memory upgrades."

Table 12-1	Funky Memory Terms Explained
Confusing Memory Acronyms	*What They Mean*
RAM	*Random Access Memory* — the main memory the Mac uses for most of its computing tasks.
ROM	*Read Only Memory* — the Mac uses this memory for unchangeable information that's loaded at the factory, such as parts of the system software.
VRAM	*Video Random Access Memory* — this memory handles the images that appear on the Mac screen.
DRAM	*Dynamic Random Access Memory* — this name is a fancy term for the kind of RAM used in desktop Macs.
PRAM	*Parameter Random Access Memory* — the very small amount of memory in your Mac that holds information like the time and date, your desktop pattern, and how fast your mouse moves the cursor across the screen. This memory gets power from a battery, so the Mac retains this information even after it shuts down.

(continued)

Table 12-1 *(continued)*	
Confusing Memory Acronyms	***What They Mean***
SRAM	*S*tatic *R*andom *A*ccess *M*emory — this memory has low power requirements, so it is used in some portable Macs. This memory is more expensive than regular RAM.
PSRAM	*P*seudo*s*tatic *R*andom *A*ccess *M*emory — a cheaper version of static RAM. This memory comes in the PowerBooks, because it has low power requirements. (Like vinyl and polyester, this RAM is cheaper because it's *pseudo*static, not *genuine* static.)
SIMM	*S*ingle *I*n-line *M*emory *M*odules — long, narrow circuit cards that hold memory chips. You install SIMMs in desktop Macs to install extra memory. PowerBooks, however, take special memory expansion cards that are different from SIMMs.

Did you know that your Macintosh contains *memory banks*, just like every sci-fi computer ever invented? Each Mac comes with two such memory banks: bank A and bank B. (Kind of like Thing One and Thing Two in *The Cat in the Hat.* We just wish we had *those* guys around to clean up for us after a rainy day in the house.) These banks are actually groupings of SIMM sockets. A memory bank can consist of one, two, or four SIMM sockets, depending on your Mac model. You can fill both banks or just one with SIMMs.

Removing and installing SIMMs

If you want to upgrade your Mac's memory, you must know how to remove and install SIMMs. You need to know how to remove existing SIMMs to make way for new ones containing more memory, and, of course, you need to know how to install those new ones.

To remove SIMMs, you need one of two particular tools: either a specialized *SIMM removal tool* . . . or the writing end of a ballpoint pen. The SIMM removal tool enables you to pull out old SIMMs very easily, and using it keeps you from damaging the delicate plastic tabs on older SIMM sockets that hold the SIMMs in place. You can buy a SIMM removal tool from many companies that sell memory. Some retailers even include a SIMM removal tool *gratis* when they sell you the memory. If you can't find a SIMM removal tool — or you don't want to spend the money to get one (assuming you bought the memory from a stingy retailer) — a ballpoint pen can do the job almost as well. All you actually need is a tool to help you push back the small tabs that hold the memory SIMMs in place. Frank has found that a ballpoint pen works well for this, because the pen is not likely to scratch or gouge circuit boards if you slip, and it is still small enough to get the job done effectively.

You find two different kinds of SIMM sockets in the memory banks on Mac logic boards — the *angled* kind and the *vertical* kind. Figure 12-1 shows these two kinds of sockets. Angled SIMM sockets come mainly in the black-and-white compact Macs, except the SE/30. The other Macs all use vertical SIMM sockets. You'll know which kind of socket your machine has after you open your Mac. (The instructions for opening and closing desktop Macs are in Chapters 17 and 18.)

The golden guide to SIMMs

To correctly install SIMMs in your Mac and make sure that the Mac recognizes its new memory, you must follow the golden guide to SIMMs.

1. Make sure that each bank is either completely full or completely empty. Macs can have memory banks made up of one socket, two sockets, or four sockets.

   If your Mac contains two memory banks consisting of four SIMM sockets each, you need to install your SIMMs in groups of four. After you install memory, therefore, you either end up with a total of four SIMMs to fill one bank or a total of eight to fill both banks. You must always have either four or eight SIMMs in such a case, never any other total.

   To obtain a total of 16 MB, for example, you install four 4MB SIMMs in bank A and leave bank B empty. For a total of 20MB, you install four 4MB SIMMs in bank A and four 1MB SIMMs in bank B.

2. Fill each bank with SIMMs of the same size and speed.

   SIMMs come in different sizes: 256K (one-quarter MB), 512K (half a MB), 1MB, 2MB, 4MB, 8MB, 16MB, and 32MB. Of course, the available sizes are always getting larger and larger as the technology develops. (Ah, progress!)

   SIMMs also have a speed rating, measured in *nanoseconds* (abbreviated as *ns*). The smaller the ns number is, the faster the memory is. Older compact Macs usually accept SIMMs rated at 120ns or faster, while newer-model Macs require them rated at 60ns or faster. You can, by the way, install faster SIMMs than your computer requires. So if you own an older Mac, such as an SE, go ahead and buy the faster SIMMs if that's all you can find. They run just fine; they just don't make your Mac run any faster. But, on the other hand, you can't install SIMMs that are slower than the minimum speed required by your Mac, because your Mac can't use them.

3. If you fill only one bank with SIMMs, fill bank A.

   For the Mac to recognize any additional installed memory, bank A must be full. You can always come back and fill bank B later if you want — or need — to.

And that is the golden guide to SIMMs — rules to live by whenever you upgrade your Mac memory.

Removing SIMMs from angled sockets

Removing a SIMM from an angled socket is a two-step process. The first step is to release the two plastic tabs that hold the SIMM in place. The second step is to pull the SIMM out of the socket. You should remove SIMMs from a bank of angled sockets by starting with the front SIMM and working toward the back SIMM until all are removed.

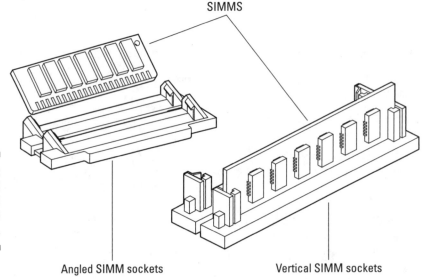

SIMMS

Figure 12-1:
Angled and vertical SIMM sockets.

Angled SIMM sockets   Vertical SIMM sockets

Be very careful not to break the plastic tabs on the SIMM sockets. These tabs are extremely delicate and require great care as you work with them. If the tabs break off, your SIMMs may not make complete contact in the socket, and your Mac may not start. You also must replace the entire SIMM socket if you break a tab. Replacing a SIMM socket usually requires replacing the entire Mac logic board — a very expensive fix for a simple plastic tab.

If you're using a SIMM removal tool, slide the legs of the tool over the ends of the foremost SIMM. After the tool is in place, pull the tool toward you and pivot the SIMM to a vertical position. Then pull the SIMM up and out of the socket.

If you're using a ballpoint pen, first use the writing end of the pen to release one of the tabs that holds the SIMM in place. Gently pull the SIMM toward you to keep the tab from slipping back in to place. Be careful not to pull too hard against the tab; it's designed to flex sideways, but not back to front. Use the pen to release the second tab. Now pull the SIMM forward into a vertical position and pull it up and out of the socket.

Installing SIMMs in angled sockets

You install SIMMs in a bank of angled sockets from back to front. To install a SIMM, you press the SIMM into the socket in a vertical position and then gently push the SIMM back into the socket so that the tabs lock the SIMM into place. (Again, be *very* gentle working with these tabs; they break easily.)

The trick to installing SIMMs correctly is to make sure that the SIMM is pressed fully into the socket before you lock it into place. You'll know the SIMM is fitting correctly in the socket because the top edge of the SIMM is sitting straight, not crooked, and you can't press the SIMM down any farther.

Removing SIMMs from vertical sockets

The two steps for removing SIMMs from vertical sockets are to release the two tabs that hold the SIMM in place and then to pull the SIMM out of the socket. This process is the same as for removing SIMMs from angled sockets; you just do the steps differently.

To remove SIMMs from a bank of vertical sockets, you must work from back to front. Newer Macs contain SIMM sockets with metal locking tabs that are much more durable than the older plastic tabs. Still, be gentle as you remove and install SIMMs in these sockets. Start with the socket at the edge of the bank where you can see the back of the SIMM. (The back of the SIMM is the side with no chips mounted on it.)

If you're using a SIMM removal tool, slide the legs of the tool over the ends of the SIMM and pull the SIMM back into an angled position. Pull the SIMM out of the socket at an angle.

If you're using a ballpoint pen, use the writing end of the pen to release the tab on one side of the SIMM. Pull the SIMM back gently with your fingers, just enough to keep the tab from clicking back into place. Be careful not to pull too hard against the tab; it's designed to flex sideways, but not back to front. Use the pen to release the second tab. Pull the SIMM back into an angled position and pull it out of the socket.

You may need to remove all the SIMMs from both banks if your Mac contains two banks of vertical SIMM sockets, one in front of the other. The Mac IIcx and IIci models, for example, use this arrangement.) Even if you want to remove only the SIMMs from bank B in these Macs, you still must first remove the SIMMs from bank A to give you enough room to remove the SIMMs from bank B.

Installing SIMMs in vertical sockets

You install SIMMs in a bank of vertical sockets from front to back. To install a SIMM, press the SIMM into the socket in an angled position and then gently push the SIMM forward into the socket so that the tabs lock the SIMM into place in a vertical position. (Again, be extremely gentle in working with these tabs, especially plastic ones, as they break easily.)

Upgrading PowerBook memory

Unlike the desktop Macs, PowerBooks don't use SIMMs for their memory upgrades. To install new PowerBook memory, you install a special memory expansion card. This PowerBook expansion card is small enough to fit inside the PowerBook and uses low-power memory chips designed for battery-powered computers. (Gee, the PowerBook battery drains fast enough as it is — thank goodness we don't need to worry about the memory upgrades sucking up all kinds of power, too!) Chapter 19 covers installing memory in the PowerBooks.

As we mentioned for angled sockets, the trick to installing SIMMs correctly is to make sure you press the SIMM completely into the socket before you lock it into place. You'll know the SIMM is fitting right in the socket because the top edge of the SIMM sits straight, not crooked, and you can't press the SIMM down any farther.

Have you ever wondered what to do with the old SIMMs you take out of your Mac? We've tried but have yet found no way to trade in these old SIMMs or even to sell them used. Once Frank had to throw away about 500 of these after he upgraded a couple hundred Macs in a large business. (Can you imagine doing this upgrade process on a *couple hundred Macs*?) Anyway, if the old SIMMs are the 256K size, well, at least they make great earrings.

Your system software and memory (especially if you use System 6)

With System 6, your Mac can use a maximum of 8MB of memory. If you run your Mac with System 6, but your Mac is maxed out on memory and you feel the need to install more, you have to switch to System 7.

After you switch to System 7 and install additional memory beyond 8MB, access the Memory control panel and turn on *32-Bit Addressing*. You may also need to upgrade your older applications, because they may not work correctly with 32-Bit Addressing turned on.

How to buy memory upgrades

In this section we tell you about buying memory. You need to know some specific information about your Mac and how much memory it's got now and how much more memory it can take. When it comes to actually laying out money for memory, you have several different options about where you buy it and for getting advice. Keep reading to find out what we think works best.

What you need to know before you buy memory

Here's what you need to know or find out before you buy new memory. We suggest that you write the information down and refer to it when you talk to a memory salesperson or to a consultant if you get someone to help you upgrade your Mac memory.

> ✔ The model of the Mac in which you intend to install the memory
>
> (You probably already know which Mac model you own, but if you're not sure, just look on the front of the case.)
>
> ✔ How much memory the Mac currently has installed
>
> To determine how much memory your Mac has now, open the Apple menu from the Finder and choose About this Macintosh. (If you use System 6, the item to choose on the Apple menu is About the Finder.) The number listed beside the Total Memory item is the amount of memory installed in your Mac. If you're using virtual memory, the amount of memory appears as Built in Memory.
>
> ✔ How much memory you want to add in your upgrade
>
> See Chapters 17 through 19, under the sections for installing memory in your Mac model, to learn the different amounts — up to the maximum — of memory you can install in your computer.

How you actually buy memory upgrades

OK, so once you know what you need to know, here's how you actually go about buying your memory upgrade.

First, try looking in the back of your favorite Macintosh magazine, such as *Macworld*, *MacWeek*, *MacUser*, or *Mac Home Journal*. You'll find numerous ads placed there by countless mail-order companies wanting to sell you Macintosh memory. (One of our favorite memory companies is TechWorks, located in Austin, Texas. The company's phone number is 800-234-5670.) Usually, the companies that specialize in memory offer better prices than the general mail-order companies do. We suggest you call several companies to compare prices before you decide on one.

When you talk to a representative on the phone, give that person the information on your Mac model, how much memory your Mac has now, and how much memory you want to install. From the information you provide, the representative can tell you how many and what size SIMMs you need to install, the price. (And as we said before, compare prices before you buy.)

To get a rough idea of what the memory upgrade should cost before you call, you can usually estimate approximately $40 to $50 per megabyte, depending on the vendor.

If you're uncomfortable relying on a company representative to tell you the SIMM size and the number of SIMMs you need, call a Macintosh user group. In most user groups, you'll find technicians and other very knowledgeable people who can help you out. For information about finding a user group near you, see Chapter 1. You'll also learn in that chapter how to work with a technician if you want someone else to install memory for you after you buy it.

If you want to learn just about everything you can know about Macintosh memory, we suggest that you order a free booklet called "Memory Solutions Guide," published by TechWorks. The phone number is 800-234-5670. This booklet is part of what TechWorks calls its "outrageous customer service."

Alternatively, you can take your Mac to a computer retail store near you, purchase the memory there, and have the store technicians install the memory. You'll probably pay two to three times more for the memory, however, than if you buy it from the mail-order companies listed in the Macintosh magazines. (Maybe you can get the store to install the memory for free to make up for the extra cost. As we always say, it never hurts to ask.)

What to do if something goes wrong

After you install new memory, it either works or it doesn't work. It if works, the sun shines, the birds sing, and we're all happy. If the memory doesn't work, well, we hope you enjoyed the installation process, because you're going to do it again. First, examine the SIMMs and make sure that you pushed them down completely into their sockets. If you're not sure whether the SIMMs are seated correctly, take out and reinstall all the SIMMs.

If reinstalling the SIMMs doesn't work, one or more of them is probably what people in technical circles call "bad." Contact the company from which you bought the SIMMs, and arrange for replacements.

Internal Storage

First off, for the basics about Mac storage, refer to Chapter 8. There you find information about the different storage devices to use with your Mac, and you also learn how to assess your storage needs.

In theory, all the types of storage devices we discuss in Chapter 8 come in internal versions. In practice, however, the storage devices you most often find installed internally are diskette drives, hard disks, CD-ROM drives, and, occasionally, a tape drive installed in a Mac used as a network server.

Every Mac made comes with an internal diskette drive, and every Mac made since the Mac SE comes with space inside for an internal hard disk, whether the hard disk is installed or not. Some of the newer, more-expensive Macs even contain enough space inside for more than one internal hard disk. Many newer Macs, such as the Performa 600, the Quadra 610, the Quadra 840, and the Power Mac 8100, come with space for an internal CD-ROM, too.

This chapter concentrates on internal hard disks, because that is the most common storage device people install in their Mac. The actual instructions for installing an internal hard disk are in Chapters 17 and 18, depending on your Mac model. If you want to install an internal hard disk in a PowerBook, we recommend that an authorized technician do the upgrade for you.

How to buy an internal hard disk

We recommend that you look for the following features in an internal hard disk. You can use this purchasing information whether or not you install the drive in your desktop Mac yourself. (This information also applies to purchasing an internal hard disk for a PowerBook.)

- *Buy a preformatted hard disk.* A preformatted hard disk comes ready to use, which means that the manufacturer has prepared the disk to handle Macintosh files and applications.

- *Buy a SCSI hard disk.* SCSI is the only kind of hard disk that works with the Mac. Those designed for use with DOS and Windows computers don't work in a Mac.

- *Buy the correct size hard disk for your Mac.* By size here we mean the physical dimensions of the hard disk, not its storage capacity (or megabytes). Desktop Macs require hard disks that are 3 ½ inches in diameter. (Note that the Mac II, IIx, or IIfx can use either the 3 ½-inch size or a 5 ¼-inch size — you can choose the size you want.)

The disk's height varies from machine to machine, but you have to buy either half height or third height. Tell the salesperson that you buy your hard disk from what model Mac you're installing the drive into so you get the right drive. PowerBooks require hard disks 2 ½ inches in diameter; only one height exists for these drives.

✔ Buy as much storage as you can afford. You'll use it.

You can buy an internal hard disk from mail-order companies or from retail computer stores. We've found that we get the best prices from mail-order companies that specialize in storage devices. One company with which we've had good luck is APS Technologies. APS is located in Kansas City, Missouri, and the phone number is 800-677-3294. We suggest that you check the ads in the back of your favorite Macintosh magazine and then call the different companies to check out the best prices.

If you buy from a computer retail store, see if you can get the store technicians to install the drive for you for free. As we said before, it never hurts to ask.

When you buy your internal hard disk, be sure to buy a hard disk mounting kit. This kit includes the hard disk carrier bracket, screws, and all the cables you need for connecting the hard disk inside your Mac. Make sure you tell the salesperson what Mac model you're upgrading so you get the right mounting kit.

After you buy your internal hard disk, but BEFORE you install it

You need to consider how you're going to transfer the files and applications from your old hard disk to your new hard disk. You have three choices:

✔ You can copy all your files and applications from your old hard disk onto diskettes and then copy them onto your new hard disk.

✔ You can copy your files and applications onto an external hard disk or another type of external storage device and then copy them onto your new hard disk.

✔ You can copy your files and applications to a network server and then retrieve them and put them on your new hard disk.

To avoid the need for copying all your files and applications, we suggest that you consider upgrading to an external hard disk instead of an internal model. That way, your original hard disk stays in your Mac, and you use your new external drive for new files and applications. If you've accumulated megabytes and megabytes of files and applications, this alternative may save you a great deal of time. (Chapter 8 includes information about external hard disks.)

If a technician upgrades your internal hard disk for you, make sure that person transfers all the files and applications from your old drive to the new one.

After you install your new internal hard drive

OK, I've installed my new internal hard disk. So what do I do with my old internal hard disk? Good question. You have a few choices. You can try to sell it to someone else at a user group meeting, or you can keep it, buy an external case, and use the hard disk as an external drive. You can buy these external cases from mail-order companies that specialize in storage. Also, how about hanging it on the wall for all to see and recognize what a skilled Mac upgrader you are? And these really do make great door stops or paper weights.

Finally, if your new internal hard disk doesn't show up on your Mac desktop or if your Mac starts up with a flashing question mark icon on-screen, refer to Chapter 8. That chapter also includes maintenance tips for storage devices.

Chapter 13

Video Upgrades

In This Chapter

▶ Getting more colors with video memory

▶ Adding a video card

▶ PowerBook video

▶ What to do if something goes wrong

*T*o display anything on a monitor, a Macintosh needs video circuitry. With newer Macs, this circuitry comes on the logic board; in older models, it comes on an expansion card.

When the circuitry comes on the logic board, we call it *built-in video*. Macs with this built-in video have a video port on the back of the machine located in the row with the other ports. To determine whether your Mac has built-in video, look for a video port at the back of the computer. You'll recognize the port by the icon that looks like a monitor.

If your machine has a video expansion card installed, you'll see a video connector in one of the expansion slots on the back of the machine.

Or, you may find both a video port and a video expansion card. With this double-video hardware setup, you can use two monitors at the same time or connect a monitor that doesn't work with the built-in video.

When You Think Video Memory, Think More Colors

Part of your Mac's built-in video is video memory. You can upgrade your built-in video capabilities by installing new video memory.

A deep dive into technical video stuff: bit depth

We're not talking underwater exploration here, we're talking about the number of colors on your Mac screen.

The color of each pixel or dot on your Mac screen is represented in the computer by a number. For black-and-white, the number is either a 1 or a 0, which can be represented by one bit, either on or off. With color or shades of gray, the more colors or shades you have, the more bits the computer uses to keep track of the color or shade.

The Mac uses the following standard bit depths:

    1 bit = black and white

    4 bits = 16 colors

    8 bits = 256 colors

    16 bits = thousands of colors (specifically, 32,700)

    24 bits = millions of colors (specifically, 16.7 million)

Once you go past 24 bits, you're beyond the number of colors the human eye can distinguish, which is millions of colors. That's a lot.

Sounds kind of like the big, huge, double-wide box of crayons we all used to covet in grade school. Besides being pretty, the more colors you use, the more the images on-screen look like real photographs. For example, 16 colors makes pictures look like a stylized poster, 256 colors look like a grainy photograph, thousands of colors look almost like a photograph, and millions of colors create photo-realistic quality.

Just as when you add more RAM (regular memory) to your Mac so that you can use more applications and larger files, when you add video memory, you can use more colors on-screen at one time.

You may hear techies kick around the term *32-bit QuickDraw*. As we said, 24-bit color gives you on-screen the maximum number of colors the human eye can see. But the Mac actually uses 32 bits of information per dot when it shuffles video information around its circuits. Only 24 bits are displayed on-screen, and the other 8 bits produce video information that you never see.

Adding video memory to get more colors

If your Mac has built-in video, you add video memory to get more colors. If your Mac does not have built-in video, refer to the section, "Adding a Video Card" in this chapter. If you're not sure whether your Mac has built-in video, look on the back of the Mac for a video port (the one with the monitor icon) or check the manual for your Mac.

How much video memory to buy

You need to find out how much video memory to purchase. The easiest way is to call 800-SOS-APPL. Before you call, gather the following information:

- ✔ Your Mac model, which you probably know

- ✔ The type of monitor you have or want to use

- ✔ How much video memory your Mac currently has, which you may not know (see "Finding out how much video memory you have" to find out how to determine this amount)

- ✔ How many colors you want, such as 16, 256, thousands, or millions.

When you call 800-SOS-APPL, be prepared to wait 20 or 30 minutes. The information you get is worth the wait. When you get the SOS-APPL operator, tell him or her that you're adding video memory to your Mac and you want to know how much memory to purchase. Give the person the information you gathered so that he or she understands your Mac and monitor system and the color results you want.

The operator will tell you how much video memory you need to buy and also what size SIMMs to buy so that you get the colors you want. In case you don't know, SIMMs are the small circuit boards that hold the video memory circuitry.

Finding out how much video memory you have

None of the Mac control panels or dialog boxes tells you how much video memory your Mac has. To find out, use a shareware program, such as MacEnvy, which you can get from user groups, on-line bulletin boards, or on-line services. The software provides a ton of information about your Macintosh hardware, such as the kind of processor running the computer, the amount of regular memory, and the amount of video memory.

If you can't get a copy of MacEnvy, here's another way to find out how much video memory you have. When you speak to the SOS-APPL operator, tell him or her what kind of monitor you use and the largest number of colors the monitor can display as shown in the Monitors Control Panel. With this information, the operator can find out from a chart how much video memory you have installed in your Mac.

Where to buy video memory

When you know how much video memory to buy, you can buy it at a computer retail store or through mail order. Usually, mail order is cheaper.

You may run into the opportunity to buy used video memory from someone who has removed it from his or her machine as part of an upgrade. The question is, should you buy used video memory? It's risky, but you can get a good price. Be sure to test the SIMMs by installing them in a Macintosh, either your Mac or the seller's, before you buy. If the computer starts up and the monitor works normally, the SIMMs are probably OK. Be sure to follow the proper electrostatic discharge prevention guidelines when you handle and transport the memory. See Chapter 3 for more information about these guidelines.

After you install new video memory, you won't see more colors on your monitor until you change the settings in the Monitors Control Panel under the Apple menu. To take advantage of all the new colors, change the settings in the Control Panel to a larger number.

When your monitor is set to use thousands or millions of colors, screen redraws may slow down somewhat because of the large amount of information required to process so many colors. If you need more speed, choose a smaller number of colors in the Monitors Control Panel. The idea is to use lots of colors only when you need them and fewer colors for everyday work.

Video memory determines the number of colors your Mac can use. The type of monitor your Mac connects to varies from model to model and depends on the built-in video circuitry or the expansion card, if one is installed. For more information about monitors, see Chapter 10.

Adding a Video Card

Another way to upgrade your Mac video is to install a video card. In this section you learn what to use a video card for and what to look for when you buy one.

What you use a video card for

Unlike video memory, which serves only the single purpose of adding colors, video cards serve four purposes:

- ✔ To use a monitor that normally wouldn't be compatible with your Mac's built-in video
- ✔ To connect a second monitor
- ✔ To accelerate video performance
- ✔ To work with more colors

The following examples illustrate the many uses for a video card:

To connect a two-page monitor to your Mac LC III, you need a video expansion card, because the LC III's built-in video doesn't work with that large a monitor.

If you find the 10-inch Color Classic screen too small and you want to work with a larger monitor, for example, you can install a video expansion card and attach a second monitor.

Because many colors means gobs of data moving around in the computer, drawing color images on-screen takes a great deal of time. Special accelerated video cards can speed up this image processing.

Suppose that you add the maximum amount of video memory that your Mac can take, and you still get only 256 colors, on your 21-inch color monitor. To work with millions of colors, you have to add a video expansion card. The setting, "Millions of colors," goes beyond the highest number of colors your eyes can see. Refer to "A deep dive into technical video stuff: bit depth" in this chapter for more information.

What to look for in a video card

When you shop for a video card, you usually find the monitor you want to use and then choose a video card to drive the monitor. To use a 16-inch color monitor with an SE/30, for example, you need to buy a video card designed for the SE/30 that will run the monitor you have in mind.

Or you may already have a monitor but you want to speed up the video performance. In this case, you should look for a video card designed for your Mac that runs the monitor you have.

Note: When should you buy an accelerated video card instead of buying a plain old video card or using the built-in video? When you have the monitor you like, and your built-in video gives you the colors you want, but the graphics just draw and redraw too slow. Then it's time to get an accelerated video card.

Sometimes the work you want to do dictates the need for an accelerated video card. For example, some accelerator cards contain special circuits to speed up certain functions in image processing applications. If you perform complex image processing regularly, you should think about getting one of these.

PowerBook Video and Adding an External Monitor

Like desktop Macs, some PowerBooks have built-in video and some don't. But unlike the desktop Macs, you can't add video memory to any PowerBook, so you can't add colors. What you buy in a PowerBook is what you get as far as the number of colors is concerned. You're probably asking, "Well, what can I do?" The major video thing you can add to a PowerBook is an external monitor.

And you really can do some cool things with a PowerBook and a second monitor. Here are a few ideas: run two programs at once and look at each one on a separate monitor; set up the external monitor as an extension of the PowerBook's built-in screen so that you have one large work area for spreadsheets or page-layout documents spread over two screens; or use the external monitor as a large mirror of the built-in screen for presentations.

PowerBooks are divided into three groups when it comes to connecting an external monitor: PowerBooks with built-in video, PowerBooks without built-in video, and Duos, which get different video capabilities by connecting to different docks.

Connecting an external monitor with the PowerBook 160, 165c, 180, and 180c

PowerBooks with built-in video include the 160, 165c, 180, and 180c. These PowerBook models are plug and play, meaning that all you need to attach an external monitor is a special cable to connect the monitor to the video port.

To find out which monitors you can connect to the PowerBooks mentioned in this section, see the manual for your model.

Connecting an external monitor with the PowerBook 100, 140, 170, 145, and 145b

PowerBooks without built in video circuitry — the 100, 140, 170, 145, and 145b — need some additional hardware to connect to external monitors. You have two options for adding this hardware: internal or external. The external upgrade is the only one you can do yourself. You need to have a technician or consultant do the internal upgrade for you. (See Chapter 2.)

With the *external* upgrade, all you do is connect a video adapter box to the PowerBook SCSI port. Then you plug the external monitor into the adapter box. Also, the adapter box comes with software that you install to enable the PowerBook to use the external monitor.

Note: Internal video expansion cards are too large to fit in the small space inside the PowerBook 100, so connecting an external monitor through the SCSI video adapter is the only option for this machine.

If you decide to do the *internal* upgrade and have a technician install the video card in your PowerBook, you should know that you will also be installing additional system memory because the PowerBook has no expansion slot inside. You install both the video circuitry and the system memory on one card into the computer's one memory connector.

After you install a video card in your PowerBook, you won't be able to install more system memory without removing the card. Make sure you get a card with as much memory as you expect to need in the future, or check that the manufacturer of the card has a trade-in program for when you want to add even more system memory.

To find out which monitors you can use with your PowerBook, see the documentation that comes with the video upgrade you choose.

Connecting an external monitor to PowerBook Duos

The PowerBook Duos have no built-in video circuitry and get their video capabilities from whatever dock they are plugged into. So upgrading Duo video is as simple as switching to a different dock. A variety of docks on the market allows you to attach an external monitor. They range in size from Apple's desktop Duo Dock to small video *micro docks,* which are small enough to fit in your shirt pocket — that is, if you have any room left in your shirt pocket next to the plastic multi-pen holder.

See the documentation that comes with your dock to find out which monitors you can use with your Duo.

What to Do if Something Goes Wrong

Here are some frequently asked questions about video, and the answers. Sometimes it's hard to differentiate between video problems and monitor problems, so be sure to look in Chapter 10, too.

I installed some video memory, and I don't see any more colors on-screen.

You probably need to reset the number of colors in the Monitors Control Panel. The tip in the section "Adding video memory to get more colors" provides information about setting the number of colors.

I installed more video memory, but no new options showed up in the Monitors Control Panel to enable me to increase the colors.

Check that the video memory SIMMs are correctly installed in the memory sockets. Make sure that they are pressed firmly into the sockets. If everything looks like it's installed correctly, you may have a faulty SIMM and need to exchange it where you bought it.

Run MacEnvy to find out whether the new video memory is registering. If the new memory registers, double-check with SOS-APPL to make sure that the amount of video memory you installed should actually give you the number of colors you want.

I installed a video expansion card, and now my monitor is blank. Help.

Make sure that your monitor is actually connected to the new card through the slot in the back of the Mac. Also, you can try zapping the PRAM (described in the section "What to Do if Something Goes Wrong," in Chapter 10.)

I installed an expansion card and connected my monitor. But when I turn on the Mac, I just see static.

A similar problem is seeing wavy lines or very distorted images after you install a video card. Double-check that the card you bought is really compatible with the monitor you connected it to. Look in the documentation that came with the card to find out this information.

You could also be using the wrong cable to connect your monitor and the card. Call the technical support department of the company that made the video card. You may need them to send you a different cable or an adapter.

Chapter 14
Speeding Up Your Mac

· ·

In This Chapter

▶ Speedup issues

▶ Free speedups

▶ Math, CAD, graphics, hard disk, and network speedups

▶ Whole Mac speedups

▶ PowerPC power

· ·

*P*ower, performance, processors. These are the words we hear when people talk about speeding up, or accelerating, their Macs. As new Macs roll off the assembly lines, the one feature they all share is that of offering more speed at a lower price than earlier models. In fact, newer, faster Macs selling for cheaper prices is a fact of life we can probably count on for some time to come. Whether you're planning to buy the newest PowerPC-based Power Mac or you just want to speed up the tried, true, trusty Mac that's seen you through project after project — this chapter's for you.

Before You Buy an Accelerator . . .

The usual hardware route to speeding up the Mac is to install accelerator hardware. Before you buy this hardware, however, you need to be aware of two factors: *compatibility* and *chain reactions*.

Accelerators and compatibility

You need to be aware that the accelerator hardware you add to your Mac may not always be compatible with the software you already own. If you've owned your Mac awhile and your software is two or three years old, you may run into problems using those programs with hardware that incorporates the newest processor chips. (Of course, you encounter the same problem if you buy a new Mac and try to run your old applications on it.) If you experience any software problems, go ahead and pick up the updated versions of these programs.

Accelerators and chain reactions

A chain reaction occurs if the hardware you buy to speed up your Mac ends up requiring you to purchase yet more hardware or new software.

Chain reactions are a problem because they often result in your spending much more money on upgrading than you planned. Suppose, for example, that you buy an accelerator because your software runs too slowly on your Mac. After you install the accelerator, you discover that it is not compatible with some vital piece of software you currently run — meaning that the program doesn't open, the program crashes, or maybe that your Mac refuses even to start. So you buy the newest version of your old program. After you have the new software version, however, you discover that you need a larger hard disk to install it and more memory to run it . . . and so on.

The moral of this chain reaction story is that sometimes all this extra hardware winds up costing the same as or more than you'd spend by just going all the way and buying a new Mac that includes a larger hard disk and extra memory. (To learn more about comparing upgrade costs to the cost of a new Mac, see Chapter 2.)

Cost-Free Speedups

So you decide your Mac is too slow. Before you go out and spend a ton of your hard-earned greenbacks, try a few of these simple cost-free speedup ideas first. Of course, because there's no such thing as a free lunch, each speedup described in this section has its own downside. We give you the pros and cons so that you can decide which are best for your situation.

We've listed these speedups in the order of fastest to slowest. Notice that the first one applies only to Macs that contain a 68040 processor.

Turn on the 68040 cache

Pros: Makes Quadras and other Macs running on the 68040 processor, including the 68LC040, run *much* faster.

Cons: Works only on Macs using 68040 or 68LC040 processors. The 68040 processor cache is also incompatible with some older software. If your software is incompatible with the 68040 processor cache, the program refuses to load or your Mac freezes up. Update the software by ordering a new version from the developer, or turn off the cache whenever you run that application.

The processor cache is what makes the 68040 processor fast. If you own a Quadra or another Mac based on the 68040 or 68LC040 processor, leaving the cache switched off is like keeping your Mac stuck in low gear — you get there eventually, but it may seem to take forever. If you aren't sure whether your Mac uses the 68040 or 68LC040 processor, look up your Mac model in Chapters 5 through 7 to find out.

To switch on the 68040 cache, pull down the Apple menu and choose Control Panels; then double-click the 040 Cache Switch control panel icon. When the control panel opens, click the button in front of the Faster (Caches Enabled) selection. After you click the button, pull down the Special menu and choose Restart to actually turn on the cache. Your Mac will shut down and start up again with the cache turned on.

If your applications crash when they didn't before you turned on the cache, go back to the 040 Cache Switch control panel and choose the More Compatible (Caches Disabled) selection to turn off the cache.

If you press and hold the Option key as you click the "Faster" or "More Compatible" buttons, you can switch the 68040 cache on and off without restarting.

Turn off virtual memory

Pros: Turning off virtual memory makes your Mac faster in virtually no time.

Cons: Without the extra memory provided by virtual memory, you may not be able to run many applications or open very large files.

Virtual memory can sometimes be very handy, but it can also really slow down your Mac, depending on the software you're running. This slowdown occurs because virtual memory uses a part of your hard disk as system memory, which means that the Mac must continually access the hard disk. And accessing the hard disk is about 1,000 times slower than accessing real memory.

To turn off virtual memory, pull down the Apple menu and choose Control Panels; then double-click the Memory control panel icon. In the Virtual Memory section of this control panel, click the button in front of the "Off" selection. After you click the button, pull down the Special menu and choose Restart. The Mac will shut down and start up again with virtual memory turned off.

Increase the size of the disk cache

Pros: Speeds up access to information on the hard disk.

Cons: Reduces the amount of system memory available for applications.

The *disk cache* is a chunk of memory set aside to store a copy of the last bit of information you used from your hard disk. Increasing the disk cache size can speed up software that requires frequent hard disk access, such as system software. As noted in the preceding section, accessing memory is much faster than is accessing the hard disk.

The larger you make the disk cache, the faster your Mac runs, because a larger disk cache decreases the number of times the Mac must access the hard disk.

In System 7, you use the Memory control panel to control the size of the disk cache. Pull down the Apple menu and choose Control Panels. Then double-click the Memory control panel icon. The top segment of this control panel is for the disk cache, and the box on the right side enables you to set the size of the disk cache. We've found that setting the disk cache from 128K to 512K provides the best gains in speed, but you could make the cache even bigger if your Mac has enough memory to spare. (Just make sure that you leave sufficient memory to run your applications.)

In System 6, you use the General control panel to control the disk cache size. You can also turn off the disk cache in System 6, whereas in System 7 the cache is always on.

Work in black and white, not color

Pros: Speeds up scrolling through documents and opening and redrawing windows.

Cons: You work in black and white, which isn't as much fun as color.

Working in black and white accelerates scrolling through documents, opening windows, and redrawing images. This is because, when you use color, the Mac has to use more information to describe the color of each dot on-screen. If you work in black and white, the Mac processes less information on-screen, so scrolling, opening windows, and redrawing goes faster.

To set your screen to black and white, pull down the Apple menu, choose Control Panels, and then double-click the Monitors control panel icon. Choose the setting for black and white from the list of settings for the number of colors available. (For more information about working with colors, see Chapter 13, and for information about color monitors, see Chapter 10.)

If most of your work on the Mac involves spreadsheets or word processing documents, for which color is not important, set your screen for black and white only. This setting provides the fastest speed for your work. If you then need to use a color application, simply change the setting in the Monitors control panel back to color while you use that application.

If you frequently work with photographic-quality images on your Mac, you probably normally set the colors to Millions in the Monitors control panel. (It's the setting just before "*Bi*llions and *bi*llions . . ." on Carl Sagan's computer.) For work that doesn't require full-color photographic quality, however, you can change your setting to 256 and realize a substantial gain in speed.

Change the settings in the Views control panel in System 7

Pros: Speeds up Finder operations such as opening and redrawing windows.

Cons: You don't see how much space each folder takes up on your hard disk, and you can't use your favorite font for document and folder titles.

You can increase system speed a bit by changing the settings in the Views control panel in System 7 back to the default settings. Pull down the Apple menu, choose Control Panels, and double-click the Views control panel icon. Choose Geneva 9 point for the Font for Views from the pop-up menus at the top of the window. Make sure that the Calculate folder sizes check box, located in the lower-left corner of the window, does not have an X in it. Close the control panel window by clicking the Close box in the top-left corner of the window. That's it — your Mac should act a bit peppier now.

Remove unused extensions and control panels from the System folder

Pros: Improved system efficiency and memory reclaimed for use by applications.

Cons: You lose the use of the extensions or control panels you remove.

Do you really know what all those cryptic icons are — the ones that appear across the bottom of the screen after your Mac starts? Your system may be bogged down with extra functions you never knew you had or that are useless for the computing you do. You can often improve performance and reclaim memory for applications by cleaning house and removing unused system extensions and control panels from your System folder.

Extensions are small pieces of system software that load automatically at start-up. Printer drivers and QuickTime are examples of extensions. You find the Mac *control panels* under the Apple menu. Among these panels are the Views, Monitor, and Memory control panels mentioned earlier in this chapter. Others include the Mouse control panel, where you adjust how your mouse functions, such as the speed at which it double-clicks, and the Sound control panel, where you can change the volume and type of your Mac's system beeps.

The best approach to removing extensions and control panels is to create a new folder outside your System folder and then move your unused extensions and control panels into that folder. Don't trash anything right away; you may discover that you removed something you really want to keep. In System 7, extensions are in the Extensions folder and control panels are in the Control Panels folder, both of which are located in the System folder. In System 6, extensions (or *INITs*) and control panels float around loosely in the System folder.

Some seldom-used system extensions include *DAL access* and the drivers for any printers you don't use with your Mac. Seldom-used control panels are Map and Easy Access. Start by removing these.

Be careful about removing extensions and control panels if your Mac runs on a network. Some network services, such as electronic mail, need specific extensions on your Mac to work correctly. Check with your network administrator before you remove any extensions from your System folder.

You Don't Have to Speed Up Everything

If you do decide to speed up your Mac, you can speed up the entire machine by accelerating the processor, or you can speed up just certain operations, such as math calculations, computer-aided design (CAD), graphics, hard disk access, or networking. Buying hardware to boost the speed of every function of your Mac gets expensive, however, so you may want to consider just speeding up the operations you really use.

Faster than a speeding calculator

If you use your Mac for mega number crunching in monster spreadsheets, consider speeding up your Mac's math abilities. You accelerate math functions by installing a chip called an *FPU*. (That stands for *Floating Point Unit*, and only real math-computer wizards understand why and where the point floats.) FPU relates to how the Mac juggles numbers. Another term for FPU is *math coprocessor* — a much easier term for most of us to understand.

In some Macs you install a math coprocessor by plugging it into a socket on the logic board; in other Macs, you install a math coprocessor expansion card. Macs running the 68000 processor, such as the Mac Plus, the Mac SE, and the PowerBook 100, can't take a math coprocessor. If you're not sure which processor your Mac uses, refer to Chapters 5 through 7.

If your Mac runs a 68020 or 68030 processor, however, you can plug a math coprocessor chip into a socket on the logic board or you can install an expansion card containing a math coprocessor. Which method you use depends on your particular Mac model, so refer to its user manual or call 800-SOS-APPL for details. Too bad, but you can't install a math coprocessor in your PowerBook.

If your Mac contains a 68040 processor or a PowerPC processor — congratulations! You already have a math coprocessor, and your math operations are running at top speed.

The exception to this golden rule, however, lies in those machines running the 68*LC*040 processor. The *LC* indicates that the math coprocessor built into the chip has been disconnected. Yeah, we know this sounds pretty weird, but that's why the 68LC040 chips cost less money than the full-blown 68040 chips do. So if you own one of these Macs and need speedy math capabilities, you must remove the 68LC040 chip from the logic board and install a standard 68040 in its place. Sorry, but a technician must handle this upgrade for you.

Only software written specifically to take advantage of a math coprocessor runs faster after you install the chip. So before you buy a math coprocessor, refer to the manual for your software to make sure that it can even use a math coprocessor's capabilities.

CAD means number crunching, too

The people who use CAD (computer-aided design) programs usually are engineers or architects. You know — the people who create blueprints and engineering drawings for cars, tools, bridges, jet engines, or the space shuttle. You may not realize it, but outrageous numbers of math calculations go into creating these drawings. The same math coprocessor that runs spreadsheet programs also speeds up CAD programs. So if you're into CAD, check out the preceding section for details.

Graphics speedups

If you're into graphics and Mac drawing applications, you've probably noticed how long an image takes to fill in on-screen after you open a file or scroll down through a drawing. This process is called *redraw*. Slow redraw is especially noticeable if your monitor is set to display thousands or millions of colors. (For more information about monitors and working with colors, see Chapters 10 and 13.)

If you use images from scanned photographs or slides or you use other photographic-quality images on a large color monitor, you definitely need to consider installing an *accelerated video card* — unless, of course, you're one of those rare, lucky people who don't need to worry about deadlines. This particular video card contains special chips that process video images *very* quickly.

Sorry to say, the downside to accelerated video cards is that they are very expensive. If your work depends on producing images quickly, however, the time you save in drawing and redrawing may well offset the cost of the card.

To use an accelerated video card, you must own a modular Mac containing a NuBus expansion slot. Check the manual for your modular Mac or refer to Chapter 6 to see if your Mac includes this type of slot.

Boosting hard disk performance

This section applies only to people who work with very large files, such as multimedia files or large databases. Feel free to skip this information if it doesn't apply to you.

Your Mac may be pretty fast when scrolling, applying font styles, rotating images, or checking spelling. But if you work with huge sound or graphics files, you may find its performance somewhat wanting. You can speed up its handling even of these files by installing an *accelerated SCSI card*. This card accelerates how the Mac brings files and portions of files from the hard disk to memory.

In techno terms, an accelerated SCSI card speeds up what is known as *hard disk access*. In theory, many large hard disks manufactured today can send files to the Mac faster than the Mac can handle them. An accelerated SCSI card enables you to tap the true potential of your hard disk. (If only tapping our own true potential were as easy as installing a card — sigh.)

To install an accelerated SCSI card, you must own a modular Mac that contains a NuBus slot.

A low-cost way to boost your hard disk's performance is to defragment your hard disk. *Defragmenting* means joining together all the individual pieces of files that are currently stored in separate locations on your hard disk. (And we don't mean gluing hard disk pieces back together after you smash it on the floor in frustration over its slow speed. You don't need super glue for this tip.)

As your hard disk fills up with files, its storage space gets smaller and smaller, so your files can get broken up and stored in separate areas on the disk. This process is called *file fragmentation*. Retrieving fragmented files takes much longer than retrieving files that are stored all together in one piece, so defragmenting your hard disk is a good idea. Unlike good ol' Humpty Dumpty, however, files *can* be put back together again. And you don't need all the king's horses and all the king's men either — just a commercial utility package designed for this purpose, such as Symantec's Norton Utilities or Central Point's MacTools.

Putting more power in your network

If you work on an AppleTalk network, you may find that moving large files from Mac to Mac takes up a great deal of time. Too bad, but AppleTalk is pretty darn slow, and you can't speed it up much beyond minor adjustments.

For really fast networking, you may want to upgrade to an Ethernet network. You can connect your Mac to an Ethernet network in any of the following three ways, depending on your model:

   ✔ If you own a newer modular Mac, such as most Quadras and Power Macs, your machine already has built-in Ethernet capability. All you need to do is buy an Ethernet transceiver and plug it into the Ethernet port on the back of the Mac.

   ✔ If your Mac has no built-in Ethernet capability but contains an open expansion slot, you can buy an Ethernet expansion card and install it in the slot.

   ✔ For Macs with neither open expansion slots nor built-in Ethernet capabilities (such as PowerBooks), you must buy an Ethernet adapter box to plug into a port on the back of the computer.

For more information about networking, refer to Chapter 11.

Total Mac Speedups

If you've tried the cost-free speedups we described earlier in this chapter, and you're not interested in speeding up specific math, graphics, hard disk, or networking functions, you're probably looking for an overall Mac speedup.

Here are four different approaches to speeding up all your Mac's functions:

   ✔ Add an accelerator card.
   ✔ Add cache memory.
   ✔ Upgrade the logic board.
   ✔ Speed up the processor timing.

The approach you should choose depends on your particular Mac model.

Adding an accelerator card

Adding an *accelerator card* is what most people mean when they talk about accelerating their Macs. An accelerator card contains a faster, more-powerful processor that bypasses the Mac's original processor. Accelerator cards can contain any processor used in the Mac, such as the 68000, 68020, 68030, 68040, or the Power PC. The card plugs into an expansion slot in your Mac. You can add an accelerator card to just about any Mac model.

Accelerator cards designed for the 128K, 512K, and Mac Plus clip onto the processor instead of plugging into an expansion slot. This clip-on style accelerator card is not as reliable as the cards that plug into a slot, and we don't recommend adding an accelerator card to Macs that require the clip-on cards.

Some accelerator cards also contain SIMM slots for extra memory, a math coprocessor, a connector for a cache memory card, or a connector for a video card to drive a larger monitor.

Adding cache memory

You also can speed up certain Macs by adding a card containing what's known as *cache memory* — and that's not something you use to remember what's printed on the back of a dollar bill. Cache memory enables your Mac to use a small amount of very fast memory to store information you use frequently so that you can retrieve that information as quickly as possible.

The advantage to adding cache memory is that it can give your Mac a 10 to 30 percent speed boost for a small amount of money compared to other accelerator options. Macs that can use cache cards include the IIci and the IIvx, the Performa 600, most Quadras, and the Power Macs. Cache cards are designed specifically for each processor chip, such as the 68030, 68040, or the Power PC.

If you're concerned about compatibility and cost, this speedup is a good one. Cache cards have no compatibility problems with either software or hardware. You can't lose by adding a cache card.

Upgrading the logic board

In a *logic board* upgrade, your existing logic board is removed and then replaced with one designed for a different Mac model. (But don't try this yourself! A technician must perform a logic board upgrade for you.)

You can upgrade certain Mac models to any newer model that shares the same case. The SE, for example, upgrades to the SE/30; the Mac II upgrades to the IIfx; the Quadra 650 upgrades to the Power Mac 7100; and so on. This logic board upgrade basically transforms your Mac into an entirely new computer. (Of course, you keep your old hard drive, diskette drive, and power supply.)

Upgrading a logic board is usually much more expensive than installing an accelerator card but is cheaper than buying a new Mac. Software and hardware compatibility issues are the same as if you were to buy the new Mac model to which you're upgrading.

Speeding up the processor timing

Speeding up the *processor timing* is probably the most technical of all the Mac speedups discussed in this chapter, so read this section carefully before you decide to go with this one. Just because this speedup is the most technical doesn't mean it's the most difficult. For some Macs, you can handle this upgrade yourself; for other Macs, you must to hire a technician. Check with the company that makes the upgrade you're installing to determine this.

This speedup involves cranking up the speed of your Mac's processor by replacing (or bypassing) the processor's original timing chip with a faster timing chip. As you may recall, processor speed is measured in megahertz — MHz — as in such numbers as 25MHz, 50MHz, and 100MHz.

This upgrade works only on Macs that are closely related to another machine in the Mac line that normally runs at the faster speed for which you're shooting. The Mac IIsi and IIci, for example, are close relatives, as are the PowerBooks 160 and 180 and the PowerBooks 140 and the 170. For example, to accelerate the Mac IIsi, you replace its processor timing chip with a faster chip designed for its close relative, the Mac IIci.

Speeding up the processor offers two major advantages. The price is cheap compared to that of an accelerator card or a logic board upgrade. And this upgrade is, in fact, the only way to accelerate the PowerBooks — although it works only on certain PowerBook models, such as the PowerBook 140 and 160, and only a technician can perform this PowerBook speed upgrade for you.

The disadvantage of speeding up the processor is that running the processor at a faster speed causes it to run hotter, as well. (Kinda sounds like a motor oil ad, huh?) This heat problem can be solved, however, by adding air conditioning for the Mac's insides in the form of either a fan to cool down the chip or a *heat sink*, which is a piece of metal that pulls the head away from the processor chip.

Although speeding up the processor's timing is less expensive than some other Mac speedups, we have mixed feelings about this upgrade, mainly because it involves messing with the logic board whenever you change the timing chip. And if you own a new Mac (less than a year old), this upgrade definitely voids the warranty.

PowerPC: Mac Power to the Max

The PowerPC is the processor running the new generation of Macs called the Power Macintoshes. The official name of the chip is the *PowerPC 601*. To put it simply, having a Power Mac is having a PowerPC chip inside.

What all this PowerPC stuff really means is that Power Mac computers are faster than older Macintosh models and represent the next step in Mac evolution. The chip's promise is to make software run up to three to four times faster than applications can run on the fastest Quadras. The chip also runs math and CAD operations up to ten times faster than on the Quadras. The catch, however, is that the software goes this fast only if it's designed specifically for the PowerPC chip. Software designed for pre-PowerPC Macs runs only at Quadra speeds, even on Power Macs.

PowerPC chip info

You'll read about two acronyms in this section — RISC and CISC. (Sounds almost as if we're talking about Nabisco cookies here, doesn't it?) Feel perfectly free to skip this processor-chip background stuff if you want to.

PowerPC chips fall into a family of what techno-in-groupers call RISC processors. RISC stands for *R*educed *I*nstruction *S*et *C*omputing.

Essentially, RISC processors streamline the internal workings of computers by reducing to a minimum the number of instructions the processors carry out, or execute. Processor speed increases as a result. The idea is to reduce any instructions the chip carries out to a bare minimum, leaving only those instructions used most often. And if a complex instruction is required, the RISC processor builds it by combining the basic instructions.

In contrast, pre-PowerPC-based Macs run on *C*omplex *I*nstruction *S*et *C*omputing processors,

known as CISC processors, for short. The official names of these Mac processors are the Motorola 68000, 68020, 68030, 68040, and 68LC040. If you don't own a Power Mac, your Mac contains one of these processors.

These CISC processors contain a wide variety of instructions that handle many different tasks, and as a result, they run more slowly than RISC processors. (In essence, the more instructions a chip must handle, the more slowly it runs.)

Until the PowerPC chip appeared in the Power Mac, RISC processors mostly were used only in engineering workstations and large database servers. Such computers usually run the UNIX operating system, which means that these machines are pretty difficult and unpleasant both to learn and to use.

Giving your Mac PowerPC power

You can travel three different paths in upgrading to the PowerPC, depending on which Mac model or models you own.

Buy a new Power Macintosh

Don't overlook the obvious. The simplest way to get PowerPC performance and power is to buy a Power Mac. Chapter 6 gives you more information about the Power Mac models.

We recommend that, if you own a Mac SE, SE/30, or Mac II series models (except for the Mac IIvx and IIvi) and want PowerPC capabilities, you buy a Power Mac. The prices are good, and you get a major speed boost in your computing even if you keep using the software you already own.

Install a PowerPC accelerator card

If you own a Mac Quadra or Centris, you can install a PowerPC accelerator card to give your Mac PowerPC speed and performance. Macs upgraded in this manner don't run as fast as genuine Power Macs, but this upgrade is a low-cost way to get true PowerPC computing.

By installing a PowerPC accelerator card, you actually do install a PowerPC processor. Because you also leave the 68040 processor in place, however, you can switch back to using that chip if necessary. (You can easily switch back and forth between the processors by changing a control panel setting and restarting your Mac.) One reason to switch back, for example, would be if your software is not native PowerPC software and it thus runs faster with the 68040 processor. (Keep reading to learn more about native software.)

Installing a PowerPC accelerator card is a good upgrade path for businesses that own many Mac Centrises and Quadras. The upgrade offers a good transition to the PowerPC, because you can protect your investment in old Macs and old software while acquiring new Macs and new software. Essentially, this upgrades enables you to get your feet wet with the PowerPC without totally committing to it.

You can perform this PowerPC upgrade yourself simply by installing the expansion card, or go ahead and have a technician do it for you if you prefer.

To take advantage of the full speed of the Power PC processor, software developers must translate their applications into what's called *native mode*. After the software is thus translated, it gains *native PowerPC status*, which means that it runs at full PowerPC speed. If you own a Power Mac but your software isn't native PowerPC software, you can't attain PowerPC speed with your applications. To take full advantage of the PowerPC, always update your software to native PowerPC versions. If you're not sure which software version you own, check with its developer.

Upgrade the logic board in your current Mac

If you own certain Quadra or Centris Macs, an Apple Workgroup Server, a Mac IIvi, IIvx, or a Performa 600, you can upgrade to the PowerPC by taking out the machine's existing logic board and replacing it with a Power Mac logic board. Logic board upgrades, however, must always be installed by an authorized technician. Sorry — you simply can't do this one yourself. (Unless, of course, you, too, are an authorized Mac technician.)

The Quadra and Centris machines that can accept a logic board upgrade are the Quadra or Centris 610, the Quadra or Centris 660av, the Quadra 650, the Quadra 800, and the Quadra 840av. (Notice that, in dealing with these machines, you can upgrade to the PowerPC in either of two ways: by installing an accelerator card, as described in the preceding section, or by replacing the logic board.)

The new logic board actually transforms your Mac into a genuine Power Macintosh — with exactly the same processor and capabilities as the Power Mac you'd buy if you walked into a computer store and bought a new one off the shelf. Table 14-1 shows you exactly which Macs can become Power Macs via a logic board upgrade. Table 14-2 demonstrates which Apple Workgroup Servers become PowerPC-based Apple Workgroup Servers via the same logic board upgrade.

Table 14-1	Power Mac Logic Board Upgrades
This Mac . . .	*Becomes This Power Mac*
Centris 610, 660av, Quadra 610, 660av	6100
Mac IIvx, IIvi, Performa 600, Centris 650, Quadra 650	7100
Quadra 800, 840av	8100

The Apple Workgroup Servers are Mac Quadras and Power Macs packaged with networking hardware and software. These machines are designed to give high performance as network servers.

Table 14-2	Apple Workgroup Server (AWS) Logic Board Upgrades	
This Apple Workgroup Server . . .	*Becomes This Power PC-Based Apple Workgroup Server*	
AWS 60	AWS 6150	
AWS 80	AWS 8150	
Quadra 900 or 950*	AWS 9150	

*The AWS 95 is not listed here, because that machine cannot upgrade to the PowerPC-based AWS 9150. The AWS 95 runs under the A/UX operating system, which is not compatible with the PowerPC processor.

Speeding up your Power Mac

After you buy your brand-new Power Mac, you may want to make it run even faster than it already does. (We Mac users are just never satisfied, are we?) You can turbo-charge your Power Mac in a couple of ways. These approaches are similar to those we describe earlier in the chapter.

Add cache memory. Plugging a cache memory card into a Power Mac is the fastest, easiest, and cheapest way to push Power Mac speed to the limit. Because the Power Macs contain an expansion slot designed especially for cache memory (known as the *level 2 cache slot*), you can install your speed upgrade in that slot and save the regular expansion slots for other upgrades.

A cache memory card provides a very significant speed improvement — in fact, you can boost the speed of a Power Mac 6100 past the speed of a standard Power Mac 7100 by installing this card. In theory, the larger the amount of cache memory you have, the bigger the speed boost, although even the smallest cache card speeds up your Mac significantly. You can buy Apple-manufactured cache cards, or you can purchase them from companies that manufacture memory for the Mac.

Speed up the processor timing. You can also upgrade your Power Mac by installing a faster processor timing chip that clips onto the original timing chip and bypasses it. You can install these clip-on devices in a Power Mac yourself by following the manufacturer's instructions. Most of these clip-on upgrades include a fan for the processor chip, because the faster speed makes the processor run hotter. (These clip-on devices are different from the ones we told you not to use with the Mac 128K, Mac 512K, and Mac Plus. The ones we talk about here are okay to use.)

This type of speedup, however, definitely voids the Power Mac warranty. But one good thing about this upgrade is that you can easily remove the upgrade hardware without leaving any trace that it was ever clipped on. Being able to easily remove the timing speedup hardware makes returning the device for a refund easy if you have problems with the upgrade.

A Few Final Words on Speeding Up Your Mac and Power Mac

You'll undoubtedly want to speed up your Power Mac even more as time goes by. A good way to learn about new accelerator hardware is to refer to various user groups, Macintosh magazine articles, and on-line services.

A good idea is to let other people try out new products first and discover any problems or glitches. Then you can benefit from their experience.

If you experience any trouble after you install your Mac or Power Mac accelerator hardware, contact the product's manufacturer. So many upgrades with so many different features exist that the manufacturer is usually the one who can give you the best advice about handling problems.

You can find information about adding other upgrades, such as more memory or an internal hard disk, to your Power Mac in Chapters 12 and 18.

The 5th Wave   **By Rich Tennant**

Dang! I told 'em a RISC-based milking machine was one upgrade too many.

Part V
Software Upgrades

"I'm afraid I don't understand all the reports of our upgrade having a delayed release date. Unless... wait a minute — How many people here DIDN'T KNOW I was speaking in dog-months?"

In this part...

What have you done with the diskettes that came with your hardware? Used them as coasters when guests came to dinner? Marked the most bizarre entry in *The Guinness Book of World Records* with them? This part tells you what to do with the software that comes on these diskettes.

We also talk about backing up your hard drive. Not a pleasant task, we agree, but one that is necessary. We provide tips for making this job easier, and we also give some information about what to do if your hard disk crashes.

So find a new bookmark and dive on in.

Chapter 15

Software for Hardware: Faking Out Your Mac

. . . .

In This Chapter

▶ Using the software that comes with upgrade hardware

▶ Faking out your Mac's memory and storage capacity

▶ Installing new system software

. . . .

*Y*ou may have wondered what to do with the diskettes that come with the hardware upgrades you buy. This chapter tells you about the software you get on these diskettes and what to do with it. If you want more Mac memory temporarily or more speed, you may want to try using virtual memory or a RAM disk. Or when a new version of the Mac system comes out, you may want to take advantage of it. This chapter tells you how.

What to Do with the Software That Comes with Hardware

In this section, you find out about the software that comes with your upgrade hardware and what you do with it. This software goes into your System folder.

Just to remind you, here are the parts of the System folder: the System file (also known as the System suitcase), the Finder, control panels, fonts, extensions (also called INITs), and Chooser resources.

When you upgrade your Mac, you change your System folder by adding extensions, control panels, or Chooser resources. These three kinds of system software are sometimes called *driver software,* or *drivers*. This software drives the hardware, so to speak.

Extensions, or INITs

Quite a few hardware upgrades use extensions to allow the new hardware to work correctly with the Mac. The extension lets the Mac know that new hardware is connected and how to work with the addition. Without the extension, the Mac's existing system software doesn't have the resources it needs to use the new hardware.

When you add an accelerator card, for example, the card comes with a diskette containing an extension that enables your Mac to use the card's capabilities. If you didn't install this software, you wouldn't get any benefit from adding the card. All that work installing the card for nothing!

If the hardware you're adding needs an extension, the manufacturer includes the software on a diskette that comes in the product package. Check the manual that comes with your upgrade for information about the extensions you need.

Control panels

Control panels function like extensions. They also allow you to choose whether to use special features of the hardware, and they let you turn the features on or off. With monitors, for example, a control panel allows you to choose the resolution you want to work with on the monitor. And with some accelerator cards, a control panel allows you to turn the acceleration on or off, depending on the work you're doing.

New control panels come on the diskette that accompanies your upgrade hardware. After you install a new control panel, choose Control Panels from the Apple menu.

Chooser resources

You get a new Chooser resource when you connect a new printer or a fax modem (but not a plain vanilla modem) to your Mac. The Chooser enables you to choose which printer, fax modem, or other output hardware you want to use. You find the Chooser under the Apple menu. If your Mac is on a network with file servers or shared Macs, the Chooser also enables you to select whether you want to use a file server, as well as which one you want to use.

What is installer software?

An installer is an application that puts the new system software parts discussed in the preceding section (such as control panels, extensions, and Chooser resources) into your System folder. This software puts the new system parts in the places in the folder where they need to be to make your upgrades work correctly.

Installer software normally comes on the diskette that accompanies your upgrade hardware. If no installer comes with the hardware, you have to copy the extensions, control panels, Chooser resources, or any other accompanying software to the right place in your System folder.

It's nice when you have the installer software to do this copying for you, but you can do the job yourself just fine. Be sure to follow the instructions in the manual that comes with your hardware. The important thing is to make sure each software item is copied into the right place in the System folder.

Memory and Storage Fake Outs

By fooling your Mac, you can use your hard disk as memory and your memory as a storage disk. You're probably asking, "And why would I want to do that?"

By using virtual memory, you can use your hard disk as memory temporarily to gain extra memory to do your work. Take, for example, a situation in which you've got several applications open. Then, when you try to open an additional application, you get a "not enough memory" message. If you turn on virtual memory, you'll be able to open the additional application just fine.

By using a RAM disk, you can get very fast access to stored files. You can also prolong the battery life of your PowerBook by reducing the amount of time the hard disk is active.

Virtual memory

The best use of virtual memory is when you need to work with several applications open at once. When you go to open one more application and get an out of memory message, one thing you can do is turn on virtual memory.

The problem with virtual memory is that it's slower than regular memory. For example, with virtual memory on, your applications open and run slowly, and spelling checking and scrolling through documents take what sometimes seems like hours.

Note: If you use System 7, you have virtual memory built into the system. If you use System 6, you can add a utility, such as Virtual from Connectix, to gain virtual memory capability.

Not only is virtual memory slow, but the more virtual memory you use, the slower your applications run. For example, Frank often visits clients who say, "My friend set me up with 32MB of virtual memory, but why does my computer run so slow?" Well, it's the virtual memory slowing things down. The solution is to add more real memory.

The virtual memory fix really is only temporary because, as we said before, virtual memory can really slow down your work. If you find yourself using virtual memory often, you should upgrade your real memory by adding SIMMs. See Chapter 12 for more information about adding memory SIMMs.

Turning on virtual memory with System 7

To use virtual memory, which is a good temporary solution to out-of-memory problems, you turn it on and set the amount in the Memory control panel. Choose Control Panels under the Apple menu; then open the Memory control panel.

When you turn on virtual memory, you use storage space from your hard disk as memory to run applications. Think carefully about the amount of memory you steal from your hard disk for virtual memory. Creating virtual memory is like robbing Petra to pay Paula.

Figure 15-1 shows the Memory control panel where you turn on virtual memory and set the amount you want to use. The number after Available on disk tells you how much hard disk space you have. But don't use all the space. The number after Available built-in memory tells you how much real physical memory you have. The text After restart has a number in the box. You can leave the number as is, or you can change it.

Note: If your hard disk doesn't have enough storage space to give to virtual memory, you'll see not enough room on disk. You won't be able to turn on virtual memory in this case.

Figure 15-1:
You turn on virtual memory in the Memory control panel.

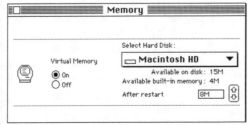

After you turn virtual memory on in the Memory control panel, you have to restart your Mac. So *before* you turn it on, you need to close the files and applications you're working with. Then you can turn on virtual memory and restart your Mac. Virtual memory stays on until you turn it off in the Memory control panel.

RAM disk

If your Mac has a great deal of memory, you can speed up performance by creating a RAM disk. No, this isn't a Frisbee for sheep; it's a way to fool your Mac into thinking that a chunk of memory is actually a storage disk.

The best use for a RAM disk is with the PowerBook. Because a RAM disk limits hard disk use, the PowerBook battery life gets prolonged. If you want to get every ounce of speed possible from your desktop Mac, however, a RAM disk can help you.

Besides tons of extra memory, you usually need special software to create a RAM disk. The exceptions are PowerBooks and some desktop Macs that have built-in RAM disk software. If your machine has built-in RAM disk software, you set up the RAM disk by using the Memory Control panel.

If you have enough memory to create a very large RAM disk, you can copy your entire System folder to the RAM disk, along with your work files and the application you want to use. When a copy of the whole System folder sits on the RAM disk, you switch control of the Mac to this copy by holding the Option key when you start the application from the RAM disk. With this setup, all access to the system software takes place on the RAM disk, increasing Mac speed and eliminating use of the hard disk.

Setting up a RAM disk

Your Mac may not have built-in RAM disk software. You can address this problem by using one of several shareware and commercial applications currently available. One shareware program is RamDisk+. You get it through user groups or from on-line bulletin boards. After you install the RAM disk software, you work with it through a control panel.

To get the maximum benefit of a RAM disk, we recommend that you copy your work files, your System file, your Finder file, and the application you want to use to the RAM disk. Then, by starting the application from the RAM disk, whenever your Mac needs to access the system software, it can use the copy on the RAM disk instead of spinning up the hard disk drive.

The contents of the RAM disk, such as files and applications, disappear when you shut down your Mac. So when you use a RAM disk, you must remember to move any files or programs you've copied to the RAM disk back to your hard disk.

One nice feature of RamDisk+ is the option to automatically copy new or modified files from the RAM disk back to your hard disk when you shut down your Mac. RamDisk+ is shareware and is available from user groups, electronic bulletin boards, and on-line services. To get access to the advanced features of RamDisk+, you must register your copy by sending the $35 shareware fee.

System software upgrades and updates

If you've had your Mac for a while, you probably noticed that Apple changes the system software periodically. You'll find that two kinds of system software changes: upgrades and updates.

System software upgrades are major changes in the system software. For example, the switch from System 6 to System 7 was a major upgrade. Minor upgrades also appear from time to time. These upgrades get labeled with decimal point numbers such as 6.0.8, 7.1, or 7.5. When you install an upgrade, completely replace your old system software.

You also may have noticed system software updates, or "tune ups," which are fixes to problems that need to be taken care of before the next decimal point upgrade comes out. When you install an update, you replace only parts of your system software.

Installing a system software upgrade is a bit different from installing an update. The following sections tell you how you do both of them.

Installing a system software upgrade

A system software upgrade comes on several diskettes. You buy the diskettes from an Apple dealer. The standard installation process adds the new system software to your old system software, which we've found does not ensure that you get clean, trouble-free system software.

So when you do a system software upgrade, we suggest that you do what's known as a *clean install*. This installation process means that you completely replace your old system software with new system software. Here's what you do:

1. De-bless your old System folder. No, we don't mean that you need priestly intervention to install new system software. You can de-bless your software yourself. You do this by opening the System folder and dragging the Finder icon out of the System folder. Don't worry about where you put the Finder icon for now — anywhere outside the System folder will do. Moving the Finder icon indicates to the Mac not to start up from the old System folder

2. Rename the System folder, but don't throw it away yet. Any name besides System Folder is fine. How about George, or Paul — Ringo, maybe? Most people name the folder *System folder.old.* That way they know exactly what it is.

3. Use the new system installer diskettes to install the new System folder on your hard disk. Insert the first installer diskette and double-click the installer application. Follow the instructions that appear on-screen. When you're done, restart your Mac.

4. After the Mac starts up, you'll see the new System folder icon on your hard disk. Now install your fonts, control panels, and extensions in the new System folder. To install these items, just drag their icons over the top of the new System folder icon, and the system will put them in the right places.

   It's best to get fresh copies of your fonts, control panels, and extensions from master diskettes, but if you can't find the diskettes, you can get these items from your old System folder. That's why we told you not to throw it away. (You might also want to look in the System suitcase for any fonts or sounds you use.)

5. Make sure you have all the fonts, control panels, and extensions you need from your old System folder; then throw it away.

Installing a system software update

You can get system software update diskettes from user groups or directly from Apple. You can call Apple at 800-SOS-APPL. Either way, you pay a small fee. When you buy the update, tell the person you talk to what system software version you're currently using so you get the latest update for that version. By the way, you can also find system software updates on electronic bulletin boards and on-line services.

It's important to install these updates, because they contain fixes for bugs and problems in the system software.

All you have to do to install an update is insert the installer diskette and run the installer application. The installer software automatically replaces the outdated parts of your system software with the new parts.

Chapter 16
Back Up, Back Up, Back Up

● ●

In This Chapter

▶ Why you should back up and some backup strategies

▶ Backup software

▶ What to do if your hard disk crashes

▶ Backup tips

● ●

*T*he best way to get up and running quickly if you have Mac hardware problems is to keep backup copies of all your work on hand.

If you have a corrupt file that won't open, open the backup file and start working again. If you can't fix your malfunctioning Mac right away, take your backups to another Mac and work there. If your hard disk crashes and you can't fix it, put your backups on a new hard disk and get right back to work.

The message plain and simple is this: back up your files.

Reasons to Back Up and Backup Strategies

Everybody will tell you to back up, and we know you know you ought to do it, but it really can take a great deal of time and planning. Backing up is easy to put off.

We're here to provide you with some ways to make backing up easier and help you make it part of your regular work routine. We'll give you suggestions, advice, tips, and information about software you can use to back up your documents and programs.

Here's a couple of examples of what can happen if you don't back up. (The names have been changed to protect the innocent — cue Dragnet theme.)

Jack had been keeping his income tax information on his Mac for the past five years. The records included all his monthly expenses and income — in short, all the background data for his tax forms. One day his hard disk crashed, and he lost all his files. Two days later, he received notice from the IRS that he was up for an audit. He knew the IRS would want to see all his records, but he didn't have any backup for his files, and he hadn't made any printouts. Jack was not a happy guy.

The HMB GMBH company was publishing its annual report. Two days before the printing deadline, the computer of the employee preparing the report suffered a hard disk crash. All the text, charts, and graphs for the report were lost. The 150-page document had to be retyped from rough draft printouts, and all the charts and graphs had to be recreated. For several days there was no joy in Mudville, the company's hometown, and no happy campers lined up at the company coffee machine.

Seriously, you have to back up, and look no further than this chapter to find as much information as we can give you to make backing up easy.

Avoiding lost data disasters

The following scenarios illustrate how individuals and companies can back up their files effectively. For more information about the hardware we talk about in these examples, see Chapter 8.

Here's the difference between backup files and archived files. Backup files are files you plan to use again only in case of an emergency. Archived files are stored files that you keep around with the expectation of using again. You store archived files knowing that you will want to access them again at a later date or time.

- ✔ Janet is a writer. She writes two to three chapters of her novel a day. At the end of the day, she copies the file with her new chapters to a diskette for backup. She also keeps a set of diskettes with all her books and outlines on them in a safe deposit box at the bank. Once a week, she adds a diskette with her new work to the set in the safe deposit box. This way, she makes sure that even in the event of a natural disaster like a fire, flood, or earthquake, she always has a copy of her valuable work.

- ✔ Bill is a graphics designer, and his Mac setup has both a hard disk and a removable cartridge drive. At the end of the day, Bill copies the files he's worked on that day to a removable cartridge for backup. This backup system also allows Bill to create an archive of graphics that he can reuse when he works on new designs.

✔ Howard has a PowerBook that he uses as his only computer. (He travels on business most of the time.) In his desk back at the office, he keeps an external hard disk. When he returns from his trips, he makes it a point to plug the hard disk into his PowerBook and transfer the work he has done on the road to the external hard disk. His coworkers used to comment that the lonely hard disk sitting on his desk looked like it needed a home. So he started locking it in a desk drawer when he left the office. He doesn't want to lose his backup system to a coworker's machine.

✔ The Human Resources department in a medium-sized company needed a simple backup system. The department staff purchased a tape backup drive. Now the people in the department each have their own supply of tape cartridges to use to back up their Macs. Each person backs up on a different day of the week and then passes the tape drive to the next person the following day. Everybody keeps his or her own backup cartridges locked in a desk drawer.

✔ The small law firm of Doolittle and Billum has about a dozen Macs linked together on a network with a file server. The file server is attached to a large hard disk on which the lawyers back up their documents each day. If they need to recover any work, they can easily retrieve their files from the server. The only problem with this backup system is that if the server goes down, anyone wanting to access his or her backup files has to wait until the server is up and running again. Once a month, the office administrator backs up the file server on a tape drive. The administrator also keeps archived files on the tape cartridges. If anyone needs a file from the archives, the office administrator retrieves the file.

✔ International Office Machines has set up a very effective automated back-up system for the fifty engineers in the company's research and development department. With the automated system, the engineers don't have to do any backing up themselves. The engineers leave their networked Macs on every night when they leave the office. From 1:00 a.m. to 3:00 a.m., a high-capacity tape drive connected to the department network server automatically backs up all the new files created that day from the engineers' computers. A system administrator archives the tapes. If anybody wants a file from the archives, the administrator supplies it.

We hope these examples give you some ideas about carrying out good backup procedures.

The cost of not backing up

Backing up may seem like an expensive and time-consuming activity. But you have to weigh this cost against the cost of restoring lost work and files. How much time and money would it cost to re-create even one week of your own work? And what if you had no hard copy at all to help your restoration? No matter what work you do — maintaining accounts receivable, monitoring inventory, or designing jet airplanes — backing up is important.

If you lose all the files on your hard disk and have no backup, you have two choices. One choice is to recreate files as best you can from memory, hard copy, or original records. The other choice is to take your hard disk to a data recovery service. These services use expensive, sophisticated equipment to try to recover the files from your hard disk. Recovery is not always successful, and the cost is very high — more than the cost of the hardware for a backup system.

Backup Made Easier with Software

One way to back up your files is to copy them to another storage medium, such as a diskette or a removable cartridge. You simply drag the files from one window to another on the Mac desktop. This method is quick and easy, and you have fast access to your backup files.

But you have to remember to do your backups, and with the Mac system software you have no way to compress the files to take up less space on your backup system. Also, you have to keep track of which files you've updated since your last backup. This stuff is easy when you work with just a few files every day, but when you work with many files, you may need some special software assistance.

We put backup software into three categories: basic backup, normal backup, and remote backup.

Tape cartridge drives require backup software. You can't back up your files onto one of these units with the Mac system software.

Basic backup: An example of basic backup software is HD Back Up, an Apple program that comes with the Macintosh Performas. This software is a very basic, no-frills backup program. It enables you to make a complete backup of your hard disk on diskettes, but not on cartridges or tape. The program is good for backing up your entire hard disk at once, but you can't select specific individual files to back up. The Mac system software works fine for backing up single files.

Normal backup: The application Retrospect is an example of what we call normal backup software. With this program, you can selectively back up the files you have changed since your last backup. This kind of backup is called incremental backup. The program determines which files have changed since your last backup and copies them to your backup hardware.

Retrospect enables you to schedule a time to do regular backups. You set a time, such as daily, weekly, or monthly. When the time comes, the software does the backup. If you're using your Mac at the backup time, the software asks whether you want to back up then or, if not, when you do want to back up. The program also enables you to compress your files so that they take up less room on your backup media, and you can back up on tape drives. In fact, as we said earlier, you can't use a tape drive without backup software such as Retrospect.

Remote backup: An example of remote backup is Retrospect Remote. This program includes the features of Retrospect mentioned previously. In addition, you can leave your Mac on after work hours and the program automatically backs up your files on a networked file server at a designated time. Isn't it nice to know your Mac is working, even when you're not? Now it's time to figure out how to get paid for it.

Preventing and Recovering from Hard Disk Crashes

A hard disk crash is when your hard disk isn't working and doesn't load any files or programs to the Mac — major bummer, huh?

Types of hard disk crashes

Two kinds of hard disk crashes can occur: hardware and software.

Hardware crashes usually mean you have to buy a new hard disk. You can tell you have a hardware problem if you hear weird screeching noises or smell a burning smell, or if the hard disk just doesn't come on at all. This type of hardware crash is not one you can solve yourself; you'll have to call a technician.

Software crashes are usually fixable. The final solution to a software crash is to reformat the hard disk, which means erasing all the files. But people usually don't want to reformat their hard disk because they don't have their files backed up.

An old computer adage says that there are two kinds of computer users: those that have had a hard disk crash and those that are going to have a hard disk crash. Don't feel alone when it happens to you. We've both had crashes, and as Frank says, Macs crash all the time.

Avoiding a hard disk crash

We suggest you do everything you can to avoid a hard disk crash. Here are some ways to do it.

Use hard disk utility software. Disk First Aid is the hard disk utility software that comes with your Mac system software. Other utilities to try are Mac Tools or Norton Utilities. We suggest you get one of these utilities and use it monthly. The utility checks your hard disk for any problems that might be developing, such as file misplacement or corruption, and makes the file repairs necessary to forestall a crash.

You might want to purchase more than one utility; not every piece of software fixes every hard disk file problem. Each program takes a different approach to fixing, which means that not every program fixes every potential problem. For more information about Disk First Aid, see Chapter 1.

One reason to get one of the commercial utilities is that they can also create a special file that contains information about the file structure of your hard disk. With this file, you can restore the files on hard disk much more easily if you have a crash. Disk First Aid doesn't create this file.

If your hard disk crashes, you should . . .

Luckily, the same utilities that you use to prevent a hard disk crash also fix most crashes. You run the utility software to try to fix any problems that the program can find and fix. Because your hard disk may not be running at the crash point, you have to start up your Mac from a diskette or another hard disk that contains the utility program.

The success rate of these programs is usually pretty high, depending on the extent of the problem. Usually, the longer the problem goes undiscovered, the less chance you have of fixing it with the utility. Hopefully, you've been using a utility regularly, as we recommended.

When you use a utility to fix a crash and the program tells you the problem is repaired, run the program again, because sometimes one problem hides another. Keep running the program until it gives you a message indicating that your hard disk has a clean bill of health.

Tips for Backing Up

As we've said before, it's easy to put off doing your backups. Here are some tips that we hope will make the process easier, faster, and more convenient.

- ✔ To make a quick backup of just a couple files, use a diskette.

- ✔ The first time you back up your hard disk, make sure that you execute a complete backup. After that, you can perform incremental backups, which back up only the files you have changed since the last backup. The first backup will take the most time, and the subsequent incremental backups will go faster, depending on how often you back up.

- ✔ Use backup software to compress your files. Compressed files save space on your backup media. They also save money, because you buy fewer backup cartridges, tapes, or diskettes.

- ✔ Be wary of encryption or passwording of backups. A backup for which you don't remember the password is as bad as no backup (thanks to M.S. for this one).

- ✔ If you travel with your PowerBook, keep a compressed version of your System folder on a diskette. This way, if you have problems with your system software, you always have a backup copy that contains your custom settings, control panels, fonts, and so on.

- ✔ Keep a set of backup files in a remote location in case of theft or natural disaster.

- ✔ For the cheapest backup, use a tape drive system, even though file retrieval is slow and inconvenient. For faster, more convenient retrieval, use removable cartridges or an external hard disk. These two backup methods are more expensive than tape, however.

Part VI
Opening Up the Mac and Installing Upgrades

The 5th Wave   By Rich Tennant

BOB WAS ONE OF THE MANY SUFFERERS OF MACINTOSH OBSOLESCENCE SYNDROME

OH GREAT! NOW THE "X3's" BEEN UPGRADED!

In this part...

Now we're to the nitty-gritty. This part tells you step by step how to perform upgrades for your particular Mac. Upgrade your hard disk, add more memory — you'll get hands-on experience in these chapters. But don't worry; just follow our instructions and it shouldn't be too difficult a task. Whether you own a Mac II, a Quadra, a PowerBook, or something in-between, this part gives you the information you need to perform the upgrade like a pro.

Roll up your sleeves, grab a screwdriver, and get going.

Chapter 17

Upgrading and Adding Great Stuff to Your Compact Mac

In This Chapter

▶ Upgrading your compact Mac with more memory, more storage, and expansion cards

▶ Safety procedures for you and your Mac

▶ Practical advice, descriptions of the tools you need, and things to watch out for as you upgrade

▶ Steps for putting your Mac safely back together again

*I*n this chapter, you get to do some hands-on upgrading. As we've said, the Macintosh, generally speaking, is easy to upgrade. The black-and-white compacts involve the most work because of their design. The color compacts, though, are very easy to upgrade. If you're not sure whether your Mac is a compact, refer to Chapter 5.

If you follow all the guidelines and instructions in this chapter, you'll be able to install your upgrade and get your Mac up and running in no time. We stick to the most common and easiest upgrades, use simple tools, and we keep the dismantling of your computer to a minimum.

Attention Mac 128K, 512K, and 512Ke users: As we said in Chapter 5, we don't recommend upgrading these Macs, so you don't find any instructions here. Sorry. If you want to open your computer and take a look inside, follow the steps in the sections "Opening your black-and-white compact" and "Discharging the CRT" in the "Black-and-White Compacts" section.

To close the case, skip to the section "Replacing the back case" at the end of the "Black-and-White Compacts" section, later in this chapter.

As you use this chapter, we suggest that you skip around from section to section, depending on the Mac model or models you want to upgrade and also on the type of upgrade you plan to do. First read the introduction to this chapter, and then read the sections "Black-and-White Compacts" or "Macintosh Color Compacts," depending on which Mac you have.

After you're in the right section, either black-and-white or color, you see that the information about opening the compacts and the safety instructions come first. The steps for opening up the computers are the same for all the compact models in the section, so you can use this information no matter which compact you have.

Then go farther in the chapter and find your particular Mac, such as the SE, Mac Classic, Color Classic, or LC 500 series Mac. Follow the steps for the upgrade or upgrades you want to do. You have your choice of three or four upgrades, such as installing a new internal hard disk, adding memory, or adding an expansion card. You can do all the upgrades at one time or do one and come back later for more.

Finally, after you install the upgrade, skip to the part about closing your Mac, at the end of the chapter, to finish the process.

To keep you and your Mac safe, remember to follow all the safety guidelines described in this chapter, and be sure to review the electrostatic-discharge prevention guidelines in Chapter 3.

Black-and-White Compacts

Chapter 5 gives you information about the black-and-white compacts, but in case you've forgotten, here are the models we talk about: 128K, 512K, 512Ke, Mac Plus, Mac SE, Mac SE/30, Mac Classic, Mac Classic II, and Performa 200.

In this section, we tell you how to open all these computers and how to close them again. And for all except the 128K, 512K, and 512Ke Macs, we tell you how to make your upgrades.

Important safety information you have to read

We have to get serious here. The compact Macs are unique in that their display screen is built into the computer. When you open the case, *you expose yourself to high-voltage components that can hold a charge even after the Mac is unplugged.* Read that last sentence again, please.

Opening a compact Mac is as serious as opening the back of your TV set. Because you face the potential for serious injury or worse (if you catch our drift), please follow some basic safety procedures (if you follow these procedures every time you open a compact Mac, you stand little chance of hurting yourself or your Mac):

1. **Always switch off the Mac and unplug it from the wall before you open the case.**

2. **Always wear safety glasses while you work inside a compact Mac.**

3. **Be extra careful when you work around the CRT (or picture tube).**

   If it's cracked or broken, the CRT can implode and shower the surrounding area with bits of broken glass. Now you see the reason for the glasses mentioned in Step 2. The narrow part at the back of the CRT, called the *neck,* is the most delicate area, so be especially careful there.

4. **Always discharge the CRT every time you open your Mac to eliminate the chance of getting a high-voltage electrical shock.**

   See the section "Discharging the CRT" later in this chapter.

If working around high-voltage components makes you nervous, take your Mac to a technician for upgrading. Better to let a trained professional take the risks for you.

Opening your black-and-white compact

You have to start at the beginning, of course, by opening the Mac. All the black-and-white compacts open the same way, so follow these instructions no matter which model or models you upgrade.

Tools you need:

- Safety glasses

- A Torx number 8 screwdriver with a 10-inch shaft (available at larger hardware stores)

- Either a Pony spring clamp or what people call a *Mac case cracker* (check the hardware store again)

- An egg carton to hold loose screws

- A flat-blade screwdriver with an insulated wood, plastic, or rubber handle

- A short piece of wire, about a foot long, with alligator clips on each end. Thicker wire is best. You use this wire and the clips for discharging the CRT. You can buy a wire with alligator clips attached to it at electronics stores, such as Radio Shack.

Things to watch out for: When you separate the back case from the front, be careful not to damage the case.

1. **Remove the reset/interrupt switch.**

   If you're working on a Classic, Classic II, or Performa 200, skip to the next step, because you cannot remove the reset/interrupt switch from your Mac.

   On the other compacts, the reset/interrupt switch is located toward the back on the lower-left side, as you face the front of your computer. Figure 17-1 shows the switch.

   If you own a Mac Plus, gently pry off the switch with a small, flat-blade screwdriver. For a Mac SE or SE/30, pull the bottom of the switch loose with your fingers and pull it away from the Mac. Unfortunately, if you don't remove this switch, the case doesn't open.

   This switch is also called the *programmer's switch* because of the rather naive assumption that only programmers use it. People restart their computer with the switch when a program *crashes,* or stops running, usually in the middle of the most important project on their to-do list. We all know that everybody's Mac crashes, not just programmers'.

   Your Mac may not have one of these switches — it was packaged loose in your Mac's original box, and you may or may not have installed it.

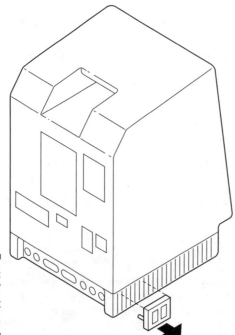

Figure 17-1:
The reset/
interrupt
switch.

2. **Lay your Mac screen on a soft surface, such as a folded towel or foam pad, and then loosen the four Torx screws on the back of the case (see Figure 17-2).**

   After you loosen the screws, you can leave them in place to keep track of them, as long as you don't turn over the back case. Or remove the screws and place them in your egg carton for safekeeping. If you decide to look at the signatures inside, remove the screws and turn the case over.

   The Mac Plus has a fifth screw, located under the battery-compartment door. The most common mistake when you open a Mac Plus is to forget this screw and then wonder why the case doesn't open.

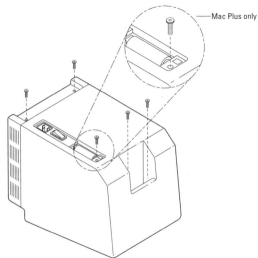

Mac Plus only

Figure 17-2:
The screw locations on the back case.

3. **Separate the back case from the front, known to some people as the *front bezel*.**

   Use the Pony spring clamp or the case cracker for this step. Insert the cracker or Pony clamp into the seam between the two sides of the case and gently pry the sides apart. Even though we use the word *pry,* do this step slowly and carefully. Work your way around the case a little at a time rather than try to pop open the case, which just gouges out chunks of the case.

   Here's a shortcut if you're upgrading a Mac Plus, Mac SE, or Mac SE/30. Remove all the screws except the ones inside the computer handle. Then unscrew the screws almost all the way. Use the Torx screwdriver to push down on a screw while you pull up on the computer handle. The case should pull apart. Then finish loosening the screws in the handle and lift the back case straight off.

Be careful not to push down too hard on the screws in the handle or else you'll strip the screw threading.

4. **Lift the back case straight up from and off the rest of the Mac.**

Be careful to avoid touching the exposed CRT.

5. **Remove the metal shield that covers the external connectors on the back of your computer.**

If you're working on a Classic, Classic II, or Performa 200, skip to the next section, which tells you how to discharge the CRT. You don't have to do this step.

The metal shield may stick inside the back case. It's important to pull it out so that you can replace it correctly when you close the case. An illustration of the inside of a compact Mac is shown in Figure 17-3.

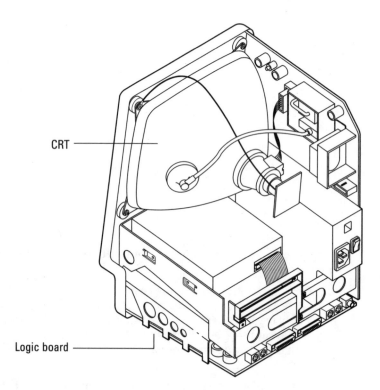

Figure 17-3:
The inside of a compact Mac.

CRT

Logic board

Discharging the CRT

Discharging the CRT continues the process of opening the Mac. Discharge the CRT as soon you remove the back cover. Don't wait. Plan your work, in fact, so that you carry out the process of opening the Mac and discharging the CRT in one complete action.

1. **Take the wire with the alligator clips and attach one clip to the metal shaft of the flat-blade screwdriver.**

   Now you're ready to discharge the CRT. Figure 17-4 shows the wire and alligator clips you use for discharging.

Figure 17-4:
Wire attached to the flat-blade screwdriver with alligator clips.

Flat-blade screwdriver with insulated handle

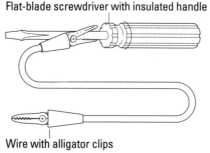

Wire with alligator clips

2. **Take off any metal jewelry, watches, or grounding wrist strap you're wearing.**

   You don't want to wear anything that might attract or conduct an electrical charge.

3. **On the upper corner of the CRT, attach the free alligator clip to the screw with a black wire attached.**

   You must attach the clip to the screw with the black wire attached to keep from frying your computer when you discharge the CRT. Figure 17-5 shows exactly where to attach the alligator clip.

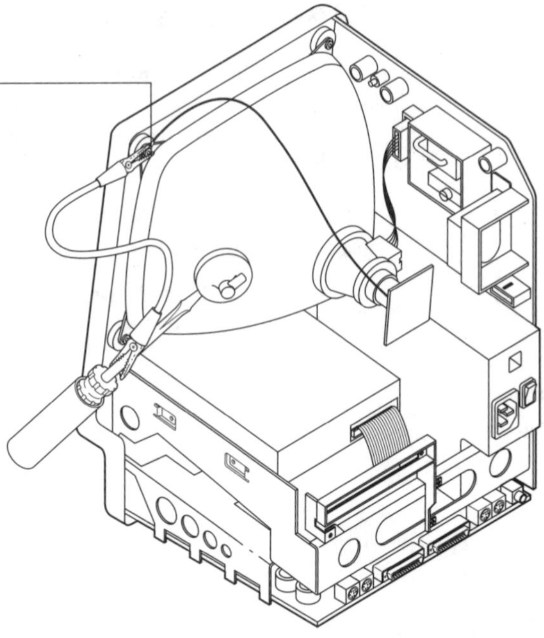

Corner Screw with wire attached

Figure 17-5:
Proper
placement
of the
alligator
clip on the
corner of
the CRT.

4. **Put one hand in your back pocket, pick up the screwdriver, and say a little prayer to the gods of high voltage.**

   Your hand goes in your back pocket because you want to make sure that the electricity moves through the wire and discharge tool, not through the discharge tool and out through your other hand that you unknowingly placed on a metal radiator or other grounding metal. This action is known as *frying yourself* (as opposed to frying your computer).

5. **Carefully place the blade of the screwdriver against the CRT next to the anode cap.**

   The anode cap looks like a suction cup with a big, red wire coming out of it.

6. **Carefully slide the screwdriver blade under the suction cup until the blade makes contact with the metal bits underneath the cup.**

   Make sure that you make contact with the metal parts under the cap. You may be rewarded with a small, popping sound as the CRT discharges. Most of the time, there isn't any noise, but if you touch the metal under there, the CRT discharges. Figure 17-6 shows the anode cap and where you place the screwdriver.

7. **Carefully slide the screwdriver blade out from under the suction cup, remove your hand from your back pocket, and detach the alligator clip from the screw with the black wire attached.**

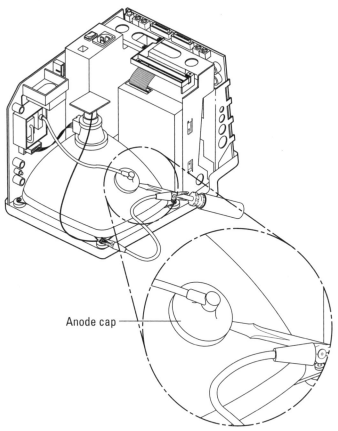

Figure 17-6:
The anode
cap and
where you
place the
screwdriver.

Anode cap

Congratulations! You have just discharged the CRT (with a rather nonchalant air and one hand in your back pocket!). With that behind you, it's time to get down to the real work of installing an upgrade or two.

You must discharge the CRT every time you open your black-and-white compact Mac.

Adding memory to your Mac Plus

Adding memory is the only Mac Plus upgrade we discuss here. Installing Mac Plus memory is really quite easy, because you simply snap a small circuit board, called a *SIMM,* into place on the computer's logic board.

Macintosh memory banks

SIMM stands for *single* *in*-line *memory module*. To put it simply, a SIMM is a circuit board with memory chips on it, and a *SIMM slot* is the connector the SIMMs plug into on the logic board.

Yes, your Macintosh has memory banks, just like every sci-fi computer ever invented. The memory banks contain four slots in which you put the SIMMs that hold the memory chips. The two back slots comprise bank A, and the two front slots comprise bank B. Sometimes installing memory (or money) in one bank or the other makes a difference, and sometimes it doesn't. We tell you when it matters and what to do about it.

Another point about SIMMs and banks is that the two SIMMs that go into a bank must match in size and speed. For more information about memory, see Chapter 12.

The standard memory configuration for a Mac Plus is 1MB. Increasing from 1MB, your upgrade possibilities are 2.5MB or 4MB. We highly recommend going directly to the 4MB maximum.

As you add memory to your Mac Plus, be sure to follow the electrostatic-discharge prevention guidelines described in Chapter 3 when you work inside your Mac.

Tools you need:

✔ A small putty knife, one to two inches wide

✔ A flat-blade screwdriver

✔ A ballpoint pen or small screwdriver to remove old SIMMs

✔ A wire cutter meant for electronics that cuts from the tip

Things to watch out for: Be careful when you work around the CRT. Keep in mind that its thinnest and most fragile points are at the neck and at the tip.

1. **Open the case and discharge the CRT.**

   For instructions, see the sections "Opening your black-and-white compact" and "Discharging the CRT," in this chapter. Figure 17-7 shows what the Mac Plus looks like after it's open. Notice the logic board and the diskette drive.

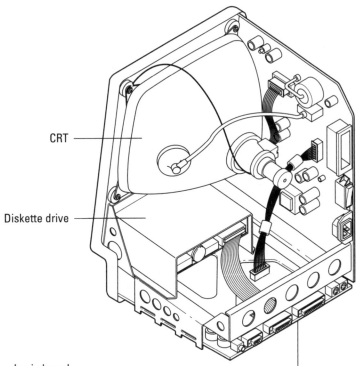

CRT

Diskette drive

Figure 17-7:
The inside of
a Mac Plus.

Logic board

2. Put on your grounding wrist strap.

See Chapter 3 for electrostatic-discharge prevention procedures and
information about the wrist strap.

3. Disconnect the disk drive cable.

The diskette drive cable keeps the logic board trapped in the chassis. You
must disconnect the diskette drive cable so that you can remove the logic
board. Figure 17-8 shows the diskette drive cable and the logic board cable
you disconnect in Step 4.

The diskette drive cable is a flat, gray cable with lots of wires inside. The
cable connects to the edge of the logic board, on which all the external
connectors are located.

Pull on the cable's plug, *not* on the cable, and wiggle it loose. After you
disconnect the cable, bend it back out of the way. OK, that's done.

4. Disconnect the logic board cable.

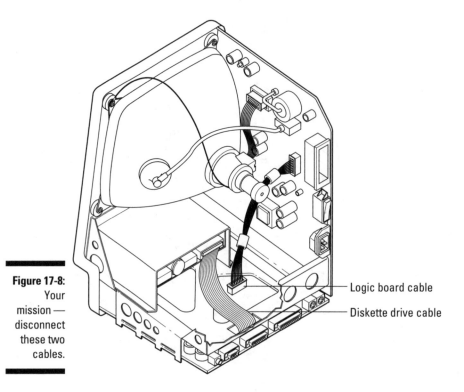

Figure 17-8:
Your
mission —
disconnect
these two
cables.

Logic board cable

Diskette drive cable

Like the diskette drive cable, the logic board cable also helps to trap the logic board in the chassis, so you must disconnect the cable. You can recognize this cable because it looks like a bundle of multicolored wires that plugs into a connector near the middle of the logic board (refer to Figure 17-8).

The logic board cable may want to stay connected, which makes pulling on it a little tough, so be careful that when the cable comes loose, your hand doesn't fly back and hit the CRT neck. ("Drat — it's that CRT thing again!")

Potential problem: The plug on the logic board cable stays in the connector because of a plastic tab along the bottom edge. The tab snaps over a little ledge on the plug and does a good job of trying to stop you from disconnecting the cable. *Solution:* Use the putty knife to keep the tab pushed away from the plug as you pull the plug free. This tab is really stiff. If necessary, use a flat-blade screwdriver on top of the putty knife for extra leverage. Be careful not to scratch the logic board with either tool. Figure 17-9 shows you how to use these tools.

When the plug is free, pull the logic board cable back out of the way.

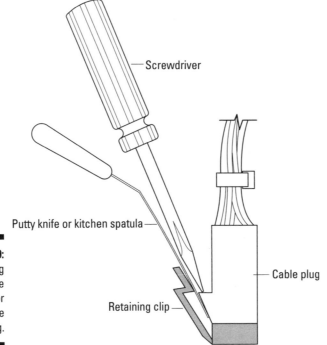

Screwdriver

Putty knife or kitchen spatula

Cable plug

Retaining clip

Figure 17-9:
Releasing
the
connector
tab from the
cable plug.

5. **Remove the logic board so that you can reach the SIMM slots to install the memory SIMMs.**

   The logic board slides out of the chassis along the rails on either side. As you pull up, pull back on the top corners of the logic board to free the metal side tabs from their slots.

   After the logic board comes out of the chassis, set the logic board on a grounded, nonconductive surface.

6. **Remove the 256K SIMMs currently in the banks.**

   You must remove some of the SIMMs already installed in your Mac Plus so that you can put in new ones. For more information, refer to the sidebar "Background information about adding Mac Plus memory."

   If you are upgrading to 4MB from 2.5MB, remove only the back two SIMMs. If you are upgrading to 4MB from 1MB, remove all four SIMMs. Figure 17-10 shows the memory banks, the home for your SIMMs.

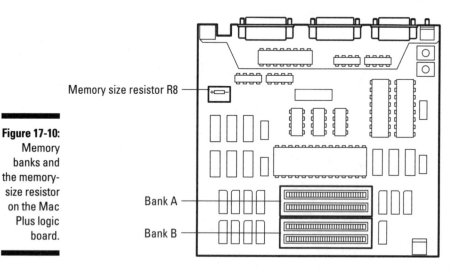

Memory size resistor R8

Bank A

Bank B

Figure 17-10:
Memory
banks and
the memory-
size resistor
on the Mac
Plus logic
board.

7. Install the new SIMMs.

To install 2.5MB, install the two 1MB SIMMs in the two back slots (bank A) and two of the 256K SIMMs in the two front slots (bank B).

To install 4MB, install four 1MB SIMMs, one in each slot. It doesn't matter whether you put them in bank A or bank B. Easy as pie.

Check that the two back SIMMs match in size and speed and that the front two SIMMs also match in size and speed. See Chapter 12 for more information about SIMMs.

8. Use the wire cutters to cut the wire on only one side of the memory-size resistor labeled R8.

This step lets the Mac know how much memory you install.

To set up the Mac to use the new, installed memory, you cut the memory-size resistor labeled R8 on the logic board. The resistor is located on the left side of the logic board, up toward the top. Before you cut, take a good look at Figure 17-11. To misquote an old saying, "Check twice, cut once." In other words, check again that the resistor you cut is labeled R8.

When 1MB of memory is on the board, the resistor is connected. Unless you or someone else has already upgraded your Mac Plus, the resistor is probably connected.

For 2.5MB or 4MB upgrades, you disconnect the resistor. All you have to do is cut the wire on one side of the resistor and bend it out of the way.

Be sure to bend the resistor wire back so that it doesn't reconnect or touch other parts of the board.

The operation's a success: with a simple snip on the resistor, your Mac gains the full use of its new memory. Good work!

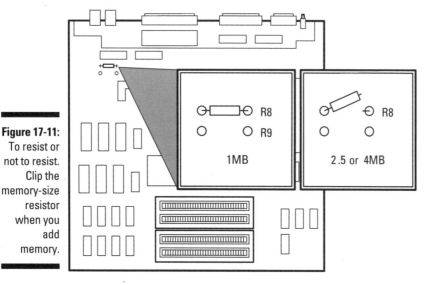

Figure 17-11:
To resist or
not to resist.
Clip the
memory-size
resistor
when you
add
memory.

Background information about adding Mac Plus memory

Before you add memory, you must know how much memory your Mac Plus contains; refer to Chapter 12 for information.

Three basic memory configurations exist for the Mac Plus: 1MB, 2.5MB, and 4MB.

One megabyte is the standard memory amount the Mac Plus contains when it's shipped from the factory. Your Mac Plus probably has this memory configuration unless you or someone else has upgraded it already.

For 1MB, 256K (¼MB) SIMMs go in all four SIMM slots. That's a total of four 256K SIMMs, with one SIMM in each slot.

For 2.5MB, use two 1MB SIMMs in the two back slots and two 256K SIMMs in the two front slots.

For 4MB, fill all four slots with 1MB SIMMs. That's a total of four 1MB SIMMs, with one SIMM in each slot.

Again, we recommend upgrading to the full 4MB. As we've said, you can never have too much memory, and you might as well do this upgrade just one time.

Putting the Mac Plus back together

It's time to put your Mac Plus back together so that you can start working with the new memory.

Tools you need: Safety glasses; Torx number 8 screwdriver with a 10-inch shaft

Things to watch out for: Remember to keep your grounding wrist strap on until your Mac is back in one piece. As always, be careful around the CRT. Also remember to reconnect all the cables or else you will have to open the Mac and discharge the CRT again to connect them. ("Not that again!")

1. **Replace the logic board.**

   The logic board slides down on the rails on either side of the chassis on which you slid it out. Slide it back into place and make sure that the metal tabs on either side engage in their slots in the chassis.

2. **Reconnect the logic board and the diskette drive cables to their connectors.**

   First reconnect the logic board cable to its connector and make sure to support the logic board from the opposite side so that it doesn't flex too much. Then reconnect the diskette drive cable. Refer to Figure 19-7 if you want help finding the cable connectors.

3. **Close your Mac Plus.**

   Close your computer by following the steps in the section "Replacing the back case," at the end of the "Black-and-White Compacts" section, later in this chapter.

Congratulations on your successful journey to the center of the Mac Plus! Your Mac should now start up normally with more memory. If you have any problems, refer to Chapter 12.

Upgrading the Mac SE and SE/30

The Mac SE and SE/30 both contain one expansion slot, which makes these Macs the most flexible of the black-and-white screen compacts for upgrading. The case and chassis for the SE and SE/30 are almost identical, so we treat them as one computer much of the time. We let you know where these computers are different and what to do about it.

Installing or upgrading an internal hard disk in the SE or SE/30

This section tells you how to install an internal hard disk in an SE or SE/30. All SEs contain one diskette drive and either a second diskette drive or a hard disk drive. Because of the size of the SE's insides, you must take out the existing upper diskette drive or remove the existing hard disk drive to make room for the upgrade. If you take out an existing hard disk, be sure to back up all your data first.

Tools you need:

- ✔ A magnetic, number 2 Phillips screwdriver
- ✔ Needle-nose pliers (where do they get these tool names?)
- ✔ A small, flat-blade screwdriver

Things to watch out for: While you're upgrading, you might have the bad luck to drop a screw or something into the heart of your Mac. With the magnetic screwdriver, you minimize your chances of doing this and then having to completely disassemble your computer just to fish out the screw. Hopefully, you can reach the screw with the tip of the magnetic screwdriver and pull the little guy out by way of the magic of magnetism.

We're sure that you have learned not to keep magnets around your computer, your hard drive, or your diskettes. A simple little magnet can wipe out all the data on your diskettes or on your hard drive. And now we're telling you to use a magnetic screwdriver. What gives? Using the magnetic screwdriver for these upgrades is OK. You don't want to set the screwdriver down on either your new hard disk or the existing one if you're taking it out, but removing and replacing the screws doesn't hurt either the drive or any data.

1. **Remove the back case and discharge the CRT.**

   See the sections "Opening your black-and-white compact" and "Discharging the CRT" for details.

2. **Put on your grounding wrist strap.**

   See Chapter 3 for electrostatic-discharge procedures and for information about the grounding wrist strap.

3. **Carefully detach the video card from the end of the CRT.**

   The video card attaches to the glass tip of the CRT where the CRT is the thinnest. Remove the card by carefully pulling it straight back from the CRT. You can leave it dangling — there's no need to disconnect the wires.

Be sure to remove the card before you continue. It's easy to knock into this video card and break off the tip of the CRT, causing the tube to suddenly de-vacuum (this is also what your carpet does when you don't clean it for a couple weeks) and possibly implode. That's $75 for a new CRT, to say nothing about shattered glass everywhere! Even after the video card is detached, be extra careful around the glass tip of the CRT.

4. Remove the three screws that hold the chassis bracket in place and set aside the screws and bracket.

It's easier to work inside the SE and SE/30 if you first remove the chassis bracket from the back of the chassis. Removing the bracket gives you much better access to all the cables inside and to the diskette drive and hard drive. Figure 17-12 shows the location of the chassis and the screws.

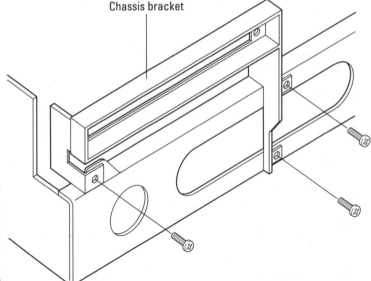

Chassis bracket

Figure 17-12:
The chassis bracket and screw locations.

5. Disconnect the cables from the existing drive.

If you are removing an existing diskette drive, disconnect only one cable. Pull the plug out of the connector on the drive and then disconnect the cable from the logic board.

If you're removing an existing hard disk, you must disconnect two cables: the wide, gray ribbon cable; and the multicolored power cable. Figure 17-13 shows the cables for the diskette drive and the hard disk.

First disconnect the wide, gray ribbon cable from the back of the hard disk. Then disconnect the cable from its connector on the logic board and set the cable aside.

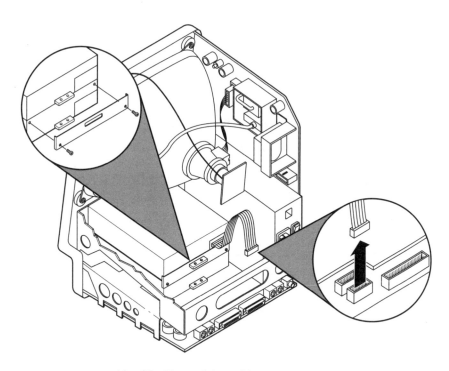

Mac SE with two diskette drives

Hard disk power cable

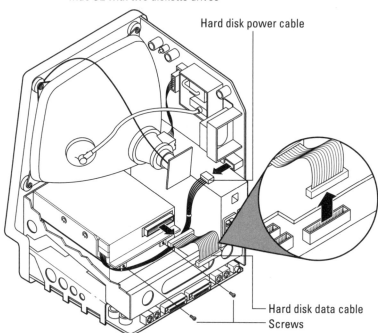

Figure 17-13:
Cable and
screw
locations on
the SE and
SE/30.

Hard disk data cable
Screws

Mac SE/30 with hard disk and diskette drive

Next, trace the multicolored power cable to its connector on the analog board and disconnect the cable there. You have to squeeze the retaining clip on the power cable plug to disconnect it. Depending on the model of the hard disk mechanism, it may be difficult to remove this cable from the hard disk, so leave it in place for now. It won't cause any trouble — we promise.

6. Remove the two mounting screws.

If you are removing a diskette drive, you also must remove the U-shaped metal bracket that holds the upper diskette drive in place. Refer to Figure 17-13 to see where the two mounting screws are located.

7. Lift up on the drive and slide it out of the SE or SE/30.

8. Prepare the new hard disk for installation.

Preparing the hard disk sounds a little daunting. All we mean is to connect some cables and attach something called a *carrier bracket* outside the SE or SE/30 before you get constricted by the small space inside your computer. Don't worry — we walk you through these steps.

Your new hard disk should come with a mounting kit that includes a carrier bracket; a wide, flat data cable; a multicolored power cable; and some screws. For more information about mounting kits, see Chapter 12.

Connect the data cable and the multicolored power cable to the hard disk mechanism. It's easier in most cases to attach these cables before you attach the drive to the carrier bracket.

Attach the carrier bracket to the hard disk. Carrier brackets come in all shapes and sizes, although every bracket has two metal tabs on both ends. The tabs with holes in them that have been bent down should go on the same end of the drive mechanism as the power cable and data cable.

If you're replacing the upper diskette drive with a hard disk, your mounting kit should include a plastic strip to cover the now-empty diskette drive opening in the front of your SE or SE/30, just below the screen.

The plastic strip does a surprising number of things after you install it. It keeps an empty opening from staring at you as you work at your computer, keeps dust from entering your Mac, and keeps you from trying to insert a diskette into an empty space. Go ahead and install that insert now.

9. Install the new hard disk in the SE or SE/30.

Two metal tabs on the front of the carrier bracket fit into two slots on top of the lower diskette drive. You have to slide the hard disk in with the back end lifted at an angle. Then engage these tabs in the slots and push the hard disk into place.

Depending on the hard disk you purchase, you may receive a drive light that lights up when you're working at your Mac to show you that your hard disk is operating. Connect the cable from the light as you complete this step. See the literature accompanying the hard disk for specifics.

You may not have to deal with the drive light at all. Some hard disks come with software that puts a display on your Mac's screen, rather than an actual light, to show that the hard disk is operating. Again, refer to the literature that comes with your new hard disk for details.

10. **Install the two mounting screws in the same place from which you removed them earlier.**

    These mounting screws secure the two metal tabs on the back of the carrier bracket to the lower diskette drive. Figure 17-13 shows you these screws.

11. **Connect the power and data cables.**

    Make sure that the power cable and data cable connect to both the hard disk and their connectors on the logic board and the analog board.

The wide, gray data cable connects to the logic board, and the multicolored power cable connects to the analog board. The cables are keyed so that they fit in the connectors in only one way. Refer to Figure 17-13 for the cable connector locations.

Finally, if you're wondering what to do with the drive you have just removed, see Chapter 12 for suggestions. If you're finished with your upgrade, skip ahead to the section "Putting your SE and SE/30 back together."

Getting ready to add memory to a Mac SE or SE/30

To add memory to an SE or SE/30, you remove the logic board. Before you can remove the logic board, you must get some cables out of the way. Don't worry — it's not as bad as it sounds. Just follow the steps we describe.

Removing the logic board is the same for both the SE and the SE/30. After you take the board out, skip ahead to either the "Adding memory to a Mac SE" section or the "Adding memory to a Mac SE/30" section, depending on which computer you're upgrading.

Tools you need: Just your hands

Things to watch out for: Be careful when you work around the CRT, especially at the neck and the very end.

1. **Remove the back case and discharge the CRT.**

    See the sections "Opening your black-and-white compact" and "Discharging the CRT" for details.

2. Put on your grounding wrist strap.

Again, see Chapter 3 for electrostatic-discharge procedures and for information about the grounding wrist strap.

3. Carefully detach the video card from the end of the CRT.

The video card attaches to the glass end of the CRT, where the CRT is the thinnest. Remove the card by carefully pulling it straight back from the CRT. You can leave it dangling — there's no need to disconnect the wires.

Be sure to remove the card before you continue. It is easy to knock into this video card and break off the tip of the CRT, causing the tube to suddenly de-vacuum (we sure wouldn't want to see that happen to our carpets) and possibly implode. That's $75 for a new CRT, to say nothing about shattered glass everywhere! Even after the video card is detached, be extra careful around the glass tip of the CRT.

4. Remove the three screws that hold the chassis bracket in place and set aside the screws and bracket.

It's easier to work inside the SE or SE/30 if you first remove the chassis bracket at the back of the chassis. Removing the bracket gives you much better access to all the cables inside and to the diskette drive and hard drive. Figure 17-14 shows the location of the chassis bracket and the screws.

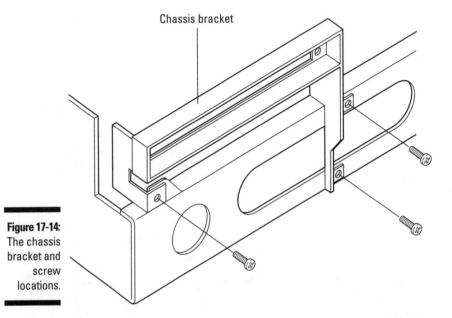

Chassis bracket

Figure 17-14:
The chassis bracket and screw locations.

5. Disconnect the hard disk cable from the logic board if your SE or SE/30 has a hard disk.

The hard disk cable is a wide ribbon cable that connects near the top edge of the logic board. Figure 17-15 shows its location. If no hard disk is installed, skip to Step 6.

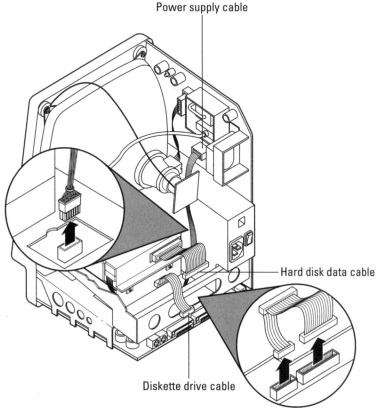

Power supply cable

Hard disk data cable

Diskette drive cable

Figure 17-15:
Disconnect these three cables before you remove the logic board.

6. Disconnect the diskette drive cable (or cables, if your SE or SE/30 has two diskette drives).

The diskette drive cable is a small ribbon cable that connects to one of two connectors beside the hard disk cable connector. Figure 17-15 shows the location. If you have two diskette drives, disconnect the two cables.

7. Disconnect the power supply cable.

The power supply cable connects to the center of the logic board. The cable really is a bundle of multicolored wires, so you can recognize it pretty easily. To remove this cable, you must squeeze the end of the retaining clip as you pull on the connector. Figure 17-16 gives you an idea about how this process works.

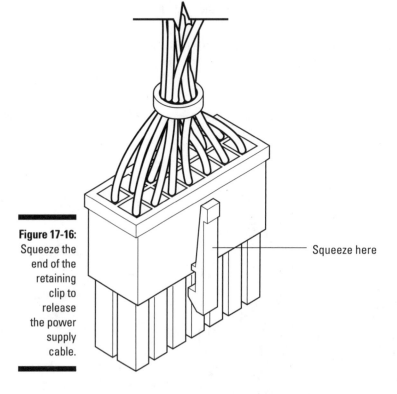

Squeeze here

Figure 17-16:
Squeeze the
end of the
retaining
clip to
release
the power
supply
cable.

When you remove the cables, especially the power supply cable, be careful not to hit the neck of the CRT when the cables pop loose. The connectors tend to give a great deal of resistance as you pull on the plug. After the cable comes loose, your hand can jerk back and hit the CRT neck. Work the cable loose slowly, by wiggling its plug from side to side. Avoid smacking that CRT.

8. Remove the logic board from the chassis.

Slide the logic board up along the rails on the sides of the chassis until the tabs on the right side of the board line up with the notches on the right-hand rail.

When the board's tabs (the ones on the right side) line up with the chassis notches, swing the right side of the logic board out toward yourself.

9. Disconnect the speaker cable from the logic board.

You'll find the speaker cable connector next to the power supply cable connector, near the middle of the logic board. Figure 17-17 shows the location.

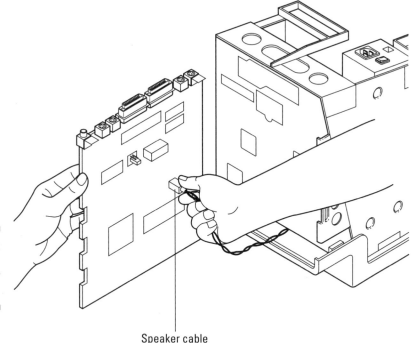

Figure 17-17:
Disconnecting
the speaker
cable.

Speaker cable

10. Remove the board and place it on your grounded work area.

Refer to Chapter 3 for information about creating a safe, grounded work area.

Now you have the logic board out and you're ready to add memory. Go directly to the next section if you want to add memory to an SE. Skip to the section "Adding memory to a Mac SE/30" if you are working with that computer.

Adding memory to a Mac SE

After the logic board is out of the SE or SE/30, adding memory requires different steps, depending on your computer. We describe the steps for adding memory to an SE here. If you are working with an SE/30, skip to the section "Adding memory to a Mac SE/30."

You work with SIMMs for this memory upgrade. For information about SIMMs and memory, refer to Chapter 12.

Upgrade the SE memory to its maximum of 4MB.

Tools you need: A ballpoint pen or a SIMM removal tool to remove old SIMMs; wire cutters meant for electronics that cut from the tip (depending on your logic board; read more to see whether you need this item)

Things to watch out for: The plastic tabs on SIMM sockets are delicate, so be extremely careful with them.

Take a look at your SE logic board. The side with all the components and connectors should face up. The edge with the external connectors faces away from you.

Two different types of SE logic boards exist. One type has a resistor with a box drawn around it that says "RAM size" behind the SIMM sockets on the left. This SE logic board is the resistor type. Figure 17-18 shows the two types of logic boards.

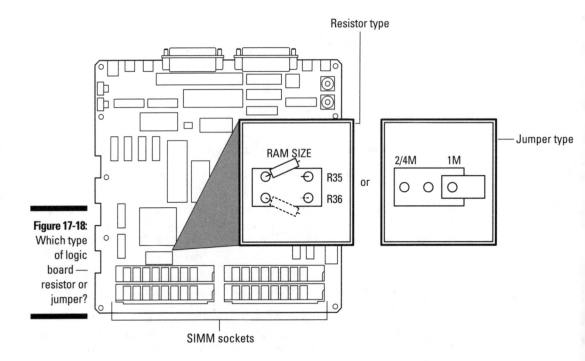

Figure 17-18: Which type of logic board — resistor or jumper?

SIMM sockets

The other logic board has a set of three jumper pins with a tiny, black, plastic block at the same location. This logic board is known as the *jumper logic board*. This type of sensible naming scheme is seldom seen in computer products, as we're sure you have noticed.

You must know whether your logic board is the resistor type or the jumper type when you upgrade to 2.5MB. Depending on which logic board you have, the two 1MB SIMMs go either in the two back slots or in the two front slots.

1. **Remove the existing SIMMs from the sockets.**

2. **Install the new SIMMs.**

   When you finish installing the new SIMMs, all the slots will be full.

   If you are installing 2.5MB and have a *resistor* type logic board, put the two 1MB SIMMs in the two back slots and the two 256K SIMMs in the two front slots.

   If you are installing 2.5MB and have a *jumper* type logic board, put the two 256K SIMMs in the two back slots and the two 1MB SIMMs in the two front slots.

   If you are installing 4MB, fill all four slots with 1MB SIMMs, no matter which type of logic board you have.

   Check that the two back SIMMs match in size and speed and that the front two also match in size and speed. See Chapter 12 for more information about SIMM size and speed.

3. **Disconnect the resistor or jumper.**

   When you upgrade to 2.5MB or 4MB, you must disconnect the resistor or jumper. The resistor or jumper stays connected only when 1MB of memory lives on the logic board.

   If you have the jumper-type logic board, disconnect the jumper, remove the tiny plastic block and push it down over just one of the pins on either end of the row.

   If you have the resistor-type logic board, cut the wire that connects the resistor to the logic board, using the wire cutters we mentioned at the beginning of this section. Cut the wire on one side of the resistor and bend the resistor out a little so that it doesn't reconnect or touch any other components.

When you disconnect the resistor, cut the wire on only one side and bend it out of the way. That way, if you ever want to "downgrade" your computer back to 1MB, you can find the resistor there and not have to look for another one to solder on.

With the jumper type logic board, when you remove the jumper, push it onto one of the edge pins so that if you need it in the future, it's right there.

You have just added memory to your SE. Good work! If this is the only upgrade you're doing, jump ahead to the section "Putting your Mac SE and SE/30 back together" for instructions on reassembling your computer.

If you want to install an expansion card or an internal hard disk, skip to the appropriate section in this chapter.

Adding memory to a Mac SE/30

The SE/30 logic board is much different from the SE logic board, so the process of adding memory is different. The reason the logic board is different is that the SE descends from the Mac Plus, and the SE/30 descends from the Macintosh IIcx. A more powerful computer genealogy, to say the least.

You have no need to worry about memory limitations on this baby. Using 16M SIMMs, the SE/30 occupies as much as a whopping 128MB of memory on the logic board. Wow.

You work with SIMMs for this memory upgrade. For information about SIMMs and memory, refer to Chapter 12.

Tools you need: A ballpoint pen or a SIMM removal tool to remove old SIMMs

Things to watch out for: The plastic tabs on the SIMM sockets are delicate, so be extremely careful with them.

1. **Remove the existing SIMMs from the sockets.**

   Figure 17-19 shows where the SIMMs are located in the memory banks.

2. **Install the new SIMMs.**

The following list gives you the guidelines for adding memory to the SE/30:

- ✔ The SE/30 logic board contains a total of eight SIMM slots grouped into two banks. Each bank contains four SIMM slots. Each bank must be completely full or empty.

- ✔ All the SIMMs in the same bank must be the same size and speed. Therefore, you need at least one set of four of the same size SIMMs (for example, you need four 256K, four 1MB, or four 4MB, if you see the pattern). You need a second set of four if you want to fill the second bank. (Don't you just love banks that are full?)

- ✔ Each SIMM should be rated at 120ns or faster. Refer to Chapter 12 for information about memory speed.

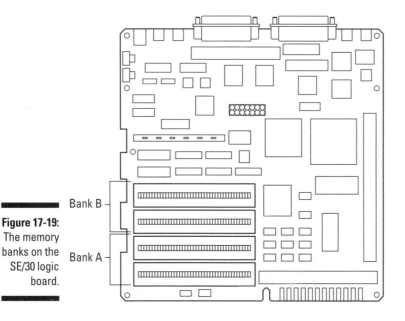

Figure 17-19:
The memory
banks on the
SE/30 logic
board.

Bank B

Bank A

✔ The larger-size SIMMs always go in bank A. These four sockets are nearest to the front edge of the logic board. Also, if you fill only one bank with SIMMs, you fill bank A.

Given these rules, the possible memory amounts using combinations of 256K, 1MB, and 4MB SIMMs are shown in this list: 1MB, 2MB, 4MB, 5MB, 8MB, 16MB, 17MB, and 20MB.

If you can afford four 16M SIMMs, you have more combinations available to you than we can list here.

When you place SIMMs of different sizes (kilobyte or megabyte sizes, that is, not physical sizes) in the slots during an upgrade, you put larger SIMMs in the front in bank A and smaller ones in the back in bank B.

The SE/30 is smart enough to figure out how much memory you install, so you don't have to set a jumper or snip a resistor on the logic board, the way you do with the SE. (Thank goodness you bought a smart computer, huh?)

For upgrades larger than 8MB, you must make a change to your system software. Install either Connectix MODE32 (System 7.0.1 or earlier) or the 32-bit enabler included with System 7.1 and later. The reason is long and boring, but the SE/30 cannot use the extra memory above 8MB without a software add-on.

That's it — your SE/30 memory upgrade is complete. Great! If you're finished upgrading, skip ahead to the section "Putting your Mac SE and SE/30 back together" for instructions on reassembling your computer.

Installing an expansion card in a Mac SE

The SE's expansion slot makes it one of the most flexible compact Macs. To add an expansion card to the SE, you remove the logic board. Don't worry — it's not as bad as it sounds.

Tools you need: A screwdriver (maybe; see the instructions that come with your expansion card)

Things to watch out for: Installing an expansion card is pretty straightforward. Just make sure that you go over the instructions that come with the expansion card before you begin. Also, some cards require that you replace the logic board in the chassis in a different way. Again, see the instructions for your expansion card for details.

1. **Remove the back case and discharge the CRT.**

   See the sections "Opening your black-and-white compact" and "Discharging the CRT" for details.

2. **Put on your grounding wrist strap.**

   Again, see Chapter 3 for electrostatic-discharge procedures and for information about the grounding wrist strap.

3. **Disconnect the cables and remove the logic board.**

   To disconnect the cables and remove the logic board, follow Steps 3 through 10 in the section "Getting ready to add memory to a Mac SE or SE/30," earlier in this chapter.

   You must go through these steps before you install an expansion card. The steps guide you through disconnecting the cables inside the SE and removing the logic board. After these steps are finished, you're ready for the expansion card.

4. **Line up the connector on the expansion card with the connector on the SE logic board and press the card into place.**

   Expansion cards in the SE install on top of the logic board to form a circuit board sandwich. (And how would that lunch taste?) The connector on the card is keyed so that it fits only one way. Figure 17-20 shows the expansion card and this connector.

Your expansion card may also have little plastic legs called *standoffs* that keep the card an even distance from the logic board. You may have to attach the standoffs to the logic board with screws placed in existing holes in the logic board. See the instructions that come with the expansion card for specific details. Figure 17-20 shows how a card plugs in to the connector on the logic board.

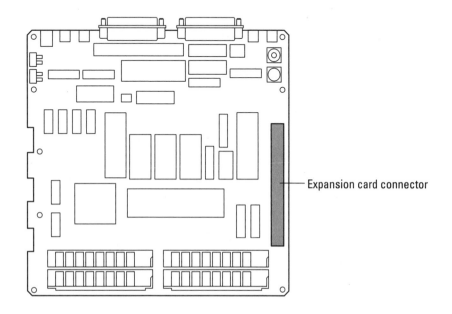

Expansion card connector

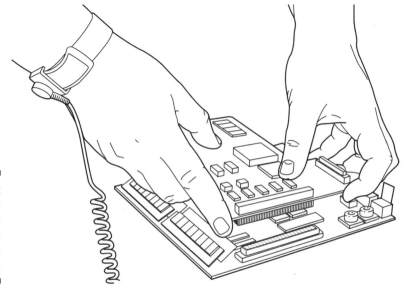

Figure 17-20:
Installing an
expansion
card on the
SE logic
board.

5. **Install in the chassis bracket any external connectors required by your expansion card.**

If your expansion card has no external connectors, skip this step.

If your expansion card is designed to let you plug something into your SE (such as a larger monitor or a high-speed network), you have to install the external connector also. This connector mounts on the chassis bracket, on a small, metal plate that attaches with one screw or bolt on either end.

Follow the instructions that come with your card about when and where to attach the cable from the external connector to the expansion card.

If the card has an external connector, you must also remove the *knockout panel* in the back case of the SE. In this panel, all the connectors show through the chassis so that you can connect cables to them. Figure 17-21 shows the external connectors.

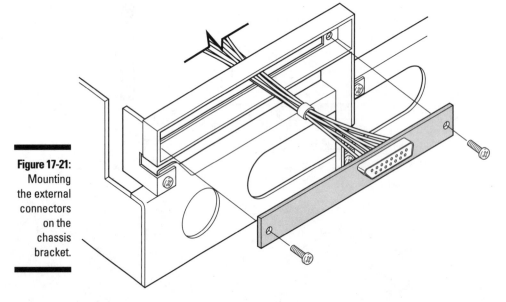

Figure 17-21:
Mounting the external connectors on the chassis bracket.

The panel pops out with a little pressure from inside the back case. If you left the screws in their holes in the back case when you opened your computer, be careful not to lose them when you remove the knockout panel.

Most expansion cards have software drivers you must install before the card will function properly. Check the instructions that come with the card. See Chapter 15 for more information about drivers.

You've installed an expansion card in your SE. Good work! If you're finished upgrading, skip ahead to the section "Putting your Mac SE and SE/30 back together."

Daughterboards

Some SE expansion cards also have a secondary connector for adding what's known as a *daughterboard* to the card. An accelerator card might come, for example, with a connector for an optional display card that drives a large external monitor.

The connectors for daughterboards are usually unique and work only with other cards made by the same manufacturer. If you add a daughterboard, you may have to add another connector that comes with the board.

Sometimes the daughterboard doesn't quite fit properly. If the board doesn't fit, you must modify the chassis a little, which sounds like a drastic change but really isn't. Just bend the rear chassis tab so that it lies flat against the chassis. The accompanying figure shows the tabs bent back.

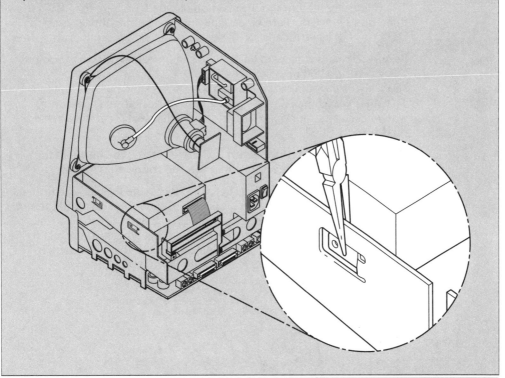

Installing an expansion card in a Mac SE/30

The interior design of the SE/30 makes it easy to add an expansion card (much easier than with the SE), because you don't have to take out the logic board.

Tools you need: None

Things to watch out for: Be careful when you're working around the neck and end of the CRT.

If you're adding memory and an expansion card to your SE/30 at the same time, add the memory first. Then reinstall the logic board and add the card.

1. **Remove the back case and discharge the CRT.**

   For details, see the sections "Opening your black-and-white compact" and "Discharging the CRT."

2. **Put on your grounding wrist strap.**

   Again, see Chapter 3 for electrostatic-discharge procedures and for information about the grounding wrist strap.

3. **Carefully detach the video card from the end of the CRT.**

   The video card attaches to the glass tip of the CRT where the CRT is the thinnest. Remove the card by carefully pulling it straight back from the CRT. You can leave it dangling — there's no need to disconnect the wires.

   Be sure to remove the card before you continue. It is easy to knock into this video card and break off the tip of the CRT, causing the tube to suddenly de-vacuum (not on my carpet, we say) and possibly implode. That's $75 for a new CRT, to say nothing about shattered glass everywhere! Even after the video card is detached, be extra careful around the glass tip of the CRT.

4. **Orient the card with the electronic thingies facing the inside of the SE/30, line up the connectors, and push the connectors together.**

   The SE/30 expansion card plugs in to the slot on the logic board through a hole in the chassis. Figure 17-22 shows the expansion card and the slot. Notice where the card plugs in to the slot. To install the card, just line up the connectors and push them together. This process is difficult to describe, but it's really easy to do. Some cards also have fasteners to secure the card to the tabs that are bent out from the chassis.

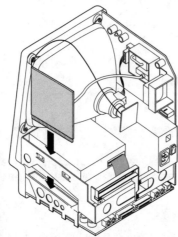

Figure 17-22:
An SE/30 expansion card.

5. **If the card you are installing has external connectors, install in the chassis bracket the small metal plate on which the connectors are mounted.**

    Before you put the case back together, be sure to connect the cables that go from the external connectors to the card. Refer to Figure 17-21 to see how the connectors mount on the chassis bracket.

    If you have external connectors, you must also remove the *knockout panel* in the back case of the SE/30. On this panel, the connectors show through the chassis so that you can connect cables to them. The panel pops out with a little pressure from inside the back case. If you left the screws in their holes in the back case when you opened your computer, be careful not to lose them when you remove the knockout panel.

Most expansion cards have software called *drivers* that you must install before the card will function properly. Check the instructions that come with the card. See Chapter 15 for more information about drivers.

Hey, you have an expansion card in your SE/30! We hope that it makes using your Mac much better.

Putting your Mac SE and SE/30 back together

This section works for putting your SE and SE/30 back together no matter which kind of upgrade you have just done, from installing a hard disk or adding 128MB of memory to putting in an expansion card with a daughterboard.

Tools you need: Phillips number 2 screwdriver

Things to watch out for: Be sure to reconnect the speaker cable.

So you've done all your upgrading and are ready to get your SE or SE/30 up and running. The following steps make sure that you don't have any parts left over after you close your computer:

1. **Replace the logic board if your upgrade involved removing it.**

    If you did not remove the logic board, skip to Step 2.

    Hold the logic board so that the external connectors face up and the side with all the components faces away from you. Place the left edge of the logic board in the left rail on the chassis.

    Reconnect the speaker cable to the logic board. The speaker cable connector is located in the center of the logic board, near the power cable connector. Refer to Figure 17-17 if you want help finding the speaker cable. If you don't reconnect this cable, the next time you start up your Mac, you won't hear the beep when your computer gets going and shows its smiling Mac on the screen.

Swing the right side of the logic board in toward the SE or SE/30 so that the tabs on the right side of the board go into the notches on the right-hand rail. Slide the logic board down into place.

2. **Make sure that you reconnect all cables you disconnected during the upgrade procedure.**

   If you removed the logic board, you must reconnect the logic board power cable, the hard drive cable, the diskette drive cable, and the speaker cable.

   If you added or replaced a hard disk, check to make sure that the data cable and the power cables connect at both ends.

   If you added an expansion card, double-check that any cables that attach to the new card are connected securely.

   When you replace the disk cable (or cables), remember that the cable from the lower diskette drive goes to the lower connector.

3. **If you removed the chassis bracket for easier access to the inside of your SE or SE/30, replace it now.**

   If you don't remember where the three screws go, look at Figure 17-14 again.

4. **Reconnect the video card to the end of the CRT.**

   The last thing you do, after you finish reconnecting and checking the cables inside the Mac, is reinstall the video card on the end of the CRT. When you replace the card, notice that the connector on the video card fits only one way on the pins around the end of the CRT.

5. **Replace the back case.**

   See the section "Replacing the back case," at the end of the "Black-and-White Compacts" section, later in this chapter.

Congratulations — you're finished! Now plug in your SE or SE/30 and use your new upgrade. We hope that it really makes your computer run better. Make sure that everything works as you expect. If you have any problems, see Chapter 12.

The Mac Classic, Mac Classic II, and Performa 200

The Mac Classic and Mac Classic II replace the Mac SE and SE/30. The Performa 200 is a Classic II, although it has a different label on the outside and sells in consumer-electronics stores. Inside, the Performa 200 mirrors the Classic II.

The Classic has the same processor and processing speed as the SE, but it is slightly faster because some parts are a little more efficient. Unfortunately, the Classic lacks the expansion slot present in the SE, so you cannot upgrade with expansion cards.

The Classic II and the Performa 200 inherited an updated logic board from the Mac LC. The Classic II and Performa 200 are also slotless, so, again, you cannot add expansion cards.

Adding or replacing a hard disk in the Classic, Classic II, and Performa 200

Tools you need: A Phillips number 2 screwdriver

Things to watch out for: This procedure is fairly straightforward. Discharge the CRT and be careful to avoid knocking into the video board on the end.

1. **Open the case and discharge the CRT.**

   For instructions, see the section "Discharging the CRT," at the beginning of this chapter.

2. **Put on your grounding wrist strap.**

   See Chapter 3 for electrostatic-discharge prevention procedures.

3. **Disconnect the hard disk data cable and the hard disk power cable.**

   Skip to Step 6 if you are adding a hard disk to a Classic, Classic II, or Performa that doesn't contain one already.

   The hard disk data cable is a wide, flat, gray cable that connects the back of the hard disk and the logic board.

   The hard disk power cable is a bundle of multicolored wires that goes between the hard disk and the power/sweep board. The power/sweep board is the large circuit board located on the opposite side of the Mac from the hard disk. You must disconnect these cables to remove the existing hard disk from the Mac. Because you install a new cable with the new hard disk, keep the old cables with the old hard disk. See Chapter 12 for suggestions about what to do with an old hard disk. Figure 17-23 shows the hard disk power cable and the power/sweep board.

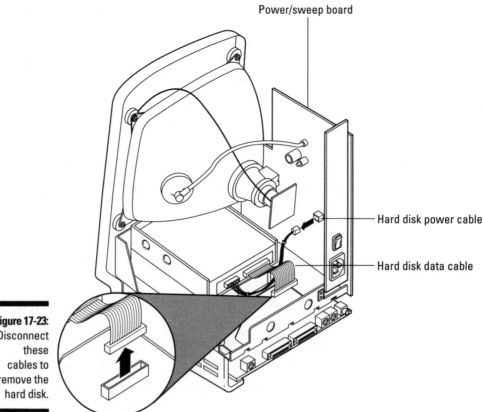

Power/sweep board

Hard disk power cable

Hard disk data cable

Figure 17-23:
Disconnect
these
cables to
remove the
hard disk.

4. **Unscrew the two Phillips screws that hold the hard disk bracket in place.**

   After these screws are loose, the hard disk just slides out of the Mac. Figure 17-24 shows where these screws hide.

5. **Lift the back of the hard disk unit slightly and slide it back and out from the Mac.**

   Set the old hard disk aside on your grounded work surface.

6. **Prepare your new hard disk.**

   The Classic, Classic II, and Performa 200 require the use of a one-inch-high, low-power hard disk unit.

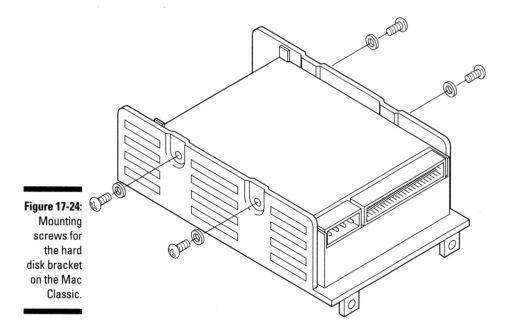

Figure 17-24:
Mounting
screws for
the hard
disk bracket
on the Mac
Classic.

As we mention in Chapter 12, you should buy a mounting kit with your new hard disk. The kit contains the cables and the bracket you need to install your hard disk.

- Connect the new data cable and power cables from the mounting kit to the hard disk. We suggest that you connect the cables while the hard disk is still outside the Mac. After you start working inside the Mac, space gets pretty tight.

- Attach the carrier bracket to the hard disk (again, working outside the Mac). This step just means that you screw in four screws to hold the hard disk on the bracket. Carrier brackets come in all shapes and sizes, so the placement of the screws varies.

- Every bracket has two metal tabs on both ends. The bent-down tabs with holes in them should go on the same end of the hard disk as the power cable and data cable.

7. **Slide the new hard disk into the Mac, right on top of the existing dis-kette drive.**

   Hold up the back end of the hard disk at an angle so that the two front tabs can slide into the corresponding slots in the top of the diskette drive. Push the hard disk into position.

8. **Install the two Phillips screws in the mounting holes on the carrier bracket.**

   Figure 17-24 shows you the screw locations on the carrier bracket. The screws keep the hard disk from sliding around inside the Mac.

9. **Connect the power cable and data cable to their connectors on the logic board and power/sweep board.**

   Be careful to support the logic board from underneath with your hand when you connect the data cable or else it might flex too much and crack. Look back at Figure 17-23 to see the cable locations.

   If you are adding memory at the same time that you install your hard disk, skip to the appropriate section about adding memory to your computer. Otherwise, if this is the only upgrade you are doing now, continue with Step 10.

10. **Replace the back case.**

   If installing a hard disk is the only upgrade you're doing, skip to the section "Replacing the back case," at the end of the "Black-and-White Compacts" section, later in this chapter.

Congratulations! You have just installed your new hard disk. If you have any problems, see Chapter 12.

Adding memory to a Mac Classic

You add memory to the Classic with a memory expansion card. This card connects to a special memory expansion slot on the Classic's logic board. The card typically comes with 1MB of memory permanently installed and two SIMMs slots to expand the Classic's memory to the full 4MB. When you add SIMMs to the memory card, you must set a jumper to let the Mac know how much memory it has. You do this by positioning a plastic block on some pins at the edge of the card.

Tools you need: None

Things to watch out for: This procedure is fairly straightforward, but be careful to avoid knocking into the video board on the end of the CRT.

Your choices for adding memory to the Classic are shown in this list:

- ✔ 1MB (the way the Classic comes from the factory)
- ✔ 2MB (with a memory expansion card)
- ✔ 2.5MB (a memory card with two 256K SIMMs installed)
- ✔ 4MB (a memory card with two 1MB SIMMs installed)

We recommend upgrading to the 4MB maximum.

1. **Open the case and discharge the CRT.**

   See the section "Discharging the CRT," earlier in this chapter, for instructions.

2. **Put on your grounding wrist strap.**

   See Chapter 3 for electrostatic-discharge prevention procedures.

3. **Prepare your memory expansion card.**

   To expand the memory to the full 4MB allowed, you must add two 1MB SIMMs rated at the speed of 120ns or faster. For 2.5MB, add two 256K SIMMs. For more information about SIMMs, refer to Chapter 12.

   For a total of 2MB, you can add the expansion card without installing any SIMMs. For a total of 2.5MB, you can add two 256K SIMMs to the expansion card. For a total of 4MB, you can add two 1MB SIMMs.

   If your Mac Classic has already been upgraded to 2MB or 2.5MB of memory, you must remove the memory expansion card before you upgrade. Remove the card by wiggling it, pulling it out of the connector, and sliding it out of its bracket.

   Install the SIMMs on the card. After the SIMMs are in place, you must position the jumper on the memory expansion card.

   The two SIMM slots on the memory expansion card are considered one bank. Therefore, both must be empty or both must be filled. Also, the size and speed of the SIMMs must match.

   If you are upgrading to only 2MB of RAM, make sure that the jumper is in the No SIMMs Installed position, and you are ready to install. If you bought a memory card with 3MB worth of chips permanently installed on the card, no other preparation is necessary and you are ready to install the card.

4. Install the memory expansion card in your Mac.

The side of the memory expansion card with the electronic parts on it should face the inside of the computer. Slide the card on the rails in the bracket and push the card into the connector on the logic board. Figure 17-25 shows you how this procedure works.

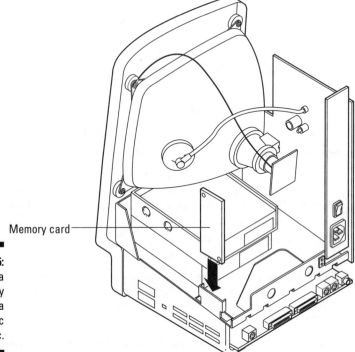

Memory card

Figure 17-25:
Installing a memory card in a Mac Classic.

5. Replace the back case.

Skip to the section "Replacing the back case," at the end of the "Black-and-White Compacts" section, later in this chapter.

Congratulations; you have just upgraded your Mac Classic's memory! Your computer should boot up normally and no longer be plagued with those annoying "out of memory" messages.

Adding memory to a Classic II or Performa 200

Adding memory to the Mac Classic II and the Performa 200 is a little more involved than installing memory in the Mac Classic, but it's still pretty easy. For these two computers, you must remove the logic board, whereas when you're adding memory to the Classic, you don't remove the board.

Tools you need: None, just your hands

Things to watch out for: Be careful to avoid knocking into the video board on the end of the CRT.

1. **Open the case and discharge the CRT.**

   See the section "Discharging the CRT" for instructions.

2. **Put on your grounding wrist strap.**

   See Chapter 3 for electrostatic-discharge prevention procedures.

3. **Disconnect the following cables from the logic board: hard disk data cable, diskette drive cable, and logic board power cable.**

   To remove the board from the chassis, you must disconnect all the cables attached to the logic board.

   The hard disk data cable is a wide, flat, gray cable that connects the hard disk to the logic board. It connects near the edge with all the external connectors. Figure 17-26 shows you the cables we're talking about.

   The diskette drive cable is also a flat, gray cable about half as wide as the hard disk data cable. It connects just below and to the side of the hard disk data cable.

   The logic board power cable is a multicolored bundle of wires that connects in the center of the logic board. Squeeze the retaining clip to release the plug as you pull it loose.

Logic board power cable

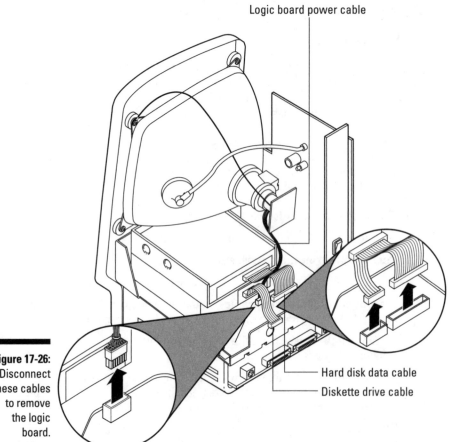

Figure 17-26:
Disconnect
these cables
to remove
the logic
board.

Hard disk data cable

Diskette drive cable

4. Slide the logic board up and out of the chassis.

The logic board just slides up and out of the chassis. No problemo. Set the
logic board on your grounded, nonconductive work surface. See Chapter 3
for information about creating a safe work surface.

5. Add two SIMMs to the on-board memory slots.

The Classic II and Performa 200 have 2MB on the logic board. The SIMM
sizes you can use are shown in this list: 1MB (for a total of 4MB); 2MB (for
a total of 6M); 4MB (for a total of 10M).

Both SIMMs must be the same size and speed, and both slots must be
either filled or empty. Figure 17-27 shows the logic board for the Classic II
and Performa 200. Notice the SIMM slots.

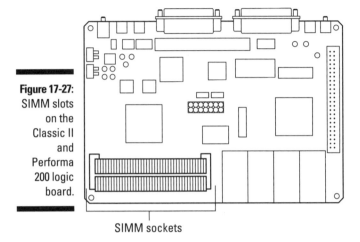

Figure 17-27:
SIMM slots
on the
Classic II
and
Performa
200 logic
board.

SIMM sockets

6. **Replace the logic board.**

   Slide the logic board down the rails in the chassis and into place.

7. **Reconnect the three cables.**

   Now is the time to reconnect the hard disk data cable, the diskette drive cable, and the logic board power cable.

   Be careful to support the bottom of the logic board when you push the cable plugs into their connectors. If you don't, the logic board can flex too much and possibly break. Refer to Figure 17-26 if you want a reminder about which cables go where.

8. **Replace the back case.**

   See the section "Replacing the back case," at the end of the "Black-and-White Compacts" section, later in this chapter.

That's it — you just upgraded your Classic II and Performa 200 memory! Pat yourself on the back, or take a little bow in front of your favorite pet. You now join the ranks of those people who have upgraded their Mac and lived to tell the tale!

In case you have any problems, See Chapter 12.

The Classic II and Performa 200 contain an expansion slot for a math coprocessor card. Installing a math coprocessor card in these two Macs is like installing a memory card in the Macintosh Classic. So if you want to install the math coprocessor, skip back to the section "Adding memory to a Mac Classic," and follow the instructions you find there. After you install the math coprocessor card, your numbers will be crunched like they've never been crunched before! Remember that only certain applications make use of a math coprocessor, so don't expect to see any speed gains with your word processor or Hungarian language-tutor program.

Replacing the back case

With your upgrade completed, next you replace the back case.

Tools you need: Safety glasses; a Torx number 8 screwdriver with a 10-inch shaft

Things to watch out for: Be careful around the CRT neck and the video card on the end of the CRT in the SEs and Classics. Make sure that you reconnect all cables before closing the case, including the speaker cable on the SE and SE/30.

If you forget a cable, you'll have to open the Mac and discharge the CRT again to connect the cable.

When you replace the case, make sure that the edges of the back case fit *inside* the edges of the front bezel all the way around. And, as always, be sure to follow the electrostatic-discharge prevention guidelines.

1. **Replace the metal shield over the connectors and the logic board.**

   If you're working on a Classic, Classic II, or Performa 200, skip to Step 2.

2. **Place the back case on the Mac.**

   Be careful of the CRT and the video card, if it's there. Make sure that the edges of the back case fit *inside* the edges of the front bezel all the way around. Push down on the back case to make sure that the front and back fit firmly together.

3. **Replace the screws on the back case and tighten.**

   Remember that the silver screws go in the handle and the black screws go on either side of the row of connectors along the bottom of the Mac.

   When you replace the screws in the handle, start by backing off the screw until you feel it engage. This action keeps the plastic screw holes from stripping out. Don't overtighten the screws in the handle or your Mac will have dimples in the plastic above the screen.

   Remember that the Mac Plus has a fifth, silver screw that goes under the battery cover. Also, if all the screws on the Mac Plus happen to be silver, look at the threads. The two with the fine threads go at the bottom, near the connectors.

4. **Replace the reset/interrupt switch, if your Mac has one.**

   If you're working on a Mac Classic, Classic II, or Performa 200, skip this step.

   Look carefully at the slots on the lower-left side of the Mac as you face the front of your computer. On the Mac Plus, you see the hole where the tabs on the switch fit. On the SE and SE/30, two slots extend higher than the rest, where the hooks on top of the switch go. On the SE and SE/30, engage the hooks and then swing the switch in toward the Mac and snap it into place.

Congratulations! You're finished. If everything went according to plan, your black-and-white compact Mac should start up normally and be ready to roll. You may have to complete some final touches, such as installing driver software if you installed an expansion card, or formatting a new hard disk — check the instructions that come with your upgrade.

Macintosh Color Compacts

If the black-and-white compact Macs are the most difficult Macs to upgrade, the color compacts are some of the easiest. These Macs were designed with upgrading in mind.

The Macintosh models we discuss in the color compact category include the ones in this list: Color Classic, Color Classic II, LC 500 series, Performa 500 series, and Mac TV.

Opening your color compact

This section, which describes how to open a color compact, may be a little disappointing to anyone expecting extensive upgrade instructions, such as all the steps we give for the black-and-white compacts. Then again, you're probably not disappointed at all. Just be glad that you chose a Mac made for upgrading.

Tools you need: A Torx number 8 screwdriver

Things to watch out for: Big Foot, Elvis, the Loch Ness monster, UFOs. Just kidding; opening these Macs is really easy.

1. **Put on your grounding wrist strap.**

   Again, see Chapter 3 for electrostatic-discharge procedures and for information about the grounding wrist strap.

2. **Remove the two Torx screws located on either side of the back door.**

   The connectors on the back of your color compact Mac are covered by a back door called the *I/O door*. This name is pronounced "eye-oh" (ee-eye-ee-eye-oh? Where do they get this stuff?) Anyway, you must remove the two Torx screws in the corners of this door. To get a look at the door, see Figure 17-28. You can also see the two Torx screws.

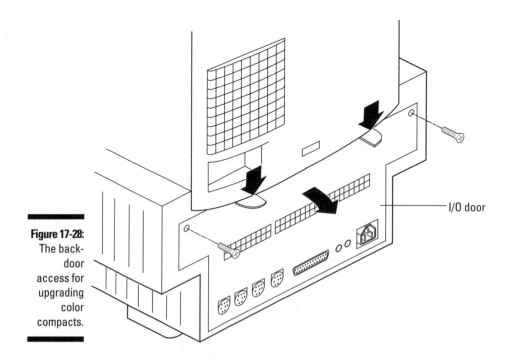

I/O door

Figure 17-28:
The back-
door
access for
upgrading
color
compacts.

3. **Push down on the two plastic tabs at the top of the door and pull the door away from the Mac.**

   That's all there is to it. Now you should see a row of undressed connectors. The connectors sit on the edge of the logic board.

4. **Grasp the edges of the logic board firmly and pull the board straight out of the Mac.**

   You must remove the logic board to do all except one of the upgrades described in this section. The exception is an internal hard disk upgrade. So you get to skip this step if you're upgrading just the internal hard disk.

   The edge of the logic board plugs into connectors near the front of the Mac, so you may feel a little resistance when you pull on the board. If necessary, wiggle the board a little from side to side to free it.

   For anybody who has removed the logic board from a black-and-white compact Mac, this step is amazingly easy. If this is the only logic board you have ever removed, again, you chose the right Mac.

   Set the logic board on your grounded work surface. Refer to Chapter 3 for electrostatic-discharge prevention procedures and for information about creating a safe, grounded work surface.

That's it — the horse is out of the barn, and you're ready to continue with your upgrade. That is, you've opened up your color compact and, unless you are upgrading just an internal hard disk, removed the logic board.

Color Classic upgrades

The slide-out design of the logic board on the Color Classic makes an easy job of upgrading memory and adding an expansion card. But getting at the hard disk is complex. In our opinion, the easiest way to expand your disk storage space on a Color Classic is to connect an external hard disk. If you really want to upgrade the internal hard disk, take it to a shop and have a technician do it. It's worth the $50 to save yourself the trouble.

If you have been lucky enough to travel to Japan, you may have purchased a Color Classic II. This computer is almost identical to the Color Classic, except for a faster processor. The upgrades we discuss for the Color Classic apply also to the Color Classic II.

Adding memory to a Color Classic

Tools you need: None

Things to watch out for: Make sure you press the memory SIMMs down completely into their sockets. A SIMM that's not all the way down inside the socket can keep the Mac from starting up.

1. **Open the I/O door and remove the logic board.**

   You must remove the logic board to access the memory slots. Follow steps 1 through 4 in the section "Opening your color compact," earlier in this chapter, to open the door and remove the logic board. Figure 17-29 shows the logic board.

2. **Insert new SIMMs in the logic board.**

   The Color Classic comes with 4MB of memory on the logic board. Your computer has two SIMM slots that accept memory upgrades, and the two slots make up one bank. You have two choices when you add memory: fill both slots with identical SIMMs or leave both slots empty. You cannot use just one slot.

   You can add two 1MB SIMMs for a total of 6M, two 2MB SIMMs for 8MB, or two 4MB SIMMs for 10MB. The Color Classic accepts a maximum of only 10M. Logically, when you add two 4MB SIMMs, you should be able to use a total of 12MB The other two megabytes that should be available are wasted. (Don't you love paying for things you can't use?)

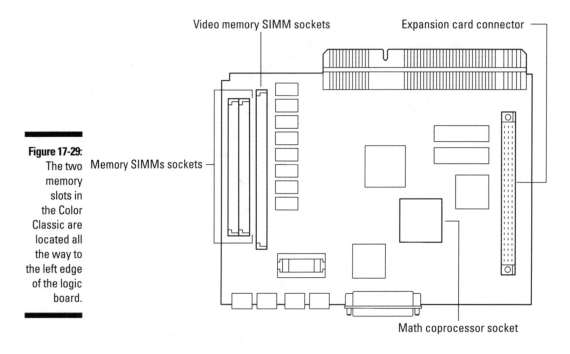

Video memory SIMM sockets

Expansion card connector

Memory SIMMs sockets

Math coprocessor socket

Figure 17-29:
The two memory slots in the Color Classic are located all the way to the left edge of the logic board.

3. Replace the logic board.

Slide the logic board in on the guide rails and push in firmly to seat the logic board in its connectors. Make sure that no bent metal tabs are there to contact the bottom of the logic board and cause a short circuit.

4. Replace the I/O door and the two screws.

Put the bottom edge of the door in place first, and then push in the top edge with the plastic tabs. Make sure that the tabs snap into place. Then replace the two screws on either side of the door.

Congratulations — you have just completed your Color Classic memory upgrade! Now you can run all your favorite applications at the same time, open more windows, and generally have more fun with your computer.

In case you have any problems, see Chapter 12 for more information about memory .

The steps in the section "Adding memory to a Color Classic" are the same steps you use to install video memory, also called *VRAM*. If you add video memory, you'll enable your Color Classic to display more colors on-screen at one time, which greatly improves the look of graphics on-screen. Photographs and digitized video will go from looking good to looking great.

The Color Classic comes with 256K of video memory on the logic board, and the video memory expands to 512K. The video memory SIMM slot is the longer connector next to the memory slots. Figure 17-29 shows the location of the video memory slot.

After you install the video memory, remember to use the Monitors control panel to change the video setting for more colors. See Chapter 13 for more information about video memory.

Adding an expansion card to a Color Classic

Tools you need: None

Things to watch out for: Be sure to read carefully the instructions that come with the card.

Be sure to follow the electrostatic-discharge prevention guidelines described in Chapter 3 when you work inside your Color Classic.

1. **Open the access door and remove the logic board.**

   You must remove the logic board to access the expansion slot. Follow Steps 1 through 4 in the section "Opening your color compact," earlier in this chapter, to open the door and remove the logic board. The expansion card slot is located on the right edge of the logic board. Figure 17-29 shows the location of the expansion slot.

2. **Prepare the expansion card for installation.**

   Each card is different, but preparing the card usually includes such tasks as attaching plastic legs, sometimes called *standoffs,* to the card.

3. **Install the expansion card.**

   Line up the connector on the card with the connector on the logic board and press down gently but firmly to match up the connectors. Make sure that the card fits all the way on the connector.

4. **Replace the logic board.**

   Slide the logic board in on the guide rails and push in firmly to seat the logic board in its connectors. Make sure that no bent metal tabs are there to contact the bottom of the logic board and cause a short circuit.

5. **Replace the I/O door and the two screws.**

   Put the bottom edge of the door in place first, and then push in the top edge with the plastic tabs. Make sure that the tabs snap into place. Then replace the two screws on either side of the door.

Congratulations! With your expansion card in place, you are ready to go boldly where perhaps none have gone before, using the new capabilities from your expansion card.

Most expansion cards come with software called *drivers* that you should install to make the card function properly. Check the instructions that came with the card to find out about the drivers.

You can upgrade your Color Classic's number-crunching capabilities by installing a math coprocessor in the computer's math coprocessor socket.

The steps you use to install a math coprocessor are the same as the steps you use for installing an expansion card. Refer to the section "Adding an expansion card to a Color Classic." Figure 17-29 shows the location of the math coprocessor socket. When you install the math coprocessor, notice that one edge of the chip looks like it has been chopped off at an angle. This edge faces away from the edge of the logic board with all the external connectors.

Because not all software is designed to use a math coprocessor, you may not notice any speed-up with some applications. Word processors and typing tutor programs probably will run about the same as before you did this upgrade. But we think that you probably will enjoy the quick calculating your spreadsheet does after the upgrade. See Chapter 14 if you have any questions about math coprocessors and speeding up your Mac.

Mac LC 500 series, Performa 500 series, and Mac TV upgrades

These Macs are an upgrader's dream! Every major component comes out easily when you simply slide it out of the case. These Macs all contain one expansion slot, but notice that the slot in the Mac TV is already filled by the TV tuner board, so you cannot add any other cards. The Performa 500s are based on the LC 500s, and, in terms of upgrading, we treat them the same.

Upgrading the internal hard disk in the LC 500s, Performa 500s, and Mac TV

This internal hard disk upgrade is probably the easiest of any Mac internal hard disk drive upgrade you can do. Of course, you would find it even easier just to add an external hard disk drive. For those of you who want all your hardware in one box, the following steps show you how to upgrade the internal hard disk.

Tools you need: None

Things to watch out for: Not much. Really, this is the easiest internal hard disk to upgrade of all.

Be sure to follow the electrostatic-discharge prevention guidelines described in Chapter 3 when you work inside your Mac.

1. **Remove the I/O door.**

   Follow Steps 1 through 3 in the section "Opening your color compact," earlier in this chapter.

   As you face the back of your Mac, the hard drive is located above the logic board and to the left.

2. **Push down on the plastic latch that holds the hard disk in place, grasp the hard disk, and pull it straight out of the Mac.**

   Figure 17-30 shows you how this step works.

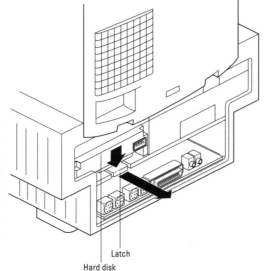

Figure 17-30:
Release the latch and pull the hard disk from the Mac.

Latch

Hard disk

3. Pull off the hard disk connector adapter.

You have to reuse this adapter on your new hard drive. Look at Figure 17-31 to see how this adapter fits on the hard disk.

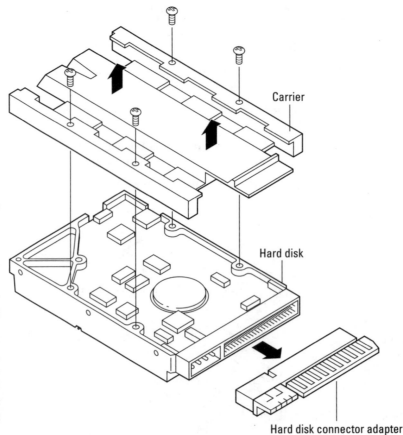

Carrier

Hard disk

Hard disk connector adapter

Figure 17-31:
The hard disk connector adapter and carrier bracket used in the Mac LC 500s, Performa 500s, and Mac TV.

4. Remove the carrier bracket and take out the four screws and set them aside.

You have to reuse the carrier bracket on your new hard drive.

5. Prepare the new hard disk.

Install the carrier bracket and connector adapter on the new drive. Look at Figure 17-31 to see how they fit on the drive. All the computers we discuss in this section need a 1-inch-high, 3 ½-inch, low-power SCSI hard disk. See Chapter 8 for more information about SCSI and Chapter 12 for information about internal hard disks.

6. **Install the new hard disk.**

   Hold down the plastic latch as you slide the new drive into place. Push firmly to be sure that the connectors fasten properly.

7. **Replace the I/O door and the screws.**

   Put the bottom edge of the door in place first, and then push in the top edge with the plastic tabs. Make sure that the tabs snap into place. Then replace the two screws on either side of the door.

Nice work — you have successfully upgraded your internal hard disk! If you're wondering what to do with your old hard disk, or if you have any problems, refer to Chapter 12.

Adding memory to the LC 500s, Performa 500s, and Mac TV

Tools you need: None

Things to watch out for: Be sure to follow the electrostatic-discharge prevention procedures outlined in Chapter 3.

1. **Open the I/O door and remove the logic board.**

   Follow Steps 1 through 4 in the section "Opening your color compact," earlier in this chapter. You must remove the logic board to access the memory expansion slot.

2. **Insert the new memory SIMM.**

   These computers come with 4MB of memory permanently installed on the logic board. The logic board has one SIMM slot. You can add one SIMM with 1, 2, 4, 8, 16, or 32MB of memory, up to a maximum of 36MB. These computers use 72-pin SIMMs rated at 80ns or faster. See Chapter 12 for more information about SIMMs. Figure 17-32 shows the location of the memory slot on the logic board.

3. **Replace the logic board.**

   Slide the logic board in on the guide rails and push in firmly to seat the logic board in its connectors.

4. **Replace the I/O door and the screws.**

   Put the bottom edge of the door in place first and then push in the top edge with the plastic tabs. Make sure that the tabs snap into place. Then replace the two screws on either side of the door.

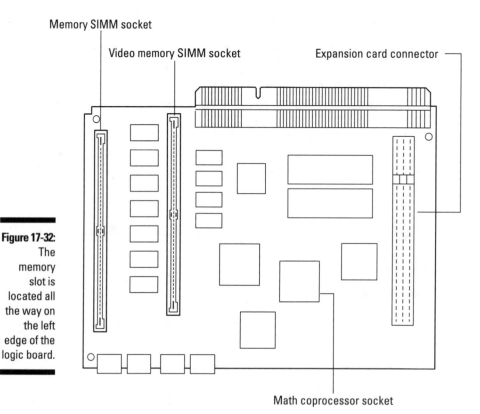

Memory SIMM socket

Video memory SIMM socket

Expansion card connector

Figure 17-32:
The
memory
slot is
located all
the way on
the left
edge of the
logic board.

Math coprocessor socket

Give yourself a big round of applause! With the new memory in place, your Mac should quit displaying those annoying "out of memory" error messages, at least until the new version of your favorite memory-hungry application comes out!

If you have any problems, refer to Chapter 12.

You might want to add video memory to your Mac so it can display more colors on-screen at a time and make graphics look better. As Figure 17-32 shows, the video memory SIMM slot is the longer connector to the right of the memory slot. To install video memory, follow the steps given in the section "Adding memory to the LC 500s, Performa 500s, and Mac TV." For more information about video memory, see Chapter 13.

Adding an expansion card to the LC 500s and Performa 500s

Tools you need: None

Things to watch out for: Be sure to follow the electrostatic-discharge prevention procedures outlined in Chapter 3. Also be sure to read carefully the instructions that come with the expansion card.

The expansion slot in the Mac TV is already filled by the tuner hardware, so you cannot add another card.

1. **Open the I/O door and remove the logic board.**

   Follow Steps 1 through 4 in the section "Opening your color compact," earlier in this chapter. You must remove the logic board to access the expansion slot.

2. **Prepare the expansion card.**

   Each card is different, but this step can include such tasks as attaching plastic legs, or standoffs, to the card. The expansion card slot is located on the right edge of the logic board (see Figure 19-32).

3. **Install the card.**

   Line up the connector on the card with the connector on the logic board and press down gently but firmly to fasten the connectors.

   Make sure that the connectors are all the way together.

4. **Replace the logic board.**

   Slide the logic board in on the guide rails and push in firmly to seat the logic board in its connectors.

5. **Replace the I/O door and the screws.**

   Put the bottom edge of the door in place first and then push in the top edge with the plastic tabs. Make sure that the tabs snap into place. Then replace the two screws on either side of the door.

Congratulations — you have just added an expansion card!

Most expansion cards have software called *drivers* that you must install before the card will function properly (check the instructions that come with the card). See Chapter 15 for more information about drivers.

You can install a math coprocessor in the Mac TV and in some of the LC 500 series and Performa 500 series Macs. The LC 500s that take the coprocessor are the LC 520 and the LC 550. The Performa 500s that take the coprocessor are the Performa 550 and the Performa 560. The others don't have a math coprocessor socket, so you can't install the chip.

The steps you use to install a math coprocessor are the same as the steps for installing an expansion card. Refer to the section "Adding an expansion card to the LC 500s and Performa 500s." Even though the Mac TV isn't mentioned in the section, you can still use the instructions to install the math coprocessor in this computer. Figure 17-32 shows the location of the math coprocessor socket. The socket is a plastic square with a depression in the center. It has metal contacts on the inside edges of the depression. When you install the math coprocessor, notice that one edge of the chip looks like it has been chopped off at an angle. This edge faces away from the edge of the logic board with all the external connectors.

By installing a math coprocessor, you upgrade the number-crunching capabilities of your Mac. But because not all software is designed to use a math coprocessor, you may not notice any speed-up with some applications. Word processors and typing tutor programs, for example, probably will run about the same as before the upgrade. See Chapter 14 if you have any questions about math coprocessors and speeding up your Mac.

Chapter 18

Upgrading and Adding Great Stuff to Your Modular Mac

● ●

In This Chapter

▶ Instructions for opening up and upgrading your modular Mac with internal storage and more memory

▶ Safety procedures for you and your modular Mac

▶ Practical advice, the tools you need, and what to watch out for as you upgrade

▶ The steps for safely putting your Mac back together again

● ●

*H*ere we go with hands-on upgrading for modular Macs. In this chapter, we take you through adding memory and internal storage to Macs, ranging from Mac IIs, LCs, and the Performa 400s to the Mac Centris, Quadra, Apple Workgroup Servers, and the latest and greatest Power Macs. The modular Mac design — with a separate monitor and a large CPU that's almost spacious inside — makes these computers especially easy to upgrade.

If you own a modular Mac, you have from one to six expansion slots inside in which you can install expansion cards for graphics, networking, or speeding up your Mac. Unlike the expansion slots in the compact Macs, you can reach the slots inside the modular pretty easily. So give yourself credit for choosing a Mac with plenty of room inside. When you install expansion cards in your Mac, the best places to go for instructions are to the manual that came with your computer and to the instructions accompanying the expansion card.

As you go through this chapter, we suggest that you skip around from section to section, depending on the Mac model or models you want to upgrade and also on the type of upgrade you plan to make, whether internal storage or memory. So, first finish reading this chapter introduction. Then proceed to the section about your particular Mac and its upgrades.

Don't worry about reading the entire chapter, however — unless you just want to. Of course, if you *do* read the whole chapter, you can impress your friends at dinner with such off-hand comments as: "Hey, did you know that the Mac II has eight memory sockets?" And: "Guess how many screws you need to remove to get the carrier bracket off of your hard disk?" (Bet you didn't know you could become a Mac trivia expert simply by reading this book, did you? Well, actually, the information provided in these pages probably doesn't make for the best dinner conversation, but the instructions are exactly what you need for installing additional memory and storage in your Mac.)

After you find your Mac's section, the first thing you see is that the information on opening up the Mac and the safety instructions for doing so come, well, *first*. The steps for opening up the Mac are the same for all the Macs in each section.

Then you can work your way farther through the section to follow the steps for the particular upgrade or upgrades you're doing, whether internal storage or memory upgrades (or both). We also offer tips for installing other types of upgrades, such as video memory upgrades. You can make all your upgrades at one time or do one now and come back later for more.

Finally, after you install the upgrade, you finish the process by following the instructions for closing up your Mac. And to keep you and your Mac safe, make sure that you carefully review the electrostatic discharge prevention guidelines listed in Chapter 3.

Mac II, IIx, and IIfx

The Mac II was the first modular Mac. In case you're wondering about the names, the *II* in Mac II differentiates it from the earlier compact Macs. The *x* in Mac IIx stands for *extended*, and the *fx* in Mac IIfx stands for *fast, extended*. Notice that you can install either a 3 ½-inch- or 5 ¼-inch-sized hard disk in the Macs we cover here.

Opening up your Mac II, IIx, or IIfx

Opening up your computer is the first step to adding an internal upgrade. Because these Macs were specifically designed to be opened and upgraded, getting inside them is much easier than getting inside a compact Mac.

Tools you need: A Phillips number 2 screwdriver

Things to watch out for: Be careful as you remove the top cover of the Mac — the plastic loops at the front edge of the cover break easily.

Electrostatic discharge — a.k.a. static electricity — can fry the delicate electronic components in your Mac, even with a zap too small for you to feel! Make sure that you read in Chapter 3 about how to prevent electrostatic discharge *before* you start any upgrade.

1. **Shut down your Mac by opening the Special menu and choosing Shut Down.**

   Always shut down your Mac correctly before you start any upgrade.

2. **Disconnect all the cables from your computer and place the main box of your Mac — but not the monitor — on your grounded antistatic work surface.**

   Use a wrist strap and a grounded antistatic mat. Make sure that you follow closely the electrostatic discharge prevention guidelines in Chapter 3 before you remove any upgrade products from their packages or touch any circuit board inside the Mac.

3. **Remove the security screw, if present.**

   The security screw is located on the back of the Mac, in the center at the top edge. (Your computer may not have this screw, because not all Macs are shipped with it in place. If your machine has been upgraded before, someone may already have removed the screw and not replaced it.) Use a Phillips number 2 screwdriver to remove the screw if it is in place.

4. **Remove the cover.**

   Two tabs at the rear corners of the cover lock the cover in place. Push in the tabs and lift the rear of the cover to about a 30 degree angle. Then push the cover toward the back of the Mac and disengage the plastic loops located at the front edge of the cover. You can't see these loops until you get the cover off, because they're inside the cover. Figure 18-1 shows the loops.

   These loops break easily if you lift the back edge of the cover more than about 45 degrees before disengaging them. If you haven't opened your Mac very often, you may find getting the loops to disengage a bit tough. Take your time and work carefully; the front edge of the case lifts up easily after the loops are free.

   Lifting the back edge of the cover more than 45 degrees can also damage the diskette drive or drives inside the Mac, so be *very* careful as you lift.

That's it — cover's off! Now skip ahead to the section that describes the exact upgrade you're adding to your Mac.

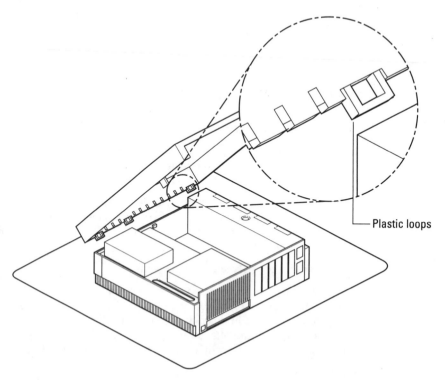

Plastic loops

Figure 18-1:
Make sure
that you free
the plastic
loops on the
front edge of
the Mac
cover.

Upgrading the internal hard disk in a Mac II, IIx, or IIfx

This section covers upgrading the internal hard disk you already have in your Mac and adding an internal hard disk if your Mac doesn't have one. Notice that, as you work on your hard disk, you can see either one or two diskette drives, depending on your Mac. And remember to back up any files you want to keep from your old internal hard disk *before* you install the new one. See Chapter 16 for more information on backing up files.

Tools you need: A magnetic Phillips number 2 screwdriver; needle-nosed pliers (optional)

Things to watch out for: The metal edges inside the Mac can be quite sharp — be careful you don't cut yourself. The large 5 ¼-inch hard disk drives used in Mac IIs can get really hot. (In fact, if you place a Mac II with one of these drives under your desk, it can double as a space heater! Well, almost.) Let the drive cool off a bit before you start your upgrade. The IIfx uses an oddball variation on the Mac SCSI system and, consequently, needs a special SCSI filter plug installed between the hard disk and the data cable that leads to the logic board. You work with this plug in Steps 2, 6, and 8.

1. **Remove the top cover by following Steps 1 through 4 in the preceding section, "Opening up your Mac II, IIx, or IIfx."**

   Set the cover aside.

2. **Disconnect the hard disk power cable and the hard disk data cable.**

   Skip to Step 5 if you are adding a hard disk to a Mac that does not currently have one. Figure 18-2 shows the location of the hard disk power cable and the hard disk data cable. Notice the two mounting screws. You may need to use the needle-nosed pliers instead of just your hands to remove the power cable from the hard disk mechanism. If you use the pliers, grip only the power cable plug, not the wires — a handful of wires ripped from the plug is not what we're after here.

   On the Mac IIfx only, you may find a SCSI filter plug installed between the hard disk and the hard disk data cable. Remove the filter plug from the hard disk and keep it handy. You reinstall it between the data cable and the new hard disk in Step 8.

Hard disk power cable

Mounting screw

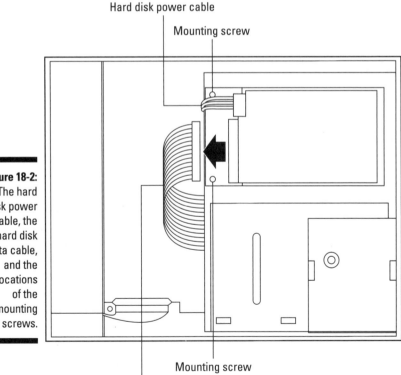

Figure 18-2:
The hard disk power cable, the hard disk data cable, and the locations of the mounting screws.

Mounting screw

Hard disk data cable

3. Remove the two mounting screws that hold the carrier bracket in place.

The *carrier bracket* is a metal plate that holds the hard disk in place inside your Mac. Refer to Figure 18-2 for the locations of the two mounting screws. Set the screws aside.

4. Remove the hard disk from the drive mount platform.

Lift the end of the hard disk where the cables attach and then slide the hard disk toward the center of the Mac. Then lift the hard disk off the metal drive mount platform that holds the hard disk and the diskette drives.

5. Attach the hard disk carrier bracket to the new hard disk.

As we pointed out in Chapter 12, whenever you buy a new hard disk for your Mac, you should also buy a mounting kit that contains a carrier bracket and cables for mounting your new hard disk in your Mac.

Use the four screws supplied in the kit to attach the carrier bracket to the hard disk. The screws attach the carrier bracket to the bottom or side of the hard disk, depending on the model.

Orient the bracket so that the end with the two protruding tabs is at the opposite end of the hard disk from the data and power connectors. These tabs fit into a set of two slots on the drive mount platform. Figure 18-3 shows the bracket correctly attached to the hard disk.

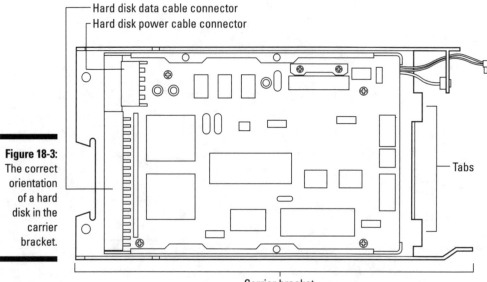

Hard disk data cable connector
Hard disk power cable connector

Figure 18-3:
The correct orientation of a hard disk in the carrier bracket.

Tabs

Carrier bracket

6. Remove the drive mount platform and connect the hard disk data and hard disk power cables.

Skip to Step 7 if you're replacing an existing internal hard disk in your Mac. Perform Step 6 *only* if you're adding a hard disk to a Mac that didn't already have an internal hard disk.

If you're installing a hard disk in a Mac that doesn't have one, disconnect the diskette drive cable or cables from the logic board. Remove the four Phillips screws located at the corners of the drive mount platform. Figure 18-4 (left) shows the location of these screws. Remove the drive mount platform with the diskette drive or drives attached and set it aside.

Locate the hard disk data and hard disk power cable connectors on the logic board. Figure 18-4 (right) points out these connectors. You may find a T-shaped terminator plug installed in the hard disk data cable connector. If this terminator plug is present, remove it. You don't need this plug again after you install the hard disk — keep it for your computer memorabilia display or just toss it out, if you prefer.

On the Mac IIfx only, you may find a SCSI filter plug installed between the T-shaped terminator plug and the hard disk data cable connector on the logic board. Remove the filter plug as you remove the terminator plug and keep the filter plug handy for use in Step 8.

Remove the wide gray hard disk data cable and the multicolored hard disk power cable from the mounting kit you ordered along with your hard disk. (You *did* order the mounting kit, didn't you? Good.) Plug in these two cables to their connectors on the logic board.

Complete this step by replacing the drive mount platform. Replace the four corner screws. Finally, reconnect the diskette drive cable or cables to their connectors on the logic board. The cable from the diskette drive on your right — that is, the one on your right as you face the front of the Mac — plugs into the right-hand connector, which is marked "Lower."

If your Mac has a second diskette drive, the cable from the diskette drive on your left plugs into the left-hand connector, which is marked "Upper." (And, yes, we know the labeling implies that the two diskette drives sit on top of each other inside the Mac. But they don't, as you can plainly see if your Mac has two diskette drives. Not exactly the best example of labeling we've ever seen — by far.)

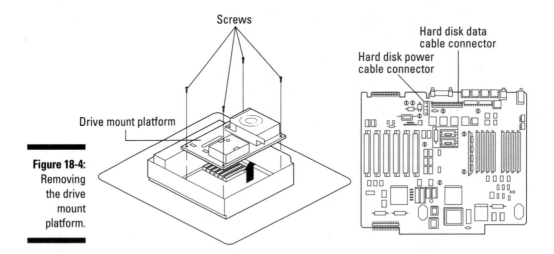

Figure 18-4:
Removing
the drive
mount
platform.

7. Install the new hard disk in your Mac.

First, position the hard disk with its carrier bracket attached to the drive
mount platform. Push the tabs on the carrier bracket into the two slots on
the drive mount platform. The drive mount platform actually has two sets
of slots. The set your carrier bracket uses depends on whether you're
installing a 3 ½-inch or a 5 ¼-inch hard disk. Figure 18-5 shows how the
different-sized hard disks fit on the drive mount platform.

Next, install the two mounting screws at the end of the carrier bracket nearest
the center of the Mac. These are the screws you removed in Step 3.

8. Connect the hard disk power cable and the hard disk data cable.

Connect the hard disk power cable and the hard disk data cable to your
new hard disk. These are the cables you unplugged from your old hard
disk in Step 2. Refer to Figure 18-2 to see how the cables connect to the
hard disk. The cables fit into their connectors only one way, so you don't
have to force them.

If you are upgrading a Mac IIfx, you also need to reinstall the SCSI filter
plug between the data cable and the hard disk. This is the filter plug you
unplugged from your Mac IIfx in either Step 2 or Step 6. (If your Mac
already had a hard disk, you removed the filter plug in Step 2; if your Mac
didn't have a hard disk, you removed the plug in Step 6.)

9. Replace the top cover.

Before you replace the top cover, however, make sure that none of the
sheet-metal tabs that run along the inside edge of the front of the cover are
bent inward toward the center of the cover. If you do find bent tabs, bend
them back into place before you replace the cover. Otherwise, the bent
tabs keep the cover from closing correctly.

3 ½-inch drive   5 ¼-inch drive

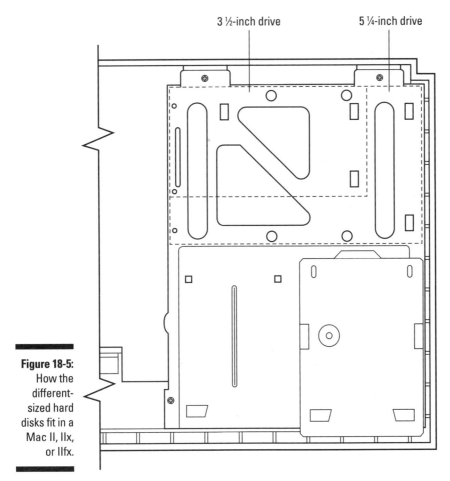

Figure 18-5:
How the
different-
sized hard
disks fit in a
Mac II, IIx,
or IIfx.

Replace the front edge of the top cover first. Pivot the back end of the cover down until the plastic tabs click into place. Press down firmly on the front edge of the cover to make sure that all the plastic loops are engaged correctly.

Can you believe it — you just installed a hard disk in your Mac! Good job! Now you're ready to start filling up that new disk with all kinds of new software goodies. (And don't forget to copy the important files you backed up from your old hard disk onto your new one.)

If you experience any problems after you complete your upgrade, see Chapters 8 and 12.

Upgrading the memory in a Mac II, IIx, or IIfx

Ah, memory — our favorite upgrade. This section shows you how to upgrade the memory in your Mac II, IIx, or IIfx. As we said in Chapter 12, if you install memory in a desktop Mac, you actually install small circuit boards that contain memory chips. Before you start your memory upgrade, refer back at Chapter 12 and the sidebar "The golden guide to SIMMs" to learn how to fill up the memory sockets correctly. Make sure that you carefully follow this guide; otherwise, the memory on which you spend your hard-earned money won't do your Mac any good. Also, read the sidebar "Guide to the specific memory needs of each Mac" in this section for details.

Table 18-1 shows you the amounts of memory each Mac covered in this section can accept in its memory banks. Check the "Possible Memory Amounts" column on the table to determine the amounts of memory your Mac model can accept. The Mac II, for example, can accept 1, 2, 4, 5, 8, 17, or 20MB of total memory. This Mac cannot, however, accept amounts that total 9, 16, or 18MB.

The table also tells you what size SIMMs work in your machine. Make sure that you buy the right size, or your Mac can't use the SIMMs after you install them. Make sure, too, that you buy the right speed of SIMM (memory speed is measured in nanoseconds and abbreviated ns). The speeds we list are the minimum speeds for each Mac. Don't buy SIMMs that run slower than the speeds listed here. Buying faster SIMMs is OK, but your Mac doesn't run any faster with the speedier SIMMs.

Table 18-1	Possible Memory Upgrades for the Mac II, IIx, and IIfx		
Mac Model	*SIMM Size This Model Can Use*	*Minimum SIMM Speed Possible*	*Memory Amounts (in MB)*
Mac II	256K, 1MB, 4MB	120ns	1, 2, 4, 5, 8, 17, 20MB
Mac IIx	256K, 1MB, 4MB	120ns	1, 2, 4, 5, 8, 16, 17, 20, 32MB
Mac IIfx	1MB, 4MB	80ns	4, 8, 16, 20, 32, 64, 128MB

Guide to the specific memory needs of each Mac

All Mac IIs: Whenever you install SIMMs in any of these Macs, you must install them in groups of four; the four SIMMs must all be the same size and speed. (See Table 18-1 to determine which SIMM sizes and speeds you need to buy.) The SIMMs must be installed in groups of four because these Macs all contain two memory banks made up of four SIMM sockets each — a total of eight SIMM sockets.

Mac II: We recommend that you add only 8MB memory to the Mac II. Passing the 8MB mark means that you enter the "black hole" of Mac II memory upgrades. For you to add more than 8MB (and enter the black hole), your Mac must have the following components installed:

✔ *New ROM chips.* You have these chips in your Mac II already if it's been upgraded with a high-density disk drive.

✔ *A PMMU chip.* This chip tells the Mac II how to use large-sized SIMMs that enable you to upgrade past the 8MB memory limit.

✔ *Special software.* You need a version of System 7 and a special system extension. For version 7.0 and 7.01, the extension is a system software product called *MODE32.* You can get this extension from a company called Connectix. The Connectix phone number is 800-950-5880. For version 7.1 and later, the extension you need is called the *32-bit system enabler.* This extension comes on your system software disk.

After these three items are installed on your machine, you can go beyond the 8MB black hole memory limit. We recommend that you have a technician install these for you.

Mac II and IIx: These two Macs share the following characteristics involving memory upgrades:

✔ If you install 1MB SIMMs, you must use SIMMs with eight chips on each SIMM. The 1MB SIMMs with only two chips do not work on these machines.

✔ If you install 4MB SIMMs, you must buy special SIMMs.

Whenever you buy memory, make sure you tell the salesperson exactly which model you own so that you get the right SIMMs.

Mac IIx only: This Mac has its own 8MB black hole, so if you want to venture past this amount in adding memory, you must use a version of System 7 and a special system extension. For Version 7.0 and 7.01, the extension is the Connectix MODE32 — the same as for the Mac II. (See the Mac II software descriptions earlier in this sidebar for the Connectix phone number.) For Version 7.1 and later, the extension you need is the 32-bit system enabler that comes on the system software disk, again, the same as for the Mac II.

Mac IIfx: You must install special 64-pin SIMMs in the Mac IIfx to upgrade its memory. These SIMMs are not used in any other Mac. To make sure that you purchase the right SIMMs, remember to tell the memory salesperson that you are installing the SIMMs in a Mac IIfx.

One last consideration: You can upgrade any of the Mac IIs only if the moon is waning. Additionally, if you upgrade the Mac II or IIfx during a neap tide, you can substitute SPAM for SIMMs — just kidding!

Tools you need: A magnetic Phillips number 2 screwdriver; a ballpoint pen or a SIMM removal tool; needle-nosed pliers (optional)

Things to watch out for: As we've cautioned previously, the metal edges inside the Mac can be quite sharp — be careful not to cut yourself. Be very careful, too, as you remove and install SIMMs, especially if your Mac uses plastic tabs on the SIMM sockets on the logic board. The plastic tabs on the sockets that hold the memory SIMMs are quite delicate. Some newer versions of the logic boards in these Macs use sockets with metal tabs instead of plastic ones.

1. **Remove the top cover by following Steps 1 through 4 in the section "Opening up your Mac II, IIx, or IIfx."**

   Set the cover aside.

2. **Remove the drive mount platform.**

   You must remove the metal drive mount platform to which the hard disk and the diskette drives are attached. You must remove this platform, because the SIMM sockets in the Mac II, IIx and IIfx live underneath it.

   In removing this platform, you also remove the drives attached to it. First, you must disconnect the hard disk data cable and the hard disk power cable. Then disconnect the cable from the diskette drive. (If two diskette drives are installed in your Mac, both attach to the drive mount platform). Next remove the four screws, located at the corners of the platform, that hold the drive mount platform in place. Figure 18-6 shows the location of all these cables and screws. Remove the platform with the drives attached and set it aside on your grounded work surface.

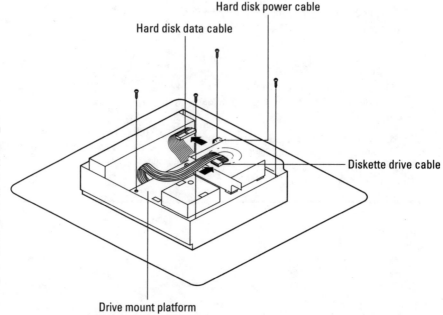

Figure 18-6: Disconnect these cables and take out the four screws to remove the drive mount platform.

Hard disk power cable

Hard disk data cable

Diskette drive cable

Drive mount platform

3. Remove the old SIMMs (if necessary).

If all the SIMM sockets on the logic board are already full, you must remove some or all of the old SIMMs to make way for the new ones. See Chapter 12 for instructions on removing the SIMMs. Figure 18-7 shows the locations of the *memory banks* on the Mac II and IIx, and on the IIfx.

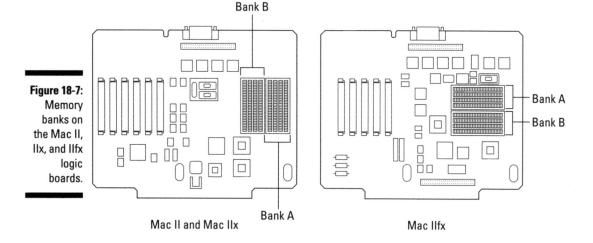

Bank B

Figure 18-7: Memory banks on the Mac II, IIx, and IIfx logic boards.

Bank A

Bank B

Mac II and Mac IIx

Bank A

Mac IIfx

4. Install the new SIMMs.

See Chapter 12 for the instructions on installing the SIMMs. Remember to follow the golden guide to SIMMs in that chapter and the information provided in the "Guide to the specific memory needs of each Mac" section, earlier in this chapter.

5. Replace the drive mount platform.

Set the drive mount platform in place. Make sure that the two small metal tabs on the back edge of the case fit in their slots in the platform. Make sure, too, that the platform is level and that all four screw holes line up. Replace the four screws in the corners of the platform.

6. Reconnect the drive cables.

Reconnect the hard disk data cable and the hard disk power cable to the hard disk.

Reconnect the diskette drive cable or cables. If your Mac has more than one diskette drive, make sure that the cable coming from the logic board and marked "Lower" plugs into the diskette drive on your right. Make sure, too, that the cable coming from the logic board and marked "Upper" plugs into the diskette drive on your left. (And, yes, from how the labels read on the logic board, you'd think the diskette drives sit on top of one another. But as you can tell from looking at your Mac, the drives actually sit side by side — so much for clear labeling.)

Notice that all the plugs on these cables are shaped so that they fit into their connectors only one way. Make sure that you orient the cable plugs correctly so that they fit into their connectors without forcing.

7. **Replace the top cover.**

Before you replace the top cover, make sure that none of the sheet-metal tabs that run along the inside edge of the front of the cover are bent inward, toward the center of the cover. If you do find bent tabs, bend them back into place before you replace the cover. Otherwise, the bent tabs keep the cover from closing correctly.

Replace the front edge of the top cover first. Pivot the back end of the cover down until the plastic tabs click into place. Press down firmly on the front edge of the cover to make sure that all the plastic loops engage correctly.

8. **Verify your upgrade.**

Reconnect your monitor, mouse, and keyboard, and start your Mac. Open the Apple menu and choose About this Macintosh. (In System 6, choose About the Finder.)

The number listed beside the words Total Memory: should equal the total amount of memory present in both banks. This number reflects both any old memory you may have left in the banks and the new memory you installed. If you have virtual memory turned on, this number is listed as Built-in Memory.

If the total memory is not what you expected or you experience other problems, refer to Chapter 12 or contact the company from which you purchased the SIMMs.

Good work; you just upgraded the memory in your Mac. How does it feel to own a Mac hock-full of memory? Wash the dust off your hands and take a well-deserved break!

Mac IIcx, IIci, and Quadra 700

The Mac IIcx and IIci are our favorite Macs to upgrade. The Quadra 700 . . . ? Well, it's a bit more complicated to upgrade than the other two. But on the Mac IIcx and IIci, all the internal parts are easily accessible — and disassembling these machines is quick and easy, too.

By the way, the c in IIcx stands for *compact*, because the Mac IIcx is the compact version of the Mac IIx. The ci in Mac IIci stands for *compact, internal video*, because the IIci was the first Mac to include built-in video circuitry on its logic board, which made connecting a monitor to your Mac easier and cheaper than with the earlier Mac IIs.

Opening up your Mac IIcx, IIci, or Quadra 700

To add any internal upgrade to your Mac IIcx, IIci, or Quadra 700, you first must open the top of the machine. And — hey! — these are modular Macs, so opening up a computer doesn't get much easier than this!

Tools you need: A Phillips number 2 screwdriver

Things to watch out for: Not much really. Opening the top on these Macs is as easy as pie.

Electrostatic discharge — a.k.a. static electricity — can fry the delicate electronic components in your Mac, even with a zap too small for you to feel! Make sure that you read in Chapter 3 about how to prevent electrostatic discharge *before* you start any upgrade.

1. **Shut down your Mac by opening the Special menu and choosing Shut Down.**

   Always shut down your Mac correctly before you start any upgrade.

2. **Disconnect all the cables from your computer and place the main box of your Mac — but not the monitor — on your grounded antistatic work surface.**

   If your Mac sits up in a vertical position, make sure that you set it on your antistatic mat in a horizontal position. You want the diskette drive slot *parallel* to the table surface and the Reset and Interrupt switches at the bottom edge of the front panel.

   Use a wrist strap and a grounded antistatic mat. Make sure that you carefully follow the electrostatic discharge prevention guidelines in Chapter 3 before you remove any upgrade products from their packages or touch any circuit board inside the Mac.

3. **Remove the security screw, if present.**

   The security screw is located on the back of the Mac, in the center at the top edge. (Your computer may not have this screw because not all Macs ship with it in place. If your machine has been upgraded before, someone may already have removed the screw and not replaced it.) Use a Phillips number 2 screwdriver to remove the screw if it is in place.

4. **Lift up on the plastic latching tabs at the rear corners of the cover and remove the cover.**

   These tabs lock the cover in place. Lift up on these tabs to release them and remove the cover.

The Quadra 700 has two rubber feet on which the Mac sits when upright. After you set this computer on its side, as described in Step 2, these feet now prevent you from removing the cover. The solution? Simply remove the two feet. Because the edges of these feet extend up over the cover, they hold the cover firmly in place if you fail to remove them.

There — you've got the cover off! Now skip to the section that describes the exact upgrade you're adding to your Mac.

Upgrading the internal hard disk in a Mac IIcx, IIci, or Quadra 700

This section describes how to upgrade the internal hard disk you already have in your Mac as well as how to add an internal hard disk if your Mac doesn't have one.

As we've cautioned you many, many times before, always remember to back up any files you want to keep from your old internal hard disk *before* you install your new one. See Chapter 16 for more information on backing up.

Tools you need: A Phillips number 2 screwdriver; a flat-blade screwdriver; needle-nosed pliers (optional)

Things to watch out for: Take care to disconnect the cables by pulling on their plugs, not on the wires.

1. **Remove the top cover by following Steps 1 through 4 in the preceding section, "Opening up your Mac IIcx, IIci, or Quadra 700."**

   Set the cover aside.

2. **Remove the power supply.**

   Taking out the power supply gives you access to the hard disk data cable and hard disk power cable connectors on the logic board. Use a flat-blade screwdriver to release the plastic latch at the back of the drive mount. Figure 18-8 shows the location of the power supply, the drive mount, and the latch.

   Hold the latch away from the power supply and pull the power supply up and out of the Mac. Removing the power supply may require a bit of effort, but if it doesn't move at all, check to make sure that the latch is released.

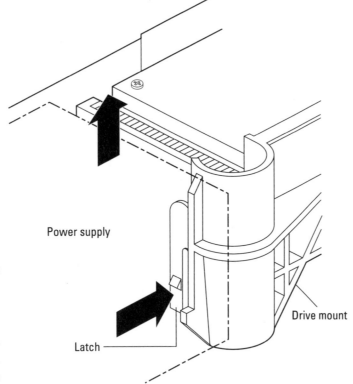

Power supply

Drive mount

Latch

3. **Disconnect the hard disk power cable and the hard disk data cable from the hard disk.**

   Skip to Step 6 if you're adding a hard disk to a Mac that doesn't currently have one installed. Figure 18-9 shows the location of the hard disk power cable and the hard disk data cable. You may need to use needle-nosed pliers to remove the power cable from the hard disk. If you do use pliers, grip only the power cable plug, not the wires.

4. **Remove the hard disk drive light from its holder on the front of the case.**

   The drive light just comes right out of its clear-plastic holder.

5. **Remove the hard disk from the drive mount.**

   Squeeze the metal tabs on either side of the hard disk together with your thumb and forefinger and pull the drive up and out of the computer. Figure 18-10 shows how to remove the hard disk.

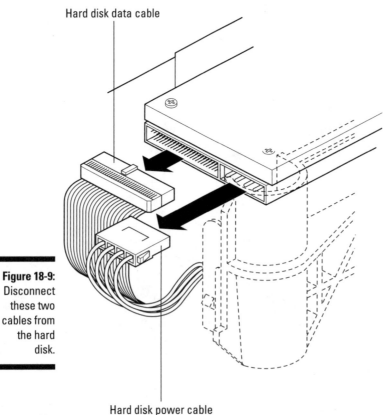

Hard disk data cable

Figure 18-9:
Disconnect
these two
cables from
the hard
disk.

Hard disk power cable

The hard disk may be wedged into the drive mount pretty tightly, so you may have to work on this a bit to get it out.

6. Attach the hard disk carrier bracket to the new hard disk.

As we pointed out in Chapter 12, whenever you buy a new hard disk for your Mac, you should also buy a mounting kit that contains a carrier bracket, a drive light, and cables. The carrier bracket is a U-shaped metal piece that holds your hard disk in the drive mount. The hard disk sits inside this U.

Use the screws supplied in the mounting kit you ordered with your new hard disk (at least, we *hope* you ordered it) to attach the carrier bracket. The four screws attach the carrier bracket to the bottom or side of your new hard disk, depending on your Mac model. Then connect the new drive light from the mounting kit to your hard disk.

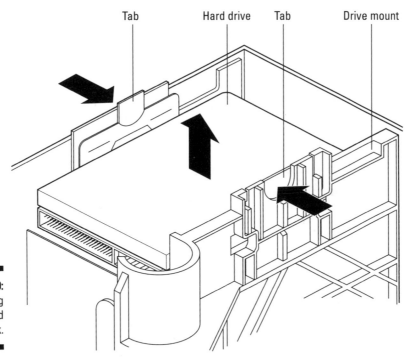

Tab   Hard drive   Tab   Drive mount

Figure 18-10:
Removing
the hard
disk.

The drive light works only if you connect it correctly. Some drive light cables have plugs that fit in the connector in the hard disk only one way. Other plugs can fit either way up. If you complete the upgrade but the drive light doesn't light up after the Mac starts or accesses a file, just plug in the connector the other way, and the light should work.

7. Connect the hard disk data and hard disk power cables to the logic board.

Skip to Step 8 if you're replacing an existing internal hard disk in your Mac. Complete Step 7 only if you're installing a hard disk in a Mac that did not already have an internal hard disk.

Locate the hard disk data and power cable connectors on the logic board. These connectors are located on the logic board below the back of the drive mount. You may also find a T-shaped terminator plug installed in the hard disk data cable connector. If a terminator plug is present, remove it. You don't need this plug again after you install the hard disk — so just throw it in your junk drawer where you can discover it someday and wonder to yourself, "What the heck *is* this thing?"

Connect the hard disk data cable and the hard disk power cables to their connectors on the logic board. The connectors and plugs are shaped so that the plugs only fit one way, so don't try to force the plugs into the connectors.

8. Install the new hard disk in your Mac.

Push the hard disk and carrier into the drive mount so that the metal tabs on the carrier bracket line up with the notches on the drive mount. The hard disk and carrier bracket click into place. Refer to Figure 20-10 to see how the hard disk fits into the drive mount.

9. Connect the hard disk data cable and the hard disk power cable.

Connect the hard disk data cable and the hard disk power cable to the new hard disk. These are the cables you unplugged from your old hard disk in Step 3. Refer to Figure 18-9 to see how the cables connect to the hard disk. The cables fit only one way into their connectors, so you don't need to force them.

10. Replace the power supply.

Align the power supply so that its fan and electrical plugs face the back of the Mac case. The plug that connects the power supply to the logic board should be on the bottom. Slide the power supply down into the right rear corner of the case so that the tabs that run along the corners of the power supply slip into the slots on the sides of the case. Push the power supply down into place until you hear the plastic latch on the drive mount click into place. Figure 18-11 shows how the power supply slides into the case.

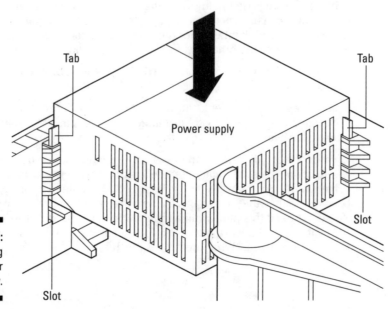

Figure 18-11:
Replacing
the power
supply.

Tab   Tab

Power supply

Slot

Slot

11. **Replace the top cover.**

> Replace the front edge of the top cover first. Pivot the back end of the cover down until the plastic tabs click into place. Press down firmly on the top of the cover to make sure that it is completely in place.

You just installed a hard disk in your Mac! Great! Just don't forget to copy the important files you backed up from your old hard disk onto your new one.

If you experience any problems after you complete your upgrade, see Chapters 8 and 12.

Upgrading the memory in a Mac IIcx, IIci, or Quadra 700

Memory — ya gotta' love it! This section shows you how to upgrade the memory in your Mac IIcx, IIci, or Quadra 700. As we described in Chapter 12, to install memory in a desktop Mac, you actually install small circuit boards that contain memory chips. Before you start your memory upgrade, refer back to Chapter 12 and its section "The golden guide to SIMMs" to learn how to correctly fill your Mac's memory sockets. Make sure that you follow the guide closely or the memory on which you spent your hard-earned money won't do your Mac any good. Also, read "Guide to the specific memory needs of each Mac," in this section for details.

Table 18-2 shows how much memory each Mac covered in this section can accept in its memory banks. Check the "Possible Memory Amounts" column on the table to determine the amount of memory your Mac model can accept. The Mac IIcx, for example, can accept 1, 2, 4, 5, 8, 17, 20, or 32MB of total memory. This Mac cannot, however, accept amounts that total 9 or 18MB.

The table also tells you what size SIMMs work in your machine. Make sure that you buy the right size, or your Mac can't use the SIMMs after you install them. Make sure, too, that you buy the right speed SIMMs. (The speeds listed in the table are the minimum speed for each Mac; remember that memory speed is measured in nanoseconds and abbreviated *ns*.) Don't buy SIMMs that run slower than the speeds listed here. Buying faster SIMMs is OK, but your Mac doesn't run any faster with speedier SIMMs.

Table 18-2   Memory Requirements for the Mac IIcx, IIci, and Quadra 700

Mac Model	SIMM Size This Model Can Use	Minimum SIMM Speed	Possible Memory Amounts (in MB)
IIcx	256K, 1MB, 4MB	120ns	1, 2, 4, 5, 8, 16, 17, 20, 32MB
IIci	256K, 512K, 1MB, 2MB, 4MB, 8MB, 16MB	80ns	1, 2, 4, 5, 6, 8, 9, 10, 12, 16, 17, 18, 20, 24, 32, . . . 64, . . .128MB (". . ." indicates many more possibilities in-between)
Quadra 700	1MB, 4MB, 16MB	80ns	4, 8, 20, 36, 68MB

Guide to the specific memory needs of each Mac

Before you install memory in your Mac, refer to the section "The golden guide to SIMMs," in Chapter 12. In addition to the guidelines offered in that chapter, the following information about memory upgrades applies to the Macs described in this section:

All Macs in this section: To upgrade memory in these Macs, you must install the SIMMs in groups of four; the four SIMMs must all be the same size and of the same speed. (See Table 18-2 to determine which SIMM sizes and speeds you need to buy.) You must install SIMMs in groups of four, because these Macs contain *memory banks* made up of four SIMM sockets each. The Mac IIcx and IIci each have two banks of four SIMM sockets, and the Quadra 700 has one bank of four.

Mac IIcx only: To upgrade past 8MB of memory in this Mac, you must use a version of System 7 and a special system extension. For Version 7.0 and 7.01, the extension is a system software product

called *MODE32*. You get the extension from a company called Connectix. The Connectix phone number is 800-950-5880. For Version 7.1 and later, the extension you need is called the *32-bit system enabler*. This extension is included on the system software disk.

Quadra 700: The Quadra 700 contains only one bank of SIMM sockets that accepts SIMMs. The computer also contains another memory bank, *bank A*, but this bank is filled with 4MB of memory chips that are permanently installed on the logic board. This leaves you only bank B for memory upgrades. This memory arrangement also means that, unless bank B is empty to begin with, you must remove the machine's old SIMMs before you can add your new ones.

Tools you need: A magnetic Phillips number 2 screwdriver; a ballpoint pen or a SIMM removal tool, needle-nosed pliers (optional)

Things to watch out for: Remove the SIMMs from their shielded packaging only at your grounded work area. Be careful to handle the SIMMs only by their edges — don't touch the chips or the metal contacts on the edge of the SIMMs. Be very careful, too, as you remove and install SIMMs, especially if your Mac uses plastic tabs on the SIMM sockets on the logic board. These plastic tabs on the sockets that hold the memory SIMMs are quite delicate. Some newer versions of the logic boards in these Macs use sockets with metal tabs.

1. **Remove the top cover by following Steps 1 through 4 in the section "Opening up your Mac IIcx, IIci, or Quadra 700."**

   Set the cover aside.

2. **Remove the drive mount.**

   Skip to Step 3 if you're upgrading a Mac IIcx or IIci. Step 2 applies to the Quadra 700 *only.*

   You must remove the drive mount because the SIMM sockets in the Mac Quadra 700 live underneath it.

   First, remove the power supply as described in Step 2 of the preceding section, "Installing or upgrading the internal hard disk in your Mac IIcx, IIci, or Quadra 700."

   Next, disconnect the hard disk data cable, the hard disk power cable, and the diskette drive cable from the logic board. The connectors for the cables are located below the back end of the drive mount. (The locations of these connectors are shown in Figure 18-12.) Remove the drive light from the clear plastic holder at the front of the case.

   Remove the Phillips screw that holds the drive mount in place. (The location of this screw also is shown in Figure 18-12.)

   Release the plastic latch at the side of the case and pull the drive mount toward the back of the case about half an inch. Lift the drive mount up and out of the case. Figure 18-12 shows how you remove the drive mount.

3. **Remove the old SIMMs (if necessary).**

   If all the SIMM sockets on the logic board are already full, you must remove some or all of the old SIMMs to make room for the new ones. See Chapter 12 for instructions on removing the SIMMs. Figure 18-13 shows the location of the memory banks that hold SIMMs on the Mac IIcx, IIci, and the Quadra 700. You can also see the video memory sockets for the Quadra 700.

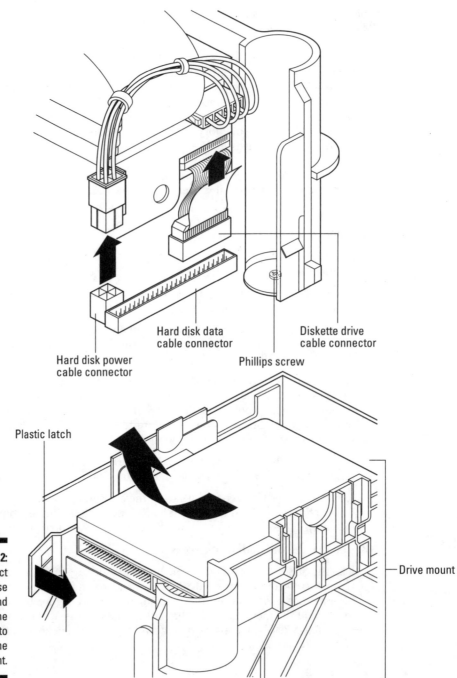

Hard disk data cable connector

Diskette drive cable connector

Hard disk power cable connector

Phillips screw

Plastic latch

Drive mount

Figure 18-12: Disconnect these cables and take out the screw to remove the drive mount.

Video memory sockets

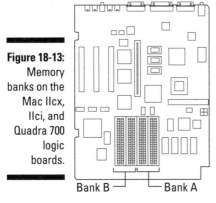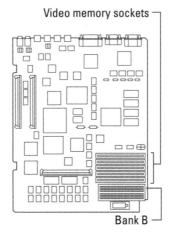

Figure 18-13:
Memory banks on the Mac IIcx, IIci, and Quadra 700 logic boards.

Bank B — └— Bank A   Bank B —

Mac IIcx & IIci   Mac Quadra 700

4. **Install the new SIMMs.**

See Chapter 12 for instructions on installing the SIMMs. Remember to follow the golden guide to SIMMs provided in that chapter and the information given in the section "Guide to the specific memory needs of each Mac" in this section.

5. **Replace the drive mount.**

Go to Step 6 if you're upgrading the Mac IIcx or IIci. Perform Step 5 for the Quadra 700 *only.*

Reverse the procedure you followed in Step 2 to replace the drive mount in the case.

6. **Replace the top cover.**

Replace the front edge of the top cover first. Pivot the back end of the cover down until the plastic tabs click into place. Press down firmly on the top of the cover to make sure that it's completely in place.

7. **Verify your upgrade.**

Reconnect your monitor, mouse, and keyboard, and start up your Mac. Open the Apple menu and choose About this Macintosh. In System 6, choose About the Finder.

The number listed beside Total Memory should equal the total amount of memory present in both banks. This number reflects any old memory you may have left in the banks and the new memory you just installed. If your virtual memory is turned on, this number is listed as Built-in Memory.

If the total memory is not what you expected or you experience other problems, refer to Chapter 12 or contact the company from which you purchased the SIMMs.

Hey — you just upgraded the memory in your Mac! Say good-bye to all those "out of memory" messages — for a while, at least. Now take a break. You deserve it.

You can install video memory in your Quadra 700 by following the same steps we give here for installing system memory. The video memory SIMM sockets are located right next to the system memory SIMM sockets on the logic board. Refer to Figure 18-13 to see where the video memory sockets are on the Quadra 700. (Sorry, but this tip doesn't apply to a Mac IIcx or IIci.)

Mac IIsi

What do you get if you cross a Mac LC with a Mac IIci? A Mac IIsi! The Mac IIsi is unique, because no other model shares its case design. The IIsi's closest relatives are the Mac IIci and the Mac LC, but the IIsi is different enough from either one that it deserves its own section. What can we say — the IIsi is in a class by itself!

Opening up your Mac IIsi

To add an internal upgrade to your Mac IIsi, the first thing you must do is open the top.

Tools you need: A Phillips number 2 screwdriver

Things to watch out for: Not much. Opening the IIsi is about as easy as opening a Mac gets.

Electrostatic discharge — a.k.a. static electricity — can fry the delicate electronic components in your Mac, even with a zap too small for you to feel! Make sure that you read in Chapter 3 about how to prevent electrostatic discharge *before* you start any upgrade.

1. **Shut down your Mac by opening the Special menu and choosing Shut Down.**

   Always shut down your Mac correctly before you start any upgrade.

2. **Disconnect all cables from your computer and place the main box of your Mac — but not the monitor — on your grounded antistatic work surface.**

   Use a wrist strap and a grounded antistatic mat. Make sure that you carefully follow the electrostatic discharge prevention guidelines in Chapter 3 before you remove any upgrade products from their packages or touch any circuit board inside the Mac.

3. **Remove the security screw, if present.**

   The security screw is located on the back of the Mac IIsi, at the top edge between the fan grill and the electrical plugs. Use a Phillips number 2 screwdriver to remove this screw, if it is in place. (Very few Mac IIsi's actually shipped with the security screw in place. And if your machine has been upgraded before, someone may already have removed the screw and not replaced it.)

4. **Remove the cover.**

   You can see four tabs on the back of the Mac. You must release the two large plastic tabs at the rear corners of the cover; you use the smaller tabs to help lift up the cover.

   Lift up on the large tabs on the cover as you use your thumbs to push down on the small, inner tabs. Pushing down with your thumbs gives you enough leverage to overcome the friction holding the case in place. Lift the back of the cover so that the cover is at an angle and then remove the cover from the Mac.

You've got the cover off! Skip ahead to the section that describes the upgrade you're making to your Mac.

Upgrading the internal hard disk in a Mac IIsi

This section covers upgrading the internal hard disk in your Mac and also describes how to add an internal hard disk to a Mac that doesn't have one. Back up the files you want to keep from your old internal hard disk *before* you install your new one. See Chapter 16 for more information on backing up.

Tools you need: A Phillips number 2 screwdriver; needle-nosed pliers (optional)

Things to watch out for: Take care to disconnect cables by pulling on the plugs, not on the wires.

1. **Remove the top cover by following Steps 1 through 4 in the section "Opening up your Mac IIsi."**

   Set the cover aside.

2. **Disconnect the hard disk power cable and the hard disk data cable from the logic board.**

   Skip ahead to Step 4 if you're adding a hard disk to a Mac that does not currently have one. Figure 18-14 shows the location of the hard disk power cable and the hard disk data cable.

Hard disk data cable

Hard disk power cable

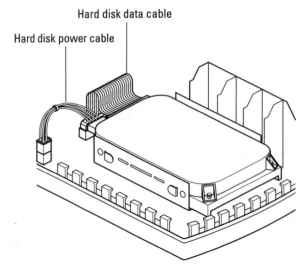

Figure 18-14:
Disconnect
these two
cables from
the hard
disk.

3. **Remove the hard disk from the computer.**

   Release the plastic tabs on either side of the hard disk and lift the hard disk out of the computer. You may need to release one side of the drive at a time. Figure 18-15 shows how the hard disk comes out of the computer.

4. **Attach the hard disk carrier bracket to the new hard disk.**

   As we pointed out in Chapter 12, whenever you buy a new hard disk for your Mac, you should also buy a mounting kit that contains a carrier bracket and cables for mounting your new hard disk in your Mac. The carrier bracket is a U-shaped metal piece that holds your hard disk in place inside your Mac IIsi. The hard disk sits inside the U.

   Use the four screws supplied in the mounting kit you ordered with your new hard disk (at least, we hope you ordered it) to attach the carrier bracket.

   The four screws attach the carrier bracket to either the bottom or side of your new hard disk, depending on the hard disk model.

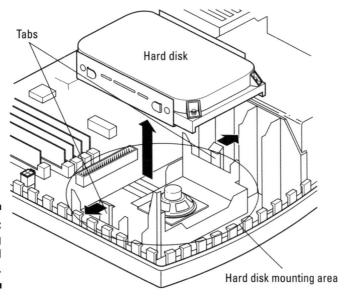

Tabs

Hard disk

Figure 18-15:
Removing
the hard
disk.

Hard disk mounting area

5. **Connect the hard disk data and power cables to the new hard disk.**

   Attach the hard disk data cable and the hard disk power cable to your new
   hard disk. These cables are included in the mounting kit you ordered with
   your hard disk.

6. **Install the new hard disk in your Mac.**

   Line up your hard disk over the hard disk mounting area in your Mac. The
   cables should face the back of the Mac. Push the hard disk down into its
   mount. The plastic mounting tabs click into place over the carrier bracket.
   Refer to Figure 18-15 to see exactly how the hard disk fits into the hard
   disk mounting area.

7. **Connect the hard disk power and hard disk data cables to the logic
   board.**

   Connect the new hard disk's data and power cables to the logic board.
   Refer to Figure 18-14 to see the location of the connectors on the logic
   board into which these cables plug. The cables fit only one way into their
   connectors, so don't force them.

8. **Replace the top cover.**

   Bring the cover straight down over the Mac. Press down until the plastic
   tabs at the back click into place. Press down gently but firmly on the top of
   the cover to make sure that it is completely in place. Check under the front
   edge of the cover to make sure that the front of the cover is all the way
   down.

You just installed a hard disk in your Mac IIsi. Great! Now you can start filling it up with new software and new files. And don't forget to copy the important files you backed up from your old hard disk onto your new one.

If you experience any problems after you complete your upgrade, refer to Chapters 8 and 12.

Upgrading the memory in a Mac IIsi

Want to install more memory in your Mac IIsi? Well, you came to the right place. This section shows you how to upgrade the memory in your Mac IIci. As discussed in Chapter 12, to install memory in a desktop Mac, you actually install small circuit boards that contain memory chips. Before you start your memory upgrade, refer back to Chapter 12 and its section "The golden guide to SIMMs" to learn how to fill up the memory sockets correctly. Make sure that you follow the guide closely; otherwise, the memory on which you spent your hard-earned money won't do your Mac any good. Also, read the section "Guide to the specific memory needs of the Mac IIsi," in this section.

Table 18-3 shows you how much memory the Mac IIsi can accept in its memory banks. Check the "Possible Memory Amounts" column on the table to determine the amount of memory your Mac IIsi can accept. (As the table shows, the Mac IIsi can accept 1, 2, 3, 5, 9, or 17MB of total memory. This Mac cannot, however, accept amounts that total 6, 12, or 20MB.)

The table also tells you what size SIMMs work in your machine. Make sure that you buy the right size, or your Mac can't use the SIMMs after you install them. Make sure, too, that you buy the right speed SIMMs. (The speed listed in the table is the minimum speed for this Mac; memory speed is measured in nanoseconds and abbreviated ns.) Don't buy SIMMs that run slower than the speed listed here. Buying faster SIMMs is OK, but your Mac doesn't run any faster with the speedier SIMMs.

Table 18-3	Memory Requirements for the Mac IIsi		
Mac Model	*SIMM Size This Model Can Use*	*Minimum SIMM Speed*	*Possible Memory Amounts (in MB)*
Mac IIsi	256K, 512K, 1MB, 2MB, 4MB	100ns	1, 2, 3, 5, 9, 17MB

Guide to the specific memory needs of the Mac IIsi

Before you install memory in your Mac, refer to the section "The golden guide to SIMMs," in Chapter 12. In addition to the guidelines in that chapter, the following information applies to the Mac IIsi.

To install SIMMs in the Mac IIsi, you must install four SIMMs at a time; the SIMMs must all be the same size and speed. See Table 18-3 to determine the SIMM sizes and speeds you need to buy.

The Mac IIsi contains only one bank of SIMM sockets to accept SIMMs. The computer does have a second memory bank, but this bank — bank A — already contains 1MB of memory chips permanently installed on the logic board. This arrangement leaves you only bank B for your memory upgrades; unless bank B is already empty, you must remove any old SIMMs before you can add your new ones.

If you're ready to do a memory upgrade, then let's go for it!

Tools you need: A Phillips number 2 screwdriver; a ballpoint pen or a SIMM removal tool

Things to watch out for: As we cautioned earlier, remove the SIMMs from their shielded packaging only at your grounded work area. Be careful to handle the SIMMs only by their edges — don't touch the chips or the metal contacts on the edge of the SIMM. Make sure that you push the SIMMs all the way into the sockets. A SIMM not correctly seated prevents the Mac from starting.

1. **Remove the top cover by following Steps 1 through 4 in the section "Opening up your Mac IIsi."**

   Set the cover aside.

2. **Remove the old SIMMs (if necessary).**

   If the SIMM sockets on the logic board are full already, you need to remove the old SIMMs to make way for the new ones. See Chapter 12 for instructions on removing the SIMMs. Figure 18-16 shows the location of the memory banks on the Mac IIsi.

3. **Install the new SIMMs.**

   See Chapter 12 for the instructions on installing the SIMMs. Remember to follow the golden guide to SIMMs provided in that chapter, as well as the information in the section "Guide to the specific memory needs of the Mac IIsi," in this section.

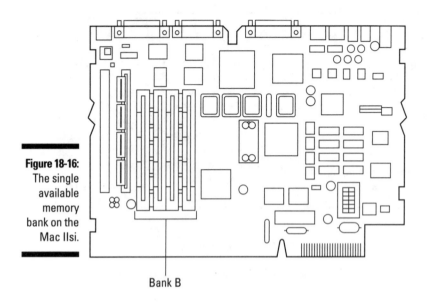

Figure 18-16:
The single
available
memory
bank on the
Mac IIsi.

Bank B

4. Replace the top cover.

Bring the cover straight down over the Mac. Press down until the plastic tabs at the back click into place. Press down gently but firmly on the top of the cover to make sure that it is completely in place. Check under the front edge of the cover to make sure that the front of the cover is all the way down.

5. Verify your upgrade.

Reconnect your monitor, mouse, and keyboard, and start your Mac. Open the Apple menu and choose About this Macintosh. In System 6, choose About the Finder.

The number listed beside Total Memory should equal the total amount of memory present in both banks. This number reflects both the 1MB of memory permanently installed in bank A and the new memory you just installed in bank B. If virtual memory is turned on, this number is listed as Built-in Memory.

If the total memory is not what you expected or you experience other problems, refer to Chapter 12 or contact the company from which you purchased the SIMMs.

Good work — you just upgraded the memory in your Mac. How does it feel to own a computer simply loaded with memory? Go ahead and take a break now. You deserve it!

Mac IIvi, IIvx, Performa 600, 600 CD, Centris or Quadra 650, and Power Mac 7100

This group of Macs is pretty amazing, because these machines come from so many different Macintosh product lines. (By the way, if you own a Mac IIvi, IIvx, Performa 600, 600 CD, or Centris or Quadra 650, and you want Power Mac capabilities, you can transform your Mac into a Power Mac 7100 via a logic board upgrade. You must get a technician to do this upgrade for you, however.)

Opening up your Mac IIvi, IIvx, Performa 600, 600 CD, Centris or Quadra 650, or Power Mac 7100

To add an internal upgrade to your Mac, you must first open the top.

Tools you need: A flat-blade screwdriver

Things to watch out for: Don't use too much force on the screw that holds the top cover in place. If you apply too much force, you may damage the top cover.

Electrostatic discharge — a.k.a. static electricity — can fry the delicate electronic components in your Mac, even with a zap too small for you to feel! Make sure that you read in Chapter 3 about preventing electrostatic discharge before you start any upgrade.

1. **Shut down your Mac by opening the Special menu and choosing Shut Down.**

   Always shut down your Mac correctly before you start any upgrade.

2. **Disconnect all the cables from your computer and place the main box of your Mac — but not the monitor — on your grounded antistatic work surface.**

   Use a wrist strap and a grounded antistatic mat. Make sure that you follow closely the electrostatic discharge prevention guidelines provided in Chapter 3 before you remove any upgrade products from their packages or touch any circuit board inside the Mac.

3. Loosen the captive screw that holds the top cover in place.

The captive screw is located on the back of the Mac, in the very center of the top edge, down inside a hole. The screw is exactly that — captive. It doesn't leave the Mac case, which is nice, because that way you can't lose it.

Use the flat-blade screwdriver to loosen the captive screw.

4. Remove the cover.

Slide the top cover forward about one inch. Lift the top cover straight up and off the Mac. Be careful not to tilt the cover as you lift it off the computer.

There. The cover's off! Now skip on to the section that describes the upgrade you're making to your Mac.

Upgrading the internal hard disk in a Mac IIvi, IIvx, Performa 600, 600 CD, Centris or Quadra 650, or Power Mac 7100

This section describes how to upgrade the internal hard disk in your Mac and also how to add an internal hard disk to a Mac that doesn't have one already. As we've mentioned before, back up the files you want to keep from your old internal hard disk *before* you install the new one. See Chapter 16 for more information on backing up your files.

Tools you need: A Phillips number 2 screwdriver; needle-nosed pliers (optional)

Things to watch out for: Take care to disconnect cables by pulling on the plugs, not on the wires.

1. Remove the top cover by following Steps 1 through 4 in the preceding section, "Opening up your Mac IIvi, IIvx, Performa 600, 600 CD, Centris or Quadra 650, or Power Mac 7100."

Set the cover aside.

2. Disconnect the power cable and the data cable from the hard disk.

Skip ahead to Step 4 if you're adding a hard disk to a Mac that does not currently have one.

Figure 18-17 shows the location of these two cables.

3. Remove the hard disk from the computer.

Remove the mounting screw that holds the hard disk in place. Then lift the back end of the hard disk and slide the hard disk back and out of the drive chassis. The arrows in Figure 18-17 show how to remove the hard disk from the computer.

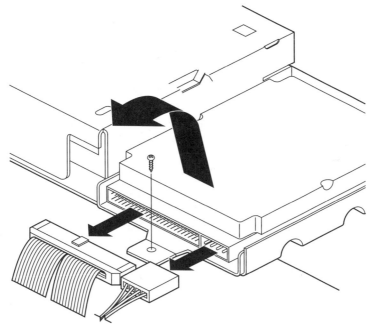

Figure 18-17:
Removing
the hard
disk.

4. Attach the hard disk carrier bracket to your new hard disk.

The carrier bracket is a metal plate that holds the hard disk in place inside
your Mac. As pointed out in Chapter 12, whenever you buy a new hard
disk for your Mac, you should also buy a mounting kit that contains a
carrier bracket and cables for mounting your new hard disk in your Mac.

The carrier bracket attaches to the bottom of the hard disk, as Figure 18-17
shows. The large tab with the hole for the mounting screw should be at the
same end of the hard disk as the connectors for the hard disk data and
power cables.

Use the screws supplied in the mounting kit you ordered with your new
hard disk to attach the carrier bracket. (You *did* order that mounting kit —
didn't you?)

5. Connect the power cable and the data cable to the logic board.

Skip to Step 6 if you're installing a hard disk in a Mac that already had one.
Perform Step 5 *only* if you are installing a hard disk in a Mac that didn't
have one previously.

The connectors for the power and data cables are located on the logic
board, below the back end of the diskette drive. Plug the cables into their
connectors. The cables fit into the connectors only one way, so you don't
need to force them.

Notice that the Macs described in this section use special power and data cables. Each cable has a connector in the middle in addition to the connectors on either end. This extra connector enables you to use the same cable to connect both a hard disk and a CD-ROM drive — a very thrifty arrangement, don't you think?

The connector at one end of each cable plugs into the logic board. The connector at the other end plugs into the hard disk. The middle connector on both cables is used for the CD-ROM drive, if your Mac has one. If your Mac has no CD-ROM drive installed, the middle connector on both cables remains unused.

6. Install the new hard disk in your Mac.

Tilt the front end of the hard disk and the carrier bracket down and slide them into place beside the diskette drive. As the tabs at the front of the carrier bracket engage in the slots in the drive chassis, lower the back end of the hard disk into place. Refer to Figure 18-17 to see exactly how the hard disk fits into the drive chassis.

After the drive is in place, install the mounting screw. Refer to Figure 18-17 to see exactly where the mounting screw goes.

7. Connect the power and the data cables to the hard disk.

Refer to Figure 18-17 to see exactly how the cables plug into the hard disk. These cables fit into the connectors only one way, so you don't need to force them.

8. Replace the top cover.

Bring the cover straight down over the Mac so that about a one-inch gap remains between the back of the cover and the back of the Mac. Slide the cover back into place.

Watch out for these components in particular as you replace the cover: the Reset and Interrupt switches and the power light. These components are located at the lower corners of the front of the Mac. Be careful not to knock them out of place as you replace the cover.

After the cover is on, tighten the captive screw at the back of the Mac. Be careful not to overtighten the captive screw, because too much force on the screw can damage the top cover.

Well, you just installed a hard disk in your Mac. Good job! The next step is to start filling up that new disk with files and applications. Remember, of course, to copy the important files you backed up from your old hard disk onto your new one.

If you experience any problems after you complete your upgrade, refer to Chapters 8 and 12.

Upgrading the memory in a Mac IIvi, IIvx, Performa 600, 600 CD, Centris or Quadra 650, or Power Mac 7100

Well, if you want to install more memory in your Mac, you've come to the right place. This section shows you how to upgrade the memory in your Mac IIvi, IIvx, Performa 600, 600 CD, Centris or Quadra 650, and Power Mac 7100. As discussed in Chapter 12, to install memory in a desktop Mac, you actually install small circuit boards that contain memory chips. Before you start on your memory upgrade, refer to Chapter 12 and its section "The golden guide to SIMMs" to learn how to fill memory sockets correctly. Make sure that you follow this guide closely; otherwise, the memory on which you spent your hard-earned money won't do your Mac any good. Also, read the section, "Guide to the specific memory needs of each Mac," in this section.

Table 18-4 shows you how much memory each Mac covered in this section can accept in its memory banks. Check the "Possible Memory Amounts" column on the table to determine the amount of memory your Mac model can accept. The Mac IIvx, for example, can accept 4, 5, 8, 12, 20, or 68MB of total memory. This Mac cannot, however, accept amounts that total 9, 16, or 18MB.

The table also tells you what size SIMMs work in your machine. Make sure that you buy the right size, or your Mac can't use the SIMMs after you install them. Make sure, too, that you buy the right speed SIMMs. (The speed listed on the table is the minimum speed for each Mac; memory speed is measured in nanoseconds and abbreviated *ns*.) Don't buy SIMMs that run slower than the speeds listed on this table. Buying faster SIMMs is OK, but your Mac doesn't run any faster with the speedier SIMMs.

Table 18-4   Memory Requirements for the Macs in This Section

Mac Model	*SIMM Size This Model Can Use*	*Minimum SIMM Speed*	*Possible Memory Amounts (in MB)*
IIvi, IIvx, Performa 600, 600 CD	256K, 1MB, 2MB, 4MB, 16MB	80ns	4, 5, 8, 12, 20, 68MB
Centris or Quadra 650	4MB, 8MB, 16MB, 32MB	80ns	4, 8, 12, 16, 20, 24, 28, 32, 36, 40, 44, 48, 52, 56, 60, 64, 68, 72, 76, 80, 84, 88, 92, 96, 104, 108, 112, 120, 136MB
Power Mac 7100	4MB, 8MB, 16MB, 32 MB	80ns	8, 16, 24, 32, 40, 48, 72, 32, 80, 136MB

Guide to the specific memory needs of each Mac

Before you install memory in your Mac, refer to the section "The golden guide to SIMMs," in Chapter 12. In addition to the guidelines in that chapter, the following information applies to each specific Mac described in this section:

All Macs in this section: You must install 72-pin SIMMs in the Mac IIvi, IIvx, Performa 600, 600 CD, Centris or Quadra 650, and Power Mac 7100. These SIMMs are different from the 30-pin SIMMs used in older Macs such as the Mac SE and the Mac IIci. So if you're thinking about using SIMMs from an older Mac in a newer Mac, check the number of pins on the old SIMMs. You can't pull SIMMs out of your Mac IIci, for example, to use in any of the Macs covered in this section. Sorry. (Normally, recycling computer parts is a good idea — just not in this case.)

Mac IIvx, IIvi, Performa 600, and 600 CD: If you install SIMMs in a Mac IIvx, IIvi, Performa 600, and 600 CD, you must install four SIMMs at a time, and the SIMMs must all be the same size and speed. (See Table 18-4 to determine the SIMM sizes and speeds you need to buy.)

These Macs contain only one bank of SIMM sockets that accept SIMMs. These computers also have another memory bank — bank A — but this bank contains 1MB of memory chips that are permanently installed on the logic board. This arrangement leaves you only bank B in which to install your memory upgrades. And unless bank B is already empty, you must remove any old SIMMs to install new ones.

Centris or Quadra 650: You can install SIMMs in any socket you want in the Centris or Quadra 650. These two Macs have four SIMM sockets on the logic board. Each socket is considered a separate bank, so you can use different-sized SIMMs in each socket. You can also skip sockets and install SIMMs in whichever sockets you like. These machines have one of the most flexible memory systems of any Mac ever built. Their sole limitation is that you can install only 4MB, 8MB, 16MB, or 32MB SIMMs. You can boost the speed of your Quadra 650 by about five to ten percent by adding memory SIMMs in matched pairs (size and speed). The reasons this can be done are really technical, so we won't go into them here, but it really does work.

Not every Centris or Quadra 650 machine, however, can use all the memory configurations listed in Table 18-4. Some Centris 650s are shipped with only 4MB of memory soldered onto the logic board; the rest of the Centris 650s and Quadra 650s are shipped with 8MB on the logic board.

Power Mac 7100: You must install SIMMs in the Power Mac 7100 in pairs. The Power Mac 7100 contains two memory banks made up of two SIMM sockets each — four sockets total. Remember that each pair of SIMMs must match in size and speed.

If you want to install video memory SIMMs in the Macs covered in this section, you can use the instructions for installing memory in the Power Mac 7100. Go to the section "Follow these steps to install memory in the Power Mac 7100" and follow Steps 1 through 8. By the way, you can't add video memory to the Power Mac 7100 itself, because that model doesn't use video memory SIMMs. This Mac instead uses system memory for its video functions.

If you're ready to rock and roll, then it's time to upgrade your Mac's memory.

Tools you need: A Phillips number 2 screwdriver (for the Power Mac 7100 only; just your hands for the other Macs); a ballpoint pen or a SIMM removal tool

Things to watch out for: Remove the SIMMs from their shielded packaging only at your grounded work area. Be careful to handle the SIMMs only by the edges — don't touch the chips or the metal contacts on the edge of the SIMM. Make sure that you push the SIMMs all the way into their sockets — a SIMM not correctly seated prevents the Mac from starting.

Follow these steps to install memory in a Mac IIvi, IIvx, Performa 600, 600 CD, or Centris or Quadra 650

1. **Remove the top cover by following Steps 1 through 4 in the section "Opening up your Mac IIvi, IIvx, Performa 600, 600 CD, Centris or Quadra 650, or Power Mac 7100."**

   Set the cover aside.

2. **Remove the old SIMMs (if necessary).**

   If the SIMM sockets on the logic board are already full, you must remove the old SIMMs to make way for the new ones. See Chapter 12 for instructions on removing and installing SIMMs. Figure 18-18 shows the logic boards for the Mac IIvi, IIvx, Performa 600, 600 CD, and Centris or Quadra 650.

Figure 18-18: The Mac IIvi, IIvx, Performa 600, and Centris or Quadra 650 logic boards.

Video memory sockets

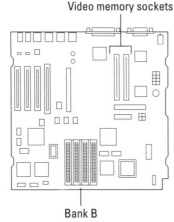

Bank B

The Mac IIvx, IIvi, and Performa 600 logic board

Video memory sockets

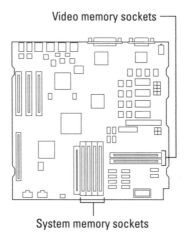

System memory sockets

The Centris Quadra 650 logic board

3. **Install the new SIMMs.**

See Chapter 12 for instructions on installing the SIMMs. Remember to follow the golden guide to SIMMs provided there, as well as the information in the section, "Guide to the specific memory needs of each Mac," in this section.

4. **Replace the top cover.**

Bring the cover straight down over the Mac so that about a one-inch gap remains between the back of the cover and the back of the Mac. Slide the cover into place.

Watch out for these components as you replace the cover: the Reset and Interrupt switches and the power light. These components are located at the lower corners of the front of the Mac. Be careful not to knock them out of place as you replace the cover.

After the cover is on, tighten the captive screw at the back of the Mac. Be careful not to overtighten the captive screw; too much force on the screw can damage the top cover.

5. **Verify your upgrade.**

Reconnect your monitor, mouse, and keyboard, and start your Mac. Open the Apple menu and choose About this Macintosh. In System 6, choose About the Finder.

The number listed beside Total Memory should equal the total amount of memory present in all the banks. This number reflects any memory permanently installed plus any memory you installed in the memory sockets. If virtual memory is turned on, this number is listed as Built-in Memory.

If the total memory is not what you expected, or you have other problems, refer to Chapter 12 or contact the company you purchased the SIMMs from.

Hey, you just upgraded the memory in your Mac. No more "out of memory" messages for a while. Congratulate yourself and take a break!

Follow these steps to install memory in a Power Mac 7100

To get at the memory banks in a Power Mac 7100, you must remove the power supply and the drive chassis. The drive chassis holds the hard disk, diskette drive, and the CD-ROM drive, if one is installed. (Figure 18-19 shows the drive chassis.)

1. **Remove the top cover by following Steps 1 through 4 in the section "Opening up your Mac IIvi, IIvx, Performa 600, 600 CD, Centris or Quadra 650, or Power Mac 7100."**

   Set the cover aside.

2. **Remove the power supply.**

   If your Power Mac 7100 has a CD-ROM drive installed, first squeeze the plastic tabs on either side of the CD-ROM drive and slide the drive forward a couple inches. Moving the drive forward opens up some working space in front of the power supply.

   Next, if a power supply strap is installed on top of the power supply, squeeze the tabs at the end of the strap and push it out through the side of the Mac. (Figure 18-19 shows the power supply strap.)

   Remove the power supply screw from the back of the Mac by using the Phillips number 2 screwdriver. Pry the latch away from the front of the power supply and then lift the power supply out of the drive chassis.

   You may feel a bit of resistance; as you lift out the power supply, you're also disconnecting it from its connector on the logic board. Figure 18-19 shows how the power supply comes out of the Mac.

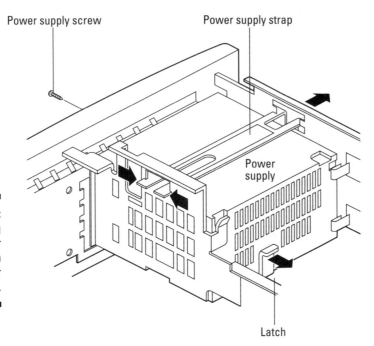

Power supply screw

Power supply strap

Power supply

Figure 18-19:
Removing the power supply from the Power Mac 7100.

Latch

3. Remove the drive chassis.

To get ready to remove the drive chassis, first disconnect all the cables from all the storage drives installed in your Power Mac 7100. Leave the cables connected to the logic board.

Disconnect the diskette drive cable from the diskette drive. Disconnect the hard disk data cable and the hard disk power cable from the hard disk. If a CD-ROM drive is installed, disconnect the data cable, the power cable, and the CD-ROM audio cable from the drive.

Now remove the two screws at the front corners of the drive chassis. One of the screws is easy to find; it's located at about the center of the front of the Mac. You may need to look around a bit to locate the other screw; it's situated down on the side of the chassis — not on the top as you may expect based on the location of the first screw. (Figure 18-20 shows these screw locations.)

Lift the front end of the drive chassis until the drive chassis is vertical. The drive chassis pivots where the chassis tabs meet the back of the Mac. Move the drive chassis forward and slide the chassis tabs out of their slots in the bottom case. Remove the drive chassis from the Mac. Figure 18-20 shows how the drive chassis comes out of the Mac.

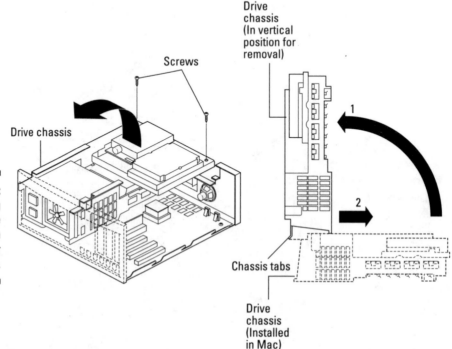

Drive chassis (In vertical position for removal)

Screws

Drive chassis

Figure 18-20: Removing the drive chassis from the Power Mac 7100.

Chassis tabs

Drive chassis (Installed in Mac)

4. Remove the old SIMMs (if necessary).

If the SIMM sockets on the logic board already are full, you must remove the old SIMMs to make way for the new ones. See Chapter 12 for instructions on removing the SIMMs. Figure 18-21 shows the memory banks on the Power Mac 7100 logic board.

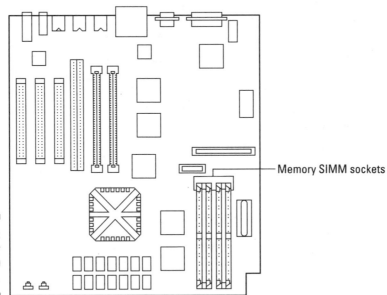

Memory SIMM sockets

Figure 18-21:
The Power
Mac 7100
logic board.

5. Install the new SIMMs.

See Chapter 12 for the instructions on installing the SIMMs. Remember to follow the golden guide to SIMMs provided there, as well as the information in the section, "Guide to the specific memory needs of each Mac," in this section.

You must install the SIMMs in the Power Mac 7100 in pairs, and both SIMMs in a pair must be the same size and speed.

6. Replace the drive chassis.

Start by holding the drive chassis in a vertical position with the drives facing up, just as the chassis was positioned when you removed it in Step 3. Guide the chassis tabs into their slots on the back case. Refer to Figure 18-20 to see where the chassis tabs fit into the back case. Lower the front of the drive chassis into place. As you lower the drive chassis, pull the drive cables from the logic board through the hole in the bottom of the drive chassis.

Replace the two screws at the front of the drive chassis.

Reconnect all the drive cables to the drives. If your computer has a CD-ROM drive installed, reconnect the data cable, the power cable, and the CD-ROM audio cable to the drive. Reconnect the diskette drive cable to the diskette drive. Finally, reconnect the data cable and the power cable to the hard disk.

7. **Replace the power supply.**

Slide the power supply down into the rear corner of the drive chassis. Push it down until it clicks into place. Replace the power supply screw at the back of the Mac. Refer to Figure 18-19 to see the location of this screw.

If your Mac has a strap on top of the power supply, replace it now. Squeeze the tabs at the end of the strap together and push the strap through the side of the case to replace it.

Push on the front of the CD-ROM drive to make sure that the drive clicks into place in the drive chassis.

8. **Replace the top cover.**

Bring the cover straight down over the Mac so that about a one-inch gap remains between the back of the cover and the back of the Mac. Slide the cover back into place.

Watch out for these components as you replace the cover: the Reset and Interrupt switches and the power light. These components are located at the lower corners of the front of the Mac. Be careful not to knock them out of place as you replace the cover.

After the cover is on, tighten the captive screw at the back of the Mac. Be careful not to overtighten the captive screw; too much force on the screw can damage the top cover.

9. **Verify your upgrade.**

Reconnect your monitor, mouse, and keyboard, and start your Mac. Open the Apple menu and choose About this Macintosh. In System 6, choose About the Finder.

The number listed beside Total Memory should equal the total amount of memory present in both banks. This number reflects any memory permanently installed plus any memory you just installed in the memory sockets. If virtual memory is turned on, this number is listed as Built-in Memory.

If the total memory is not what you expected or you experience other problems, refer to Chapter 12 or contact the company from which you purchased the SIMMs.

Great! You just upgraded the memory in your Power Mac. How does it feel to have your computer loaded with memory? Go ahead — take a well-deserved break!

Mac Centris or Quadra 610, Centris or Quadra 660AV, AWS 60, Power Mac 6100, and WGS 6150

These desk-hugging flat Macs feature reasonable computing muscle for a bargain price. All the components inside these Macs are easily accessible, so any upgrade you want to make goes smoothly.

Opening up your Mac Centris or Quadra 610, Centris or Quadra 660AV, AWS 60, Power Mac 6100, or WGS 6150

The first step to any internal upgrade is to pop the cover off your Mac.

Tools you need: Nothing but your hands!

Things to watch out for: This part is just opening the top — nothing to watch out for yet.

Electrostatic discharge — a.k.a. static electricity — can fry the delicate electronic components in your Mac, even with a zap too small for you to feel! Make sure that you read in Chapter 3 about how to prevent electrostatic discharge *before* you start any upgrade.

1. **Shut down your Mac by opening the Special menu and choosing Shut Down.**

   Always shut down your Mac correctly before you start any upgrade. Use the power button on the front of the Mac to turn off the power.

2. **Disconnect all the cables from your Mac and place the main box of the computer — but not the monitor — on your grounded antistatic work surface.**

   Make sure that you use a wrist strap and a grounded antistatic mat and that you follow closely the electrostatic discharge prevention guidelines provided in Chapter 3 *before* you remove any upgrade products from their packages or touch any circuit board inside the Mac.

3. **Remove the cover.**

   Position your Mac so that the back panel faces you. Find the tabs on either side of the top cover at the back of the Mac. To remove the cover, use your thumbs to push up on the tabs. You hear the tabs click as they disengage. Tilt the cover up and remove it from the Mac.

There. You've got the cover off! Now go on to the section that describes the exact upgrade you're making to your Mac.

Upgrading the internal hard disk in a Mac Centris or Quadra 610, Centris or Quadra 660 AV, AWS 60, Power Mac 6100, or WGS 6150

This section describes how to upgrade the internal hard disk in your Mac. You can never have enough storage space. Believe us, you'll fill it up with files and applications — and do so much faster than you think! Remember to back up the files you want to keep from your old internal hard disk before you install your new one. See Chapter 16 for more information on backing up.

Tools you need: A Phillips number 2 screwdriver; needle-nosed pliers (optional)

Things to watch out for: Take care to disconnect cables by pulling on the plugs, not on the wires.

1. **Remove the top cover by following Steps 1 through 3 in the section "Opening up your Mac Centris or Quadra 610, Centris or Quadra 660AV, AWS 60, Power Mac 6100, or WGS 6150."**

   Set the cover aside.

2. **Disconnect the hard disk power cable and the hard disk data cable from the hard disk.**

   Figure 18-22 shows the location of these two cables. You may need to use needle-nosed pliers to pull the power cable plug out of its connector on the hard disk. Always pull on the plug, not on the cable.

3. **Remove the metal hard disk shield from the front of the computer.**

   Pull the top edge of the metal shield away from the computer. Then push the shield down to disengage the tabs at the bottom of the case. Set the shield aside.

4. **Remove the hard disk from the computer.**

   Push down on the plastic tab at the front of the hard disk and slide the hard disk forward and out of the computer. Figure 18-23 shows how to remove the hard disk from the computer.

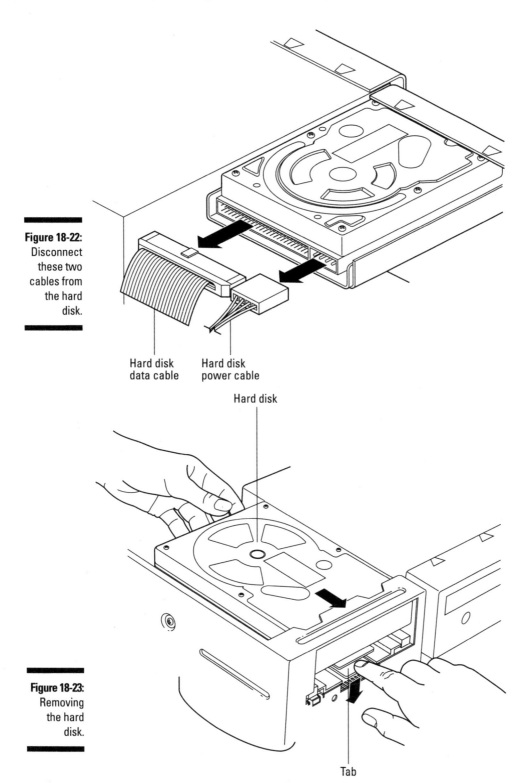

Figure 18-22: Disconnect these two cables from the hard disk.

Hard disk data cable

Hard disk power cable

Hard disk

Figure 18-23: Removing the hard disk.

Tab

5. Remove the hard disk carrier bracket from your old hard disk.

The carrier bracket is the plastic piece that attaches to the underside of the hard disk and holds the disk in place inside the Mac. As suggested Chapter 12, whenever you buy a new hard disk for your Mac, you should also buy a mounting kit that contains a carrier bracket and cables for mounting your new hard disk in your Mac.

Remove the four screws that attach the carrier bracket to the hard disk. (Figure 18-24 shows the carrier bracket and the hard disk and how they attach.)

6. Attach the hard disk carrier bracket to your new hard disk.

Figure 18-24 shows how the hard disk attaches to the hard disk carrier bracket.

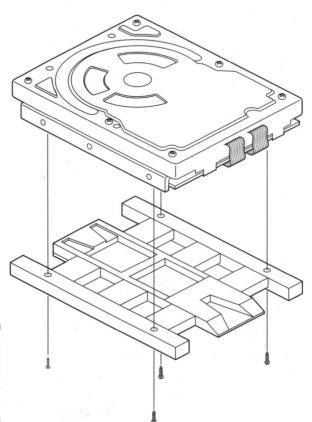

Figure 18-24:
The hard disk and the carrier bracket.

7. **Install the new hard disk in your Mac.**

   Position the hard disk so that the connectors on the back of the hard disk face the back of the Mac and the carrier bracket is on the bottom. Slide the hard disk into place until the tab on the carrier bracket clicks into place.

8. **Connect the hard disk power cable and hard disk data cable to the hard disk.**

   Connect the hard disk data cable and hard disk power cable to the hard disk. Refer to Figure 18-22 to see where the cables attach to the back of the hard disk. The cables fit into their connectors only one way, so you don't need to force them.

9. **Replace the metal hard disk shield on the front of the computer.**

   Fit the bottom of the metal shield into place first. Then push the top edge into place.

10. **Replace the top cover.**

    Lower the cover over the Mac at an angle so that you put the front edge in place first. Then lower the back edge of the cover down until the plastic tabs at the back click into place. You may need to push against the front edge of the cover while you lower the back edge into place to make sure that the tabs engage correctly — having three hands helps in performing this operation, by the way.

You just installed a hard disk in your Mac. Good work! You're ready now to fill it with new files and applications. Remember — always! — to copy the important files you backed up from your old hard disk onto the new one.

If you experience any problems after you complete your upgrade, see Chapters 8 and 12.

Upgrading the memory in a Mac Centris or Quadra 610, Centris or Quadra 660AV, AWS 60, Power Mac 6100, or WGS 6150

Are you ready to install more memory in your Mac? Well, you came to the right place. The table in this section lists all the possible memory configurations for the Mac Centris or Quadra 610, Centris or Quadra 660AV, AWS 60, Power Mac 6100, and WGS 6150. As discussed in Chapter 12, to install memory in a desktop Mac, you actually install small circuit boards that contain memory chips.

Before you start your memory upgrade, refer back to Chapter 12 and the section "The golden guide to SIMMs" to learn how to fill your Mac's memory sockets correctly. Make sure that you closely follow the guide provided in that chapter; otherwise, the memory on which you spent your hard-earned money won't do your Mac any good. Also, read the section "Guide to the specific memory needs of each Mac" in this section.

Table 18-5 shows you how much memory each Mac covered in this section can accept in its memory banks. Check the "Possible Memory Amounts" column on the table to determine the possible memory amounts your Mac model can accept. The Centris 610, Quadra 610, and AWS 60, for example, can accept 4, 8, 12, 16, 20, 24, 28, 36, 40, 44, 52, or 68MB total memory. These Macs cannot, however, accept amounts such as 9 or 18MB.

The table also lists the size of SIMMs that work in your machine. Make sure that you buy the right size, or your Mac can't use the SIMMs after you install them. Make sure, too, that you buy the right speed SIMMs. (The speed listed in the table is the minimum speed for each Mac; memory speed is measured in nanoseconds and abbreviated *ns*.) Don't buy SIMMs that run slower than the speeds listed in the table. Buying faster SIMMs is OK, but your Mac doesn't run any faster with the speedier SIMMs.

Table 18-5   Memory Requirements for the Macs in This Section

Mac Model	SIMM Size This Model Can Use	Minimum SIMM Speed	Possible Memory Amounts (in MB)
Centris or Quadra 610, AWS 60	4MB, 8MB, 16MB, 32MB	80ns	4, 8, 12, 16, 20, 24, 28, 36, 40, 44, 52, 68MB
Centris or Quadra 660AV	1MB, 2MB, 4MB, 8MB, 16MB, 32MB	70ns	4, 8, 12, 16, 20, 24, 28, 36, 40, 44, 48, 52, 56, 68MB
Power Mac 6100, WGS 6150	4MB, 8MB, 16MB, 32MB	80ns	8, 16, 24, 40, 72MB

Guide to the specific memory needs of each Mac

Before you install memory in your Mac, refer to the section "The golden guide to SIMMs," in Chapter 12. In addition to the guidelines provided in that chapter, the following information applies to the specific Macs in this section:

All the Macs covered in this section: You must install 72-pin SIMMs in all the Macs covered in this section. These SIMMs are different from the 30-pin SIMMs used in older Macs such as the Mac SE and the Mac IIci. So if you're thinking about using SIMMs from an older Mac in a newer Mac, check the number of pins on the old SIMMs. You can't pull SIMMs out of your Mac IIci, for example, to use in any of the Macs covered in this

section. Sorry. Under normal circumstances, recycling is a good idea — just not in this case.

Mac Centris or Quadra 610, Centris or Quadra 660AV, AWS 60: In these Macs, you can use different-sized SIMMs in each socket. Each socket is considered a bank all by itself. Each machine contains two SIMM sockets on the logic board.

Power Mac 6100 and WGS 6150: With these two Macs, you must fill the two memory sockets on the logic board with matching SIMMs — and both SIMMs must match in size and speed.

If you want to add video memory SIMMs to a Quadra or Centris 610 or AWS 60, just follow the instructions in this chapter for adding system memory. The video memory SIMM sockets are located just behind the system memory sockets on the logic board. Sorry, but the video memory in the Quadra or Centris 660AV, the Power Mac 6100, and the WGS 6150 cannot be upgraded.

Are you ready to install memory? OK, then — go for it!

Tools you need: A ballpoint pen or a SIMM removal tool

Things to watch out for: Remove the SIMMs from their shielded packaging only at your grounded work area. Be careful, too, to handle the SIMMs only by their edges — don't touch the chips or the metal contacts on the edge of the SIMM. Make sure that you push the SIMMs all the way into the sockets. A SIMM not correctly seated prevents the Mac from starting.

1. **Remove the top cover by following Steps 1 through 3 in the section "Opening up your Mac Centris or Quadra 610, Centris or Quadra 660AV, AWS 60, Power Mac 6100, or WGS 6150."**

   Set the cover aside.

2. **Disconnect the SCSI data cable from the logic board.**

   The SCSI data cable is the flat, wide, gray cable that connects the CD-ROM drive and hard disk to the logic board. Disconnecting the SCSI data cable enables you to access the SIMM sockets. Just pull the cable plug out of its connector on the logic board and bend the cable out of the way toward the front of the Mac.

3. **Remove the old SIMMs (if necessary).**

   If the SIMM sockets on the logic board already are full, you must remove the old SIMMs to make way for the new ones. See Chapter 12 for instructions on removing and installing SIMMs. Figure 18-25 shows the locations of the memory sockets on the Mac Centris or Quadra 610, Centris or Quadra 660AV, AWS 60, Power Mac 6100, and WGS 6150.

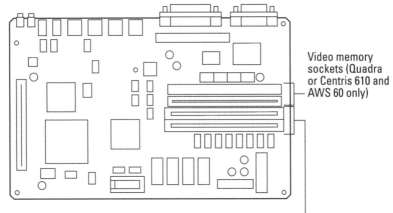

Figure 18-25: Now where does that SIMM go? In the memory sockets on the logic board.

Video memory sockets (Quadra or Centris 610 and AWS 60 only)

Memory sockets

4. **Install the new SIMMs.**

   See Chapter 12 for the instructions on installing the SIMMs. Remember to follow the golden guide to SIMMs in that chapter, as well as the information in the section "Guide to the specific memory needs of each Mac" in this section.

5. **Reconnect the SCSI data cable to the logic board.**

   This cable is the one you disconnected in Step 2. Remember to reconnect this cable — or your Mac can't start.

6. **Replace the top cover.**

   Bring the cover down over the Mac at an angle so that you put the front edge in place first. Then lower the back edge of the cover down until the plastic tabs at the back click into place. To make sure the tabs engage correctly, you may need to push against the front edge of the cover while you lower the back edge into place.

7. **Verify your upgrade.**

   Reconnect your monitor, mouse, and keyboard, and start up your Mac. Open the Apple menu and choose About this Macintosh. In System 6, choose About the Finder.

   The number listed beside Total Memory should equal the total amount of memory present in both sockets. This number reflects any memory permanently installed plus any memory you just installed in the memory sockets. If virtual memory is turned on, this number is listed as Built-in Memory.

   If the total memory is not what you expected or you experience other problems, refer to Chapter 12 or contact the company from which you purchased the SIMMs.

Good for you! You just installed new memory in your Mac. Go out and brag a little to your friends about your newly loaded-up Mac. And take a well-deserved break!

Mac Quadra 800, 840AV, AWS 80, Power Mac 8100, and WGS 8150

These appealing tower-style Macs pack some major computing muscle under the hood. If you're looking for a high-end graphics workstation, these Macs fill the bill. The downside to upgrading these models is that you need to remove the logic board to add memory — the only modular Macs to make you do so.

Opening up the Mac Quadra 800, 840AV, AWS 80 Power Mac 8100, or WGS 8150

To add an internal upgrade to your Mac, you first must open the top.

Tools you need: A flat-blade screwdriver

Things to watch out for: Not too much. Just be careful not to bang the cover on the insides of the Mac as you remove it.

Electrostatic discharge — a.k.a. static electricity — can fry the delicate electronic components in your Mac, even with a zap too small for you to feel! Make sure you read about how to prevent electrostatic discharge in Chapter 3 *before* you start any upgrade.

1. **Shut down your Mac by choosing Shut Down from the Special menu.**

   Always shut down your Mac properly before you start any upgrade.

2. **Disconnect all the cables from your computer and place the main box of your Mac — but not the monitor — on your grounded antistatic work surface.**

   Use a wrist strap and a grounded antistatic mat. And make sure that you follow the electrostatic discharge prevention guidelines in Chapter 3 before you remove any upgrade products from their packages or touch any circuit board inside the Mac.

3. **Loosen the captive screws that hold the cover in place.**

   Four screws are located on the back side of the Mac at the corners — called *captive screws*. (These screws are exactly that — captive. They don't leave the Mac case, which is nice because you can't lose them.)

   Use the flat-blade screwdriver to loosen the captive screws.

4. **Remove the cover.**

   Slide the top cover forward about one inch. Lift the cover straight up and off the Mac.

That's it; you've got the cover off! Now skip on to the section that describes the exact upgrade you're installing in your Mac.

Upgrading the internal hard disk in your Mac Quadra 800, 840AV, AWS 80, Power Mac 8100, or

This section describes how to upgrade the internal hard disk in your Mac. You can't go wrong with a storage upgrade — nobody ever seems to have enough room for files and applications. As we continue to say, back up any files you want to keep from your old internal hard disk before you install your new one. See Chapter 16 for more information about backing up.

Tools you need: A Phillips number 2 screwdriver

Things to watch out for: Take care to disconnect cables by pulling on the plugs, not on the wires.

1. **Remove the top cover by following Steps 1 through 4 in the section "Opening up your Mac Quadra 800, 840AV, AWS 80, Power Mac 8100, or WGS 8150."**

   Set the cover aside.

2. **Disconnect the hard disk data cable and the hard disk power cable from the hard disk.**

   These two cables are located at the back of the hard disk. Make sure that you pull on the plug, not on the cable.

3. **Remove the hard disk from the computer.**

   Push down on the plastic tab at the front of the hard disk and slide the hard disk forward and out of the Mac. Figure 18-26 shows how to remove the hard disk from the computer.

4. **Remove the hard disk carrier bracket from your old hard disk.**

   The carrier bracket is the plastic piece that attaches to the underside of the hard disk and holds the hard disk in place inside the Mac. As suggested in Chapter 12, whenever you buy a new hard disk for your Mac, you should also buy a mounting kit that contains a carrier bracket and cables for mounting your new hard disk in your Mac.

   Remove the four screws that attach the carrier bracket to the hard disk. (Figure 18-27 shows the carrier bracket and hard disk and how they are attached.)

5. **Attach the hard disk carrier bracket to your new hard disk.**

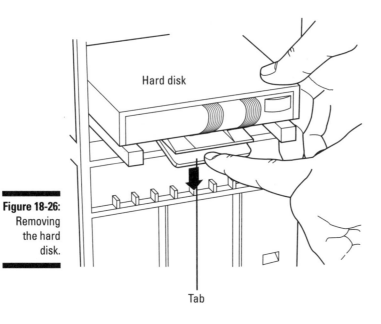

Figure 18-26:
Removing
the hard
disk.

Hard disk

Tab

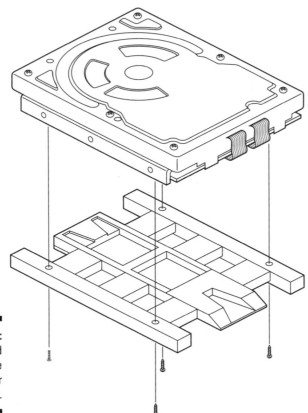

Figure 18-27:
The hard
disk and the
carrier
bracket.

6. **Install the new hard drive in your Mac.**

   Orient the hard disk so that the connectors on the back of the hard disk face the back of the Mac and the carrier bracket is on the bottom. Slide the hard disk into place until the plastic tab clicks into place.

7. **Connect the power and data cables to your hard disk.**

   Connect the data cable and power cable to the hard disk. These are the cables you disconnected in Step 2. The cables fit into their connectors only one way, so don't force them.

8. **Replace the top cover.**

   Bring the cover straight down over the Mac, leaving a one-inch gap where the cover meets the back of the Mac. Push the cover back so that it is flush with the back of the Mac and then tighten the four captive screws. Make sure as you tighten the screws that they line up with the threaded holes in the cover.

Good for you. You just installed a hard disk in your Mac! Now you're ready to start filling it with all sorts of new software goodies! Make sure, too, that you copy the important files you backed up from your old hard disk onto your new one.

If you experience any problems after you complete your upgrade, refer to Chapters 8 and 12.

Upgrading the memory in a Mac Quadra 800, 840AV, AWS 80, Power Mac 8100, or WGS 8150

If you're ready to install more memory in your Mac, you've found the right section.

This section shows you how to upgrade the memory in your Mac Quadra 800, 840AV, AWS 80, Power Mac 8100, and WGS 8150. As noted in Chapter 12, to install memory in any desktop Mac, you actually install small circuit boards that contain memory chips.

Before you start your memory upgrade, refer to Chapter 12 and its section "The golden guide to SIMMs" to learn how to fill up the memory sockets correctly. Make sure that you follow the guide carefully; otherwise, the memory on which you spent your hard-earned money won't do your Mac any good. Also, read the section "Guide to the specific memory needs of each Mac" in this section.

Table 18-6 shows how much memory each Mac covered in this section can accept in its memory banks. Check the "Possible Memory Amounts" column on the table to determine the amount of memory your Mac model can accept.

The table also tells you what size SIMMs work in your machine. Make sure that you buy the right size, or your Mac can't use the SIMMs after you install them. Make sure, too, that you buy the right speed SIMMs. (The speed listed in the table is the minimum speed for each Mac; memory speed is measured in nanoseconds and abbreviated *ns*.) Don't buy SIMMs that run slower than the speeds listed here. Buying faster SIMMs is OK, but your Mac doesn't run any faster with the speedier SIMMs.

Table 18-6   Memory Requirements for the Macs in This Section

Mac Model	*SIMM Size This Model Can Use*	*Minimum SIMM Speed*	*Possible Memory Amounts (in MB)*
Quadra 800, AWS 80	4MB, 8MB, 16MB, 32MB	60ns	4, 8, 12, 16, 20, 24, 28, 32, 36, 44, 48, 52, 56, 60, 64, 68, 72, 76, 80, 84, 88, 92, 96, 104, 108, 112, 116, 120, 132, 136MB
Quadra 840AV	1MB, 2MB, 4MB, 8MB, 16MB, 32MB	60ns	8MB to 128MB (comes with one 8MB SIMM — no permanent memory)
Power Mac 8100, WGS 8150	4MB, 8MB, 16MB, 32MB	80ns	8MB to 264MB (has 8MB permanent memory on the logic board)

If you own a Quadra 800, AWS 80, or Quadra 840AV, you can follow the instructions we give for installing system memory to add video memory SIMMs. More video memory SIMMs enable you to work with more colors on the Mac screen. The Power Mac 8100 and the WGS 8150 do not use separate video memory, so you can't do this upgrade on these guys.

Are you ready to do a memory upgrade? Then here we go.

Tools you need: A Phillips number 2 screwdriver; a ballpoint pen or a SIMM removal tool

Things to watch out for: Remove the SIMMs from their shielded packaging only at your grounded work area. Be careful, too, to handle the SIMMs only by their edges — don't touch the chips or the metal contacts on the edge of the SIMM. Make sure that you push the SIMMs all the way into the sockets. A SIMM that is not correctly seated prevents the Mac from starting.

Guide to the specific memory needs of each Mac

Before you install memory in your Mac, refer to the section "The golden guide to SIMMs," in Chapter 12. In addition to the guidelines provided in that chapter, the following information applies to each specific Mac:

All the Macs covered in this section: You must install 72-pin SIMMs in all the Macs covered in this section. These SIMMs are different from the 30-pin SIMMs used in older Macs such as the Mac SE and the Mac IIci. So if you're thinking about using SIMMs from an older Mac in a newer Mac, check the number of pins on the old SIMMs. You can't pull SIMMs out of your Mac IIci, for example, to use in any of the Macs covered in this section. Sorry. Recycling is usually a good idea — but not in this case.

All the Macs covered in this section, except the Quadra 840AV, come with 8MB of memory soldered onto the logic board. The Quadra 840AV

has no soldered-on memory; instead, the standard configuration comes with one 8MB SIMM already installed in one of the sockets.

Mac Quadra 800, 840AV, AWS 80: You can use different-sized SIMMs in each socket on these Macs; in these machines, each socket is considered a bank.

Quadra 800 or AWS 80: You can boost the speed of your Quadra 800 or AWS 80 by about five to ten percent by adding memory SIMMs in matched pairs (size and speed). The reasons this can be done are really technical, so we won't go into them here, but it really does work.

Power Mac 8100 and WGS 8150: You must install SIMMs for these Macs in pairs, and both SIMMs must match in size and speed. These Macs have four banks of two SIMM sockets, for a total of eight sockets.

To add memory to the Macs covered in this section, you need to remove the logic board. The following steps describe how to remove the logic board, how to add memory, and how to put your Mac back together again.

1. **Remove the cover by following Steps 1 through 4 in the section "Opening up your Mac Quadra 800, 840AV, AWS 80, Power Mac 8100, and WGS 8150."**

   Set the cover aside.

2. **Remove the reset and interrupt switch actuator.**

   The *reset and interrupt switch actuator* is located inside the Mac, on the side containing the logic board. The actuator is the plastic piece at the front of the Mac that actually presses the reset and interrupt switches on the logic board. Pull this piece out and set it aside.

3. **Remove the screw that holds the logic board in place.**

   The screw is located just above center of the plastic frame that holds the logic board. Use the Phillips number 2 screwdriver to remove this screw.

4. Release the logic board from the Mac.

Slide the logic board forward until the slot on the logic board nearest the
front of the Mac lines up with the plastic tab that holds the logic board in
place. Then lift the plastic latch at the back of the logic board to release
the logic board from the Mac. Figure 18-28 shows the location of the slot
and the latch.

Slot   Latch

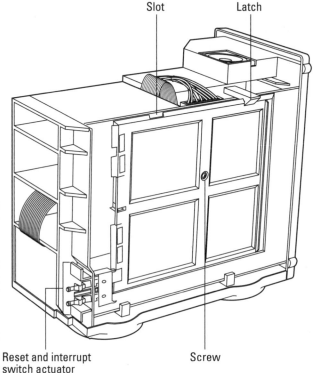

Figure 18-28:
Remove the
reset and
interrupt
switch
actuator
and the
screw.

Reset and interrupt   Screw
switch actuator

5. Disconnect all the cables from the logic board.

Pivot out the front edge of the logic board so that you can access all the
cables connected to the logic board. Disconnect all the following cables:

- Logic board power cable
- Speaker cable
- LED cable
- SCSI data cable
- Diskette drive cable
- CD-ROM audio cable (if present)

Most of these cables connect across the top edge of the logic board. Make a mental note of where the cables plug in for reconnecting them later.

6. Set the logic board on your grounded work surface.

After you disconnect the cables, you can take the logic board out of the Mac. Lay the logic board down flat so that you can install the memory SIMMs.

7. Remove the old SIMMs (if necessary).

If the SIMM sockets on the logic board already are full, you must remove the old SIMMs to make way for the new ones. See Chapter 12 for instructions on removing and installing SIMMs. Figure 18-29 shows the locations of the memory banks on the Mac Quadra 800 and AWS 80, the Quadra 840AV, and the Power Mac 8100 and WGS 8150.

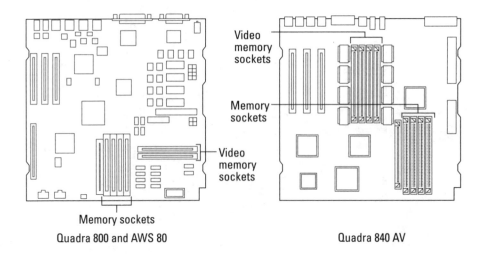

Quadra 800 and AWS 80

Quadra 840 AV

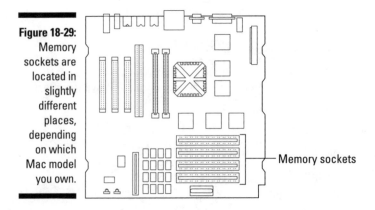

Figure 18-29: Memory sockets are located in slightly different places, depending on which Mac model you own.

Power Mac 8100

8. **Install the new SIMMs.**

   See Chapter 12 for instructions on installing the SIMMs. Remember to follow the golden guide to SIMMs section in that chapter as well as the information in the section "Guide to the specific memory needs of the Mac," in this section.

9. **Reconnect all the cables to the logic board.**

   Set the logic board down next to the chassis, with the top side of the board facing in toward the Mac. Reconnect all the cables you disconnected in Step 5.

10. **Replace the logic board in the chassis.**

    Align the logic board so that the front slot on the top edge of the logic board lines up with the tab on the chassis. Put the bottom edge of the logic board into place. Then lift the plastic latch at the back of the chassis and push the top edge of the logic board into place. Make sure that the logic board fits into the slot in the latch. Finally, slide the logic board toward the back of the Mac and into place. (Really, you don't need three hands for this step.) Refer to Figure 18-28 for the location of the slot and the latch.

11. **Replace the screw that holds the logic board in place and then the reset and interrupt actuator.**

    Refer to Figure 18-28 for the locations of the screw and the reset and interrupt actuator.

12. **Replace the top cover.**

    Bring the cover straight down over the Mac, leaving a one-inch gap where the cover meets the back of the Mac. Push the cover back so that it is flush with the back of the Mac and then tighten the four captive screws. As you tighten the screws, make sure that they line up with the threaded holes in the cover.

13. **Verify your upgrade.**

    Reconnect your monitor, mouse, and keyboard, and start your Mac. Open the Apple menu and choose About this Macintosh. In System 6, choose About the Finder.

    The number listed beside Total Memory should equal the total amount of memory present in all the banks. This number reflects any memory permanently installed plus any memory you just installed in the memory sockets. If virtual memory is turned on, this number is listed as Built-in Memory.

    If the total memory is not what you expected or you experience other problems, refer to Chapter 12 or contact the company from which you purchased the SIMMs.

Great! You just installed new memory in your Mac. How does it feel to own a computer that's absolutely loaded with memory? Hey, take a well-deserved break!

Mac Quadra 900, 950, and AWS 95

The Macs in the 900 series are the big boys of the Quadra and Apple Workgroup Server lines. These machines make ideal network servers or image-processing workstations.

Many possibilities exist for installing internal storage drives — up to as many as five hard disks, a tape drive, and/or a CD-ROM drive. We recommend that you hire a technician to install these internal storage devices in your Mac, as well as to determine exactly where to put them and how to connect them. The logistics of connecting so many devices are complex.

If you want to upgrade the storage yourself, go ahead and add external storage devices. They simply plug into the back of the Mac. (See Chapter 8 for details.)

Note: Although the WGS 9150 fits in with the other Macs in this section, we're skipping that machine, because upgrading its memory requires near complete disassembly of the Mac. We recommend that you hire a technician for upgrades to both internal storage and memory in this Mac.

Adding memory to a Mac Quadra 900, 950, or AWS 95

Fortunately, all you need do to add memory to these Macs is to take off the cover and plug in the SIMMs. Keep the following information in mind if you're adding memory to the Mac Quadra 900, 950, or AWS 95.

As noted in Chapter 12, to install memory in any desktop Mac, you actually install small circuit boards that contain memory chips. Before you start your memory upgrade, refer back to Chapter 12 and its section "The golden guide to SIMMs" to learn how to fill the memory sockets correctly. Make sure that you follow that guide closely; otherwise, the memory on which you spent your hard-earned money won't do your Mac any good. Also, be sure to read the section, "Guide to the specific memory needs of each Mac," in this section.

Table 18-7 lists how much memory each Mac covered in this section can accept in its memory banks. Check the "Possible Memory Amounts" column on the table to determine the amount of memory your Mac model can accept.

The table also tells what size SIMMs work in your machine. Make sure that you buy the right size, or your Mac can't use the SIMMs after you install them. Make sure, too, that you buy the right speed SIMMs. (The speed listed in the table is the minimum speed for each Mac; memory speed is measured in nanoseconds and abbreviated *ns*.) Don't buy SIMMs that run slower than the speeds listed here. Buying faster SIMMs is OK, but your Mac doesn't run any faster with the speedier SIMMs.

Table 18-7   Memory Requirements for the Macs in This Section

Mac Model	SIMM Size This Model Can Use	Minimum SIMM Speed	Possible Memory Amounts (in MB)
Quadra 900, Quadra 950, AWS 95	1MB, 2MB, 4MB, 8MB, 16MB	80ns	Up to 256MB

Are you ready to get your hands dirty? OK, let's go!

Tools you need: A ballpoint pen or a SIMM removal tool

Things to watch out for: Remove the SIMMs from their shielded packaging only at your grounded work area. Be careful, too, to handle the SIMMs only by their edges — don't touch the chips or the metal contacts on the edge of the SIMM. Make sure that you push the SIMMs all the way into the sockets — a SIMM not correctly seated prevents the Mac from starting.

Electrostatic discharge — a.k.a. static electricity — can fry the delicate electronic components in your Mac, even with a zap too small for you to feel! Make sure that you read in Chapter 3 about how to prevent electrostatic discharge *before* you start any upgrade.

Guide to the specific memory needs of each Mac

Before you install memory in your Mac, refer to the section "The golden guide to SIMMs," in Chapter 12. In addition to the guidelines in that chapter, the following information applies to each specific Mac in this section:

You must add memory to these machines in groups of four matching SIMMs. All the Macs in this section have four memory banks containing four SIMMs sockets each, for a whopping total of 16 sockets! These are really far out memory-socket-to-the-max machines!

1. **Shut down your Mac by opening the Special menu and choosing Shut Down.**

   Always shut down your Mac correctly before you start any upgrade.

2. **Disconnect all cables from your computer and place the main box of your Mac — but not the monitor — on your grounded antistatic work surface.**

   Use a wrist strap and a grounded antistatic mat. Make sure that you carefully follow the electrostatic discharge prevention guidelines in Chapter 3 before you remove any upgrade products from their packages or touch any circuit board inside the Mac.

   The cover on these Macs is on the right hand side as you face the Mac. Lay the Mac down on its side on your mat so that the cover is on top. You want the back of the Mac facing you and the bottom side with the feet facing your left.

3. **Press in on the two plastic release buttons and then remove the cover.**

   The two plastic latch-release buttons are located just a bit in from the rear corners of the cover. These buttons release the latches that lock the cover in place. Press in the two tabs, lift the rear of the cover, and then remove the cover from the Mac.

4. **Remove the old SIMMs (if necessary).**

   If the SIMM sockets on the logic board are full already, you must remove the old SIMMs to make way for the new ones. See Chapter 12 for instructions on removing and installing SIMMs. Figure 18-30 shows the locations of the memory banks on the Mac Quadra 900, 950, and AWS 95.

   Notice that these banks consist of four groups of four SIMM sockets each, starting with the front four (bank A) and moving toward the back of the logic board and the last four (bank D).

5. **Install your new SIMMs.**

   See Chapter 12 for the instructions on installing the SIMMs. Remember to follow the golden guide to SIMMs section in that chapter as well as the information in the section "Guide to the specific memory needs of each Mac" in this section.

6. **Replace the top cover.**

   Replace the edge of the cover nearest the front of the Mac first. Then lower the rear of the cover into place. Make sure that the cover latches click into place.

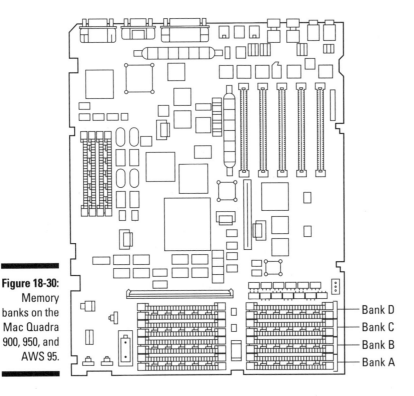

Figure 18-30:
Memory
banks on the
Mac Quadra
900, 950, and
AWS 95.

Bank D
Bank C
Bank B
Bank A

7. Verify your upgrade.

Reconnect your monitor, mouse, and keyboard, and start your Mac. Open
the Apple menu and choose About this Macintosh. In System 6, choose
About the Finder.

The number listed beside Total Memory should equal the total amount
of memory present in all the banks. If virtual memory is turned on, this
number is listed as Built-in Memory.

If the total memory is not what you expected or you experience other
problems, refer to Chapter 12 or contact the company from which you
purchased the SIMMs.

Good work — you just upgraded the memory in your Mac. How does it feel to
own a computer that you loaded-up with memory yourself? Wash your hands
and take a break!

Mac LC, LC II, LC III, LC 475, Quadra 605, and Performa 400 series

The LCs and their relatives are among the most popular Macs ever made. The Performa 400 series includes all the various and sundry LC-based Performas that show up in department stores and consumer electronics chains. The 400 series includes models such as the Performa 400, 405, 410, 430, 450, 460, 466, 467, 475, and 476.

Opening up your Mac LC, LC II, LC III, LC 475, Quadra 605, or Performa 400 series

The first step to any internal upgrade is to pop the cover on the Mac.

Tools you need: A Phillips number 2 screwdriver

Things to watch out for: We're just opening the top; nothing to watch out for yet.

Electrostatic discharge — a.k.a. static electricity — can fry the delicate electronic components in your Mac, even with a zap too small for you to feel! Make sure that you read in Chapter 3 about how to prevent electrostatic discharge before you start any upgrade.

1. **Shut down your Mac by opening the Special menu and choosing Shut Down.**

   Always shut down your Mac correctly before you start any upgrade. Use the power switch on the back of the Mac to turn off the power.

2. **Disconnect all cables from your computer and place your the main box of your Mac — but not the monitor — on your grounded antistatic work surface.**

   Use a wrist strap and a grounded antistatic mat. Make sure that you carefully follow the electrostatic discharge prevention guidelines in Chapter 3 before you remove any upgrade products from their packages or touch any circuit board inside the Mac.

3. **Remove the security screw (if present).**

   A very small number of the Macs described in this section have a security screw installed at the back — right in the dead center of the top edge. It's the only screw you see back there. If your Mac has such a screw, remove it now.

4. Remove the cover.

Face the front of the Mac, reach over the top, and grab the tabs on either side of the back of the case. Lift up on the tabs to release the cover and then lift the cover up and off the Mac.

Hey — you've got the cover off! Now skip to the section that describes the exact upgrade you're adding to your Mac — storage or memory.

Upgrading the internal hard disk in your Mac LC, LC II, LC III, LC 475, Quadra 605, and Performa 400 series

This section covers how to upgrade the internal hard disk in your Mac. You can never have enough storage space. Believe us, you'll fill it up — faster than you think! Remember to back up any files you want to keep from your old internal hard disk *before* you install your new one. See Chapter 16 for more information on backing up files.

Tools you need: A Phillips number 2 screwdriver; needle-nosed pliers (optional)

Things to watch out for: Take care to disconnect cables by pulling on the plugs, not on the wires.

1. **Remove the top cover by following Steps 1 through 4 in the preceding section, "Opening up your Mac LC, LC II, LC III, LC 475, Quadra 605, and Performa 400 series."**

   Set the cover aside.

2. **Disconnect the hard disk power cable and the hard disk data cable from the logic board.**

   See Figure 18-31 for the location of these two cables.

3. **Remove the hard disk from the computer.**

   Pull back the plastic tabs on one side of the hard disk and lift the side a bit to keep the tabs from clicking back into place. Release the tabs on the other side of the hard disk and lift it out of the Mac. Figure 18-31 shows how the hard disk comes out of the computer.

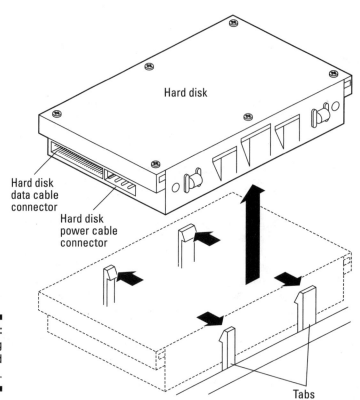

Hard disk

Hard disk
data cable
connector

Hard disk
power cable
connector

Tabs

Figure 18-31:
Removing
the hard
disk.

If you own an original Mac LC with two diskette drives and no hard disk installed, this tip is for you. To add a hard disk to this type of LC, you must permanently remove one of the diskette drives — the one on the left as you face the Mac. You replace this diskette drive with the new hard disk. Your final internal storage configuration after the upgrade is a hard disk and one diskette drive. To remove the diskette drive, follow the steps for removing the hard disk, beginning with Step 3.

4. Attach the hard disk carrier bracket to your new hard disk.

As suggested in Chapter 12, whenever you buy a new hard disk for your Mac, you should also buy a mounting kit that contains a carrier bracket and cables for mounting your new hard disk in your Mac. Figure 18-32 shows the carrier bracket and hard disk and how they attach.

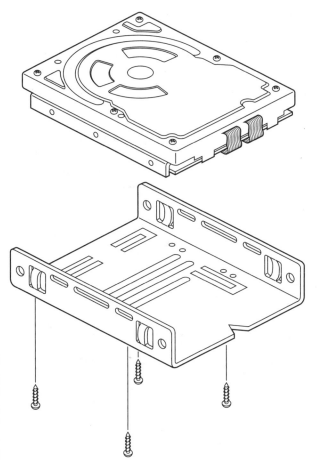

Figure 18-32:
The hard
disk and the
carrier
bracket.

5. **Connect the hard disk data cable and hard disk power cable to your hard disk.**

   The cables connect to the back of the new hard disk. Refer to Figure 18-31 to see how these cables attach to the back of the hard disk. The cables fit into their connectors only one way, so you don't want to force them.

6. **Install the new hard drive in your Mac.**

   Orient the hard disk so that the connectors on the back of the hard disk face the back of the Mac and the carrier bracket is on the bottom. Push the hard disk straight down into its mounting area until the plastic tabs click into place on both sides.

7. **Connect the hard disk power cable and hard disk data cable to the logic board.**

   Connect the two cables from the back of the hard disk to their connectors on the logic board. Refer to Figure 18-31 for the location of these connectors on the logic board. The cables fit into their connectors only one way, so you don't want to force them.

8. **Replace the top cover.**

   Bring the cover straight down over the Mac. Push against the front edge to make sure that the cover is all the way back on the Mac. Push down on the cover until the tabs at the back click into place. Push down on the front of the cover to make sure that it is all the way down on the Mac.

Well, you just installed a new hard disk in your Mac. Great! You're ready now to start filling it with new files and applications. But remember to copy the files you backed up from your old hard disk onto your new one, too.

If you experience any problems after you complete your upgrade, check Chapters 8 and 12.

Upgrading the memory in a Mac LC, LC II, LC III, LC 475, Quadra 605, or Performa 400 series

If you're adding more memory in your Mac, you've come to the right place. This section shows you how to upgrade the memory in your Mac LC, LC II, LC III, LC 475, Quadra 605, and Performa 400 series. The table in this section shows you the possible memory configurations for these machines. As noted in Chapter 12, to install memory in a desktop Mac, you actually install small circuit boards that contain memory chips.

Before you start your memory upgrade, refer back to Chapter 12 and its section "The golden guide to SIMMs" to learn how to fill the memory sockets in these Macs correctly. Make sure that you follow this guide closely; otherwise, the memory on which you spent your hard-earned money won't do your Mac any good. Also, read the section "Guide to the specific memory needs of each Mac," in this section.

Table 18-8 describes how much memory each Mac covered in this section can accept in its memory banks. Check the "Possible Memory Amounts" column on the table to determine the amount of memory your Mac model can accept.

The table also tells what size SIMMs work in your machine. Make sure that you buy the right size, or your Mac can't use the SIMMs after you install them. Make sure, too, that you buy the right speed SIMMs. (The speed listed in the table is the minimum speed for each Mac; memory speed is measured in nanoseconds and abbreviated *ns.*) Don't buy SIMMs that run slower than the speeds listed here. Buying faster SIMMs is OK, but your Mac doesn't run any faster with the speedier SIMMs.

Table 18-8   Memory Requirements for the Macs in This Section

Mac Model	SIMM Size This Model Can Use	Minimum SIMM Speed	Possible Memory Amounts (in MB)
LC, LC II, Performa 400, 405, 410, 430	1MB, 2MB, 4MB	100ns	2, 4, 6, 8, 10MB
LC III, LC 457, Quadra 605, Performa 450, 460, 466, 467, 475, 476	1MB, 2MB, 4MB, 8MB, 16MB, 32MB	80ns	4, 5, 6, 8, 12, 20, 36MB

Guide to the specific memory needs of each Mac

Before you install memory in your Mac, refer to the section "The golden guide to SIMMs," in Chapter 12. In addition to the guidelines in that chapter, the following information applies to each specific Mac:

Mac LC, LC II, Performa 400, 405, 410, 430: You must add SIMMs to these Macs in pairs, and they must also match in size and speed. These Macs contain only one bank of two SIMM sockets on the logic board. You add 30-pin SIMMs to the Mac LC, LC II, Performa 400, 405, 410, and 430.

Mac LC III, LC 457, Quadra 605, Performa 450, 460, 466, 467, 475, 476: These Macs contain just one SIMM slot for adding memory. So if a SIMM is already in this socket, you must remove it to add more memory.

You must install 72-pin SIMMs in the Mac LC III, LC 457, Quadra 605, Performa 450, 460, 466, 467, 475, and 476. These SIMMs are different from the 30-pin SIMMs used in older Macs such as the Mac SE and the Mac IIci. So if you're thinking about using SIMMs from an older Mac in a newer Mac, check the number of pins on the old SIMMs. You can't pull SIMMs out of your Mac IIci, for example, to use in any of the Macs covered in this section. Sorry. Recycling computer parts is a good idea — but not for these machines' memory upgrades.

To add video memory SIMMs to the Macs covered in this section, simply follow the instructions for installing system memory. Adding more video memory SIMMs enables you to work with more colors on the Mac screen.

Are you ready for a memory upgrade? Let's go.

Tools you need: A ballpoint pen or a SIMM removal tool

Things to watch out for: Remove the SIMMs from their shielded packaging only at your grounded work area. Be careful, too, to handle the SIMMs only by their edges — don't touch the chips or the metal contacts on the edge of the SIMM. Make sure that you push the SIMMs all the way into the sockets — a SIMM not correctly seated prevents the Mac from starting.

1. **Remove the top cover by following Steps 1 through 4 in the section "Opening up your Mac LC, LC II, LC III, LC 475, Quadra 605, and Performa 400 series."**

   Set the cover aside.

2. **Remove the old SIMMs (if necessary).**

   If the SIMM socket or sockets on the logic board are already full, you must remove the old SIMMs to make way for the new ones. See Chapter 12 for instructions on removing and installing SIMMs. Figure 18-33 shows the locations of the memory sockets on the Mac logic board.

3. **Install the new SIMMs.**

   See Chapter 12 for the instructions on installing the SIMMs. Remember to follow the golden guide to SIMMs section there and the information in the "Guide to the specific memory needs of the Mac" in this section.

4. **Replace the top cover.**

   Bring the cover straight down over the Mac. Push against the front edge to make sure that the cover is all the way back on the Mac. Push down on the cover until the tabs at the back click into place. Push down on the front of the cover to make sure that it is all the way down on the Mac.

5. **Verify your upgrade.**

   Reconnect your monitor, mouse, and keyboard, and start up your Mac. Open the Apple menu and choose About this Macintosh. In System 6, choose About the Finder.

   The number listed beside Total Memory should equal the total amount of memory present in all the banks. This number reflects both any memory permanently installed and any memory you just installed in the memory sockets. If virtual memory is turned on, this number is listed as Built-in Memory.

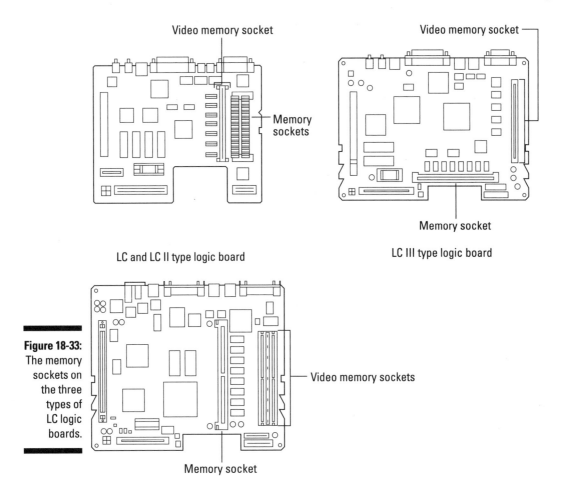

Figure 18-33: The memory sockets on the three types of LC logic boards.

If the total memory is not what you expected or you experience other problems, refer to Chapter 12 or contact the company from which you purchased the SIMMs.

Well, you just upgraded the memory in your Mac. Good work! Say "Good-bye" to those "out of memory" messages for a while — and take a break. You deserve it!

Chapter 19

Upgrading and Adding Great Stuff to Your PowerBook

....

In This Chapter

▶ Adding more memory or an internal modem

▶ Safety procedures for you and your PowerBook

▶ What tools you need and what to watch out for as you upgrade

▶ The steps for safely putting your PowerBook back together again

....

This chapter shows you how to add internal upgrades to your PowerBook. We provide step-by-step instructions for installing the easiest and most useful upgrades — memory and an internal modem. Upgrading PowerBooks requires careful attention to detail because of their small size and the delicate components inside. But we show you what to watch out for and tell you in detail how to perform the upgrades correctly and successfully.

To upgrade your internal hard disk, we recommend getting a qualified technician to do it because of the complexity of this upgrade and because of the many complications that can arise. If you own a PowerBook Duo and want to upgrade the internal hard disk or even just install an internal modem, we also suggest that you get a professional to perform the upgrade for you.

As you use this chapter, we suggest that you skip around from section to section, depending on the exact type of PowerBook you want to upgrade, such as the PowerBook 100, the other 100-series PowerBooks (the 140, 145, 145b, 170, 160, 165, 165c, 180, and 180c), or the Duos. After you locate the appropriate section for your machine, you'll find that information on opening up the PowerBook comes first. Then farther into the section are specific instructions for installing the desired upgrade or upgrades. Finally, each section ends with steps for closing up your PowerBook.

PowerBooks are more sensitive to electrostatic discharge than any other Macs. Their small, low-power components are easily damaged by even the smallest static electrical charge. Whenever you upgrade a PowerBook, therefore, always work on a grounded work surface, always wear a grounding wrist strap, and *always* follow the electrostatic discharge prevention guidelines we list in Chapter 3. An antistatic mat and wrist strap, after all, are *much* cheaper than a new motherboard. (By the way, the PowerBook *motherboard*, called the logic board in other Macs, is the main circuit board in the machine. It contains the circuitry that runs the computer. For more information about Mac hardware and parts, see Chapter 4.)

PowerBook 100

In this section we show you how to add more memory and an internal modem to your PowerBook 100.

We haven't included instructions for upgrading the original Macintosh Portable. We believe that, instead of spending money to upgrade an old portable, your hard-earned cash is much better spent on buying a new PowerBook.

Opening up the PowerBook 100

Before you add your internal upgrades, you need to open up your PowerBook 100 — ahhhh! — and remove its display assembly and keyboard. Removing these components enables you to access the inside of your PowerBook 100.

Tools you need: A Phillips number 2 screwdriver

What to watch out for: Be very careful as you work with the cables inside the PowerBook 100. These cables are very thin, and they tear easily. The thin, flat wires inside the cables can also can break if you bend the cables too much. Make sure that you remove all the batteries from the PowerBook and that you unplug the power adapter and turn off the power switch *before* you open up the machine. And follow carefully the safety procedures we provide in Chapter 3.

To open your PowerBook 100, follow these steps:

1. **Put on your grounding wrist strap.**

   See Chapter 3 for electrostatic discharge procedures and for information about the grounding wrist strap.

2. Shut down your PowerBook by opening the Special menu and choosing the Shut Down command.

You need to make sure that your PowerBook is really shut down, not just sleeping. By using the Shut Down command, you ensure that you quit all your applications and save all the changes you've made to your documents *before* the computer shuts off.

3. Unplug the power adapter.

Make sure that you disconnect the power adapter from your PowerBook. (Some people call the power adapter the *AC adapter.*)

4. Close the PowerBook display so that the computer locks together.

Make sure that you close your PowerBook securely.

5. Move the power switch on the back of the computer to the Off position.

The power switch doesn't really turn your PowerBook on and off. Actually, the switch disconnects all the batteries so that not even a tiny amount of power flows through the PowerBook's circuits. To perform your upgrade, you must turn off *all* the power. Even a tiny amount of electricity can damage the internal components if something shorts out as you install your upgrade.

The power switch is located on the back panel of your PowerBook, right next to where the power adapter plugs in. If the switch is in the up position, the batteries are connected. If the switch is in the down position, the batteries are disconnected. (Figure 19-1 shows the location of the power switch.)

Make sure that you use the Shut Down command to shut down your PowerBook 100 *before* moving the power switch to the off position. If you don't do this, you may black out the entire East Coast power grid or inadvertently short-circuit your cable TV box so that all you can pick up for the rest of the season are Barney reruns.

6. Remove the backup batteries.

Rotate the "feet" at the back of your PowerBook to the down position — a simple feat, really. Press down on the latch and open the plastic door that covers the ports on the back of your PowerBook. You should now see the edge of the backup battery door, next to the sound-out port. Open the backup battery door and pivot out the battery holder. Now carefully remove the three disk-shaped backup batteries.

In case you're interested, these batteries are the standard CR2430 lithium batteries used in calculators and are available at most electronics shops. Figure 19-1 shows how to remove the backup batteries.

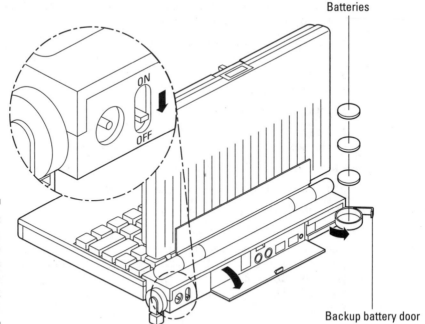

Batteries

Backup battery door

Figure 19-1:
Removing
the backup
batteries
from the
PowerBook
100.

7. Remove the main battery.

Rotate the feet at the back of your PowerBook to the up position. Slide the battery cover to the right. After you slide the battery cover over, you can use the protruding edge to pull the battery straight out of the PowerBook.

8. Remove the display assembly.

Your PowerBook should still be closed from your actions in Step 4. Turn your PowerBook upside down. Use your fingernail to gently pull out the three round rubber plugs that cover the three Phillips screws on the bottom of the computer. If your fingernails aren't long enough, well, try some other lengthy, very thin, stiff object, such as a needle or a nail file.

Unscrew and remove these three screws. Because you just removed the screws that secure the top and bottom case, you must now hold the PowerBook together as you turn it right-side up. Rotate the feet at the back of your PowerBook back to the down position. Unlatch the computer and lift up the display assembly. Keep a good grip on the display assembly and disconnect the display cable from the motherboard.

Figur 19-2 shows the location of the display cable and its connector on the motherboard. After you disconnect the cable, set the display assembly aside in a safe place. (And no, your cat's favorite nap spot is *not* a safe place.)

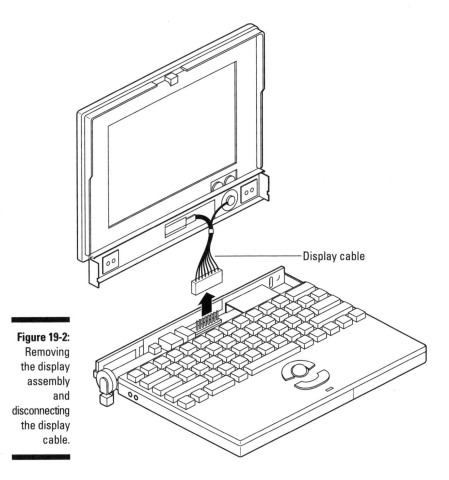

Display cable

Figure 19-2:
Removing
the display
assembly
and
disconnecting
the display
cable.

9. **Remove the keyboard and disconnect the keyboard cables.**

   Lift the rear edge of the keyboard as high as the cables allow you. Slide the
   keyboard back until the front edge of the keyboard clears the edge of the
   palm-rest cover. Then lift up and hold the keyboard in a vertical position
   so that you can unlock the cable connectors; remove the two keyboard
   cables.

   Figure 19-3 shows the location of the keyboard-cable connectors. You may
   need to pull up one side of the connector at a time to release the cable. Set
   the keyboard aside in a safe place.

Well, you've successfully gained access to the inside of your PowerBook. Good
work! Now you're ready to continue with the steps described under the specific
upgrade you are performing — installing additional memory or an internal
modem. Go to the appropriate section and continue your upgrade.

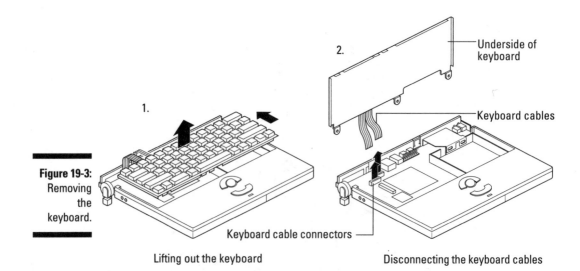

Figure 19-3:
Removing
the
keyboard.

Lifting out the keyboard

Disconnecting the keyboard cables

Installing memory in the PowerBook 100

To add memory to your PowerBook 100, you plug in a special memory expansion card in the memory card connector. To access the connector, you must partially disassemble your PowerBook 100. Don't worry, however. Disassembling the machine is a fairly simple process, believe us. The most exotic tool you use for this upgrade is a Phillips screwdriver.

Tools you need: A Phillips number 2 screwdriver

What to watch out for: Again, be very careful as you work with the cables inside the PowerBook 100. These cables are very thin, and they tear easily. The thin, flat wires inside the cables also can break if you bend the cables too much. Make sure that you remove all the batteries from the PowerBook and that you unplug the power adapter and turn off the power switch. And make sure that you carefully follow the safety procedures we provide in Chapter 3.

To add more memory to your PowerBook 100, follow these steps:

1. **Follow Steps 1 through 9 as described in the preceding section "Opening up the PowerBook 100."**

   These steps show you how to open up your PowerBook so that you can then install a memory card.

PowerBook 100 memory amount choices

The PowerBook 100 has 2MB built-in memory and a memory expansion connector to which you can install a memory card if you upgrade. You can upgrade to a total of 8MB of memory by installing the appropriate memory expansion card. (Only one memory card can go in the PowerBook at a time.) How much memory you install depends on how much you can afford to buy. We always recommend loading up your computer with as much memory as you can. See Chapter 12 for more information about buying memory.

To upgrade, you must remove the currently installed memory card and replace it with a card containing more memory. If no memory card is currently installed, you simply add one to the memory expansion connector.

Memory expansion cards are available in versions of 2MB, 4MB, or 6MB. To determine total memory after an upgrade, just add the amount of memory on the expansion card to the 2MB already in the PowerBook. Use a 6MB card, for example, to upgrade to the full 8MB (6MB + 2MB = 8MB).

2. Remove the palm-rest cover.

The *palm-rest cover* is the piece that includes the palm rest and the trackball buttons. After you complete the steps in the section "Opening up the PowerBook 100," you can just grab the back corners of the palm rest cover and lift it up and off the computer. Set the palm-rest cover aside in a safe place.

3. Install the memory expansion card in your PowerBook 100.

The memory expansion card connector is located on the motherboard on the side of the PowerBook 100, opposite the main battery compartment. Figure 19-4 shows where the memory card fits into the PowerBook 100.

The memory card fits into the small space inside the PowerBook 100 in only one way. The memory expansion card connector is shaped so that the card fits into the connector only if it is oriented the right way. Gently but firmly press the memory card into the connector on the motherboard.

4. Replace the palm-rest cover.

Start by holding the palm-rest cover vertically in front of the front edge of the PowerBook. Move the back of the cover down and back until it locks into place. Check that all the edges are correctly seated.

5. Close up your PowerBook.

Skip to the section "Closing up your PowerBook 100," later in this chapter and follow the steps in that section. Then return to Step 6 of this section for information about verifying your memory upgrade.

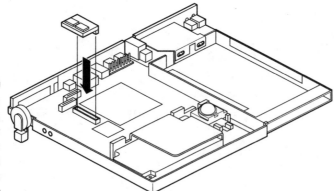

Figure 19-4:
Installing a
memory
card in a
PowerBook
100.

6. Verify your memory upgrade.

Start your PowerBook 100. Open the Apple menu in the Finder and choose About this Macintosh. The total memory displayed should equal the 2MB built into the computer, plus the amount of memory you just added with the memory expansion card.

Congratulations! You've just upgraded the memory in your PowerBook 100. You're ready to run all your favorite applications all at once or to set up a RAM disk. (If you want more information about RAM disks, see Chapter 15.)You'll be the envy of all your friends with all that new memory in your PowerBook. Good job!

If you experience any problems in performing the upgrade, see Chapter 12 for additional information on memory upgrades or refer to the documentation that came with your memory card.

Installing an internal modem in the PowerBook 100

As we've said previously in this book, a modem is what really puts the Power in PowerBook. Installing an internal modem card in a PowerBook 100 is literally a snap, because the modem card simply snaps into place on the motherboard.

PowerBook internal modems are cards that you install inside the machine. Most PowerBook users prefer internal modems because all the hardware is contained inside the PowerBook, so you don't need to carry around any extra hardware and cables. (Chapter 11 offers more information about external modems and communications software.)

Many PowerBook modems are not compatible with the PowerBook 100. Make sure that the modem you choose is compatible with the PowerBook 100 *before* you buy.

To install a modem in your PowerBook 100, follow these steps:

1. **Follow Steps 1 through 9 as described in the section "Opening up the PowerBook 100," earlier in this chapter.**

   These steps show you how to open up your PowerBook so that you can install the modem.

2. **Remove the metal modem shield.**

   The modem shield is located at the rear of the PowerBook, behind the main battery compartment. Push the metal prongs that hold the shield in place toward the back of the computer and then remove the modem shield. Figure 19-5 shows the modem shield.

3. **Remove the plastic modem-connector cover.**

   The *modem-connector cover* is a small, square piece of plastic on the back panel of the PowerBook. The modem-connector cover slides up and out of the PowerBook to leave an opening for the modem's phone line connector. (Figure 19-6 shows the location of the modem-connector cover.)

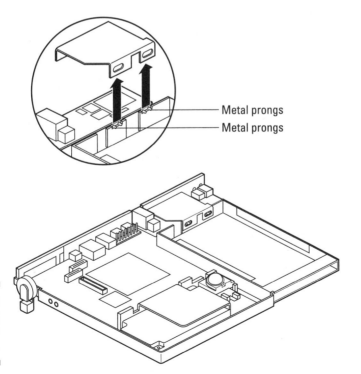

Metal prongs
Metal prongs

Figure 19-5:
Removing
the modem
shield.

4. Press the modem card into place on the motherboard.

Position the modem card so that all the chips face up. Line up the small connector on the bottom of the modem card with the connector on the motherboard. The phone jack on the modem should line up with the opening left after you removed the modem-connector cover in Step 4.

The two holes in the modem card should line up with the two plastic *standoffs* on the motherboard. The standoffs hold the modem card in place and keep the modem from touching the motherboard and causing short circuits. After the card is aligned correctly, gently but firmly press down until it locks into place on the two standoffs. Figure 19-6 shows how the internal modem card fits in a PowerBook 100.

5. Replace the modem shield.

Replace the modem shield on top of the modem. Push the metal prongs toward the back of the computer so that you can replace the modem shield. Make sure that no part of the modem shield extends into the main battery compartment; otherwise, the battery could short out and damage your PowerBook.

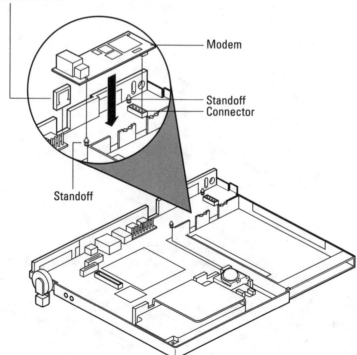

Modem-connector cover

Modem

Standoff
Connector

Standoff

Figure 19-6:
The correct alignment of the modem card in a PowerBook 100.

6. **Close up your PowerBook.**

   Follow the steps in the following section, "Closing up your PowerBook 100."

Hey, good job! You just installed an internal PowerBook modem! Not too many people can claim to have done that. You're now ready to hook up to on-line services, download files from bulletin boards, or send and receive faxes. Have fun! (For more information about modems and communications, see Chapter 11.)

Closing up the PowerBook 100

The next six steps cover closing up your PowerBook 100. You'll replace the keyboard, the display assembly, and the batteries. You'll also move the power switch back to the on position so you'll be able to power up your PowerBook after the upgrade.

Tools you need: A Phillips number 2 screwdriver

What to watch out for: Be careful that the fine wires of the display cable aren't pinched as you replace the display assembly, and be *very* careful as you replace the keyboard cables.

To close up your PowerBook 100, follow these steps:

1. **Replace the keyboard.**

   Hold the keyboard vertically as you replace the two cables in their connectors and lock the cables in place. Slide the front edge of the keyboard under the palm-rest cover and slide the keyboard forward and down into place. (Be careful not to pinch or stress the keyboard cables.)

2. **Replace the display assembly.**

   Rotate the feet at the back of your PowerBook to the down position. Hold the display assembly above the rest of your PowerBook as you reconnect the display cable to the logic board. Refer to figure 19-2 for the location of the display cable connector.

   Replace the display assembly on top of the rest of the PowerBook and latch the PowerBook closed.

   Be especially careful to keep the display cable from getting pinched by the case as you close your PowerBook. The fine wires in the display cable break easily if they are pinched by the case.

After the display assembly is in place, hold the top and bottom of the PowerBook together and turn it over. Replace the three case screws, taking care not to overtighten the screws. Replace the three round rubber plugs on top of the screws. Turn your PowerBook right-side up.

3. Replace the main battery.

Slide the battery into the main battery compartment, with the gold-colored metal contacts facing down. Slide the battery cover to the left to lock the battery in place.

4. Replace the backup batteries.

Rotate the feet at the back of your PowerBook to the down position. Open the plastic door that covers the ports on the back of your PowerBook by pressing down on the latch. Open the backup battery door the same way that you did to remove the batteries. Now carefully replace the three disk-shaped CR2430 lithium backup batteries. Make sure that the positive side of each battery (marked by a "+" symbol) faces up. Close the backup battery door and the door that covers the ports on the back of your PowerBook. Refer back to figure 19-1 for the location of these backup batteries.

5. Move the power switch on the back of the computer to the on position.

The power switch is located on the back panel of your PowerBook, right next to where the power adapter plugs in. If the switch is in the up position, the battery is connected. If the switch is in the down position, the battery is disconnected. You must remember to turn on this switch; otherwise, your PowerBook can't start up from the battery.

6. Start your PowerBook and verify that your upgrade works correctly.

If you experience any problems with your upgrade, check the documentation that came with the hardware.

The Other 100-Series PowerBooks

This section shows you how to add memory and an internal modem to the rest of the 100-series PowerBooks (the 140, 145, 145b, 170, 160, 165, 165c, 180, and 180c).

Opening up a 100-series PowerBook

Before you add your internal upgrades, you need to open up your PowerBook and remove the top case and display assembly. Removing these components enables you to access the inside of your PowerBook so that you can add memory or an internal modem.

Tools you need: Torx number 8 and Torx number 10 screwdrivers

What to watch out for: As we've warned you before, always be very careful as you work with the cables inside your PowerBook. These cables are very thin, and they tear easily. The thin, flat wires inside the cables can also break if you bend the cables too much. Make sure that you remove all the batteries from the PowerBook and that you unplug the power adapter and turn off the power switch. Because the low-power components inside PowerBooks are very sensitive to electrostatic discharge, always work on a grounded work surface, and follow carefully the safety procedures we provide in Chapter 3.

1. **Put on your grounding wrist strap.**

   Again, see Chapter 3 for electrostatic discharge procedures and for information about the grounding wrist strap.

2. **Shut down your PowerBook by opening the Special menu and choosing the Shut Down command.**

   You need to make sure that your PowerBook is really shut down and not just sleeping. By using the Shut Down command, you ensure that you quit all your applications and save all the changes you've made to your documents before the computer shuts off.

3. **Unplug the power adapter.**

   Make sure that the power adapter is disconnected from your PowerBook. (Some people call the power adapter the *AC adapter*.)

4. **Close the PowerBook display so that the computer locks together.**

   Make sure that your PowerBook is securely closed.

5. **Remove the main battery.**

   The battery is located on the left side as you look at the front of the PowerBook. Slide the battery door toward you. After you slide the door toward you, you can pull on the protruding edge of the door to slide the battery out of the PowerBook. Set the battery aside.

6. **Remove the plastic door that covers the ports on the back of the PowerBook.**

   Open the plastic door by carefully bending the door outward and slipping one of the pegs that holds the door on out of the hole. After you detach the first peg, the door slips out easily. Remove the door and set it aside.

   These door pegs are the most delicate part of the PowerBook. So be *extremely* gentle as you remove the door. Many PowerBooks out there are now missing this door, so if you notice the door missing on somebody's PowerBook, you'll know why.

7. Remove the case screws.

Use the Torx number 8 screwdriver to remove the small screw located next to the ports on the back of the PowerBook. Then turn the PowerBook over and use the Torx number 10 screwdriver to remove the four screws on the bottom of the case. See Figure 19-7 for the locations of these screws.

8. Remove the top case and display assembly.

Carefully turn your PowerBook over so that you're holding it right-side up. Because you removed the case screws in the preceding step, you now must hold the top and bottom parts of the case together as you turn it over. Lift up the rear of the top case and disconnect the *interconnect cable*, as shown in Figure 19-8. By the way, the interconnect cable connects the PowerBook display to the motherboard. Lift the top case and display assembly off the rest of the PowerBook and unhook the two tab fasteners at the front edge of the bottom case. Figure 19-8 shows the location of these tab fasteners.

OK, you've opened your PowerBook, and you're ready to install your upgrade. Go to the section that tells you how to install the upgrade you're performing and follow the steps in that section.

Installing memory in a 100-series PowerBook

To add memory to your 100-series PowerBook, you simply plug in a special memory expansion card. To access the memory card connector, you must partially disassemble your PowerBook. To disassemble your machine, you follow Steps 1 through 8 in the preceding section, "Opening up a 100-series PowerBook."

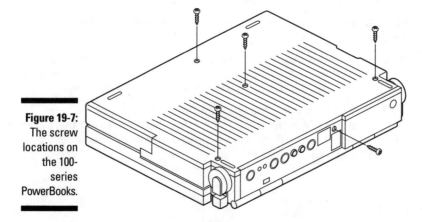

Figure 19-7:
The screw locations on the 100-series PowerBooks.

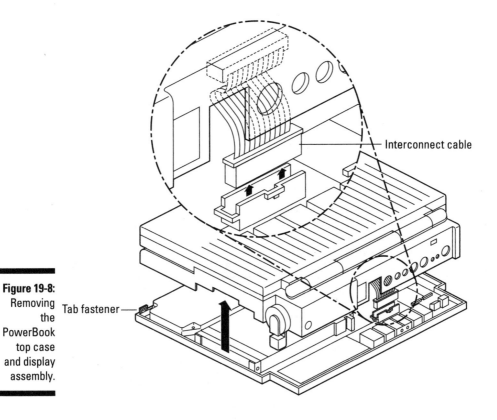

Interconnect cable

Figure 19-8:
Removing
the
PowerBook
top case
and display
assembly.

Tab fastener

Tools you need: Torx number 8 and Torx number 10 screwdrivers

What to watch out for: Again, be very careful as you work with the cables inside the PowerBook. These cables are very thin, and they tear very easily. The thin, flat wires inside the cables also can break if you bend the cables too much. Make sure that you remove all the batteries from the PowerBook and that you unplug the power adapter and turn off the power switch. And make sure that you carefully follow the safety procedures we provide in Chapter 3. Because the low-power components inside PowerBooks are so sensitive to electrostatic discharge, always work on a grounded work surface, as described in Chapter 3.

100-series PowerBook memory amount choices

The PowerBooks 140, 145, and 170 come with 2MB memory on the motherboard and upgrade to a total 8MB. The PowerBook 145b comes with 4MB memory and also upgrades to a total 8MB. The PowerBooks 160, 165, 165c, 180, and 185c come with 4MB memory and upgrade to a total 14MB.

Only one memory card can be installed in a PowerBook at a time. To upgrade, you must remove the currently installed memory card and replace it with a card containing more memory. If no card is currently installed, simply add one to upgrade your machine's memory.

Memory expansion cards for the 100-series PowerBook come in several different versions: 2MB, 4MB, 6MB, and so on. To determine the total memory after upgrading, just add the amount of memory on the expansion card to the amount already on the motherboard. For example, installing a 6MB upgrade card into a PowerBook 170 yields a total of 8MB (6MB + 2MB = 8MB).

To add additional memory to your 100-series PowerBook, follow these steps:

1. **Follow Steps 1 through 8 as described in the preceding section, "Opening up a 100-series PowerBook."**

   These steps show you how to open up your PowerBook so that you can install the memory card.

2. **Press the memory expansion card into its connector.**

   Align the memory card and carefully press it into the connector. Figure 19-9 shows the location of the memory expansion card connector.

   The memory expansion card connector is shaped so that the memory card fits in only one way. Don't try to force the memory card into place; if you do, you may damage the card — and your PowerBook.

   Press down only on the area of the memory card directly on top of the connector. Pressing down on the components or other areas of the card may damage the card. Make sure that you don't bend or flex the card, either.

3. **Close up your PowerBook.**

   Skip to the section "Closing up your 100-series PowerBook" later in this chapter and follow the steps listed there. Then return to Step 4 of this section to verify your memory upgrade.

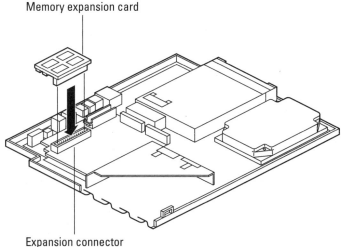

Memory expansion card

Expansion connector

4. Verify your memory upgrade.

Start your PowerBook. Open the Apple menu in the Finder and choose About this Macintosh. The total memory displayed should equal the amount built into your PowerBook, plus the amount of memory you just added by installing the memory expansion card. If you have virtual memory turned on, this number is listed as Built-in Memory.

Nice work! You just finished installing more memory in your 100-series Power-Book. (See Chapter 12 for more information on memory upgrades or refer to the documentation that came with your memory card.)

Installing an internal modem in a 100-series PowerBook

A PowerBook without a modem is just a computer. But *with* a modem, why, it's a travelin', file-accessin', telecommunicatin', awesome information tool! (No wonder adding an internal modem to a PowerBook is such a popular upgrade.)

Tools you need: Torx number 8 and Torx number 10 screwdrivers

What to watch out for: As we've mentioned several times by now (but it definitely bears repeating), be *very* careful as you work with the cables inside the PowerBook. These cables are very thin, and they tear quite easily. The thin, flat wires inside the cables can also break if you bend the cables too much.

Make sure that you remove all the batteries from the PowerBook and that you unplug the power adapter and turn the power switch off. And make sure, too, that you carefully follow the safety procedures we provide in Chapter 3. Because the low-power components inside PowerBooks are so sensitive to electrostatic discharge, always work on a grounded work surface, as described in Chapter 3.

1. **Follow Steps 1 through 8 as described in the section "Opening up a 100-series PowerBook" earlier in this chapter.**

   These steps show you how to open up your PowerBook so that you can install an internal modem card.

2. **Remove the plastic modem-port cover.**

   Locate the modem-port cover on the top case and display assembly you set aside when you opened up your PowerBook. The modem-port cover is a small, square piece of plastic on the back panel of the PowerBook.

   Two plastic tabs hold the modem-port cover in place. Pinch the tabs together and push out the modem-port cover. Removing this cover leaves a small square opening. This is where the modem's phone line connector goes.

3. **Press the modem card into place in the PowerBook.**

   Position the modem so that all its chips face up. Line up the small connector on the bottom of the modem card with the connector on the motherboard. The two holes in the modem card should line up with the plastic standoffs on the motherboard. Carefully press the modem card into the connector on the motherboard. After the modem card is in place, install the mounting screws through the two holes. Figure 19-10 shows how the internal modem card fits in a 100-series PowerBook.

4. **Close up your PowerBook.**

   Follow the steps in the following section, "Closing up your 100-series PowerBook."

Great! You just installed an internal PowerBook modem! Now you can link up to on-line services, download files from bulletin boards, or send and receive faxes. (See Chapter 11 for more information about modems and communications.)

Closing up your 100-series PowerBook

Tools you need: Torx number 8 and Torx number 10 screwdrivers

What to watch out for: As you replace the interconnect cable, make sure that it is folded, as illustrated back in Figure 19-8. As you replace the small screw in the back panel of your PowerBook, be careful not to tighten it too much, because this could crack the case.

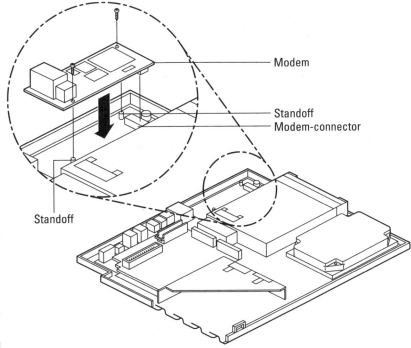

Modem

Standoff
Modem-connector

Standoff

Figure 19-10:
Installing an
internal
modem in a
100-series
PowerBook.

1. Replace the top case and display assembly.

Lower the top case and display assembly onto the bottom case. Engage the two tab fasteners on the front edge of the bottom case first. Then reconnect the interconnect cable. Make sure that the cable is folded, as shown back in Figure 19-8. If the cable is folded incorrectly, it could get pinched, short out, and damage your PowerBook. Lower the back of the top case into place.

2. Replace the case screws.

Hold the top and bottom parts of the case together and turn your PowerBook over. Replace the four larger case screws in their holes in the bottom case and tighten them by using the Torx number 10 screwdriver. Replace the small case screw in the back panel and tighten it by using the Torx number 8 screwdriver.

Don't overtighten the small screw on the back panel near the ports. If you tighten this screw too much, it can crack the plastic on the back panel. Tighten only until the screw is snug.

3. **Replace the plastic door that covers the ports on the back of the PowerBook.**

   Carefully bend the door outward so that you can slip the little pegs on the bottom corners of the door into their holes. Be extremely gentle in doing this; as we stated when you were taking them off, these pegs are the most delicate part of the PowerBook.

4. **Replace the main battery.**

   Slide the battery into its compartment on the left side of the PowerBook. Then slide the battery door toward the back of the PowerBook to lock it into place.

That's it; your upgrade is complete! Your PowerBook is back in one piece and better than ever. You're ready to hit the road!

PowerBook Duos

Doing inside upgrades on a PowerBook Duo is, in most cases, a real pain in the neck, even for experienced technicians. Only one internal Duo upgrade is easy enough to perform yourself — adding memory.

Note: The reason the Duos are so difficult to open and upgrade is that, to add an upgrade like a new internal hard disk or a modem, you must completely disassemble the Duo. Some of the parts you must remove to disassemble the Duo are considered disposable by Apple. Technicians are supposed to simply replace any parts that break or get damaged, and the professionals all have "PowerBook Duo Disposable Parts Replacement Kits" to help make these replacements. As a result, most Duo upgrades are better left to the technicians — who are, of course, specially trained in the correct swear words to use to ensure a successful Duo upgrade.

Adding memory to the Duo is, in fact, the only upgrade that doesn't involve tearing out the Duo's insides. Actually, this memory upgrade is pretty much on par with adding memory to a 100-series PowerBook. Because we cover only one upgrade for the Duos in this section, we are combining the opening, closing, and the upgrade all into one procedure.

Installing memory in your PowerBook Duo

All Duos come with 4MB of memory on the motherboard. All the Duos except the 270c upgrade to a maximum of 24MB of memory. The 270c upgrades to a maximum of 32MB of memory.

Tools you need: Torx number 8 screwdriver; jeweler's flat-blade screwdriver

What to watch out for: Again, be very, very careful as you work with the cables inside the Duo. These cables are very thin, and they do tear easily. The thin, flat wires inside the cables can also break if you bend the cables too much. Make sure that you remove the battery from the Duo and that you unplug the power adapter. Because the low-power components inside Duos are so sensitive to electrostatic discharge, always work on a grounded work surface and carefully follow the safety procedures provided in Chapter 3.

1. **Put on your grounding wrist strap.**

   Again, see Chapter 3 for electrostatic discharge procedures and for information about the grounding wrist strap.

2. **Shut down your Duo by opening the Special menu and choosing the Shut Down command.**

   Make sure that your Duo is really shut down and not just sleeping. By using the Shut Down command, you ensure that you quit all your applications and save all the changes you've made to your documents before the computer shuts off.

3. **Unplug the power adapter.**

   Make sure you that disconnect the power adapter from your Duo. (Some people call the power adapter the *AC adapter.*)

4. **Close the Duo display so that the computer locks together.**

   Make sure that you close the Duo securely.

5. **Remove the main battery.**

   The battery is located on the left side, at the front of the Duo. Press the battery release button and slide the battery door to the left. Pull the battery straight out of the Duo. Set the battery aside.

6. **Remove the three case screws nearest the back of the Duo.**

   Turn the Duo over so that you're holding it upside-down. Use the Torx number 8 screwdriver to remove the two screws at the back corners and the screw in the center of the case. Leave the fourth screw, in the center of the front edge of your Duo, in place. Set the screws aside in a safe place. Figure 19-11 shows the screw locations.

7. **Remove the keyboard.**

   Turn your Duo right-side up. Open up the display. Carefully tilt the computer toward you and lift out the keyboard. Turn the keyboard over and set it on the palm rest. Figure 19-12 illustrates this procedure. Use the jeweler's screwdriver to push out the release tabs on the keyboard cable connectors and then remove the keyboard cables. Set the keyboard aside.

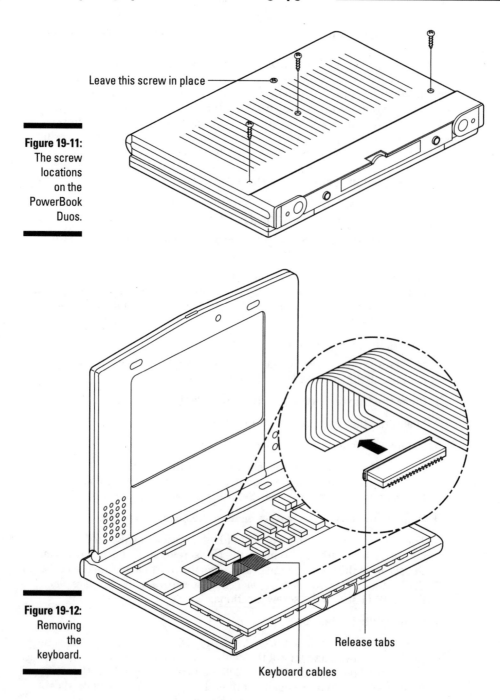

Leave this screw in place

Figure 19-11:
The screw
locations
on the
PowerBook
Duos.

Figure 19-12:
Removing
the
keyboard.

Release tabs

Keyboard cables

Be *very* careful as you handle the keyboard cables. They are very delicate and tear easily. Do not pinch or crease the cables. The small, flat wires in the cable break easily if you bend or flex them excessively.

8. **Connect the memory expansion card to the motherboard.**

   Hold the memory expansion card by the edges. Slide the card into its connector on the logic board, as shown in Figure 19-13.

9. **Replace the keyboard.**

   Place the keyboard face down on the palm rest. Push the keyboard cables into their connectors. Lock the cables into place by using the jeweler's screwdriver to push in the tabs on the connectors. Carefully turn the keyboard over and replace it in the Duo.

10. **Replace the three case screws you removed in Step 6.**

    Turn your Duo over so that you're holding it upside-down. Use the Torx number 8 screwdriver to replace the two screws at the back corners and the screw in the center of the case. Refer to Figure 19-11 for the screw locations.

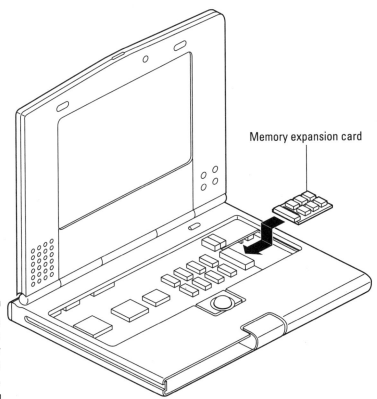

Memory expansion card

Figure 19-13:
Installing a
memory
expansion
card.

Be extremely careful not to overtighten the screws holding the keyboard in place. If you tighten these three screws too much, the keyboard can warp, and certain keys may not work correctly. Check the movement of the keys after you replace the screws. If you notice any keys that stick or feel wrong, back the corresponding screw out just a bit until the problem is corrected.

11. **Replace the main battery.**

    Slide the battery into the Duo. Slide the battery door to the right to lock the battery in place.

12. **Verify your memory upgrade.**

    Start your Duo. From the Finder's Apple menu, choose About this Macintosh. The total memory listed should equal the 4MB of memory on the motherboard, plus the amount of memory you added on the expansion card. If you have virtual memory turned on, this number is listed as Built-in Memory.

That's it; you just performed a memory upgrade on a PowerBook Duo! Give yourself a well-deserved pat on the back. Your Duo is now ready to take on all those memory-intensive tasks you have lined up for it.

If you experience any problems with your memory upgrade, see Chapter 12 for help.

Part VII
The Part of Tens

New Age Macintosh Repair

"QUIET EVERYONE – LET THE CRYSTAL DO ITS WORK."

In this part...

This is the fun part. Browse through these chapters to find out the ten hardest upgrades. Or what about the best PowerBook upgrades? Check out Chapter 21. Increase your PowerBook's battery life or find out some general tips to make your Mac run better. And what about the Power Macs? There are tips in here regarding those, too.

This part provides some valuable snippets of information presented in a way that's easy to digest. So whether you've just performed an internal upgrade or if you always begin a new book by reading the end first, pick a chapter and start reading.

Chapter 20
The Ten Hardest Mac Upgrades

● ●

In This Chapter

▶ Accelerating a Mac Plus

▶ Making a Mac SE into an SE/30

▶ Upgrading the Mac Color Classic's internal hard disk

▶ Installing an internal modem or hard disk in a PowerBook Duo

▶ Adding memory to a black-and-white compact Mac

● ●

*T*he upgrades noted in the preceding list are all possible but complicated, and we're outlining them here for you so that you know what you're getting into if you decide to do them. The processes are long, involved, take many steps, and include a bunch of pieces of hardware to look out for and take care not to break. We suggest that you hire a technician if you want to try these upgrades, and because of the difficulty level, we don't even include instructions for most of them in this book.

Installing an Accelerator in a Mac Plus

This upgrade may seem attractive because it makes your Mac Plus go faster. But installing an accelerator in a Mac Plus is a complex operation involving many steps. Many things can cause trouble, such as poor electrical connections.

After you install the accelerator, you run the risk of overloading the power supply because of the additional chips you install and the power demands of the accelerator. Also, if you make this upgrade, software that ran fine before may no longer be compatible. In short, we think that installing an accelerator in the Mac Plus causes more problems than it solves. (For more information about accelerators and speeding up your Mac, see Chapter 14.)

If you really want to speed up your Mac Plus, the one speed upgrade we do recommend is the Brainstorm Accelerator from Brainstorm Products. You cannot install this upgrade yourself, though; only Brainstorm resellers are authorized to install it.

Upgrading a Mac SE to an SE/30

In theory, only authorized service providers can purchase the hardware to convert the SE to an SE/30. The reason is that performing this upgrade is the Macintosh equivalent of replacing the engine in your car. It involves completely disassembling the SE and putting it back together correctly. You may be able to find a reseller to sell you the hardware to perform this upgrade, but take it from us, this one is complicated — have a technician do it.

Upgrading the Internal Hard Disk in a Mac Color Classic

This upgrade, which seems like it should be straightforward, involves opening up the Color Classic and working near the color picture tube and other high voltage electrical components. Working near this machine's color picture tube is even more dangerous and complicated than working inside the black-and-white compacts. You also have to disconnect and then reconnect about ten cables.

If you want to upgrade the internal hard disk in this Mac, leave it to a technician. Any other upgrade for the Color Classic is a piece of cake. Chapter 17 contains the instructions for upgrading the Color Classic with memory, video memory, an expansion card, and a math coprocessor.

Installing an Internal Modem or Hard Disk in a PowerBook Duo

Because of the PowerBook Duo's design, installing an internal modem or an internal hard disk involves completely disassembling the machine. What makes these upgrades even worse is that some parts of the computer cannot be removed without breaking them. Authorized Apple technicians learn that these parts are considered disposable, and they keep a supply on hand to replace the ones they break when they take the Duo apart.

The only internal Duo upgrade that doesn't require complete disassembly is installing a memory card, which is about the same difficulty level as installing memory on any other PowerBook. For the instructions for installing memory in a Duo, refer to Chapter 19.

Installing Memory in a Black-and-White Compact Mac

Adding memory to a black-and-white compact Mac is probably the most complicated upgrade we show you how to do in this book. You'll find the instructions in Chapter 17. No one step is extremely difficult, but the upgrade involves removing the back case and taking the Mac apart. It also involves working around high voltage components, although we show you how to do this work safely.

If, after looking over the instructions in Chapter 17, you feel uncomfortable about performing this upgrade yourself, hire a technician to do it for you. Many computer stores install memory for free if you purchase the memory in the store. Just make sure that the price for memory is not higher than the cost of memory you buy elsewhere plus the installation fee.

Chapter 21
The Top Ten PowerBook Upgrades

*H*ere is the top ten list of our favorite PowerBook upgrades.

Buy a Carrying Case

One of the first things you need is a case to carry your PowerBook and all its accessories. Look for a case that offers good protection for your PowerBook and has room for all your equipment. We suggest you purchase your case at a computer store, not through mail order, so that you can get a good look at the case and make sure it has the features you want in terms of size, protection for your PowerBook, and, of course, the right color to go with most of your outfits.

Add Memory

As we said before, no Mac or PowerBook ever contains too much memory, especially when you're running many applications and using large documents. And if your PowerBook contains enough memory, you can create a RAM disk, which will extend the machine's battery life. Chapter 15 provides more information about RAM disks.

Install a Bigger Internal Hard Disk

You may have experienced the phenomenon where the things you take with you on a trip expand to fill all your available luggage space. Likewise, your computer files and applications always expand to fill the available hard disk space. Our advice is buy the biggest hard disk you can afford — you will use the space. We also advise you to hire a technician to do this upgrade for you. It falls in the pretty difficult category, because things get pretty crowded inside the PowerBooks, and your hands and any tools you use can just take up too much space and potentially cause too much trouble in there.

Try connecting an external hard disk or CD-ROM drive to your PowerBook. To plug in the drives, you need either a PowerBook SCSI cable or a PowerBook SCSI adapter to use with a regular SCSI cable. If you're interested in this upgrade, see Chapter 8 for more information on SCSI. You can handle this upgrade yourself.

Add a Fax Modem

We once heard someone say that a modem is what puts the power in PowerBook because it connects your PowerBook to the world of on-line services, bulletin boards, and your office e-mail system. You can buy a modem with or without fax capabilities. These days, the price difference is so little that you may as well go ahead and get a modem with fax capabilities. Then you can fax a document you create on your Mac as easily as you can print it.

Suppose that you're on the road with your PowerBook but don't have a printer, and you need a quick printout of a document. Here's a trick. Use a fax modem to send a copy of the document to yourself via the fax machine in your hotel. If the hotel fax isn't convenient, fax the document to a copy shop that has a fax machine. Voila! You have a hard copy.

Connect an External Mouse

Some people find the PowerBook trackball annoying to use. You can use an external mouse with your PowerBook by plugging it into the ADB port on the back panel. The only hitch is that you need to use a low-power mouse, which is marked with a symbol on its underside, near the serial number. The symbol looks like a circle that's open at the top with a line across the opening. If you don't use a low-power mouse, your battery will drain quickly, even with the power adapter plugged in.

Our favorite eight-year-old has this to say about upgrading her family's PowerBook trackball: "Even I can upgrade the PowerBook with a new trackball. Adding a pink trackball or one with a smiling face and other designs is fun." Here's what you do to add a new trackball:

1. **Rotate the circular plastic piece that surrounds the trackball counter-clockwise.**

   When you look closely at the circular plastic piece, you'll see two raised edges, one on either side of the trackball. The raised edges help you rotate the plastic piece.

2. **Pull the plastic piece away from the PowerBook.**

3. **Remove the trackball.**

   You'll probably have to turn your PowerBook upside down and let the trackball fall out into your hand.

4. **Put the new trackball into the opening.**

5. **Put the circular plastic piece back in place and rotate it clockwise until you hear a click.**

Then try out your new trackball. We hope smiling faces or yin-yang symbols make your computing faster and easier.

You can purchase colored and decorated trackballs from APS Technologies, the makers of APS PowerBalls. APS is located in Kansas City, Missouri, and the phone number is 800-677-3294.

Buy an AppleTalk Network Connector

An AppleTalk connector enables your PowerBook to link up to most Macintosh networks. It also enables you to access the laser printers and file servers on the network.

You should buy an AppleTalk PhoneNet-style connector that uses a phone cord. Almost all AppleTalk networks can use this PhoneNet-style connector. A second benefit is that you can use the same cord to connect your modem to the phone jack in the wall.

Even if you don't normally use your desktop Mac on a network, buy two AppleTalk connectors and use them to create a mini-network between your PowerBook and your desktop Mac. You can then transfer documents between the two machines by using this network and the file sharing feature of System 7. If you're interested in setting up this kind of network, see Chapter 11 for more information.

Connect an External Monitor

By plugging your PowerBook into an external monitor, you can view your work on a large screen, perhaps in color.

Or have you thought about connecting the PowerBook to a large monitor or video projector to give a presentation to a room full of people? This capability comes built into the latest PowerBooks, such as the 160, 180, and later machines. Older machines like the 140, 170, and 145b, need special hardware to connect to external monitors. You can either install a PowerBook video board or use an external video box connected to the SCSI port.

To connect a PowerBook Duo to an external monitor, you need external hardware, such as the Apple Duo Dock or the MiniDock, that can connect monitors. If you're not using a dock, you can purchase a video adapter from companies other than Apple.

Buy a PowerBook SCSI Cable or an Adapter

We find it useful to carry a PowerBook SCSI cable or an adapter for regular SCSI cables with our PowerBooks, and you may, too. With this cable or the adapter, you can connect your PowerBook to hardware like external hard disks, external CD-ROM drives, or scanners. Carrying the cable equipment with you is definitely easier than trying to find it when you're traveling.

Some PowerBooks can connect to a desktop Mac and serve as an external hard disk. Check the documentation for your PowerBook to determine whether the computer has this capability.

To get your PowerBook to act like a hard disk, you need a PowerBook SCSI cable or an adapter for the regular SCSI cable. This cable equipment is different from the equipment mentioned previously, so carefully explain what you want to do to the salesperson in the computer store. After the PowerBook connects as a hard disk, the internal hard disk on the PowerBook shows up as an external hard disk on your Mac desktop.

Connect an External Diskette Drive

If you own a PowerBook Duo or a PowerBook 100, you know that these computers come without an internal diskette drive. You may not need a diskette drive all the time, but when you need it, you need it.

For the PowerBook 100, just plug the external diskette drive into its port on the back of the Mac.

For the Duos, you need a piece of hardware called the PowerBook Duo Floppy Disk Adapter. The adapter attaches to the back of a Duo and supplies the connectors you need to attach an external diskette drive and also a mouse or a keyboard.

Buy a Printer Adapter Cable

A printer adapter cable enables you to connect your PowerBook to practically any printer made for IBM PCs and IBM-compatible computers. The advantage is that you can print from almost any printer you run across when you travel. The cable also comes with a collection of software drivers for hundreds of different printers. The drivers are the software that enable your PowerBook to send your documents to a printer for printing.

Attach a Numeric Keypad

The number keys in the top row of the PowerBook keyboard make entering lots of figures hard to do. We don't even like calculating something small like check-book entries with these keys. So, depending on how much number crunching you do, this upgrade could be what you need.

Chapter 22

Ten PowerBook Tips for Better Battery Life

- -

In This Chapter

▶ Some of the best power saving tips

▶ To keep your PowerBook running longer

▶ On the road, or anywhere away from an outlet

- -

*T*he PowerBook gets electrical power from one of two sources: the internal battery or the power adapter. You know the power adapter — it's the gray brick that plugs your PowerBook into the wall. Some people call the power adapter the *AC adapter*. You also know the battery. That's what gives you and your PowerBook the mobility to compute on a plane, on a camping trip, or on your sun porch.

Plug in the Power Adapter Whenever Possible

In other words, work with your PowerBook plugged into an electrical outlet as much as you can, and avoid using the battery unless you're working far away from an outlet.

Charge the Battery Overnight

To charge the battery, use a PowerBook battery recharger or keep your PowerBook plugged in with the power adapter overnight.

Put Your PowerBook to Sleep

Use the Sleep command in the Special menu or the Sleep button in the Battery desk accessory as often as possible. This sleep period gives you time to collect your thoughts while you're working without draining the battery. When you're ready to work again, press any key to bring your PowerBook out of Sleep. If you know you'll be away from your PowerBook for a while, use the Shut Down command from the Special menu instead of Sleep.

Adjust the Screen Brightness

Turn the brightness controls below the screen to keep the screen readable, but no brighter than necessary.

Turn Off the PowerBook's Speaker

Set the sound to zero in the Sound control panel. The zero setting turns the internal speaker off and saves the power the speaker uses to produce sounds.

Turn Off Virtual Memory

Open the Memory control panel under the Apple menu and set virtual memory to off. Virtual memory uses part of the PowerBook's internal hard disk as RAM, which means that every time you work with a file or an application loaded into virtual memory, the hard disk needs to spin. This almost constant hard disk access drains the battery in no time.

Virtual memory is the opposite of a RAM disk, which uses part of the Power-Book memory as a virtual disk to prolong battery life. See Chapter 15 for more information about RAM disks and virtual memory.

This tip doesn't apply to PowerBook 100s.

When You're Not Using AppleTalk, Turn It Off

When you're working on your own with no need to use a printer or to communicate with other people on your AppleTalk network, or if you're just feeling anti-social, go ahead and turn off AppleTalk in the Chooser desk accessory.

Disconnect Any Unused External Hardware

External hardware, such as printers, hard disks, or CD-ROM drives, can drain battery power. So disconnect anything that you're not actually using.

Note: If you have several devices connected in a chain to the SCSI port and you're only using one of them, be sure that every device in the chain is turned on. Power can leak from your battery through attached power supplies that aren't even turned on.

Use the Diskette Drive As Little As Possible

Eject any diskettes in the drive that you're not using. Accessing the diskette drive uses power, and just keeping a diskette in the drive causes the system software to check it periodically.

Quit Communications Software When You're Done with It

Most communications software keeps the modem in a standby state that uses power, even if you're not using the modem. So when you finish with your modem, quit the communications software right away.

Open Applications and Files while Using the Power Adapter

Opening applications and documents requires hard disk access that uses power. The trick here is to start up and do all your hard disk accessing before you unplug your PowerBook from the outlet. After you open all the documents and applications you plan to use, put your PowerBook to sleep. Then when you wake up the PowerBook by using the battery, all your work is loaded into memory, and no hard disk access is necessary.

If you plan a morning at the beach with your PowerBook, use the power adapter before you go to load the applications and documents you're going to use. Then put the machine into sleep mode by using the Sleep command. When your machine comes out of sleep mode at the beach, your applications will be running with your documents appearing on-screen. Of course, you want to be sure you keep sand out of your PowerBook, and don't let sunscreen drip into it. Flying Frisbees and beach balls shouldn't be much of a problem, though.

Use Only Low-Power Mice or Keyboards

Make sure that you use only low-power ADB hardware designed for Power-Books. This tip also applies to other input devices that plug into the ADB port, such as pens or trackballs.

Completely Discharge the Battery Every 90 Days

You can maximize the life of your PowerBook battery by completely discharging it once every 90 days.

The nickel-cadmium type batteries used in the PowerBooks 140 through 180c can develop a condition known as a *memory effect*. Memory effect, you ask? Is that a halo around my PowerBook or a mirage on-screen? Memory effect means that the battery lasts only a short time, even after a full recharge. Luckily, the condition is not permanent. All you need to do is completely discharge the battery before recharging it again.

To discharge your PowerBook completely, just use the computer as you normally would, but ignore the low power messages that appear on-screen and be sure to save your work. Let the power in the battery run out. When the computer goes to sleep automatically, recharge the battery completely before using that battery again.

Never completely drain the battery in the PowerBook 100 or Duos. These PowerBooks use a different type of battery that can be damaged if it's completely discharged. The batteries in these machines are content to be left charging through the power adapter when you're not using them, which is just the opposite of the other PowerBooks.

Remove the Battery from Your PowerBook for Storage

If you're not planning to use your PowerBook for a month or more, you should remove the battery. Fully charge the battery, remove it from the PowerBook, and place it in the plastic slip cover that comes with the machine.

Even after your PowerBook shuts down, it still drains a small amount of power to maintain the date and clock setting. If your battery sits in your PowerBook for more than a few weeks without recharging, it can discharge to the point where it cannot recharge. If left long enough, the battery can leak, or even explode and destroy your PowerBook. All this electro-charge-o info ought to convince you to remove the battery when you leave your PowerBook alone for an extended time.

If you store your PowerBook for a while, remember to recharge the battery about once a month to keep it from completely dying.

Chapter 23

Ten Ways to Make Your Mac Run Better

*T*his chapter helps you get the maximum performance possible from your Mac. With your Mac running at top speed, you can get your work done faster and better. Five of the tips are things you can do with the control panels under the Apple menu and with your system folder. The other three concern hardware to install in your Mac.

Install More Memory

To quote our friend Grog the caveman, "Memory gooood!"

Adding memory is, without a doubt, the best upgrade value for your Mac. The benefits of adding memory include the following: keeping more applications running at one time, opening larger files, an increase in system speed, and the general warm fuzzy feeling that comes from having gobs of memory.

Eliminate Unused System Extensions

From your system folder, remove the system extensions and control panels that you don't use. Extra system extensions and control panels hog memory and decrease system speed. By removing these parts of your system, you increase system efficiency and reduce the possibility of a crash occurring because of conflicting extensions.

Seldom-used system extensions and control panels include DAL access, Map, easy access, and drivers for printers that you don't use. We suggest that you keep only the extensions you absolutely must have to accomplish your work. For more information on system extensions and control panels, see Chapter 15.

The best strategy when you remove extensions and control panels is to create a new folder outside the system folder; then move the extensions and control panels you don't want into this folder. Don't trash the extensions and control panels until you're sure you can live without them.

If your Mac is on a network, check with your network administrator before you remove any system extensions to make sure that you keep everything you need for network services.

Turn Off Virtual Memory

For best system performance, turn virtual memory off in the Memory control panel under the Apple menu. Virtual memory uses part of your hard disk as extra memory, which means you loose a chunk of storage space to gain working memory — robbing Pedro to pay Pablo. The drawback to keeping virtual memory on is that accessing the hard disk takes much longer than accessing real, physical memory, so the whole system runs slower.

Note: If you can't work without the extra memory that virtual memory gives you, it's high time you added more memory SIMMs to your system. Virtual memory works best as a temporary supply of memory and isn't meant to be used full-time. Chapter 12 gives you more information about memory.

Install a Math Coprocessor

Install a math coprocessor if you use spreadsheets to crunch numbers or burn through drawings created in CAD programs (that's *computer aided design,* in case you're wondering).

This upgrade is not for everyone, but a math coprocessor can provide amazing speed gains. Remember, only applications designed specifically to look for and use a math coprocessor will show a speed increase, so check the manuals for your applications to find out whether your software can benefit.

Set the System 7 Views Control Panel for Maximum Speed

If you use System 7, check the settings in the Views control panel. Certain settings can really slow your Mac down.

For the fastest speed, set the "font for views" pop-up menu to Geneva 9 point and leave the "calculate folder sizes" box unchecked. These settings enable your Mac to open and redraw windows as quickly as possible.

Increase the Disk Cache

Increasing the size of the disk cache is one good way to speed up your Mac. The increased cache gives the Mac quick access to your most recently used files, data, applications, and system software, which means that your work, or your play if you're into games, goes faster.

You change the size of the disk cache by using the control panels under the Apple menu. Use the Memory control panel if you use System 7, or use the General control panel if you use System 6. Usually, the bigger the cache, the bigger the speed gain.

Setting the cache to between 128K and 512K seems to give the best results, but if you have a bunch of memory available in your machine, you can make the cache even bigger. You can make the cache as large as you want, but be sure to leave enough memory to run applications. If your Mac contains 8MB of memory, for example, and you set the cache for 7, you won't have enough memory left for applications. For more information on the disk cache, see Chapter 14.

If you run low on memory, you can decrease the size of the cache. You sacrifice a little performance, but you get more memory.

Use Fewer Colors On-Screen

Use the Monitors control panel to reduce the number of colors that appear on-screen. We suggest you set the control panel to black-and-white even if you have a color monitor. On the Mac, things runs faster in black and white. You probably won't do all your work without color, but your word processing and spreadsheet applications will scroll much faster with this setting.

Install a Processor Accelerator

Install a processor accelerator if you try all the previous suggestions and still need more speed.

If your Mac has one or more empty expansion slots, installing an accelerator simply involves adding an expansion card to your Mac. If you don't have any free slots, you're out of luck as far as adding an accelerator is concerned. Chapter 14 provides more information about accelerators.

Before you buy an accelerator, be aware of what it does and does not do:

✔ An accelerator will not give you a bigger hard disk or an improved screen.

✔ An accelerator will speed up your present Mac.

If you get an accelerator, you may also end up spending money on more memory and on software upgrades or updates to achieve compatibility with the new processor. Speaking of compatibility, check with the company that makes the accelerator you're thinking of buying for information about compatibility with the software you use. For more information on accelerators, see Chapter 14.

Or maybe you need a new Mac. After considering an accelerator, take a look at new Mac prices. You may be surprised at how much prices fall every year. It's almost a sure thing that you can find a Mac that will run at least twice as fast as your current Mac for less than half the money you originally spent. The accelerator and any memory or software upgrades you need for your current Mac may cost almost as much as a new Mac.

Chapter 24

Ten Easy PowerBook Power Supply Upgrades

· ·

In This Chapter

▶ Purchasing an extension cord

▶ Adding an extra battery

▶ Using a battery recharging plate

▶ Adding a second power adapter

▶ Using an external battery pack

▶ Buying an adapter for the cigarette lighter plug in your car

▶ Getting a solar panel

· ·

*T*he following PowerBook upgrades will help you keep electrical power flowing to your machine, whether you compute at home, in the office, in the woods, or on the commuter train.

Buy an Extension Cord

The power adapter for the PowerBook has a very short cord. To get yourself working a reasonable distance away from electrical outlets, go to the grocery store and get a six- to eight-foot extension cord and keep it with your Power-Book. The one we used for writing this book is long and dark brown. You know the kind we're talking about.

A good friend of ours always takes his PowerBook with him to meetings, and he swears the extension cord is the best upgrade he owns. When he makes a presentation, he no longer has to say, "Excuse me, can you all gather around the outlet?"

The extension cord also allows you to sit in a chair in the airport while you wait for your plane instead of sitting cross-legged on the floor next to an outlet.

Keep an Extra Battery on Hand

The PowerBook battery lasts about two hours at most, if you're lucky. We suggest that you buy an extra battery or two to keep on hand.

Buy a Battery Recharging Plate

An external battery charger lets you keep two batteries charging near an outlet while you work farther afield. The recharging plate uses the same power adapter that plugs into your PowerBook and can recharge a completely drained battery in three or four hours. Some rechargers even condition your battery, which means that the recharger fully discharges the battery before recharging.

Buy a Second Power Adapter

A second power adapter can be useful if you divide your PowerBook's time pretty equally between two main locations. You can leave an adapter plugged in at both places so you won't have to crawl on your hands and knees to grab the plug every time you switch locations.

It's easy to leave the power adapter behind at an office or in a hotel room when you travel. Tape your business card to the adapter. Then the people in the office where you worked or the hotel staff can send the adapter to you or at least contact you when they find it.

Buy an External Battery Pack

Instead of carrying six extra batteries, buy one external battery pack. If you need several hours of computing time between battery charges, a battery pack may be just the ticket. Most battery packs are a flat plate that fits under your PowerBook or a box that sits beside it. Both types plug into the power adapter port and can give up to 12 hours of continuous use before needing recharging.

Buy an Adapter for the Cigarette Lighter Plug in Your Car

If you spend lots of time using your PowerBook in the car, why not let the car power the computer? Plug your PowerBook into the cigarette lighter plug with a PowerBook DC adapter, sometimes called an *auto adapter*. You can find this adapter in most computer stores.

This strategy is useful for repair people or technicians working out of vans. Also, you might catch up on some work while you drive to the office in your vanpool, and maybe your kids will use the PowerBook to play games on a long car trip.

Buy a Solar Panel

Live up in the mountains with no utilities hook ups? Going on an expedition to the Sahara? Trekking in the Himalayas? If you'll be away from an electrical outlet for an extended time but still need your PowerBook, you can power your computer with a solar panel.

As you can imagine, this power source is not the kind of thing you find at your local computer store. Check with shops that specialize in alternative energy devices; for solar panels designed especially for the PowerBook, check out SunPack PB from Keep It Simple Software at 800-327-6882. This upgrade is a bit on the wild side, but we want you to know you can take your PowerBook anywhere.

Chapter 25

Ten Things to Remember about PowerPC and Power Macs

. . . .

In this Chapter

▶ Power Mac means PowerPC inside

▶ PowerPC means fast!

▶ Only "native" software gives you PowerPC speed

▶ Upgrading to PowerPC power

▶ System 7 and the Power Mac

▶ Your software and the Power Mac

▶ Your hardware and the Power Mac

▶ Why today's Power Macs are sure to get faster with age

. . . .

So, you've heard of the PowerPC and the Power Mac, but what are they really all about? This chapter describes some of the most important things to know about the Power Macs and the PowerPC.

The Power Mac Has a PowerPC Chip Inside

The Power Macintosh computers are driven by the PowerPC processor. The computer is the *Power Mac*, and the processor chip inside is the *PowerPC*. (The processor's official name is *PowerPC 601*.) Newer versions of the chip are designated as the PowerPC 603, the PowerPC 604, and the PowerPC 620.

The PowerPC Chip is Fast

People get exited about the PowerPC chip because it's fast. The chip makes software designed for Power Macs run up to three to four times faster than applications running on the fastest Quadras. The chip also makes math and CAD applications run up to ten times faster than the same applications running on Quadras. New software developed for the Power Macs is expected to deliver features that integrate the computers with modems, fax machines, and telephones. Graphics and video processing features are also likely to become available.

To Get PowerPC Speed, Your Software Must Be "Native"

To run at the promised PowerPC speeds, however, your software must be designed especially for the PowerPC chip. Software designed for pre-Power Macs runs at Quadra speeds, even on Power Macs. To take advantage of the full speed of the PowerPC chip, software must be translated by developers into what's called *native mode*. If you own a Power Mac and want to make sure that you realize its full speed and power, update your software to native PowerPC versions. Check with the software developer about obtaining updates.

Upgrading to the PowerPC

To get PowerPC power, you can either buy a Power Mac or you can upgrade your current Mac to Power Mac status (depending on the model).

If you own a Mac Quadra or Centris, you can install a PowerPC accelerator card. Macs upgraded this way don't run as fast as a genuine Power Mac, but this upgrade gives you a low-cost way to upgrade to the PowerPC. This upgrade also is one you can make yourself — no technician is required. See Chapters 14 and 18 for more information.

You can upgrade the following Macs to the PowerPC by having the computer's current logic board removed and then replaced with a Power Mac logic board: the Quadra or Centris 610; the Quadra or Centris 660AV; the Quadra 650; the Quadra 800; the Quadra 840AV; Apple Workgroup Servers; the Mac IIvi and IIvx; and the Performa 600. You can't make this upgrade yourself on these machines; you must hire a technician to do it for you. For more information, see Chapter 14.

System 7 is the Operating System for the Power Mac

The operating system for Power Macs is System 7. So if you buy a Power Mac, you don't need to learn a new operating system. You can copy files, open and close windows, and launch applications the same way as you do now. If you now use System 6, however, you must move up to System 7 to operate a Power Mac. Moving to System 7, however, really isn't much of a switch in terms of what you need to learn. You just get new system software features.

Your Current Software and the Power Mac

The software you use currently on your Mac with System 7 runs fine on the Power Mac. You just don't get PowerPC speeds with your old applications and utilities — but you can still run them on a Power Mac. If you have native PowerPC software, too, you can run both the native software and your old Mac software on a Power Mac at the same time.

Your Current Hardware and the Power Mac

The Macintosh hardware you currently use with your Mac runs with a Power Mac, too. If you buy or upgrade to a Power Macintosh, you can expect all the Macintosh printers, hard disks, scanners, mice, keyboards, trackballs, networking cards, video cards, and other hardware you use with your current Mac also to work with the new or upgraded machine.

Expect Today's Power Macs to Become Even Faster

After Apple releases new versions of the system software, the Power Macs should become even faster than they already are! Some parts of the current system software still haven't been converted to native mode. As the remaining parts of the system are converted, the Power Macs will be fine-tuned to run at their top speeds.

Index

IDG's bestselling ...For Dummies Quick Reference Series provides a quick and simple way to remember software commands and functions, written in our down-to-earth, plain English style that guides beginners and experts alike through important commands and hidden troublespots.

Fun, Fast & Cheap!

"Thanks for coming up with the simplest idea ever, a reference that you really can use and understand."

Allison J. O'Neill, Edison, NJ

WORDPERFECT FOR DOS FOR DUMMIES™ QUICK REFERENCE
by Greg Harvey

With this guide you'll never have to worry about deciphering cryptic WordPerfect commands again!

ISBN: 1-56884-009-8
$8.95 USA/$11.95 Canada
£7.99 UK & Eire

WORD FOR WINDOWS FOR DUMMIES™ QUICK REFERENCE
by George Lynch

End your stress over style sheets, mail merge, and other pesky Word features with this quick reference. Covers Word 2.

ISBN: 1-56884-029-2
$8.95 USA/$11.95 Canada

ILLUSTRATED COMPUTER DICTIONARY FOR DUMMIES™
by Dan Gookin, Wally Wang, & Chris Van Buren

This plain English guide to computer jargon helps with even the most techie terms.

ISBN: 1-56884-004-7
$12.95 USA/$16.95 Canada
£11.99 UK & Eire

1-2-3 FOR DUMMIES™ QUICK REFERENCE
by John Walkenbach

Keep this quick and easy reference by your desk and you'll never have to worry about forgetting tricky 1-2-3 commands again!

ISBN: 1-56884-027-6
$8.95 USA/$11.95 Canada
£7.99 UK & Eire

WINDOWS FOR DUMMIES™ QUICK REFERENCE
by Greg Harvey

The quick and friendly way to remember Windows tasks & features.

ISBN: 1-56884-008-X
$8.95 USA/$11.95 Canada
£7.99 UK & Eire

EXCEL FOR DUMMIES™ QUICK REFERENCE
by John Walkenbach

A fast, fun and cheap way to remember bothersome Excel commands.

ISBN: 1-56884-028-4
$8.95 USA/$11.95 Canada
£7.99 UK & Eire

DOS FOR DUMMIES™ QUICK REFERENCE
by Greg Harvey

A fast, fun, and cheap way to remember DOS commands.

ISBN: 1-56884-007-1
$8.95 USA/$11.95 Canada
£7.99 UK & Eire

WORDPERFECT FOR WINDOWS FOR DUMMIES™ QUICK REFERENCE
by Greg Harvey

The quick and friendly "look-it-up" guide to the leading Windows word processor.

ISBN: 1-56884-039-X
$8.95 USA/$11.95 Canada/£7.99 UK & Eire

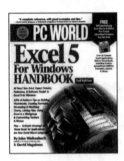

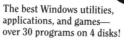

Order Form

Order Center: (800) 762-2974 (8 a.m.-5 p.m., PST, weekdays) or (415) 312-0650

For Fastest Service: Photocopy This Order Form and FAX it to: (415) 358-1260

Quantity	ISBN	Title	Price	Total

Shipping & Handling Charges

Subtotal	U.S.	Canada & International	International Air Mail
Up to $20.00	Add $3.00	Add $4.00	Add $10.00
$20.01-40.00	$4.00	$5.00	$20.00
$40.01-60.00	$5.00	$6.00	$25.00
$60.01-80.00	$6.00	$8.00	$35.00
Over $80.00	$7.00	$10.00	$50.00

In U.S. and Canada, shipping is UPS ground or equivalent.
For Rush shipping call (800) 762-2974.

Subtotal

CA residents add applicable sales tax

IN and MA residents add 5% sales tax

IL residents add 6.25% sales tax

RI residents add 7% sales tax

Shipping

Total

Ship to:

Name _____

Company _____

Address _____

City/State/Zip _____

Daytime Phone _____

Payment: ❑ Check to IDG Books (US Funds Only)   ❑ Visa   ❑ Mastercard   ❑ American Express

Card# _____ Exp._____ Signature_____

Please send this order form to: IDG Books, 155 Bovet Road, Suite 310, San Mateo, CA 94402.

Allow up to 3 weeks for delivery. Thank you!